Before Freedom Came

AFRICAN-AMERICAN LIFE IN THE ANTEBELLUM SOUTH

Plate 1.
Virginia's capital, Richmond, was the second largest slave-trading market in the South, and many visitors witnessed auctions there. An English artist, Levevre J. Cranstone, painted one such Richmond sale. The view is probably based on a work by the artist Eyre Crowe that was widely reproduced in contemporary illustrated newspapers in both the United States and England.

Before Freedom Came

AFRICAN-AMERICAN LIFE IN THE ANTEBELLUM SOUTH

To accompany an exhibition
organized by The Museum
of the Confederacy

Edited by
Edward D. C. Campbell, Jr.,
with Kym S. Rice

Essays by
Drew Gilpin Faust
David R. Goldfield
Charles Joyner
Theresa A. Singleton
John Michael Vlach
Deborah Gray White

The Museum of the Confederacy, Richmond,
and the University Press of Virginia, Charlottesville

First edition

Third printing.

**Library of Congress
Cataloging-in-Publication Data**
Before freedom came: African-American life in the antebellum South: to accompany an exhibition organized by the Museum of the Confederacy / essays by Drew Gilpin Faust . . . [et al.]; edited by Edward D. C. Campbell, Jr., with Kym S. Rice

Exhibition held at the Museum of the Confederacy from July to December 1991, the McKissick Museum from January to March 1992, and the National Afro-American Museum and Cultural Center from April to June 1992.

Includes bibliographical references (p.) and index.
ISBN 0-8139-1332-2 (paper)

1. Slaves — Southern States — Social conditions — Exhibitions. 2. Afro-Americans — Southern States — Social conditions — Exhibitions. 3. Plantation life — Southern States — History — 19th century — Exhibitions. 4. Southern States — Social life and customs — 1775-1865 — Exhibitions. I. Faust, Drew Gilpin. II. Campbell, Edward D. C., 1946– . III. Rice, Kym S. IV. Museum of the Confederacy (Richmond, Va.) V. McKissick Museum. VI. National Afro-American Museum and Cultural Center (U.S.)
E443.B44   1991
975 — dc20   91-14386
                                                    CIP

Designer: Douglas W. Price
Goochland, Virginia

Production Managers: Tucker H. Hill,
Director of Museum Programs
John M. Coski, *Staff Historian*

Principal Photographer: Katherine Wetzel

Printer: Carter Printing Company
Richmond, Virginia

This book was published on the occasion of the exhibition *Before Freedom Came: African-American Life in the Antebellum South,* organized by Kym S. Rice, guest curator, and the staff of The Museum of the Confederacy, Richmond, Virginia. The exhibition was on view at The Museum of the Confederacy from July to December 1991; the McKissick Museum, of the University of South Carolina, Columbia, from January to March 1992, and the National Afro-American Museum and Cultural Center, Wilberforce, Ohio, from April to June 1992.

This book and the exhibition were made possible by generous grants from the National Endowment for the Humanities, Washington, D.C.

Contents

HAULING THE WHO

Plate 2.
During an 1842 visit to Nitta Yuma, a cotton plantation near Vicksburg, Mississippi, artist William Henry Brown created several collages depicting everyday plantation life for the children of the Vick family. In one scene, field hands bring in the "whole weeks picking," including large baskets full of cotton balanced on the heads and shoulders of male and female slaves.

EEKS PICKING

Notes on Contributors

Edward D. C. Campbell, Jr., is a former director of The Museum of the Confederacy and currently editor of *Virginia Cavalcade* magazine at the Virginia State Library and Archives, Richmond. He is the author of *The Celluloid South: Hollywood and the Southern Myth* (1981) as well as numerous essays on southern popular and material culture.

Drew Gilpin Faust is Annenberg Professor of History at the University of Pennsylvania. Her many publications include *The Sacred Circle: The Dilemma of the Intellectual in the Old South, 1840–1860* (1977), *The Ideology of Slavery: Proslavery Thought in the Antebellum South, 1830–1860* (1981), *James Henry Hammond and the Old South: A Design for Mastery* (1982), and *The Creation of Confederate Nationalism: Ideology and Identity in the Civil War South* (1988).

David R. Goldfield is Robert Lee Bailey Professor of History at the University of North Carolina at Charlotte. His many publications include *Urban Growth in the Age of Sectionalism: Virginia, 1847–1861* (1977), *The City in Southern History: The Growth of Urban Civilization in the South* (edited with Blaine A. Brownell, 1977), *Cotton Fields and Skyscrapers: Southern City and Region, 1607–1980* (1982), *Promised Land: The South Since 1945* (1987), and *Black, White, and Southern: Race Relations and Southern Culture 1940 to the Present* (1990).

Charles Joyner is Burroughs Distinguished Professor of Southern History at the University of South Carolina, Coastal Carolina College, and the author of numerous essays on southern folklore as well as *Folk Song in South Carolina* (1971)

and the highly acclaimed *Down by the Riverside: A South Carolina Slave Community* (1984).

Kym S. Rice served as guest curator for The Museum of the Confederacy's exhibition *Before Freedom Came: African-American Life in the Antebellum South* and has organized exhibitions for the Library of Congress, the New York Public Library, and the Virginia Women's Cultural History Project.

Theresa A. Singleton is an anthropologist and associate curator of historical archaeology at the National Museum of Natural History, Smithsonian Institution. She is the author of numerous essays on the archaeology of slave sites and the editor of *The Archaeology of Slavery and Plantation Life* (1985).

John Michael Vlach is professor of American civilization and director of the Folklife Program at the George Washington University, Washington, D.C.. His publications include *The Afro-American Tradition in Decorative Arts* (1978, reprint 1990), *Charleston Blacksmith: The Work of Philip Simmons* (1981), *Common Places: Readings in American Vernacular Architecture* (edited with Dell Upton, 1986), *Folk Art and Art Worlds* (edited with Simon Bronner, 1986), *Plain Painters: Making Sense of American Folk Art* (1988), and *By the Work of Their Hands: Studies in Afro-American Folklife* (1990).

Deborah Gray White is associate professor of history at Rutgers University and associate editor of the journal *Gender and History*. She is the author of the award-winning *Ar'n't I a Woman?: Female Slaves in the Plantation South* (1985).

Foreword

efore Freedom Came was a project conceived and organized by The Museum of the Confederacy. The exhibition, book, and the wide range of programming about African-American life in the antebellum South is evidence of the continued broadening of the Museum's interpretive mission over the last quarter century. Opened to the public in 1896 as a memorial endeavor, the Museum today seeks to collect, preserve, and interpret aspects of nineteenth-century southern life, especially the Confederate experience and the American Civil War.

In 1976 the Museum entered a new era with the opening of its museum building featuring three levels of modern gallery spaces. While the Museum presented its rich military collections in *The Confederate Years* on the main entrance level, a third of the upper gallery was devoted to its first social history exhibition, *People of the Confederacy*, which included the often overlooked experiences of African Americans and women. In the mid-1980s, the Museum presented two major exhibitions, *Women in Mourning* and *Victory in Defeat: Jefferson Davis and the Lost Cause*. These explored the role of women in the wartime and postwar South and examined the postwar Confederate memorial period.

At that time, the Museum was restoring Jefferson Davis's executive mansion, popularly known as "the White House of the Confederacy." Opened in 1988, this historic house represents the Museum's most ambitious project to expand its interpretive programs. All the while, the Museum has continued its role as one of the nation's principal repositories for objects and documents interpreting the Confederate experience.

For over a decade The Museum of the Confederacy considered plans to explore the long-neglected history of antebellum African-American life in the South. Not only was slavery the prewar South's "peculiar institution," but

African Americans also represented 40 percent of the population of the states that eventually made up the Confederate States of America.

Accordingly, in 1987 the Museum engaged the nationally respected curator Kym S. Rice to study the feasibility of mounting a major exhibition on the subject. Rice's inquiries to other museums and private collections revealed not only the existence of a significant number of artifacts but also a broad-based interest in the project and its success. We are grateful to those lending institutions and individuals for their cooperation. We are especially grateful to the National Endowment for the Humanities for two generous grants, which made this possible, and for its ongoing encouragement.

After opening at the Museum in 1991 and traveling to two other venues, *Before Freedom Came* was adapted by the Smithsonian Institution into a traveling exhibition that has been on display across the country since 1993. The Museum followed *Before Freedom Came* with such exhibitions as *Embattled Emblem: The Army of Northern Virginia Battle Flag, 1861–Present* and, most recently, its centennial exhibition, *A Woman's War: Southern Women, Civil War, and the Confederate Legacy*. Like *Before Freedom Came*, *A Woman's War* features an illustrated companion volume of essays published with the University Press of Virginia and is supported by major grants from the National Endowment for the Humanities.

The trustees and staff of The Museum of the Confederacy are proud of its diverse programming and especially pleased by the warm reception given *Before Freedom Came* in both its exhibition and published forms. This third printing of the first edition is evidence of its enduring success.

Robin Edward Reed
Executive Director
April 1997

Plate 3 (left).
A New Orleans city ordi-
nance required all black fe-
male residents to wear a
kerchief, or tignon *(a local*
variation of the word chi-
gnon), over their heads.
The subject of a ca. 1840
portrait, the well-dressed
New Orleans slave
adorned with a red tignon
is identified only as a maid
of the Douglas family.

Plate 4.
Adolph Rinck, a German artist, painted an unidentified femme de couleur libre, *or free*
woman of color, wearing an elaborate tignon in New Orleans in 1844. The subject is possi-
bly Marie Laveau, the famous voodoo priestess. An elderly former slave recalled that as a
child he had seen Laveau: "She come walkin' into Congo Square wit' her head up in the air
like a queen. Her skirts swished when she walked and everybody step back to let her pass.
All the people—white and colored—start sayin' that's the most powerful woman there is."

Preface

As public institutions concerned with the teaching of history, museums have struggled with ways to integrate the so-called New Social History into their interpretation of American life. In a speech summarizing recent interpretive exhibitions and programs, historian Gary Kulik dubbed history museums "agents for inclusion" ("History Museums and the Cultural Politics of the 1980s," *History News* 45, no. 5 [1990]: 22). The American museums he described actively include the story of women, immigrants, the poor and disadvantaged, native Americans, and other groups in their presentations to the public. Within the twenty-year period Kulik addressed, many institutions, large and small alike, have shifted with remarkable alacrity to follow current historical thinking, often forming partnerships with academics for the purpose of improving interpretation.

For all Kulik's praise, museums have yet to explore one of the central paradoxes in our history—African-American slavery. Using such resources as slave narratives and the techniques of archaeology and material culture, scholars have been able to reconstruct the lives of African-Americans—slave and free—in the antebellum South. But, perhaps because the subject remains so troubling and complex, slavery has never been the subject of a comprehensive exhibition.

This book and the exhibition it accompanies represent an effort to take advantage of recent scholarly achievements. They are offered to further our understanding of the important contributions to American culture made by antebellum slaves and free black people. As Louis F. Gorr, director of The Museum of the Confederacy, notes in his introduction, this project is an important step in the Museum's expanding interpretive scheme. It is an equally important step in the treatment of this subject. *Before Freedom Came* demonstrates that it is possible for a "majority" institution to take a critical look at this subject and to produce a book that displays both objectivity and integrity.

Before Freedom Came is intended for a broad audience, for the general reader as well as the student and scholar. The authors of the essays were asked to draw on original research and to synthesize the historical literature to provide an overarching view of African-American life in the South within a critical seventy-five-year period of great change. As each essayist demonstrates, the conditions of life for any individual slave or free black under the South's "peculiar institution" were far from homogeneous and were, in fact, subject to wide variation depending on such factors as geographic region, the prevailing staple crop, sex ratios and demographics, and the nature of the African-Americans' relationship with whites.

In her introduction, Drew Gilpin Faust, of the University of Pennsylvania, surveys the historiography of American slavery and race relations and the problems both have posed for American values. John Michael Vlach, of the George Washington University, describes the physical setting—the natural and built environments—and how the plantation landscape shaped the daily routines of slaves. Charles Joyner, of the University of South Carolina, Coastal Carolina College, offers a wide-ranging view of "the world of the plantation slaves" throughout the antebellum South. Deborah Gray White, of Rutgers University, summarizes her seminal work on the lives of slave women. The essay by David R. Goldfield, of the University of North Carolina, Charlotte, analyzes the lives of slaves and free blacks in urban settings and focuses on the changing relationships between blacks and whites in southern cities during the 1850s. The book concludes with a pioneering essay by Theresa A. Singleton, of the Smithsonian Institution, that presents the significant findings of a decade of archaeological investigation of slave sites across the South. Historical archaeology offers some of the most tantalizing—and controversial—evidence concerning the creation of African-American culture.

This project was initiated by the Board of Trustees of The Museum of the Confederacy and supported by two generous grants from the National Endowment for the Humanities, funding which permitted the project director to consult collections at numerous institutions and to draw materials from many different sources. The illustrations selected for this book reveal the range of visual materials and objects available to enhance our understanding of the antebellum African-American experience. Many are published here together for the first time. Particularly remarkable are the photographs taken during the Civil War, images that capture the transformation of southern slaves into free men and women.

As the essays suggest, historians themselves disagree over how best to understand the black experience in the South, and their interpretations undoubtedly will continue to develop, be refined, and change. Suggestions for further readings, compiled with the assistance of the authors, are included with the hope that the interested reader will wish to learn more. Primary source materials are many and diverse. Of particular interest are the slave narratives—interviews with elderly former slaves recorded largely in the 1930s under the auspices of the Work Projects Administration and its Federal Writers' Project. These offer a memorable and moving memoir of slavery from those who experienced it.

This book, in fact, takes its title from the phrase "before freedom" that appears in so many of the narratives. Slaves were fully aware of how emancipation changed their lives. One ex-slave in Texas compared her life before and after freedom: "In slavery I ownes nothin' and never ownes nothin'. In freedom I's own de home and raise de family. All dat cause me worryment and in slavery I have no worryment, but I takes de freedom."

Kym S. Rice
Project Director

Plate 5.
A well-known view of a southern plantation illustrates the distinct life slaves created for themselves in the quarter apart from their owners. While the specific entertainment is unknown, it is probably African in origin. One of the musicians plays a banjo made in the method of many central and West African stringed instruments. To his left, a man beats a drum made from a skin-covered gourd and identified as a quaqua *by early traveler J. F. D. Smyth.*

Plate 6 (right).
France was but one of several European nations engaged in the eighteenth-century slave trade between Africa and the Caribbean. An unknown artist in 1773 depicted the slave ship Marie Séraphique, *of Nantes, moored off Cap Français in the French colony of Saint Domingue, the western portion of the island of Hispaniola. On board, white gentlemen and ladies enjoyed a festive picnic astern while others examined the human cargo just arrived from Angola. Cap Français was later the site of a bloody slave revolt that led to years of conflict against both French and later British occupation.*

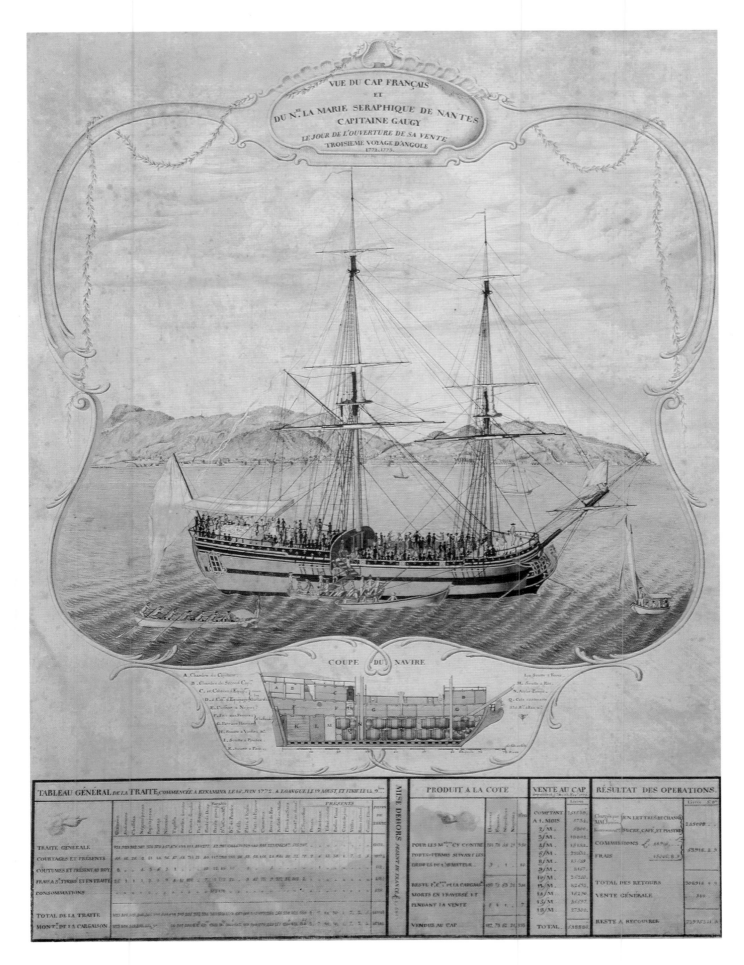

SLAVERY IN THE AMERICAN EXPERIENCE

Drew Gilpin Faust

Fig. 1.
A group of former slaves posed for a photographer at Saint Helena Island, South Carolina, shortly after receiving their freedom.

Fig. 2.
In his late-eighteenth-century narrative, Olaudah Equiano recorded the horrors of the Middle Passage: "The closeness of the place, and the heat of the climate, added to the number in the ship, being so crowded that each had scarcely room to turn himself, almost suffocated us. . . . The shrieks of the women, and the groans of the dying, rendered it a scene of horror almost inconceivable."

Founded upon ideals of liberty only imperfectly understood, the United States has struggled to define its conception of freedom. In the writings of the Founding Fathers, *slavery* served as the antithesis of the much cherished notion of liberty. It was, after all, from *slavery* to Great Britain that the colonists were most determined to escape. Yet many of these founders were themselves slaveholders and in the Constitution and in subsequent legislation established human bondage as a legal reality in the new nation. The force of this paradox has made understanding our experience with slavery central to grasping the changing meaning of American freedom—not just as it appeared to our forebears, but as we, too, perceive liberty and human rights.[1] Slavery may have ended with the Thirteenth Amendment in 1865, but the questions it raised about America's national identity have persisted in the troubling realities of twentieth-century racism and oppression.

Slavery came to the Americas as part of Europe's general political and commercial expansion between the fifteenth and nineteenth centuries. An ancient institution that had flourished in Greece and Rome, slavery by 1500 was all but moribund within most of Europe, surviving only in the Mediterranean states of Spain and Portugal. But the growing desire of European nations for global power stimulated a contest for worldwide trading empires based on the production and exchange of exotic crops. It was this economic expansionism that encouraged systems of unfree labor in colonies beyond the European continent. The growth of slavery on the European periphery made the provision of slave laborers itself a central part of international commercial exchange, and directed the attention of European states to sources of supply in Africa.[2]

Various forms of domestic dependency known as slavery existed across much of the African continent, but these institutions did not involve the same scale, market orientation, or social alien-

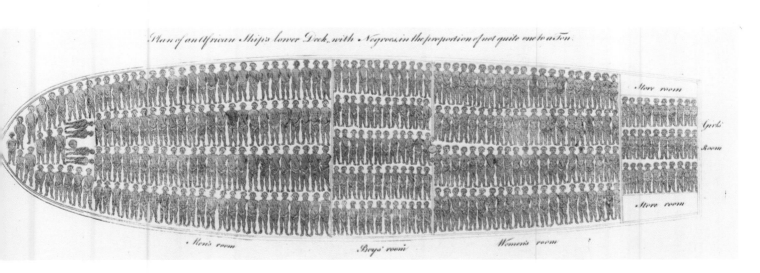

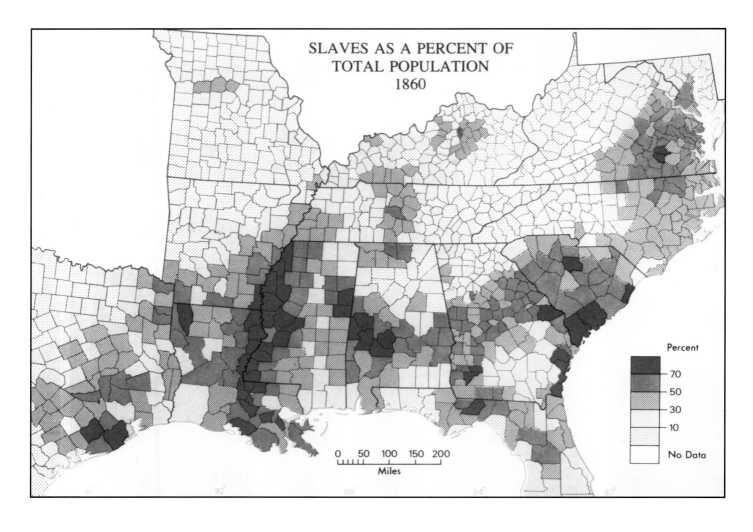

SLAVES AS A PERCENT OF
TOTAL POPULATION
1860

Percent
— 70
— 50
— 30
— 10

No Data

0   50 100 150 200
└┴┴┴┴┘
Miles

Fig. 3.
By 1860 nearly four million African-American slaves lived in the South, with the largest percentage concentrated in the areas of sugar, rice, and cotton production.

ation that would characterize the New World's slave systems. International demand for ever-increasing numbers of blacks, however, transformed the character of slavery even within certain regions of Africa at the same time it produced a new order of "unfreedom" in the Western Hemisphere. In pursuit of profits and power, Africans responded to the European demand for labor by creating a much-expanded internal market in humans. Particularly in West Africa, tribal and national conflict erupted specifically over the effort to seize war captives for sale to European traders. Over the four centuries of its existence, the Atlantic slave trade between Africa and the Americas is estimated to have involved not just the twelve million Africans who were shipped westward, but perhaps almost as many who died in Africa from the cruelties of capture and their initial enslavement.[3] Scholars still vehemently debate the actual numbers of Africans taken from their homelands, as well as the significance of their removal for Africa's subsequent history and development, but there can be little doubt that the Atlantic slave trade constituted one of the largest forced movements of population in recorded history.[4]

The present-day United States became the northernmost destination of a trade that touched the Caribbean as early as a decade after Christopher Columbus's voyage of discovery. By the middle of the sixteenth century, the trade had populated Brazil with sugar workers. Indeed, most of the early importations involved only the Portuguese and Spanish, by then long engaged with slavery in their own homelands as well as in Old World plantation colonies such as Cyprus, Madeira, and Sao Tome, an island just off Africa's west coast.[5] The English and French, who were to settle most of North America, had little direct knowledge of either African or plantation slavery and in the late-sixteenth and early-seventeenth centuries had no plans to establish the institution in their colonies.

At the outset, the English hoped their 1607 settlement at Jamestown might prosper through trade with native Americans. It soon became clear, however, that Virginia would of necessity be an agricultural colony instead, one based initially on the labor of indentured servants immigrating from the motherland. But when a Dutch man-of-war wandered up the James River in 1619 seeking provisions in exchange for a cargo of "23 and odd

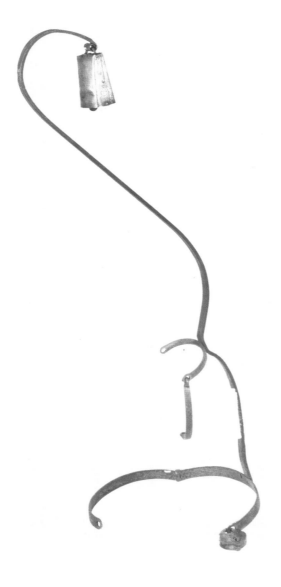

Fig. 4.
Mississippi ex-slave John Crawford recalled that his master constructed a harness, similar to the example shown here, to control troublesome slaves: "Five feet over they heads he hung a brass bell on the top where they can't reach it. Then he turned them loose and told them, 'Don't you let me hear that bell leavin' this place, or God have mercy on your black hides.'" The slaves thwarted their master by muffling the sound of the bell clappers with mud.

Negroes," a seemingly chance encounter initiated the slow transformation of Virginia society and of the land that would eventually become the United States. The Virginians' purchase of these Africans did not, however, inaugurate a fully structured slave system. Instead, for more than a half century, the status of these unwilling immigrants remained unclear. In most instances they were at first probably treated like white indentured laborers. But by 1660 a series of provincial laws in England's Chesapeake colonies indicated that Africans had come to occupy a social position quite different from that of whites. Unlike white indentured servants, who were freed after four to seven years, the blacks' term of service—and their children's—was to be for life. Racial slavery had come to British North America.[6]

Thus, although slaves were present throughout English North America by about 1640, the formal institution of slavery grew slowly, in part because of the difficulty and expense of obtaining African slaves from a trade dominated by the Spanish and Portuguese and in part, too, because of English preferences for laborers of their own nationality and ethnicity so long as such workers were readily and cheaply available. By the last three decades of the seventeenth century, however, such preferences could no longer prevail. Improved economic conditions in England together with increasingly constrained opportunities for quick wealth in the Chesapeake region greatly reduced the number of white workers willing to risk their destinies abroad.[7]

Serendipitously, the English Royal African Company in 1672 entered into the slave trade, thus making available the ever-increasing number of African laborers required to meet the growing demand. In all, between five hundred thousand and six hundred thousand blacks were imported into mainland North America. These numbers, however, represent only about 5 percent of the total Atlantic trade. Unlike their counterparts in Latin America and the Caribbean—whose numbers were sustained only though massive, continuing imports—North American slaves increased naturally at about the same rate as the white population.

Slaves destined for the Atlantic colonies came chiefly from the West African coastal areas between Senegambia and Angola. An extensive area encompassing a great diversity of soils, climate, and ethnic groups, the region included Africans of widely varied cultural and linguistic attributes, attributes that influenced price and salability in the Atlantic market. A knowledge of rice cultivation among Africans from parts of Upper Guinea and the Niger Delta, for example, made such slaves highly desirable to South Carolina rice planters. Because of the African market's own preference for female slaves, regarded as the most productive laborers, and a reverse prejudice for male workers among American buyers, almost twice as many men as women were transported across the Atlantic, an imbalance that delayed the establishment of stable black family life in the New World.[8]

The dramatic growth in the number of slaves imported into the southern colonies in the late seventeenth century was to have both a qualitative and quantitative impact upon the nature of both colonial society and the institution of slavery itself. From the earliest voyages, the largest importations of slaves went to the southern colonies, in large part because of their geographic proximity to the already thriving Caribbean trade. Even more significant, the South's emerging plantation-based agriculture also promised the highest profitable use of slave labor. As the proportion of blacks to whites began to change,

both groups found themselves in a new, evolving relationship.

For whites, the rising number of blacks often aroused anxiety, especially in areas such as the South Carolina low country where by the early eighteenth century slaves outnumbered whites by as much as four or five to one. Such realities, represented most strikingly by the emergence of a black majority in South Carolina by 1708, motivated whites to exert more systematic control over blacks, to regulate interracial contact more closely, and to curtail insofar as possible all forms of black autonomy. Laws appeared forbidding blacks to bear arms, requiring slaves to acknowledge their servitude and inferior status by wearing certain kinds of clothing, and prohibiting slaves from learning to read or write.

The growing availability of slaves brought a transformation of labor patterns as well, for many individual masters acquired dramatically larger holdings. Masters who had once worked side by side with just one or two slaves now owned a dozen or more. The process was especially striking as plantation agriculture became established in the malaria-infested South Carolina coastal parishes, areas shunned by whites during much of the year. Scores of blacks labored in the coastal rice fields under the supervision of only one or two white overseers. Although in the Chesapeake colonies blacks did not comprise such a high proportion of the population, tobacco culture in Virginia and Maryland similarly moved toward larger work units, involving gangs of black slaves isolated from constant and direct interaction with white masters.[9]

The significance of these demographic shifts for blacks extended beyond the loss of freedom and status entailed by the rigid codifying of the slave institution. For many Africans, the increased number of fellow slaves meant the opportunity to establish black communal life, find marriage partners and create families on their home planta-

Fig. 6, Fig. 7.
Taken at Stirrup Branch plantation near Bishopville, South Carolina, an 1857 tintype captured members of the Rembert family on the front porch of their house. In a second, companion tintype, their slaves are organized by rank, with the driver in the mid-foreground, followed by the house servants and the field hands. The woman to the right is identified as a cook.

tions, and preserve their African beliefs and customs in a New World setting. The massive increase in slave importations in the late seventeenth and early eighteenth centuries thus made possible a distinct African-American culture born of the slaves' own diverse experiences.[10]

The nature of this African-American culture has been of enormous interest to scholars during the past three decades. Until the late 1950s, most historians assumed that very little of the African past had survived among American slaves—slaves who were thought to have largely, if imperfectly, adopted the beliefs and standards of their white masters. Such views grew almost naturally out of a scholarship that reflected American culture's racist assumptions. The leading early-twentieth-century historian of slavery, Ulrich B. Phillips, defended the peculiar institution as benign and benevolent, a school designed to train inferior and benighted Africans in the superior ways of the white race, while at the same time protecting blacks from the harsh realities of the wider world.[11]

As views shifted about the place of African-Americans in contemporary life, conceptions about the black past also began to change. While World War II discredited racism by associating it with the Nazi enemy, and as civil rights in the postwar decade became part of the national agenda, Americans' understanding of slavery's significance began to change. In 1956, in the wake of the U.S. Supreme Court's *Brown* v. *Topeka Board of Education* decision calling for school integration, a young and politically committed historian named Kenneth M. Stampp published *The Peculiar Institution,* a direct challenge to Phillips's conception of slavery. Like Phillips, Stampp focused on the system's impact upon the slave, but reached strikingly different conclusions. Detailing the physical realities of slave life—describing slave diet, housing, work routines, and punishment—Stampp concluded that rather than a benevolent institution, slavery had been harsh and exploitative.[12]

Three years later, Stanley Elkins published a study intended to transcend what he perceived as the inherent limitations of the Stampp-Phillips debate over the physical treatment of slaves. The most interesting question about slavery, Elkins asserted, a question left almost entirely unaddressed by its historians, was the nature not of its physical but its psychological impact upon its victims. Using a variety of innovative approaches, including comparative history and psychological theory, Elkins argued that slavery had been as devastating emotionally as Stampp had shown it to be physically. Slave culture and identity, he believed, had been destroyed by the cruelties of capture, transportation, and forced labor. Consequently, slaves retained almost nothing of African culture or any other foundations for independent selfhood. Moreover, in North America institutions such as the church and crown did not effectively protect the slave—in contrast, Elkins argued, to the constraints both exercised upon the planters' arbitrary power in Latin America. As a result, he concluded, southern slaves almost completely accepted their masters' views of them, acknowledging their own inferiority as "Sambos." Slavery, Elkins contended, transformed blacks into permanently infantilized and dependent human beings with no significant figures—except their oppressive masters—to serve as sources of identity and self-worth.[13]

Elkins's startling—and, to many, offensive—assertions generated almost immediate controversy and ultimately led to a generation of new scholarship undertaken to refute his claims.[14] Elkins's insistence upon the master as the African-American's only important influence led scholars to ask new questions about the role of black families, religion, and the slave community in providing a counterweight to white psychological power. The portrait of the docile slave also prompted renewed scholarly interest in black resistance and rebellion. And as other historians looked again at Latin American slavery and especially Elkins's comparatively favorable assessment of the Spanish and Portuguese slave systems, the field of comparative slave studies emerged.[15]

The intense debate and criticism that greeted Elkins's book coincided with further shifts in twentieth-century American race relations. Although Elkins had in important conceptual ways gone beyond the work of both Phillips and Stampp, all three historians shared one fundamental and, in the political atmosphere of the 1960s, increasingly debatable assumption. Each perceived the slave as largely passive and powerless, as one acted *upon* by the institution of slavery. Although Phillips regarded slaves as the beneficiaries while Stampp and Elkins saw them as the victims of white power, all three scholars assumed that the slave experience was shaped almost entirely by white masters. With the emergence in the mid-1960s of Black Power to challenge the integrationist principles of the earlier Civil Rights movement, historians began to look differently at their own scholarly projects, responding to the question perhaps most forcefully posed by black novelist Ralph Ellison. "Can a people," he demanded, "live and develop over three hundred years simply by reacting? Are American Negroes simply the creation of white men or have they . . . helped create themselves out of what they found around them?"[16]

Fig. 8.
An unidentified African-American is included in an album of formal portraits taken of Robert E. Lee's slaves.

The portrayal of slaves as empowered actors with the means and motivation to shape their own destinies thus reflected political priorities of the 1960s and 1970s and transformed the nature of historical scholarship about slavery. In books such as John Blassingame's *The Slave Community,* Herbert Gutman's *The Black Family in Slavery and Freedom,* Lawrence Levine's *Black Culture and Black Consciousness,* and in Eugene Genovese's massive and synthetic *Roll, Jordan, Roll,* historians explored what Genovese advanced as the subtitle of his important work: "the world the slaves made."[17] The search for the voice of the slave led scholars to new sorts of sources—architecture, archaeology, songs, folklore, material objects—appropriate to the study of a people forbidden by law the literacy necessary for the production of conventional historical evidence such as manuscript letters and diaries.

Central to this newly recognized slave culture and identity were the family ties that slaves established as soon as sizable plantation communities and a more even sex ratio emerged from the chaos of forced immigration. With the first native-born generation, kinship networks and a particular African-American family culture began to appear. More recent scholarship suggests that eighteenth- and nineteenth-century slave families were strong, even if often rendered unstable by sale or forcible migration. One scholar has estimated that during the 1800s such separations destroyed as many as one in three first marriages in the Upper South, a figure that indicates how ever-present the fear, as well as the reality, of forced separations must have been.[18]

Despite the devastating effects of such white interference, and despite the refusal of American law to recognize slave marriages, most slaves born in North America grew up with two parents. Yet these families varied in significant ways from those of southern whites. Naming patterns and marital choices, such as a prohibition on first-cousin unions, for example, reflected African influences, and the importance of widely extended kinship networks represented both the persistence of an Old World tradition and a means of adaptation to the ever-present threat of family separations.

The conditions of slavery and the practices of African-American family life shaped the experience of slave women in ways that distinguished their lives from those of both white women and black men. Slave women bore a double burden of gender and race. Their obligations as laborers outside the home made both their domestic and work roles unlike those of most white southern women, while their central role within family life in most cases still left them with more extensive family duties than slave men. Unlike eighteenth- and nineteenth-century white fathers and husbands, black men exerted no legal control over their women and children. This in one sense freed slave women from the oppressions of patriarchal marriage. But slave women were directly subjected to the power of white men, a less constrained and thus ultimately more devastating form of domination.[19]

Just as they derived solace and support from family life, so slaves drew comfort from strong religious ties. While white masters often encouraged a form of Christianity that emphasized obedience and acceptance, African-Americans appropriated a different side of Christianity, one emphasizing the religion of Moses and the exodus of the Israelites from bondage in Egypt. Moreover, the Christian emphasis upon freedom in the world to come offered many slaves a hope of freedom here and now, a sense of ultimate if not immediate self-justification and self-worth. And in fostering the role of preacher, slave religion provided an opportunity for black leadership, for personal aspiration and achievement. Slaves who served as preachers, like those who distinguished themselves as artisans, midwives, healers, musicians, or even slave drivers, demonstrated the inaccuracy of the "Sambo" stereotype.[20]

Rebellious blacks like Nat Turner, Gabriel Prosser, and Denmark Vesey, all of whom planned large uprisings during the nineteenth century, similarly challenged the notion of slave docility. From the earliest days of their captivity until the eve of emancipation, slaves in North America plotted and executed insurrections. Yet their record of rebellion does not compare to that of slave societies in the Caribbean and Latin America where massive, destructive revolts occurred throughout the slave era. In North America, a number of factors—including a smaller proportion of slaves within the population, the presence of a resident, as opposed to an absentee master class, and the absence of nearby runaway slave communities—hampered such outbursts. North American slaves were realistic in assessing the difficulties of mounting a successful rebellion. As a result, they more often expressed their resistance in less revolutionary, less organized, less overt forms, ranging from self-emancipation, through running away, to breaking tools, to stealing provisions, even to poisoning the food of the master's family.[21]

Much of black-white interaction within the South's peculiar institution made clear that whites were far from all-powerful. Especially during the last six or seven decades of slavery, whites sought to make the system consistent with the new humanitarianism that characterized the age. Historian Willie Lee Rose has written of the "domestication" of southern slavery in the nineteenth century, explaining that "the Old South was actually engaged in a process of rationalizing slavery, not only in an economic sense, but also in emotional and psychological terms."[22] Slaves were not to be dominated by simple brute force; instead, masters endeavored through persuasion, manipulation, and negotiation to elicit blacks' acquiescence—which whites often chose to regard as consent—to the conditions of their bondage. "Inspire a negro with perfect confidence in you & learn him to look to you for support," one planter explained, "& he is your slave."[23]

The doctrines of paternalism, widely embraced by the southern master class, prescribed that whites' power over slaves be tempered by responsibility for their dependents' welfare. Paternalism defined slavery as a system of mutual obligations—of slave to master and of master to slave—thus offering southern planters a moral justification for their exploitation of black labor. But this ideology of reciprocity at the same time ensnared white southerners in a web of duty and imbued slaves with a doctrine of rights.

It is important to recognize, as did white southerners themselves, that these paternal, humane ideals were far from realized in the antebellum South. Both the masters' records and the slaves' testimony taken in the years after emancipation reveal that brutal whippings, insufficient food and clothing, rape of slave women by white men, and forcible separation of families were far from rare occurrences. Yet, however much violated in the day-to-day operations of slavery, the ideology of paternalism represented at least an abstract white commitment to some fundamental level of humanity and black welfare. This in turn provided slaves with considerable leverage—even negotiating power—over their masters, who in the evangelical South found themselves deeply invested in the ideals—if not always the practice—of Christian stewardship.[24]

The white ideology of paternalism and the flourishing of black community and culture were alike products of the maturing slave system in the years surrounding the American Revolution. The ideals Americans articulated as the foundation of their new nation necessarily placed slavery under close scrutiny. Revolutionary rhetoric had stressed the evils of colonial enslavement to Great Britain, compelling Americans to question the legitimacy of racial slavery in their own midst.[25] And during the war, hundreds of blacks themselves seized opportunities for freedom from the chaos of invading armies and social disruption. Blacks also served in both the British and Continental forces,

Fig. 9.
The possibility of sale always threatened whatever measure of family life a slave might achieve. Upon her purchase and separation from her mother, brothers, and sisters, one woman recollected, "it seem like I griebe ter death . . .one mornin' dey took me off an' I never see'd one of 'em again." A Canadian traveler sketched this view of a Charleston slave auction.

Fig. 10.
The relationship between master and slave shifted daily. Bondspeople carefully preserved a life apart from their owners. "One life they show their masters and another life they don't show," recalled former slave Robert Smalls in 1862.

Fig. 11.
In describing his life as a field hand, a former slave from North Carolina remembered, "We hated to see the sun rise in slavery time, 'cause it meant another hard day; but then we was glad to see it go down."

Fig. 12.
Carrying loads of cotton balanced on their heads, field laborers at Woodlands plantation, near Charleston, followed the driver back from the fields at sunset.

often winning their freedom in return for military service.[26]

The period's revolutionary ideals influenced many individual southern masters to manumit their own slaves, leading to a dramatic growth in the free black population, especially in the Upper South. Although several northern states had sizable slave populations during the colonial period (slaves had comprised as much as 15 percent of New York's population, for example), the Revolution inaugurated a process of abolition that reduced the North's unfree population to fewer than three thousand by 1830.[27] The antislavery impulses of the revolutionary generation were, however, ultimately limited in their impact. The task of building a nation took clear precedence in the minds of the Founding Fathers over any commitment to abstractions of human equality. And racist assumptions shared throughout eighteenth-century American society made it impossible for white Americans to contemplate a biracial society of equals. Much of the opposition to human bondage, moreover, arose from fears about the corrupting influence of absolute power upon whites, rather than concerns about the situation of the black slave.[28]

During the debates over the Constitution a clearly defined slavery interest emerged, articulated most forcefully by representatives from South Carolina and Georgia. Politicians concerned about national unity thus struggled to compromise on the place of slavery within the new national order, restricting its growth by providing for the end of the transatlantic slave trade by 1808, yet at the same time recognizing the institution by counting slaves in the apportionment of congressional seats as "three-fifths of all other persons."[29] Perhaps the most important result of the revolutionary generation's ambivalent legacy concerning slavery, however, was its effective restriction of the institution to the southern states. In the new nation, slavery became a "peculiar" institution, a system increasingly on the defensive in the face of expanding national boundaries and power.

Yet if slavery was in some ways weakened by the Revolution and its aftermath, the exponential growth in cotton production after 1790 made slavery even more important to southern identity and prosperity. Cotton production increased steadily in those areas of the South with at least a two-hundred-day annual growing season, creating a realm that stretched from southern North Carolina across central Tennessee into Arkansas. Output tripled in the single decade after the War of 1812, the flush times for settlement of the rich cotton areas to the southwest, areas that soon became the states of Alabama and Mississippi. With the movement of slaves to the southwest averaging more than two hundred thousand each decade between 1820 and the Civil War, the institution of slavery spread across the South.

The political implications of such changes were soon evident. Acrimonious debates between 1819 and 1821 over the admission of Missouri to the Union exposed the consolidation of an aggressive slave interest, an interest made increasingly assertive by the growing yields of slave agriculture. The North and South were all the more

Fig. 13.
Picking cotton required strength and dexterity. Scales measured each laborer's work, with some hands able to pick three hundred pounds a day.

distinctive and divergent. It was, as Thomas Jefferson put it, like the sounding of "a firebell in the night," an alarming portent of greater conflicts to come.[30] Slavery had become peculiar to the South and the South peculiar within the nation. "Slavery," wrote antebellum South Carolinian William Henry Trescot, "informs all our modes of life, all our habits of thought, lies at the basis of our social existence, and of our political faith."[31]

Throughout antebellum southern history, the strength of political support for slavery varied with the predominance of the institution itself from place to place. Slaves were unevenly distributed geographically, with much heavier concentrations in the Deep South states of the Cotton Kingdom where on the eve of the Civil War there were eighty-two blacks to every one hundred whites. In the Upper South, the system was less firmly entrenched, with only thirty blacks for every one hundred whites. Within individual states as well, patterns of slave ownership varied. The coastal areas of the South Atlantic states, regions

like the Eastern Shore of Maryland, the tidewater of Virginia, the low country of South Carolina, and the Sea Islands of Georgia, retained sizable populations of slaves even after the heavy movements of population to the Southwest, while piedmont and mountain areas of the same states were primarily farming areas, settled largely by whites, rather than plantation regions containing substantial numbers of black slaves. In the Deep South, too, divisions appeared within states, most often expressed as conflicts between fertile Black Belt and less richly productive hill-country areas. Across the South, these differences assumed political expression as the sectional conflict intensified after 1830. The heaviest slaveholding areas were the very regions that ultimately voted most enthusiastically for secession, while the predominantly white areas were more likely to resist southern independence and, in some instances, to produce subversive pockets of wartime Unionist sentiment.[32]

Slaves were also unevenly distributed among owners, a reality with profound meaning for the slave's experience. In 1860 approximately 24 percent of white southerners were members of slaveholding families and, of these, 49 percent owned fewer than five slaves. Only 12 percent of owners possessed more than twenty slaves, the number usually considered the minimum necessary to comprise a plantation. Only 1 percent held more than one hundred. For owners, therefore, slavery was most often experienced on a fairly small scale. But because of the existence of some large concentrations, the majority of slaves in fact lived in plantation-size units. By 1860 the South contained more than forty-six thousand such holdings. Thus most southern blacks lived within groups large enough to make community

Fig. 14.
On the Bayside plantation, Bayou Teche, Louisiana, slaves earned money or merchandise for completing extra jobs or for raising produce for sale on their own time. The plantation ledger included the slaves' accounts.

Fig. 15.
By 1860 approximately 250,000 free blacks resided in the South, chiefly in North Carolina, Virginia, and Maryland. Although frequently regarded with suspicion and distrust by whites, many were able to fashion lives for themselves and their families on the periphery of southern society. But not always. In one instance, two whites kidnapped, tortured, and killed a Maryland free black.

and family life possible.[33]

Although the plantation, and the cotton plantation in particular, was the black laborers' most characteristic experience in the nineteenth century, the system of bondage encompassed considerable diversity as well. Although three-fourths of all southern slaves worked in cotton on the eve of the Civil War, unfree workers also cultivated wheat in Virginia and Maryland, tobacco in those same states as well as in North Carolina and Kentucky, sugar in Louisiana, rice along the South Carolina and Georgia coasts, hemp in Kentucky, and foodstuffs, especially corn, almost everywhere. Work routines differed according to the size of a particular slaveholding, which in turn helped determine whether slaves labored under the direct supervision of a master, that of a white overseer, or perhaps of a black driver.

But labor patterns also varied from crop to crop. Sugar production, because of the necessity of promptly refining the newly harvested crop, included industrial processes unique in southern agriculture and employed a disproportionate number of males. Rice cultivation, requiring extensive hydraulic engineering to provide ditches and gates for flooding the crop, encouraged a task system of labor, with slaves assigned differentiated, individualized jobs rather than being worked together in a gang. Because a task was defined by an average worker's ability to complete it within a single day, enterprising and skillful slaves often found themselves finished with their obligations early enough to claim independent time. Task labor was thus not only subject to less direct supervision than gang work but also

gave slaves something of a life apart from constant white demands. In the South Carolina low country, for example, some slaves even used the time to plant and market their own crops and thus accumulate considerable holdings of their own property. Slaves with claims of ownership to goods and livestock represented a reality strikingly at odds with the struggle by Carolina masters from the early eighteenth century on to perfect their domination over the black population by excluding slaves from the market economy.[34]

The diversity of the Old South's slave system encompassed more than just varieties of agriculture. As much as 5 percent of the region's slave population in 1850 worked in industry, especially in the manufacture of textiles and iron, in the processing of tobacco, and in mining. The great majority of these workers were male, usually owned by the companies that used their labor, although perhaps 20 percent were hired on an annual basis from individual masters. Skilled slaves often offered themselves for hire as well, paying their wages to their masters, but possessing considerable independence in managing their own hours and work. Slave hiring flourished particularly in southern cities, where the practice proved well adapted to the varied and changing economic needs of an urban environment.

More than 140,000 slaves lived in cities in 1860, and because the region's population of free blacks was also concentrated in urban areas, the South's largest cities were more than 20 percent African-American. Although the system of hiring-out introduced a degree of flexibility to the South's labor system, southerners worried

Fig. 16.
Prosperous free blacks, mostly Creoles of color called gens de couleur libre, *composed a significant percentage of New Orleans society. One, a young woman identified as Marie Lassus, the daughter of a black mother and a Parisian father, posed for a visiting French photographer in 1860.*

that it also represented the insidious encroachment of a free labor system as well as a challenge to the alleged paternalism and mutuality of the master-slave relationship. One who rented a slave simply did not have the same investment and interest in the slave's welfare as one who owned him.[35]

Even more forcefully than the system of work for hire, the presence of free blacks served as an ever-present reminder of the unavoidable contradictions present in a system of racial slavery. From the colonial period onward, white Americans treated free blacks as not entirely free, constraining them with laws designed to keep them in subordination. Although individual regulations varied from state to state, in most cases free blacks were prohibited from testifying against whites in court, from marrying or engaging in sexual relations with white women, from voting, and from claiming equal access to public accommodations. Nevertheless, some free blacks, particularly in the privileged urban communities of New Orleans and Charleston, managed to accumulate sizable property holdings.[36]

As mounting sectional conflict compelled southerners to defend slavery against ideological attack from the North, as well as from possible subversion from within, the position of the free person of color seemed a growing threat to the logic upon which the system rested. Free black David Walker's 1829 publication of an appeal to slaves to revolt and the discovery in 1822 of a planned uprising by a Charleston free black,

Denmark Vesey, only reinforced growing white fears.[37] New laws greatly restricted manumission, prohibited contact between free blacks and slaves, and generally circumscribed the independence of the free black population. On the eve of the Civil War these oppressive measures intensified, and many whites urged that all free people of color be forced into slavery. Unlike most other slave societies in the Western Hemisphere, the American South struggled to limit the possibilities for attaining freedom and to restrict the meaning of that freedom once realized.[38] There was thus no real exit from slavery; free blacks were largely, as one historian has characterized it, "slaves without masters," subject not to the domination of a single individual, but to that of society as a whole.[39]

Historians' recent emphasis on the autonomy and diversity possible within slavery has provided an important corrective to a historical literature that had cast slaves either as passive victims or beneficiaries of white domination. Yet some scholars are now suggesting that the interpretive pendulum may have swung too far. Slavery was a cruel and oppressive institution that in constraining its subjects' freedom must inevitably have shaped their lives in ways we have yet fully to understand. If "oppression" did not necessarily, as one fugitive from slavery put it, drive "the wise man mad," bondage must at least have had an impact on slave personality and culture, an impact that is crucial to our understanding of the slave experience.[40] "We simply cannot," Bertram Wyatt-Brown has recently suggested, "continue expatiating on the riches of black culture without also examining the social and psychological tensions that slavery entailed."[41]

In an intriguing exploration of these issues, Peter Kolchin has used comparative history to evaluate the character of southern slave culture. By looking simultaneously at the lives of Russian serfs and American slaves, he has concluded that we may have exaggerated "the strength and cohesion of the slave community."[42] Southern slaves lived, he reminds us, on holdings that were small in comparison with those in Latin America or the Caribbean, as well as with the settlements of serfs in Russia. Building a community was difficult on farms with ten or fewer slaves, for even finding a marriage partner and establishing a family often proved impossible. Most southern slaveholders tended, again unlike Russian lords and Latin American masters, to reside on their plantation, impinging on the slaves' world in ways that severely limited black autonomy. The intrusiveness of the accompanying paternalism constrained the independence of both masters and slaves. In the United States, moreover, slaves lacked the economic independence of many serfs as well as the institutional autonomy Russian peasants obtained through the recognized formal structures of their *mir*, or village community, in which families cultivated jointly owned land.[43] The institutions of southern slave society, such as the black church, thus necessarily remained invisible.

The scholarly revisions and counterrevisions generated by Stanley Elkins's provocative assertions compel us to consider the forces both encouraging and circumscribing the power of both masters and slaves. Blacks and whites struggled unceasingly within the slave system, with each race endeavoring to extend its control to maximum possible limits. Each group defined its

unity in large part by its contentious relationship with the other. Neither existed in autonomy. Each was defined by its opposition to the other.

For southern whites, the implication of this reality, the undeniability of black power, became ever more alarming as antislavery forces to the North threatened to reinforce the system's internal instability. Although individual Americans had spoken out against slavery from the earliest days of its existence, most such critiques offered only gradualist solutions, if indeed they advocated any specific program of change at all. By the 1830s, encouraged by lingering revolutionary sentiment and by the identification of slavery as exclusively southern, a new and more aggressive antislavery

Fig. 17.
Frederick Douglass, the former Maryland slave who emancipated himself in 1838, became one of the most compelling of the northern abolitionists.

Fig. 18.
Many male slaves accompanied their Confederate masters into the army. "Whenever there was fighting," one ex-slave recalled, "all of us Negroes had the camp to look after and when the shooting was over we had to help bring in the wounded. In between battles we had to keep all our masters' boots polished, the horses and harness cleaned and the rifles and swords spic and span." Posing for a wartime ambrotype, Marlboro, the manservant of Major Raleigh S. Camp, of Georgia, wore a Confederate frock coat and a variety of other accoutrements, some of which were perhaps battlefield souvenirs.

spirit emerged. Rejecting cautious, evolutionary approaches, the new abolitionists called for immediate freedom for blacks, without compensation for their owners. Confined to northern states, the abolitionist movement was highly unpopular even there and aroused mobs that attacked antislavery meetings and activists. Still, the petition campaigns and public meetings of slavery's opponents drew continuing national attention and placed the South ever more firmly on the defensive.[44]

It was not abolitionism, however, but the territorial issues raised by the Mexican War that made sectional confrontation over slavery unavoidable. From the first months of the conflict, the question of the slave's status in the new lands won from Mexico troubled the nation. While each section had been more or less content to permit the other to determine slavery's status within its own regional borders, commonly held territories presented a more complex and troubling dilemma. The South believed the exclusion of slavery from the West would represent a stigma, an indictment of the southern way of life, while

Fig. 19.
As part of his plan to mount an insurrection in Virginia, John Brown commissioned a Connecticut blacksmith to make a thousand pikes with which to arm the slaves he hoped would follow him. Brown's October 1859 attack to seize the federal arsenal at Harpers Ferry was a failure. Townspeople afterwards sold many of the weapons as souvenirs.

Fig. 20.
When asked by a Union officer why he had fled slavery, one slave replied, simply, "Cause I want to be free." The army settled many newly liberated slaves—whom the Federal government dubbed "contraband of war"—in hastily constructed camps such as one at the Baton Rouge Female Seminary in Louisiana.

Fig. 21.
More than 180,000 African-Americans from the South served in the Union army in various capacities.

Fig. 22.
The Confederate government impressed slaves as wartime laborers for the construction of fortifications around southern cities and military posts. An estimated ten thousand African-Americans worked on Georgia's military defenses alone.

most northerners were equally unwilling to yield their position. During most of the nation's short history, members of Congress had agreed not to permit formal discussion of the volatile issue of slavery. But after 1848 Congress seemed to talk of little else. While only a small minority of northerners sympathized with the principles of immediate abolition, a great many more did identify with the doctrines of free soil, the belief that slavery should be extended no farther across the continent, the belief that the northern way of life should prevail.

Consumed by territorial battles, the 1850s was a decade of heightened national conflict over slavery, a struggle reflected in the South's efforts to tighten its control over the slave system. As part of its territorial compromise, the region de-manded a stronger fugitive slave law, one that would invoke federal power to compel reluctant northerners to return escaped slaves.[45] At the same time southern fears of abolitionist-inspired slave violence mounted, until John Brown's unsuc-cessful effort to spark a slave insurrection by seizing the federal arsenal at Harpers Ferry in October 1859 seemed nothing more than, as

one secessionist put it, "fact coming to the aid of logic."[46]

Southerners' anxieties about the insecurities of their slave property only increased as sectional conflict gave way to armed strife. When war erupted in April 1861, southerners held almost four million slaves, comprising approximately 33 percent of the region's population. These blacks would prove to be an important labor resource for the Confederacy, working in jobs ranging from the customary agricultural labor, to build-ing fortifications, to hospital nursing, that re-leased thousands of whites for active military service.[47] But the war also brought severe prob-lems to the institution that Confederate vice-president Alexander Stephens described as the "cornerstone" of the new nation.[48] The depar-ture of many planters and overseers for the war left slaves without close supervision and encour-aged increasing black independence and asser-tiveness. "I lay down at night," one Alabama plantation mistress complained, "& do not know what hour . . . my house may [be] broken open & myself & children murdered. . . . My negroes very often get to fighting."[49] And when the

Confederate government seized slaves for use on public works and fortifications, many masters regarded the action as an assault on their control and thus a dangerous intrusion upon the master-slave relationship, which had served as a stabilizing as well as a legitimating force within southern slavery.[50]

Although the North's position on slavery's ultimate fate remained unclear during the first year and a half of the war, Abraham Lincoln's Emancipation Proclamation, issued in preliminary form in the fall of 1862, explicitly tied Union war aims to abolition. The significance of the event was not lost on Southern slaves, who frequently responded to the approach of Union troops by fleeing from their masters. More than one hundred thousand ex-slaves claimed their freedom in an even more dramatic way, fighting as soldiers in the Union army.[51] As one South Carolina volunteer exclaimed, "Now we sogers are men — men de first time in our lives. Now we can look our old masters in de face. They used to sell and whip us, and we did not dare say one word. Now we ain't afraid, if they meet us, to run the bayonet through them."[52]

During most of the war, black troops were given less pay than whites and placed under the command of white officers.[53] But the risks they took on the battlefield were considerably higher than those faced by their white counterparts, since the Confederate government regarded black soldiers as insurrectionists, unentitled to the rights of prisoners of war. For the most part, fear of Northern reprisal prevented Southerners from actually acting on this premise, but in a number of instances Southerners clearly violated the laws of just warfare. At Fort Pillow, Tennessee, in April 1864, Confederate troops killed nearly three hundred black soldiers who had already surrendered.[54]

Still, they fought in sizable numbers and with great distinction. Perhaps the most famous black military figure was Robert Smalls, a Charleston slave who had been hired out before the war as a sailor and pilot. Impressed into Confederate service on the steamer *Planter*, Smalls with his black crew mates stole the ship and sailed to the Union fleet, after which he was commissioned an infantry officer in the United States Colored Troops. "I thought the *Planter* might be of some use to Uncle Abe," he explained.[55] Smalls serves as a dramatic example of the many and ingenious ways in which southern slaves claimed their liberty amid the upheaval of civil war.

The fall of the Confederacy brought an end to slavery in the rebellious states, although some masters struggled to fend off the inevitable by withholding from their laborers any knowledge of their just-won freedom for as much as a year.[56] The border states that had remained loyal to the Union moved individually toward abolition as the fate of the South became self-evident. Maryland passed a constitutional referendum in 1864; Missouri voted first for gradual then immediate abolition in 1865. By the end of the war slavery remained legal only in Kentucky and Delaware. In December 1865, ratification of the Thirteenth Amendment prohibited servitude within the entire United States.

For those just-freed people, the long-awaited "Day of Jubilo" was one of confusion, uncertainty, anxiety — as well as joy. No one, black or white, seemed fully to grasp the implications of freedom. "Dey all had diffe'nt ways o' thinkin' 'bout it," one Mississippian remembered of his fellow slaves. "Mos'ly though dey was jus' lak me, dey didn' know jus' zackly what it meant."[57] In some ways the struggle had just begun. Slavery had been abolished, but Reconstruction and the years to follow would continue to raise issues about the place of blacks in American society and the meaning of their hard-won freedom. □

PLANTATION LANDSCAPES OF THE ANTEBELLUM SOUTH

John Michael Vlach

Fig. 24.
Part of the Bennehan-Cameron plantation complex outside Durham, North Carolina, Horton Grove Quarter consists of four well-constructed slave houses built by slave carpenters in 1851.

By the time *Gone With the Wind* premiered in 1939, Americans generally imagined the southern plantation as a pillared mansion surrounded by cotton fields. One just like Twelve Oaks. Margaret Mitchell described Ashley Wilkes's fictional home as a white house "tall of columns, wide of verandas, flat of roof, beautiful as a woman is beautiful who is so sure of her charm that she can be generous and gracious to all," a house with a "stately beauty, a mellowed dignity" far beyond even Scarlett O'Hara's beloved Tara.[1] Evoking the glory and romance of a lost age, the plantation of the popular imagination has long been perceived as an icon of success and attainment.[2] In reality, few plantations ever equalled the visual splendor of the places described in *Gone With the Wind*.

The fictional notion of the plantation as a large agricultural estate with an elegant house set amid a long string of various outbuildings can be traced back at least to 1832 and John Pendleton Kennedy's *Swallow Barn; or, A Sojourn in the Old Dominion*. In the novel's opening chapter the author describes "an aristocratical old edifice" from which its master, Frank Meriwether, commands an extensive tract extending three or four miles along the James River. The planter's house, the novelist comments, has thick brick walls, a porch "upheld by massive columns of wood," "an ample courtyard," and a "rather ostentatious iron gate . . . swung between two pillars of brick surmounted by globes of cut stone."[3] Similar images of a massive Greek Revival mansion staffed by a host of black servants have been repeated in works of fiction, art, music, and cinema for the last 150 years, in many minds thus merging the South and the great plantation into a single identity.[4]

In such a South it follows that there were only two white social classes: rich planters and poor whites. In that view, the region then lacked a noticeable middle class—a perception vigorously countered by the revisionist studies of Frank L. Owsley. The typical nineteenth-century southerner, he argued, was, in fact, a member of the "plain folk," a farmer or herdsman who worked a small landholding of about two hundred acres without the aid of slave labor. Owsley claimed that these nearly six million southerners had been totally forgotten because of a pervasive "plantation mythology."[5] Equally revisionist were the findings of James C. Bonner. In his study of plantation architecture he declared that "a great house of classic design in a rural setting was a rare phenomenon, even among the more prosperous planters." In fact, travelers "were frequently astounded at the great number of wealthy men they found living in miserable dwellings."[6] The typical planter's abode was apt to be nothing more than the plainest log house consisting of two rooms with a shed behind it and a long porch on the front. Minimal, ramshackle buildings were indeed so common that in 1845 one Alabaman remarked that it appeared to him as if a shower of rails had fallen one day and a shower of houses the next.[7]

If so few southerners were ever planters and, further, if most planters lived in modest wooden houses lacking even the slightest gesture toward the current architectural taste, then clearly the great slaveholding estate was only a minor element in the southern experience. A sifting of the region's prewar census data lends support to this claim. If, as historians have agreed, one had to own at least twenty slaves to merit the title *planter*, then the great planter who controlled vast lands and gangs of slaves while living luxuriously in a

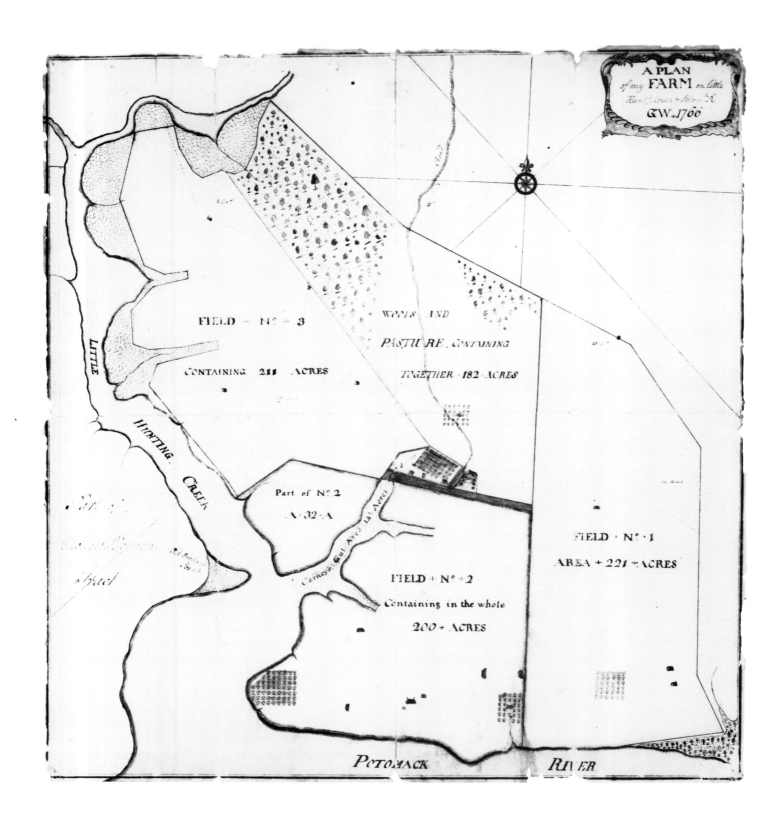

A PLAN
of my FARM on Little
Hun[?] Creek & Potow[?]k
GW 1766

LITTLE HUNTING CREEK

FIELD · N° · 3

CONTAINING 211 ACRES

WOODS AND

PASTURE CONTAINING

TOGETHER 182 ACRES

Part of N° 2
A · 32 · A

Carneys Gut Area 18 Acres

Part of
Bartlet Boure
Tract

FIELD · N° · 2

Containing in the whole

200 + ACRES

FIELD · N° · 1

AREA · 221 · ACRES

POTOMACK   RIVER

Fig. 25.
Radiating out from the
home plantation of
Mount Vernon, George
Washington's property
consisted of four sur-
rounding farms amount-
ing to some eight thousand
acres. One of Washington's
maps depicted the small
houses and outbuildings of
a single Quarter on which
several hundred slaves
lived scattered in areas
adjacent to their work.

large house was a member of a very small, hardly representative minority. In 1860, for example, only about twenty-three hundred owned more than one hundred slaves.[8] Moreover, the plantation estates created by this group were equally uncommon as elements of the southern landscape.

Yet even though the grand plantation was an atypical landscape for whites, it was for enslaved blacks, on the other hand, a significant and common environment. Historian John B. Boles, after reviewing census counts for 1850 and 1860, explained the apparent paradox by using a theoretical group of just ten slaveholders. Of those ten, Boles suggested, imagine

eight owning two slaves apiece, one owning twenty-four, and the tenth possessing sixty. Obviously most slaveholders (80 percent) would own fewer than five slaves, but most slaves (84 out of a 100) would reside in units of more than twenty. Such an imaginary model suggests what the numbers reveal. In 1850, when 73.4 percent of the slaveholders held fewer than ten slaves, exactly 73.4 percent of the slaves lived in units numbering more than ten. Over half, 51.6 percent, resided on plantations of more than twenty bondsmen. These figures were more pronounced in the Deep South, and still more so in 1860, when fully 62 percent of the slaves in the Deep South lived in plantation units, and one-third on really substantial plantations of more than fifty slaves.

"It is clear," Boles concluded, that within the Deep South "most slaves lived on plantations in close proximity to numerous other slaves."[9] Thus by 1860 when some two million blacks were living on plantations, almost seven hundred thousand were held in groups of fifty or more. These statistics are highly revealing. In short, although the plantation was a source of economic and political power for white elites, demographically it was a black institution. That blacks living on plantations were gathered into such large groups explains, in part, how they were able to develop such strong family allegiances and ultimately forge a distinct culture. Well known African-American expressions of music, oral literature, dance, and folk art and craft, for example, took shape on plantations.[10] Through the first half of the nineteenth century the plantation was thus the crucible for a large portion of the black experience.

Southern plantations are perceived today as having been devoted almost exclusively to cotton, which throughout the nineteenth century was, after all, the region's leading commodity.[11] Actually, however, "King Cotton" dominated only the middle portions of South Carolina, Georgia, Alabama, the lower Mississippi River valley, and a few counties in east Texas. Cotton was therefore characteristic of only a sub-region of southern plantation activity. Other areas of the South featured other crops: tobacco in the Chesapeake regions of Virginia and Maryland, rice in the Carolina and Georgia low country, and sugar in Louisiana. Because different plants have different growing conditions and cycles, the schedule and conduct of farming varied from region to region according to the commodity produced.

The size and layout of tobacco fields, for example, were different than those for cotton. The sorts of barns, sheds, and equipment were different as well. Consequently, it is necessary to speak not of the southern plantation but of southern *plantations*, estates that varied not only with the commodity produced but to some extent also with the size of the work force employed, the productivity of the soil, and the willingness of the owner to embrace up-to-date methods of cultivation, harvest, and processing. Moreover, there were also some inevitable sub-regional differences within an area as large as the South, a zone commonly understood to extend from the Atlantic Ocean to central Texas and from the Gulf of Mexico to the Ohio River. The character of plantations in a given locale reflected the immediate ecology as well as the consequences of a particular settlement history. Put another way, plantation buildings evolved from a set of regional architectural customs rather than from an overall plantation style.

There were, in short, differing plantation landscapes, the term *landscape* denoting neither a visual scene nor an environmental setting but a cultural construction, one that includes buildings and structures, fields, gardens, and pathways. Since the inhabitants of these landscapes also created their living spaces, it follows that these features collectively convey deeply entrenched ideas regarding social order and well-being, ideas often not expressed as forcefully or clearly in words.[12] A survey of plantations can reveal both what the planter had in mind and how his slaves may have found within his plans the means to create a landscape of their own.

Considering colonial Virginia's early success with cultivating tobacco, the Indian weed, it is not surprising that by the early eighteenth century there was a small but highly prosperous class of planters, a group that developed large plantation tracts along the principal rivers that drained into the Chesapeake Bay. Apparently following the precedent of English countryside estates, these

Fig. 26.
Located along the Roanoke River in Campbell County, Virginia, Green Hill's "Upper Town" consisted of a large group of service buildings adjacent to the planter's house and included a double laundry, an office, kitchen, barn, icehouse, and slave quarters.

Fig. 27.
Cobblestone pathways linked the outbuildings at Green Hill to the main house and were symbolic of the degree of control the planter wielded over his physical world.

planters situated their houses on the highest point. There they dominated the vista. William Hugh Grove, who sailed along the York River in 1732, found "pleasant Seats on the Bank which Shew Like little villages." The "villages" were, in fact, single plantations. They resembled small towns because so many buildings made up a single holding. Grove noted that it was common for these "Seats" to consist of "Kitchins, Dayry houses, Barns, Stables, Store houses, and . . . 2 or 3 Negro Quarters all Separate from Each other but near the mansion houses."[13] Even so, Grove as he passed by aboard his ship could form only a partial impression. Early Virginia plantations were often made up of several farms, or Quarters.[14] What Grove and other visitors saw was only the homeplace and its adjacent grounds; the rest of the plantation stretched out over what a planter such as Landon Carter called his "backlands."[15]

Virginia's early plantations were organized in a diffuse pattern with an array of Quarters set at some distance from the mansion house. Landon Carter's Sabine Hall, for example, followed such a plan. Beyond the "home" fields lay several Quarters: Mangorike, the Fork, Jammy's, and Davis's. At George Washington's Mount Vernon, the Mansion House Farm was surrounded by Dogue Run Farm, Union Farm, River Farm, and Muddy Hole Farm. Similar divisions were common on other great estates along the James, Rappahannock, and Potomac rivers. There, interspersed among the irregularly shaped fields, were woodlots, marshes, and other untamed lands. An overall unity of place was to the planter probably more a mental than a visual reality. A planter knew from maps, deeds, and other documents what was his, for he rarely was able to stand in one place and see all that he owned.

Agricultural production on Virginia plantations was divided between tobacco and other grains, mainly corn and wheat. Grain fed the plantation, but tobacco made the money, at least at first. A portion of a designated plantation Quarter set aside for cultivation, rather than for livestock grazing, was certain to be planted in tobacco. The barn, or "tobacco house," for curing the harvested leaves was often in the fields close to the plants. Slaves assigned to a particular Quarter usually lived close to their work in a cluster of rough cabins. Adjacent to these dwellings were garden plots, sometimes as much as an acre in size, in which slaves grew vegetables to supplement the food allowances provided by their master.[16] A plantation Quarter thus consisted of a variety of spaces and buildings: fields, barns, dwellings, and gardens. Some served the planter, while others were understood as part of the slaves' domain.

The homeplace site, the core of the plantation, was more complex. Besides the planter's residence and its landscaped grounds, it included a number of service buildings, workshops, and quarters for the slaves employed in the "big house." George Mason, of Gunston Hall, owned many slaves who worked as carpenters, sawyers, coopers, blacksmiths, tanners, shoemakers, spinners, weavers, and knitters; another was even a distiller. One can easily imagine the number of workshops and warehouses Mason needed to shelter his laborers and their finished products.[17]

While much of the work was done at the homeplace, the mansion was intended to be the ceremonial centerpiece of the planter's world. Hence it was whenever possible tastefully decorated and its grounds contrived to highlight its importance. Philip Fithian's description of Robert Carter's Nomini Hall underscores the importance of grounds and gardens as a means of establishing social hierarchy. The main house, he wrote, "is large, & stands on a high piece of Land [and] it may be seen a considerable distance; I have seen it at the Distance of six Miles." Nearby,

"Due East of the Great House," he continued are two Rows of tall, flourishing, beautiful, Poplars, beginning on a Line drawn from the School to the Wash-House; these Rows are something wider than the House, & are about 300 yards Long . . . These Rows of Poplars form an extremely pleasant avenue, & at the Road, through them, the House appears most romantic, at the same time that it does truly elegant.[18]

The homeplace and its Quarters while different were nevertheless inexorably linked. Planter William Byrd II referred to his "Bond-men and Bond-women" as "a large family of my own." In his mind, such people—and all his other possessions as well—were united as in one large "Machine."[19] In reality, within his plantation, he and they lived by different rules and expectations.

The later, nineteenth-century plantations that developed farther inland in the foothills of the Blue Ridge were generally smaller than the great river estates. They contained hundreds rather than thousands of acres. William Massie's Pharsalia plantation, established in Nelson County on land given Massie in 1815, is a good example of the type. The plantation consisted of six fields, each about one hundred acres, worked by a corps of between twenty and twenty-five slaves. Although Massie raised tobacco until his death in 1862, he was often disappointed in the price he got for his crop and thus also experimented with hemp, wheat, and rye. While he never gave up on tobacco, he did diversify his operation by selling hams and bacon from the two hundred to three hundred hogs he slaughtered each year. An 1847 map of Pharsalia reveals a centralized organization of space. From the main house located in the middle, six fields radiated out to the plantation's boundaries almost like spokes. Closest to the house were gardens and orchards. Just beyond these spaces were the stable, barns, the slaves' houses and their garden lot, and the mill.[20] To move away from the center of this plantation was to move down a scale of power and significance.

Pharsalia and other piedmont plantations like it followed the same general landscape as tidewater estates, even though the latter are more accurately characterized as diffuse rather than clustered. In their design, the piedmont's smaller holdings basically duplicated the homeplace environs of a Mount Vernon or a Gunston Hall. What they lacked were the backlands Quarters. While some piedmont planters did acquire large tracts of land—William Massie in time owned eight thousand acres—most of their property remained undeveloped for farming. The middle-Virginia plantation thus represents the tidewater ideal at an early stage; it is the planter's seat with its service buildings and grounds and nearby fields and pastures.

Estates of this sort have largely vanished from the countryside, but one survives relatively intact. Samuel Pannill acquired Green Hill in southern Campbell County in 1797 when he purchased six hundred acres from William and Moses Fuqua. By Pannill's death in 1864, Green Hill had grown to include five thousand acres. Moved by a strong entrepreneurial spirit, Pannill developed not only his plantation but milling and shipping businesses as well. Green Hill was said to consist of an "Upper Town" set atop a bluff overlooking the Roanoke River and a "Lower Town," an industrial village near the water's edge.[21]

Today only the "Upper Town"—Pannill's house, grounds, and service buildings—remains. At its center is a boxwood garden surrounded by a stone wall and some eighteen structures. Most stand along the northern edge of the garden and include the main house, kitchen, laundry, icehouse, office, a duck house (more recently used as a pigsty), two slave quarters, and the ruins of possibly two others. Connected to the main house by cobblestone pathways are two small barns, a carriage house, stable, granary, and a large tobacco barn. Green Hill's surviving service buildings and main house outline a rectangular yard that in turn echoes the rectangular shape of the boxwood garden. Along the southern edge of the garden Pannill positioned buildings in which he stored his produce. His mills, warehouses, toll

bridge, and other slave quarters he located down the bluff in "Lower Town." The overall plan follows a hierarchy similar to that described by Fithian for Nomini Hall. Both the central location and decoration of his house site and its elevation established Pannill's image of control. And even though his residence was a modest I-house of only four rooms and an attic, in Green Hill's setting it conveyed a message equal to any gentleman's seat along the James.[22]

While rice was grown successfully on the barrier islands and along the banks of the estuarial rivers of both South Carolina and Georgia as early as the 1690s, the region's plantation landscape did not develop its special characteristics until the mid-eighteenth century.[23] Because planters from the start intended to establish large slaveholding plantations, the number of Africans imported was very high. In fact, by the mid-1700s, slaves outnumbered whites by five to one, causing one observer to remark in 1737 that "Carolina looks more like a negro country than like a country settled by white people."[24] Landholdings were equally extensive. In one parish near Georgetown, South Carolina, for example, an average rice plantation contained approximately fifty-three hundred acres, eight hundred of which were cleared for cultivation. In 1860, the slave work force on the usual rice plantation included almost 150 men and an equal number of women.[25]

Rice fields were "created" lands—tracts of land laboriously reclaimed from the marsh. Unlike crops for which workers cleared and prepared an existing field, for cultivating rice the laborers had to first construct the field itself. Gabe Lance, an ex-slave from the Mount Arena plantation on Sandy Island, South Carolina, recalled that "all dem rice field been nothing but swamp. Slavery people cut kennel [canal] and cut down woods—and dig ditch through raw woods. All been clear up for plant rice by slavery people."[26] He spoke with justifiable pride. To convert the tidal marshes into productive rice paddies required a keen knowledge of irrigation as well as a prodigious effort. Moreover, the slaves' African background as rice cultivators may well have been a factor in their considerable success.[27]

A number of conditions restricted the location of rice plantations: the distance from the ocean, the flow of fresh water in an adjacent river or stream, and the difference in elevation between the high and low tides, what the planters called "pitch." Since it was the tidal lift that brought water to the paddies, a rice field had to be lower than the high tide to allow for irrigation, but higher than the low tide to allow for drainage. Further, the paddies had to be just far enough inland to avoid saline or briny water, but not so

Fig. 28.
The cultivation of rice involved considerable proficiency and hard work, beginning with the transformation of swamps into productive fields. Slaves performed nearly all of the labor in growing rice by hand.

Fig. 29.
On the Limerick plantation on South Carolina's Cooper River, the slave housing was located midway between the planter's residence and the rice fields. The eight houses set in two facing rows formed a short street as well as a small community for the slaves who lived there.

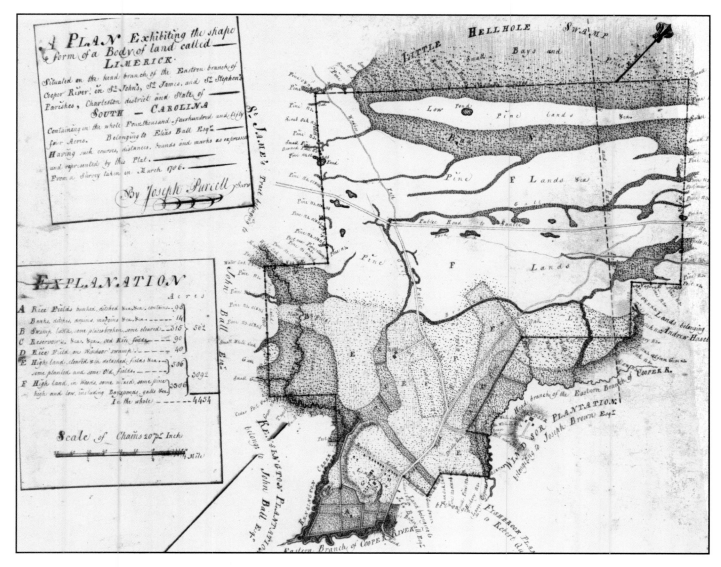

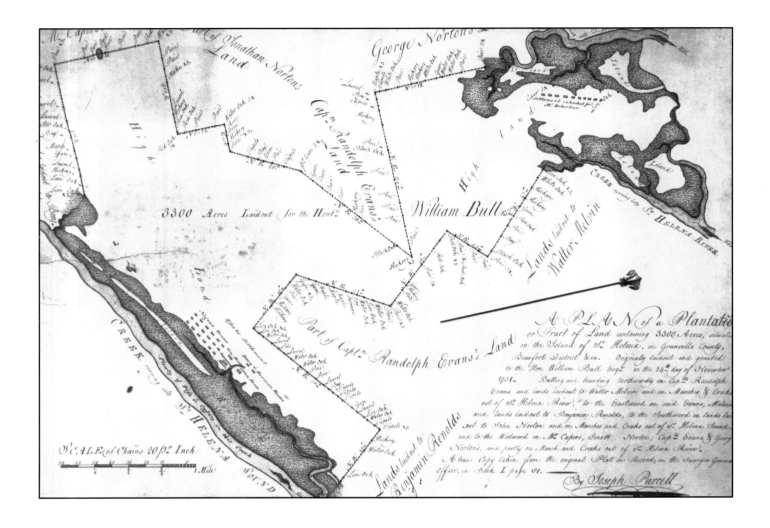

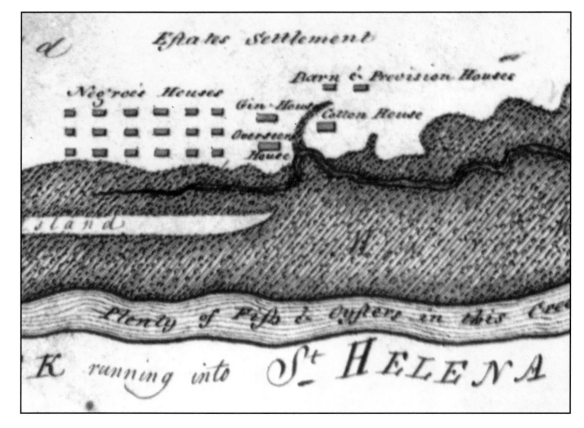

Fig. 30 (detail right). The slave quarter on one low-country cotton plantation on Saint Helena Island, South Carolina, was the size of a village. In addition to the eighteen slave houses, the complex included a residence for the white overseer and four work-related outbuildings.

Fig. 31 (right), Fig. 32. Arranged in a broad arch and exactly twelve feet apart, the tabby cabins on Kingsley plantation, Fort George Island, Florida, are differentiated by size. Four cabins, larger than the others, probably served as quarters for the drivers.

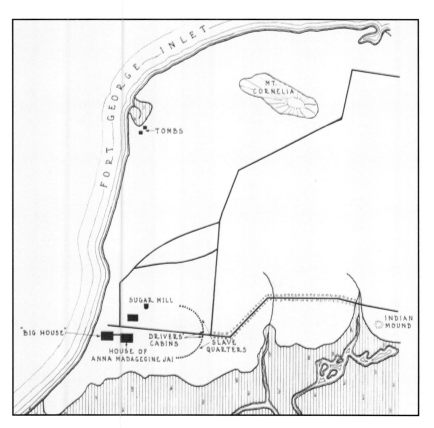

Fig. 33.
The relative isolation from white owners and the close living conditions of the quarter undoubtedly strengthened the slave community.
Timothy O'Sullivan photographed the Mills plantation quarter on Port Royal Island, South Carolina, in 1862.

far that the pitch was too low. Planters thus constructed large dikes to hold back the tidal floods. Inside these dikes were squared-up and leveled fields at varying heights so that once the irrigating flow reached the rice fields, the water via internal canals dropped progressively from one sector to the next. In 1858 Frederick Law Olmsted reported that the fields of a Georgia rice plantation seemed to him a "Hollandlike" network of sluices, gates, channels, and culverts.[28] One planter characterized the low country rice plantation as "a huge hydraulic machine, maintained by constant fighting against the rivers," an apt summation of both the artificiality and fragility of the rice-producing landscape.[29]

The engineered soil on which the profits of a rice plantation depended was hard-won and precious and rarely devoted to any other use, although later some plantations raised long-staple Sea Island cotton and sugar cane in rotation with rice.[30] Given the fields' high value, plantation buildings had to be carefully placed. They might be adjacent to the fields, or some place convenient to the master, but never actually in the fields as was the case in Virginia.

Building arrangements followed several patterns. In one, slave houses were set near the main house in a long, single row, a design used in 1838 at the E. M. Seabrook plantation on Edisto Island, South Carolina, for eleven buildings and earlier for twenty houses at the Julianton plantation in Georgia. A map of a Combahee River plantation in Colleton County, South Carolina, indicates that its slave quarters were arranged in two parallel rows forming a "street" between them. In fact, there were so many dwellings that, apparently for some administrative reasons, the planter separated them into two sets, one on either side of his mansion. Pierce Butler distributed his 582 slaves principally among four slave villages evenly spaced along the southern edge of Butler's Island. He also kept a large group near the main house to operate and maintain the plantation's shops and machinery. Another pattern, seemingly set up for an absentee planter, appears on a 1798 plat map of Saint Helena Island in Beaufort County, South Carolina. The only buildings indicated are the slave quarters, an overseer's house, a cotton house and gin, a barn, and a provision house; no residence is shown. The eighteen slave dwellings are arranged in a distinctive rectangular grid six houses wide and three deep.

A low country plantation not only sheltered the owner and his slaves but also served as a production center for refining the raw product for shipping to a nearby town or city. Consider the range of buildings mentioned in an 1825

advertisement in the *Charleston City G*[ ] the sale of the Point Plantation on th[ ] River. The property included a six-room o[ ] house, kitchen, overseer's house, cotton [ ] corn house, fodder house, carriage house and stable, mule stable, ox house, a dairy, well, and "negroes houses for 50 to 60."[31] A similar list in the 1858 inventory of Robert F. W. Alston's Guendalos plantation in Georgetown County, South Carolina, mentions a ten-room dwelling house, steam thrasher, two barns, a corn and fodder house, plantation storeroom, cart house and mule stable, an overseer's house, stable, smokehouse, servant's house, hospital, potato cellar, plantation kitchen, and forty houses for two hundred slaves.[32] These ensembles suggest that one portion of the plantation was designed to serve the master, another to manage production, and a third to care for the slave population.

Since the rice planters owned such large groups of slaves, the slave quarters were often one of the more prominent features of the plantation landscape. Among the most unique was a group of thirty-six cabins set in a semicircle at the plantation of Zephaniah Kingsley on Fort George Island in northern Florida, the southernmost end of the rice coast. Constructed in the 1820s or 1830s with tabby, a primitive sort of oyster-shell concrete, this arc of slave houses perhaps reflects Kingsley's appreciation of geometry but more likely reveals the absolute control he exercised over his property.[33]

Linear arrangements of slave houses were much more commonplace. Olmsted noted this preference during his tour of Georgia rice plantations and their slave villages. One of these villages "consisted of some thirty neatly-whitewashed cottages, with a broad avenue, planted with Pride-of-China trees between them." The cottages themselves, he wrote, "were framed buildings, boarded on the outside, with shingle roofs and brick chimneys; they stood fifty feet apart, with gardens and pig-yards, enclosed by palings, between them." One dwelling "was evidently the 'sick house,' or hospital."[34] At a neighboring plantation he encountered the same sorts of houses set in the same double-row pattern—except that the slaves had their own well and a milling house where they ground their corn. An overseer's house at the end of the row marked the top of a T-shaped intersection from which one road led to the barns while another led to the owner's mansion.[35]

The largest slave settlement Olmsted noted contained houses measuring forty-two by twenty-one feet set on opposite sides of a two-hundred-foot-wide common. Spaced at two-hundred-foot intervals, the houses were separated by areas "in-

Fig. 34, Fig. 35.
The technology of rice pro-
duction changed during the
antebellum period. In
time, steam-powered rice-
threshing mills (below)
replaced the distinctive
winnowing houses used to
separate the chaff from
the grain.

closed with palings, in which are coops of fowl with chickens, hovels for nests, and for sows with pig."[36] Within settings like these slaves lived essentially in the company of other slaves. While they certainly performed their assigned tasks, African-Americans also had ample opportunity to pursue personal initiatives, ranging from raising and selling one's own livestock to developing a distinctive musical culture.[37] Moreover, these large slave settlements were of incalculable importance in the post–Civil War era: it was in these settlements that many blacks first experienced independence if not freedom.

Several structures that existed only on rice plantations deserve mention. One was the winnowing house, a small building, perhaps ten feet square topped by a pyramidal roof, set up as much as fifteen feet off the ground on four corner-posts and reached by an external stairway. There slaves threshed rice from the fields by separating the heads of grain from the stalks, flailing them on a large level area of the yard called the "rice floor." Next, workers pounded the grain with wooden pestles in large mortars to remove the outer husk from the rice kernel. The rice was then taken into the winnowing house and dropped through a grating in the floor. As the wind blew the chaff away, the heavier grain fell to the ground below, where the slaves gathered it up into barrels or sacks.[38] In the 1830s steam-powered rice mills bypassed this set of tasks on the larger plantations. Machinery housed in a large two- or three-story building processed the grain and as it reached the last stage, according to planter Robert Alston,

> The rice, now pounded, is once more elevated into the attic, whence it descends through a rolling-screen, to separate whole grains from the broken, and flour from both; and also through wind-fans, to a vertical brushing screen, revolving rapidly, which polishes the flinty grain, and delivers it fully prepared into the barrel or tierce, which is to convey it to market.[39]

Steam power did not completely eliminate the need for the old winnowing houses. Since machine-threshed rice would not germinate, seed rice for the following year's crop still had to be threshed by hand. Thus both the mills and winnowing houses remained the chief focal points in the work yards.

Located out in the rice fields were still other specialized buildings known as storm towers—round, conical-roof structures approximately thirty feet in diameter and twenty feet high. Looking more like small barns than towers, they provided emergency refuge from hurricanes unexpectedly blowing in off the Atlantic. In Georgia, these structures were called "hurricane houses." Since rice fields were in low-lying terrain—the Santee Delta, for example, is not more than five feet above sea level—and generally some distance from other shelter, the storm towers provided much-needed protection from the assault of wind and tidal wave. That they were necessary is evident. An 1822 report from the Santee River area noted that a storm took 127 lives. Many of the dead were field slaves caught out in the open.[40] While these towers stand today only as ruins, in the nineteenth century every field hand noted their location if there was an ominous shift in the weather.

The rice plantations' large size alone made them regional landscape features. Where there were rice plantations there was little other economic activity. Further, where there were rice plantations, slaves constituted between 75 percent and 80 percent of the population. The rice coast was essentially a landscape of irrigation, a great "hydraulic machine," marked by buildings and devices used nowhere else in the United States. Recently described as "ingenious," the rice plantations of the Southeast were a unique achievement in the history of American agriculture.[41] They were also important as the context in which black cultural traditions remained archaic and strongly tied to Mother Africa. The rice coast was pulled then in two directions: the planters pushed ahead to develop a modern technological design; the slaves held back as they tried to create a sensible human order.

In the Deep South it was cotton that spurred the development and expansion of plantations into the piney forests to the west. A variety of cotton had been grown in early Jamestown and small stands were generally cultivated in the eighteenth century for domestic use. However, not until 1793 when Eli Whitney invented a machine—an engine or, in common speech, a gin—that separated the clinging seeds from the tufts of cotton fiber did cotton become a major commodity.[42] The demand for cotton fiber rose dramatically in the first half of the nineteenth century, encouraging the clearing and planting of more and more land. Even as late as 1827 a Georgia newspaper reporter found the entire region from Charleston to Saint Louis obsessed with cotton. It was, he said, "a plague" in which he "found cotton land speculators thicker than locusts in Egypt."[43]

The entire South seemed to be rushing into the southwestern territories. Census records confirm that a cotton mania profoundly affected the region. In 1815 the Carolinas produced 45 percent of the region's cotton, but by 1850 they produced only 15 percent while Alabama, Mississippi, Louisiana, Arkansas, and Texas accounted for 55 percent of the crop.[44] The change suggests that the more representative cotton plantations were to be found in the fast-growing, newly opened frontier section of the South where land was available and cheap and the soil was fertile enough to produce almost a four-hundred-pound bale of cotton per acre.

Cotton farming required a particular regimen but none of the technical complexities encountered with rice, for example. Land, labor, and seed were its prime requirements and thus a small farmer or a large planter raised cotton equally well. Indeed, farmers owning few or no slaves grew at least half the cotton raised during the antebellum period.[45] Nevertheless, the planter class dominated a cotton belt stretching from South Carolina to eastern Texas.

The promise of great profits from the cotton market encouraged the development of a single-crop system. Only the owners of the largest estates, in their efforts to be self-sufficient, devoted appreciable acreage to corn, wheat, or peas and other vegetables. Consequently, the soil of the cotton belt was rather quickly depleted and production levels reduced. The solution was simply to clear new, and hopefully more fertile, lands. Thus cotton plantations were generally quite large with many surplus acres as a hedge against the sterility of over-cultivation. In Edgefield County, which ranked first in South Carolina cotton production, James Henry Hammond, the county's largest planter, owned 5,500 acres in 1859 of which only 750 were devoted to cotton.[46] The average Edgefield farm in 1860 included almost 600 acres with less than 180 actually cultivated. In 1850, when Edgefield farms averaged 100 fewer acres, the amount of tilled land totaled roughly 130 acres.[47] A nineteenth-century cotton plantation was essentially a tract of new land worked progressively to exhaustion. Against this background of land use—or, to put it more accurately, land abuse—is the cotton plantation to be considered.

Since a rush of speculation created the cotton economy, there was much variation in the way owners layed out their plantations. Clear differences are particularly evident in the recollections of ex-slaves recorded in the 1930s. Ned Walker, who worked on the plantation of Henry Gaillard near Winnsboro, South Carolina, remembered its careful spatial organization as "a little town," one "laid out wid streets wide 'nough for a wagon to pass thru. Houses was on each side of de street. A well and church was in de center of de town. Dere was a gin-house, barns, stables,

cowpen and a big bell on top of a high pole at de barn gate."[48] The degree of order was even more pronounced on the plantation in Tuscumbia, Alabama, where William Henry Townes lived. He recalled that

the Big House was a two-story house; white like mos' houses endurin' dat time. On the north side of the Big House set a great, big barn, where all de stock an' stuff dat was raised was kep'. Off to de southwes' of de barn an' wes' of de Big House was 'bout five or six log houses. These houses was built facin' a space of ground in de center of a squa'e what de houses made. Anybody could stan' in his front do' an' see in at the front of de yuther houses.[49]

No fixed rules of organization seem to have been employed. The pattern on the North Carolina plantation where Manus Robinson worked, for example, was quite different. He stated that

Ole Mars had his slave cabins scattered all 'round over his plantation, he lacked 'em dat way, he wanted 'em convenient to der different parts. Some ob 'em wuz clos' ter de barn an' stables, den dey wuz two or three close ter de big house fer de servents an' maids ter live, uders wuz near de fields an' pastures.[50]

The clearest distinction in the cotton plantations' landscape was one of scale, which separated older, more established plantations from newer ones. A newer plantation in northern Louisiana visited by Olmsted proved to be a bleak collection of log structures. The main house, which could hardly be distinguished from its slave dwellings, was "a small square log cabin, with a broad open shed or piazza in front, and a chimney, made of sticks and mud, leaning against one end." "The house," Olmsted added, "had but one door and no window, nor was there a pane of glass on the plantation." Meager though this cabin was, it did serve as the headquarters for a plantation. It marked one end of the administrative core of the planter's landholdings; at the other end, some three hundred yards away, were the gin house and the stable. In the intervening space were two rows of slave cabins.[51]

In contrast was the Trentham plantation near Camden, South Carolina, as described by one of its former slave hands: "Marster's plantation was a awful big plantation with 'bout four hundred slaves on it. It was a short distance from the Wateree River. The slave houses looked like a small town and dere wus grist mills for corn, cotton gin, shoe shops, tanning yards, and lots of

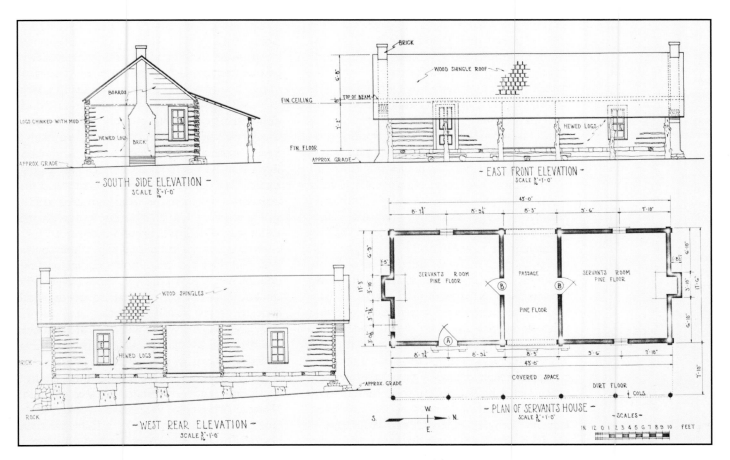

Fig. 36.
The arrangement of slave housing frequently was hierarchical. At Thornhill, an Alabama cotton plantation, the planter located the lodgings for domestic servants or artisans within sight of the main house while the two other quarters for field hands were located off in the distance.

Fig. 37.
As many as ten slaves shared the living space in each of the Thornhill plantation's "dog-trot" cabins, characteristically built with two rooms divided by a central breezeway passage.

looks for weavin' cloth." "Dere was," he added, "a jail on de place for to put slaves in."[52] The nameless plantation visited by Olmsted was only slightly larger than the common slaveholding farm and was most representative of the typical cotton estate. The Trentham plantation, however, comes closer to our contemporary idea of what a cotton plantation should be.[53]

The surviving buildings at Thornhill in Greene County, Alabama, in the center of the cotton belt, provide a good example of a major plantation. Established between 1833 and 1835 by Virginia native James Innes Thornton, the estate once included twenty-six hundred acres. In the 1930s the surviving structures included, besides the mansion, a schoolhouse, kitchen, dairy, smokehouse, a well and cistern, carriage house, barn, six log dwellings for slaves, and a cabin designated as a slave hospital. Five of the slave houses were examples of the "dog-trot" type, two rooms with an open breezeway between them. Assuming that each housing unit sheltered the usual average of five persons, then Thornton may have kept approximately fifty slaves to work the fields near his house. (He quartered another

one hundred field hands at two other locations on the plantation.) Thornton arranged his buildings in a line with his mansion at one end, near the road, and the other structures running back to his barn; he set only the school off to one side. The service buildings near the house, including a cabin for the slave cook, form a small work yard. Beyond this area are houses for the field hands. Interesting to note, the slave quarters and the mansion house share the same high ground, the same elevation. Hierarchy is, nevertheless, still signaled by visibility, scale, and decoration.[54]

Since it was imprudent to raise more cotton than could be harvested, planters tended to gauge how much to plant by the size of their plantation's labor force. A planter expected a mature field hand to harvest at least five bales, at a bale an acre. Still, since slaves could cultivate twice as much cotton as they could pick, planters frequently put out as much seed as possible and hoped they could coerce a superhuman effort from their hands. As one former slave recalled, "Dere wasn't so much foolishness at cotton pickin' time." All hands, including artisans such as blacksmiths and carpenters, even the overseers, went down the rows gathering cotton bolls at harvesttime.[55] The single-minded devotion to cotton was extraordinary. Many planters ordinarily set off plots of ground on which slaves raised their own vegetables but some even granted their laborers enough land to put in small crops of their own cotton. In 1851 Hugh Davis, the proprietor of Beaver Bend plantation in Perry County, Alabama, planted 173 acres of cotton. He reserved 9 acres for "negro patches," and with good reason. A year earlier, eight of his slaves had produced 3,404 pounds of cotton, which Davis purchased from them.[56]

Marking the fields of the most prominent cotton plantations were two specialized production machines, the gin and the press. Ex-slave Salomon Oliver noted that his Mississippi plantation was particularly well equipped with two of each.[57] Before the introduction of steam power, a cotton gin was horse- or mule-operated. Below the gin, raised about eight feet off the ground on wooden pillars, draft animals harnessed to a vertical axle plodded in a circular path. The shaft's rotation turned large gears, which in turn furnished power to the wheels and belts of the gin itself.

The press was a more spectacular structure. Standing perhaps as much as thirty feet high, the press's sturdy frame supported a great threaded screw, more than a foot in diameter, positioned over a box holding the loose cotton lint. From the top of the screw, two long beams stretched out and then down almost to the ground like arms. Mules harnessed to these beams, or "levers" as they were sometimes called, walked a circular path, turning the screw and compacting the cotton into a tight bale. The screw was sometimes made of cast iron, but wooden screws were preferred since they were less prone to break suddenly under the tremendous strain. Some slave carpenters, such as Jordan Goree, of Huntsville, Texas, gained great fame for their skill at carving screws for cotton presses.[58]

The pattern of the cotton plantation thus varied. Since cotton was the South's predominant crop during the nineteenth century, it was grown across a broad area by all classes of farmers on holdings both large and small. But while cotton was typical of the South, there was, on the other hand, no typical way in which it was produced. The most certain mark of a cotton plantation was the presence of cotton, perhaps little else, in its fields. The focus on one crop also indicated that the nineteenth-century southern plantation was increasingly less a type of farm than a production center for distant factories.

In 1795 Jean Etienne Boré conducted an ex-

Fig. 39.
Built in 1857 on a grand scale, Bellegrove, near Donaldsonville, Louisiana, was a variation on the linear-plantation model. In addition to twenty double-cabins for the slaves, the outbuildings included a dormitory for 150 laborers, with three to a room.

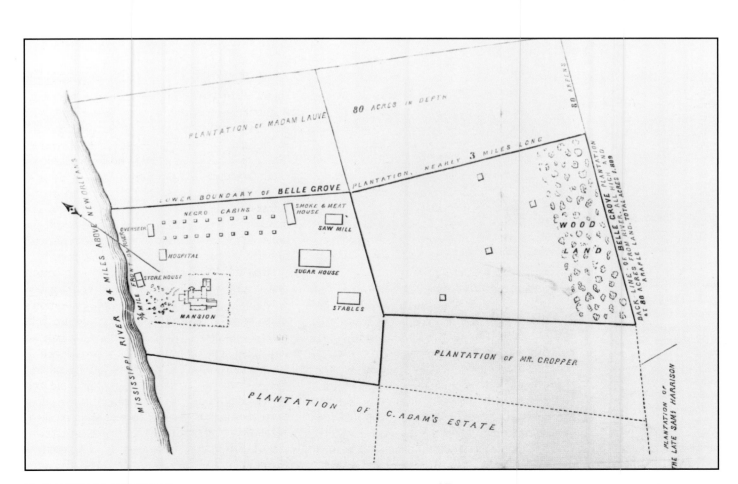

Fig. 40.
In Louisiana, planters whenever possible established their sugar plantations along the Mississippi River, the principal transportation route for their annual crop. Typically, each plantation had a warehouse—for storing processed sugar in hogsheads—and a wharf at the river's edge.

periment to determine whether the syrup pressed from Louisiana cane could be converted to granulated sugar. Because his experiment proved successful he was hailed as a "savior" and the lower half of Louisiana was soon regarded as a "sugar bowl."[59] Within thirty years there were more than three hundred Louisiana sugar plantations, collectively holding some 21,000 slaves. By 1858 the number of sugar plantations had grown to almost thirteen hundred and the slave labor force stood at more than 180,000 hands.[60] The sugar plantation, like the rice plantation, was generally

a large holding, its vastness, in fact, being one of its significant identifying characteristics.

The largest sugar plantation in Louisiana, actually a combination of holdings in two adjacent parishes, belonged to John Burnside. In 1860 he owned twenty-two thousand acres, seventy-six hundred of which were considered improved. On these fields, laid out across prairie, forest, and swampland, 937 slaves raised enough cane to produce 3,266,000 pounds of sugar. Also produced on the plantation were the considerable quantities of corn, potatoes, and livestock needed

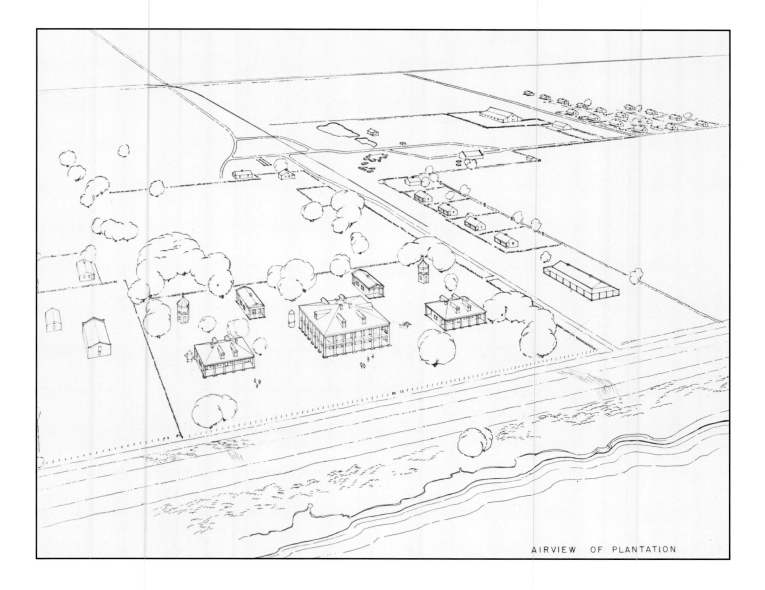

AIRVIEW OF PLANTATION

to feed its huge work force.[61] In 1863, W. H. Russell, an English visitor to Burnside's plantation, wrote approvingly of the mansion and its grounds. He was even more impressed with the crops.

> If an English agriculturist could see six thousand acres of the finest land in one field, unbroken by hedge or boundary, and covered with the most magnificent crops of tasselling Indian corn and sprouting sugarcane, as level as a billiard-table, he would surely doubt his senses. But here is literally such a sight . . . .[62]

Not as large, but equally impressive, was the plantation of Valcour Aime located on the Mississippi River about sixty miles above New Orleans. In 1852 Aime owned 15,000 acres of which 800 were in cane, 300 in corn, and 150 in slave gardens. From the remaining forested lands, his slaves cut the two thousand to three thousand

cords of firewood that his sugar mill and boiling house required per year.[63] Olmsted provided further evidence of the grand scale of the Louisiana sugar plantation. "Fronting upon the river," but removed from the road, he wrote, "was the mansion of the proprietor: an old Creole house, the lower story of brick and the second of wood, with a broad gallery, shaded by the extended roof, running all around it." Inside, the "parlors, library, and sleeping rooms of the white family were all on the second floor." Outside, Olmsted observed that

> Between the house and the street was a yard, planted formally with orange-trees and other evergreens. A little on one side of the house stood a large two-story, square dove-cot, which is a universal appendage of a sugar-planter's house. In the rear of the house was another large yard, in which, irregularly placed, were houses for the family servants, a kitchen, stable, carriage-house, smoke-house,

PLANTATION LANDSCAPES

etc. Behind this rear-yard there was a vegetable garden, of an acre or more, in the
charge of a negro gardener.

"From a corner of the court," he added, "a road
ran to the sugar-works and the negro settlement,
which were five or six hundred yards from the
house." The slaves' houses "were provided with
broad galleries in front" and "were as neat and
well-made externally as the cottages usually provided by large manufacturing companies in New
England."[64] As Olmsted so accurately noted, in
the first half of the nineteenth century when the
American demand for sugar was great and its
market price was high, sugar planters commanded
impressive estates. As yet another observer,
Estwick Evans, noted in 1818, the sugar plantations were "superb beyond description."[65]

Given the bulky weight of a hogshead of sugar,
the difficulties of overland transportation, and
thus the need for an easier route to markets, the
planters first developed lands along the Mississippi River. These riverfront plantations dominated
a region extending from Baton Rouge to about
fifty miles below New Orleans. There land boundaries followed lines established by the "long lot"
survey—a colonial system of land measure with
property boundaries perpendicular to the river's
edge at intervals of approximately forty yards and

with fields divided into narrow, but long, strips.
As a consequence, sugar estates along the lower
Mississippi all tended to share a similar landscape.[66]

The owner's mansion, set close to the levee,
was aligned with the plantation's sugar house,
located as much as a half mile behind it in the
cane fields. Between these two main structures
was a road flanked by fields and slave quarters.
Called "linear plantations" by geographer John
B. Rehder, their growth also coincided with a
major nineteenth-century migration of Haitian
refugees to Louisiana. The plantations' landscape
configuration may thus have links to precedents
in the French West Indies.[67]

Along the waterways west of the Mississippi,
particularly along bayous Terrebonne and Teche,
sugar plantations took a different form. On what
Rehder calls "bayou block plantations," buildings were clustered together near the water's
edge with the fields spread out in all directions.
The owner's "big house" was separated from the
slaves' dwellings by the sugar house and other
production buildings, but the distance between
them was not pronounced. One senses in the
plan the strong use of a focused center and a grid
pattern. On sugar plantations located on Bayou
Lafourche, the tight block pattern gave way to a
form Rehder names the "nodal-block plantation," with buildings clustered about the fields in

Fig. 43.
Fig. 43.
The most dominant land-
scape form on a Louisi-
ana sugar plantation was
the mill for processing the
slave-harvested cane.

groups. The mansion and its service buildings were, however, still close to the waterway—still the prime means of public access—but the quarters were grouped according to the workers' occupations. Thus mill hands lived near the sugar house while field hands were closer to their assigned tasks out in the cane or possibly closer to the woodlot. While the nodal-block plan was less rigid than the block form, it also followed a grid outline. Compatible with the federally sanctioned rectangular township and range survey systems, both landscape designs dominated areas settled extensively by Anglo-Americans, particularly from the Chesapeake's tidewater region.[68]

These three plantation forms were essentially working concepts that proprietors and managers followed more or less. Features of all three plans are found in the layout of Uncle Sam Plantation near Convent in Louisiana's Saint James Parish. Its mansion, a house of grand proportions, was surrounded by two *garconnieres*, or dormitories, two offices, two *pigeonneieres*, or dovecotes, and planted gardens. These buildings constituted the planter's domestic space. To one side of this ensemble was a row of seven slave buildings consisting of a hospital and six cabins. At the end of the row was the plantation's production center: the sugar mill, boiling house, scale, and blacksmith shop. About two hundred yards to

the south of the sugar house were barns and another set of slave houses arranged in two parallel rows. The plan thus appears to follow the French linear model from its mansion house to the sugar house as well as the nodal-block plan in the location of its second set of slave houses. And since none of the buildings are very far apart—all collectively set in a continuous L-shaped pattern—the cohesive clustering of the block ideal is also evident. If the linear and block modes are understood to represent respectively French and Anglo-American plantation designs, then perhaps the plan for Uncle Sam Plantation is a synthesis of traditions born of decades of cross-cultural contact.

Regardless of a plantation's arrangement, the broad acreages required much the same care. For the cane fields, workers dug and cleared drainage canals sometimes as much as two miles long. Since water had to be removed quickly for fear the cane might rot if the soil remained damp too long, ditches and cross-drains neatly bounded rectangular, four-acre fields. The work was both onerous as well as dangerous to the slaves' health. Thus, whenever possible, planters hired white immigrant laborers for the task. In the opinion of one overseer, "It was much cheaper to have Irish do it, who cost nothing to the planter, if they died, than to use up good field-hands in such severe employment."[69]

Fig. 44.
*In antebellum southern
cities, slaves and masters
often lived in close
proximity in compounds
such as at the Waring
House in Mobile that, to
some extent, replicated
plantation models.*

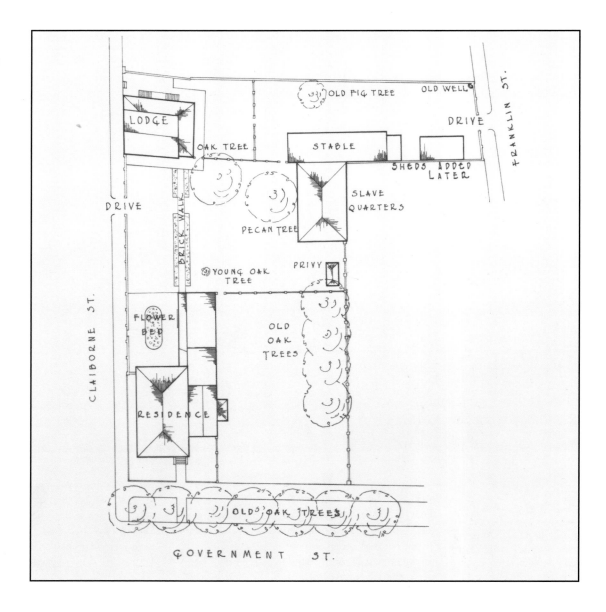

The persistent ditching and clearing of land gave the fields a manicured aspect much admired by visitors. The only sight that competed with such a view was the burning of these same fields once the harvest was complete. According to an eyewitness in the early 1840s, the deliberately set fires produced "the most sublime sight that I ever beheld, a solid sheet of fire extending for miles up and down the stream. . . . At one time it looked like a lake of fire agitated by a tempest, and then again like a burning city."[70] The ashes supposedly fertilized the soil, but the benefits were never conclusively demonstrated. The routine, however, at least marked a stage of sugar production, when a fiery spectacle consumed once-productive fields.

Harvesting the cane required much hauling to get the stalks to the mill. Mule- or ox-drawn carts usually transported the crop. However, heavy rains during the harvest often made plantation roads impassible. To solve this problem, planters constructed small-gauge railroads across their fields. In 1830 a Madam Poefarre built a permanent track bed down the middle of her plantation to which movable rails could be attached when and where they were useful. While the cars on her railroad were still mule-drawn, small locomotives were soon in wide use throughout the sugar country.[71] These rail systems—hauling cane or firewood from distant fields easily and with little risk—allowed the planters to clear and cultivate even more land.

The sugar house, despite its lack of ostentatious architectural ornamentation, was with its size and highly visible central location the dominant building on a sugar plantation. Often a two-story building measuring 100 to 134 feet in length and 50 to 60 feet in width, it sheltered both the mill, which pressed the juice from the cane, and the boilers and cooling vats, which converted the juice first into syrup and then into sugar. In the early nineteenth century, horses or

Fig. 45.
Often visible from the street, urban slave quarters frequently were far more detailed and finished than plantation quarters in order to complement the design of the owner's home. The Ward mansion, on Charleston's East Bay Street, is flanked by two large brick service dependencies.

mules turned the rollers in the mill, but by 1861 some 80 percent of Louisiana's sugar houses were powered by steam engines. Over the same period the traditional open kettle-boilers were replaced by closed vacuum-pan evaporators, heated by furnaces burning crushed cane stalks called *bagasse*.[72] The sugar house was thus a large shed punctuated by tall chimneys spewing smoke and venting steam while machinery clanked and wheezed inside. During the harvest season, it was a hive of activity where workers—engineers, greasers, firemen, wood haulers, and kettle men—swarmed to their tasks around the clock. Without question the pulse of the plantation was to be found in its sugar house.

The landscape of sugar was on a scale sure to instill respect or awe in the viewer. In 1818 Estwick Evans wrote that Louisiana sugar plantations were "formed and decorated with much taste," observing further that "planters here derive immense profits from the cultivation of their estates." Their wealth was immediately apparent in the extent of their fields, the number and size of their buildings, and the number of slaves at work. But Evans could not have guessed at that early date how successful Louisiana sugar planters would become. By 1853 they were producing one-fourth of the world's exportable sugar.[73]

As on the plantation, slaveholding was com-

monplace in the South's major cities. By 1860, for example, the population of Charleston included almost fourteen thousand slaves, or roughly one-third the city's residents. The proportion of slaves to the total population was the same in Richmond, Savannah, and Mobile as well.[74] Generally employed as domestic servants, urban slaves also proved their worth in various skilled trades. The decided concentration of black craftsmen in the building trades, for example, suggests that some of the best available carpenters, masons, plasterers, and blacksmiths must have been bondsmen.[75]

Urban slaves were, for the most part, housed in the homes of their owners. However, if a slave was expertly skilled, he might be hired out and allowed to live in the house or shop of his employer. There was, then, little architectural differentiation between the living quarters of blacks and whites as both groups occupied the same spaces. Slaves might be kept separate from the family in an attic area or in a room at the back of the kitchen, but there was rarely an external sign that slaves lived in a particular house.

If a family was especially large, a household sometimes had more slaves than could be reasonably kept within the usual dwelling house. The cook, butler, and other servants, and their children, too, might then be housed in a separate

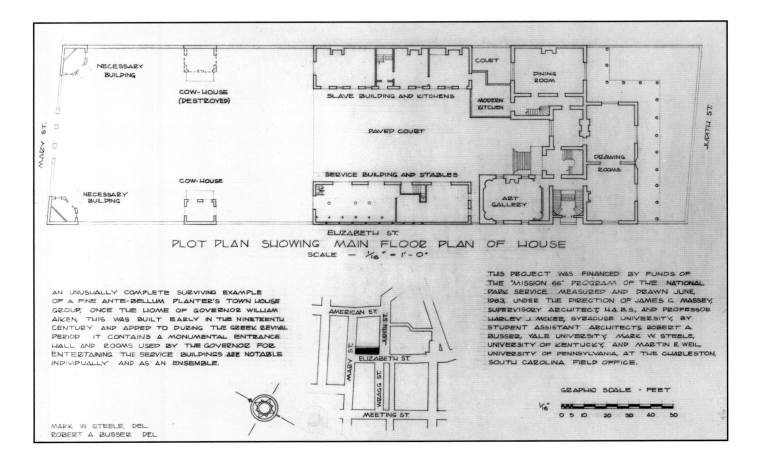

PLOT PLAN SHOWING MAIN FLOOR PLAN OF HOUSE
SCALE — 1/16" = 1'-0"

AN UNUSUALLY COMPLETE SURVIVING EXAMPLE OF A FINE ANTE-BELLUM PLANTER'S TOWN HOUSE GROUP, ONCE THE HOME OF GOVERNOR WILLIAM AIKEN, THIS WAS BUILT EARLY IN THE NINETEENTH CENTURY AND ADDED TO DURING THE GREEK REVIVAL PERIOD. IT CONTAINS A MONUMENTAL ENTRANCE HALL AND ROOMS USED BY THE GOVERNOR FOR ENTERTAINING. THE SERVICE BUILDINGS ARE NOTABLE INDIVIDUALLY AND AS AN ENSEMBLE.

MARK W. STEELE, DEL.
ROBERT A. BUSSER, DEL.

AMERICAN ST.
JUDITH ST.
MARY ST.
ELIZABETH ST.
WRAGG ST.
MEETING ST.

THIS PROJECT WAS FINANCED BY FUNDS OF THE "MISSION 66" PROGRAM OF THE NATIONAL PARK SERVICE. MEASURED AND DRAWN JUNE, 1963, UNDER THE DIRECTION OF JAMES C. MASSEY, SUPERVISORY ARCHITECT H.A.B.S., AND PROFESSOR HARLEY J. McKEE, SYRACUSE UNIVERSITY, BY STUDENT ASSISTANT ARCHITECTS ROBERT A. BUSSER, YALE UNIVERSITY, MARK W. STEELE, UNIVERSITY OF KENTUCKY, AND MARTIN E. WEIL, UNIVERSITY OF PENNSYLVANIA, AT THE CHARLESTON, SOUTH CAROLINA FIELD OFFICE.

GRAPHIC SCALE - FEET
1/16"   0 5 10   20   30   40   50

Fig. 46.
Covering an entire Charleston city block, the Robinson-Aiken house duplicated a plantation arrangement on a smaller urban scale. The 1860 census listed nineteen slaves living in the household.

building behind the main house. These were often two-story structures with kitchens, laundries, and other work rooms on the first floor and the slaves' bedrooms on the second. Such slave quarters were usually substantial buildings finished in a manner compatible with the owner's house.

In New Orleans, a distinctive pattern evolved in which the quarters were generally set against the back of the house's lot and thus, along with the main house, visually enclosed the slave owner's domain. The main house together with the kitchen building, the yard between them, and the enclosing side walls—often more than ten feet high—constituted a discrete spacial unit. With free whites placed in front of the enslaved blacks, the environment clearly reflected an image of social control.[76] According to historian Richard C. Wade,

The sole route to the street lay through the house or a door at the side. Thus the physical design of the whole complex compelled slaves to center their activity upon the owner and the owner's place. Symbolically, the pitch of the roof of the Negro quarters was the highest at the outside edge and then slanted sharply toward the yard—a kind of architectural expression of the human relationship involved. The whole design was concentric,

drawing the life of the bondsman inward toward his master.[77]

When space was less restricted, the relationship between a town house and its slave quarters was occasionally more loosely structured. Such was the case with the Moses Waring house in Mobile. The house and its outbuildings, as they stood in the 1930s, were spread over a generous L-shaped lot more than 240 feet deep. The space was divided into four zones, each one dominated by a different building. At the front facing Government Street, the primary thoroughfare, was the main dwelling house and its gardens. Directly behind sat the "lodge," or bachelors' quarters, built in 1852 for Moses Waring's older sons. Between these two buildings, but off to one side, was a two-story slave quarters and its work area. Fenced in at the rear of the lot were the stable and stable yard, all together forming an urban compound.[78]

Some of Charleston's slaveholding compounds were so large they might appropriately be called plantations. Many of the city's wealthy merchants kept more than twenty slaves in their households. In some cases up to fifty people were crowded into dormitories behind their owner's house.[79] While such a barracks-like slave quarters strongly resembled plantation housing in wide use in the

Caribbean, the layout of other Charleston properties closely followed the pattern seen on plantations in the surrounding low country. At the Ward house on East Bay Street, for example, two large brick buildings intended to shelter both slaves and their labor mark a wide yard behind the main house and are much like the flanking dependencies found at the nearby Middleton and Drayton Hall plantations just up the Ashley River. Indeed, the arrangement at the Ward house replicates the usual geometry of a rural big house and its adjacent buildings and grounds.[80]

The Robinson-Aiken house provides an even more vivid instance of a plantation arrangement in an urban setting. The house and its outbuildings are situated on a lot that runs through an entire city block, from Judith Street to Mary Street. The house, built sometime between 1817 and 1826 for John Robinson, was acquired by William Aiken in 1842. Aiken, then a prosperous rice planter and soon-to-be governor, used this Charleston town house as his summer retreat and escape from the malarial fever endemic to the coastal plantation region. The three-story brick house, while generous in its proportions and fashionable in its late-Federal decoration, was actually rather modest by Charleston standards. Nevertheless, it suitably met Aiken's needs for seasonal quarters.

He did, however, make some important changes. First, he added a wing to serve as a new dining room. Next, he updated the grand entrance hall and staircase with Greek Revival elements. It was probably at this time that he began to add six service buildings on the north side of the house. The two largest, measuring approximately seventy by twenty feet, define the edges of the service yard. The eastern building, closest to the dining room wing of the main house, contained two kitchens on the ground floor with at least three rooms for slave quarters and two storage rooms above. The building to the west served

Fig. 47.
A large, two-story, ten-bay, stuccoed kitchen and slave quarter (right), and a stable, carriage house, and slave quarter (left), originally detached from the Robinson-Aiken House, frame the service yard.

Fig. 48.
Surviving outbuildings at the Robinson-Aiken house in Charleston include a brick cow-house with stalls for two animals.

as a barn with a stable as well as harness and carriage rooms. Two living spaces shared the second floor with a hayloft. Beyond and in line with these two large structures were two small milking houses or cow barns. At the end of the lot were two substantial privies. All these outbuildings were constructed of brick and embellished with Gothic motifs.

The Aiken family's service yard contained most of the buildings commonly associated with rural plantation houses; only food production and preservation buildings, such as a smokehouse, springhouse, or chicken coop, were missing.[81] These sorts of buildings were probably not needed since groceries could be purchased from any number of nearby stores or from local street vendors. Aiken had essentially transported the administrative center of his Jehossee Island plantation to Charleston.

The federal census of 1860 listed nineteen

slaves, including eleven adults and eight children, living on Aiken's town property. In the previous year Aiken had paid a city tax for only twelve slaves.[82] Since there was no tax assessed for a carriage or any livestock, the sort of property for which his outbuildings were intended, clearly the taxes reflected a period during which Aiken was not in residence and only a minimum number of servants were needed to maintain the house. Just how many slaves might have lived and worked on Aiken's back lot is difficult to determine; at least twenty-five could have been comfortably quartered there if he observed the prevailing standards for slave housing. The size of the main house and its numerous outbuildings certainly suggest that the former governor needed twenty-five servants, or more, to run the household. According to agricultural journalist Solon Robinson, Aiken kept about seven hundred slaves on Jehossee Island to cultivate fifteen hundred acres of rice and five hundred acres of corn, oats, and potatoes. He thus had a large pool of workers from which to pick an entourage to accompany him to Charleston.

Robinson also noted of Aiken's plantation residence that it was "a very humble cottage, embowered in dense shrubbery, and making no show, and is, in fact, as a dwelling for a gentleman of wealth, far inferior in point of elegance and convenience, to any negro house upon the place, for the use and comfort of that class of people."[83] However, his preference for plain living while on the plantation needs to be understood within the context of the grandeur of his Charleston property. In Charleston he had a suitable planter's mansion with large drawing rooms opening out onto a two-story veranda. There he took sumptuous meals in a specially designed dining room and strolled with his guests through an octagonal art gallery fitted with a skylight. Aiken, in following the migratory habit of the planter class, had two residences. But unlike most of his peers, his big house was located in Charleston rather than on his sea-island plantation. The house and service buildings as positioned along Elizabeth Street provided him with the architectural imagery that effectively confirmed his status as a man of wealth and power. For Aiken, then, his plantation landscape was one that linked rural and urban settings into one estate.

Thus while Thomas Jefferson envisioned the United States as a nation of farmers, his fellow southerners had greater dreams. They saw themselves as potential owners of large estates. They soon called themselves "planters" even if their holdings were small and their crop production meager.[84] Indeed, by the nineteenth century only a few families were able to attain the wealth, independence, and self-sufficiency emblematic of full planter status. To be a planter was to be a member of the gentry, and in a nation where half the wealth in 1850 was held by less than 2 percent of the population, the social circle of planters was very small. Plantation ownership may have been the dream for many, but it was, in fact, a reality for very few.

The very design of their plantations reveals a vigorous participation by planters in the national and international economies. Decisions about what and how much to plant, and when to do it, were tied directly to the market price of a particular crop. The single-crop cultivation that characterized the plantation routine was, then, less like farming and more like industrial production. In fact, many contemporary observers compared southern plantations to New England factory towns, an evaluation that was particularly appropriate for large rice and sugar plantations outfitted with steam-powered mills and other machinery.

Moreover, planters rarely cared to work within the given limits of climate, soil conditions, or topography, a trait seen repeatedly, for example, in the abandonment of land on cotton plantations after only a few seasons. In both the rice and sugar regions, planters reconfigured huge tracts of land into vast "growing machines" with more effort being directed toward the maintenance of the machine's parts—dikes, levees, and canals—than to cultivation. Finally, the commodity sent to market was more important than the look of the land. While visitors were often quite rhapsodic in their descriptions of certain plantations, the planters evaluated their estates primarily by the size of their harvests. To a great extent, planters' perceptions of their estates were tied to the prevailing market prices.

While plantations varied from region to region with the commodity produced, their physical arrangements conveyed a unified message, that the master had tremendous power. The scale and style of his domestic buildings and grounds clearly set him above and apart from the overseers and slaves living behind the big house. He was also clearly above the majority of common folk who lived beyond his fence lines. Access to his domestic arena was contrived in order to make the best impression. There was never even the slightest doubt about who was in charge.

The planter's degree of control was, however, somewhat undercut by the great distances encompassed within a vast holding. Since at least most of his field slaves were generally kept out of sight, there was adequate opportunity for them to think and act in ways not in keeping with the planter's ideal. On all plantations there were two domains: one for whites and one for the slaves. Out in the quarters, particularly on large plantations, slaves created a social circle with its own schedule of appropriate behavior. Thus while slaves were held captive on their plantations, they still managed to find certain measures of independence because they were held so far away from the master's daily authority. Their cabins were not always comfortable, but reinforced by a feeling that they had some control over their lives, the slaves sensed that in their quarters they were at home. They developed a sense of ownership over their cabins, gardens, tools, and clothing even if these were provided by their owners. They formulated their own sense of place—one the master could hardly imagine. □

Fig. 49.
Standing on the roof of an Edisto Island plantation house in 1862, a photographer captured the contrast between the world the slaves created for whites and, in the background, the fields and quarters in which the slaves worked and lived.

49

THE WORLD OF THE PLANTATION SLAVES

Charles Joyner

Fig. 50.
A group of contrabands posed at "Mr. Foller's House," Cumberland Landing, Virginia, in May 1862 for one of Mathew Brady's photographers.

Little Jacob was a slave. At the age of eight he was assigned to help take care of his master's stable of fine horses. One day a groom began to beat him with a switch for no apparent reason. It was the first time he had been whipped by anyone except his parents. He cried out in pain, but he thought to himself that he would tell his father. Father would take care of that groom. When at last his oppressor quit beating him, Jacob ran to his father. His father, William, told him there was nothing he could do. He told Jacob to be a good boy and go back to work. But Jacob's mother, Chloe, complained to the groom. The groom took his whip and began to flog her. Jacob ran back and forth between them until the groom stopped beating her and gave him another whipping.

Soon Jacob's whippings became daily ordeals. Eventually he told his parents he would put up with the whippings no longer. He would fight back. William forbade him; the master would think his parents had advised him to fight. That would make life harder for the whole family. William told Jacob to keep silent and do his work as well as he could. Frustrated, Jacob complained that he did not know why he should be whipped. He had done nothing wrong. The groom simply whipped him because he felt like it. William replied sadly that the only thing he could do was to pray to the Lord to hasten the time when such things should all be done away.

Chloe burst into tears when she saw the wounds upon Jacob's back, but there was little she could do to comfort him. She said she would not mind it so much except that Jacob was so small. If she told the master, she believed he would forbid the groom from treating the child so cruelly. She had

grown up with her master, she said, and he would listen to her. But William was skeptical. If the master stopped the groom from whipping Jacob, William said, the groom would only avenge himself through the overseer. The best thing for him to do would be to pray over it. The time would come when the children would be free, though their parents might not live to see it. Chloe cried out that she wished they would take her son out of this world so he would be out of pain. If he were in heaven, his parents would not have to fret so about him. William told the boy not to worry, he would be a man eventually. Jacob thought if small boys are treated so cruelly, how much worse would it be when he became a man?

Suddenly Jacob realized for the first time what slavery really meant, realized that he and the rest of his fellow slaves were doomed to arbitrary treatment throughout their lives. And there was nothing he could do about it. Not only was he unable to defend himself, his parents could not defend him either. They, too, were forced to submit to the same degradation. At bedtime the family knelt in prayer. To Jacob, William's prayer that night seemed more anguished and more genuine than ever before, especially when he prayed that the Lord would hasten the time when the children would be free men and women. Jacob expected that the Lord would answer his father's prayer in two or three weeks at the latest. He could not know then that his father would die the following year, or that it would be six more years before emancipation.[1]

Cotton was the dominant crop of the Old South, but some regions with the highest concentrations of slaves were not part of the Cotton Kingdom. There were tobacco plantations in the

Fig. 51.
The sound of a horn or bell signaled both the beginning and end of the workday. A slave, William B. Randolph, probably a driver, used this horn on a Bolivar County, Mississippi, plantation.

Chesapeake, rice plantations in the low country of South Carolina and Georgia, and sugar plantations in Louisiana. But whether on cotton, tobacco, rice, or sugar plantations, most slaves worked in the fields. Slave workdays began before dawn. The sound of a bell, horn, or conch summoned the slaves to the fields. At harvesttime virtually all the slaves, regardless of their occupations, worked in the fields.

Cotton was a hazardous crop. Cato, a Georgia driver, wrote to his master that "the heavy rains in August & hot Sun has damaged us in the cotton much[.] All the unmannured ground is more or less blighted & in Spots looks like winter but the manured ground though diseased holds on well." But sometimes success came when least expected. With a justifiable note of pride, Cato added that "the marsh has astonished Every boddy that has seen it it is very fine cotton & Especially all the oldest Stocks from the first planting, we have now all the women picking cotton & from appearance will have no more time to do anything else[;] it is opening finely & is very white & pretty cotton. I think we will make Thirty Bales unless I am much dicieved."[2]

Former slaves, interviewed by field-workers of the Federal Writers' Project in the 1930s, remembered their work vividly. Ebenezer Brown, a slave on a Mississippi cotton plantation, recalled that "when de slaves wuz wurkin good" they sang

Watch de sun; see how she run;
Niver let her ketch yo wid yer wurk undun.[3]

Slaves on cotton plantations "listed" the ground—that is, broke it up with a broad cotton-field hoe. A full-grown hand was expected to "list" a half acre per day. "June month's," the slaves agreed, "a ha'd month." The sun was hot and the weeds grew fast in June. As the slaves moved across the cotton fields, keeping time to the rise and fall of their hoes, they sang a favorite tune.

What y'u gwine t'do fo' June month?
  Jerusalem Jerusalem.
Pull off y'u coat an' go t'work.
  Jerusalem Jerusalem.
June month's a ha'd month.
  Jerusalem Jerusalem.
Jerusalem in the mornin'.
  Jerusalem Jerusalem.

At harvesttime, a field hand was expected to pick at least ninety pounds of cotton a day.

Way down in the bottom—whah the cotton
  boll's a rotten
Won' get my hundud all day
Way down in the bottom—whah the cotton
  boll's a rotten
Won' get my hundud all day[4]

If the master owned a cotton gin, male slaves usually operated it. Packing the cotton in with their feet was hard and tiring work.

Virginia slaves had vivid memories of setting out the tobacco plants in the spring.

Dey w'uld 'ave de land all hilled up fur de plants, an' de 'bacco plants w'uld be put in a wagon an' de wagon w'uld be drawn by six oxen. De 'bacco rows w'uld be one mile long. I 'ave seen 50, 60 or 75 'ands settin' ert 'bacco plants. Dey always had one or two plants in their 'ands, so if one want good dey w'uld use de 'toter one. Aftur de 'bacco grew dey w'uld prime de le'ves off, de lower ones, le'vin de good ones on. Den dey w'uld worm 'hit e'ery day.[5]

It was very important to keep worms off the tobacco during the growing season. Young children each day examined the tobacco leaves, pulled off the worms, if there were any, and killed them. Simon Stokes said that his overseer "wuz de meanes ole hound you'se eber seen, he hed hawk eyes fer seein' de worms on de terbaccer." If a slave did not get them all, he or she would "habe ter bite all de worms dat yo' miss into, or git three lashes on yo' back wid his ole lash." The overseer's lash, he recalled, "wuz powfull bad, wusser dan bittin' de worms, fer yo' could bite right smart quick, and dat wuz all dat dar wuz ter it; but dem lashes done last a pow'full long time." Simon Stokes "sho' didn't like dat job, pickin' worms off de terbaccer plants."[6]

"Guess I was a girl 'bout five or six," Nancy Williams remembered, "when I was put wid de other chillun pickin' de bugs off de terbaccy leaves. Gal named Crissy was wukin' on nex' row, an' kep' whisperin' to me to pick em all off. Didn'

Fig. 52.
Frank Bell recalled that his Virginia master "put everybody in de field, he did, even de women" during harvesttime. "Growed mostly wheat on de plantation, an' de men would scythe and cradle while de women folks would rake and bind. Den us little chillun, boys an' girls, would come along an' stack." Edwin Forbes sketched this harvest scene outside Culpeper, Virginia.

pay no 'tention to her, any dat fell off I jus' let lay dere." Soon her master came by, checking on the children's progress. He saw that she had been missing some of the tobacco worms. Nancy Williams would never forget what happened next: "Picked up a hand full of worms, he did, an' stuffed 'em inter my mouth; Lordy knows how many of dem shiny things I done swallered, but I sho' picked em off careful arter dat."[7]

By midsummer it was harvesttime. "Got to pick dem leaves what's jus' startin to brown," Gabe Hunt pointed out. "Pick 'em too soon dey don't cure, an' you pick 'em too late dey bitters." Matilda Perry agreed. One would "git a lashin' too," she said, "effen you cut a leaf fo' its ripe." It was important to break the tobacco leaves off cleanly at the stem and not twist them. If they were bruised they would spoil. Hunt never forgot the tactile sensation of tobacco: "Hands git so stuck up in dat old tobaccy gum it git so yo' fingers stick together. Dat ole gum was de worse mess you ever see. Couldn't brush it off, couldn't wash it off, got to wait tell it wear off." After picking the tobacco leaves, slaves spread them on a cart and dragged it to the tobacco barn. There slave women placed the stem of each between two pieces of board and tied the ends together. "Den hand 'em all up in dat barn an' let it smoke two days an' two nights," Hunt explained. "Got to keep dat fire burnin' rain or shine, 'cause if it go out, it spile de tobaccy. Ev'ybody happy when de tobaccy curin' is done, 'cause den ole Marse gonna take it to market an' maybe bring back new clothes fo' de slaves."[8]

Rice culture was labor intensive. Rice plantations had a larger number of slaves per unit than did cotton or tobacco plantations. Work was apportioned according to the task system, with each day a certain task allotted to a slave. When the slave had completed the task to the driver's

Fig. 53.
Slaves followed methods of rice cultivation and processing first developed in Africa. Mortars and pestles, employed by slaves to husk the rice grain, were traditional tools used in Africa.

satisfaction, the worker had the rest of the day to use for his or her own purposes. The hoe, as in Africa, was the principal all-purpose tool for preparing the soil. But slaves on rice plantations also used gourds for sowing, sickles for harvesting, wooden flails for threshing, and mortars and pestles for pounding the rice. Much of the work was drudgery. At its best, rice culture was exacting hand labor. The slaves' constant exposure to extremely unhealthy conditions appalled a visitor. "The labor required for the cultivation is fit only for slaves," she wrote, "and I think the hardest work I have seen them engaged in."[9]

The annual cycle began in December or January. During the winter slaves prepared the fields by turning and hoeing; they also cleaned trunks, canals, and ditches. Planting began in mid-March and continued through April. Workers dropped seed rice into shallow trenches some three inches wide at twelve-inch intervals. Then the slaves opened the floodgates—or trunk docks—at the next high tide and flooded the fields. A sequence of flooding and draining followed until harvesttime.

> John say you got to reap in the harvest what
>   you sow
> John say you got to reap in the harvest what
>   you sow
> If you sow it in the rain, you got to reap it
>   jus' the same
> You got to reap in the harvest what you
>   sow.[10]

Once the water drained away, the slaves cut the rice stalks with sickles. They bound the dried rice stalks in sheaves about a foot thick and brought the sheaves to the threshing ground. Threshers, armed with wooden flailing sticks, began to separate the grain from the husk.

At first, nearly all plantations used the mortar and pestle to hull and polish the rice for market, although eventually some plantations had pounding mills. Pestles had a sharp end for bruising and removing the rice husks and a flat end for polishing the grain. Mortars were hollowed out of cypress or pine logs. Women or boys would hold the pestles in the middle, raising and lowering them quickly and evenly to a rhythmic chant.

> I gwine t' beat dis rice
> Gwine t' beat 'um so
> Gwine t' beat 'um until the hu'ks come off
> Ah hanh hanh [nasal sound]
> Ah hanh hanh.[11]

Slaves did not finish harvesting, threshing, and pounding the rice until early November. The four winter months were scarcely long enough for the amount of work that had to be accomplished before March, when planting first began. Threshing, pounding, and shipping to market had to be completed. Then the stubble had to be burned, the land turned, and the annual cycle began again.

On sugar plantations, planting began in January and continued through April, employing three

Fig. 54.
On sugar plantations in Louisiana and Texas the day was long and the labor demanding. "Lawd knows how much sugarcane my old marse had," an ex-slave commented. "To dem dat work cuttin' de cane, it don't seem lak much, but to dem dat work hour in, hour out, dem sugarcane fields sho' stretch from one end of de earth to de other."

Fig. 55.
On larger plantations, the driver was the slave designated by the owner as the supervisor of field work—and it was to him that the administration of harsh punishment often fell. One former slave characterized his driver as "de meanest devil dat ever lived on de Lord's green earth."

Winter
Plantation —
Men each 2 shirts, & either
2 pants or 1 coat & 1 pants.
Women 2 chemises & 1 frock.
Those who take their cloth
6 1/2 yds. for each frock, thread,
buttons, & 1 1/2 yds. cotton lining —
When convenient, those who
work out, have sacks like
their frocks —
Rhina has 4 1/2 yds. red flannel
every other winter — (had Dec. 185[illegible])
Sukey takes just what the
yard women have —
Children, each 3 shirts & 2 outside
suits of woollen cloth —
Women with infants have 3 yds
calico & 3 shirting for baby clothes

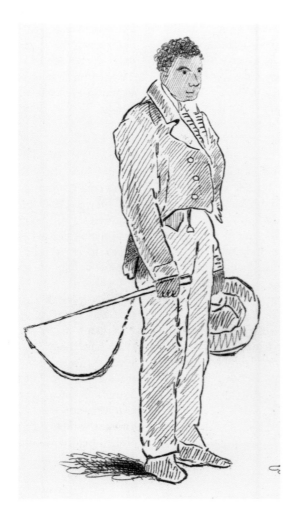

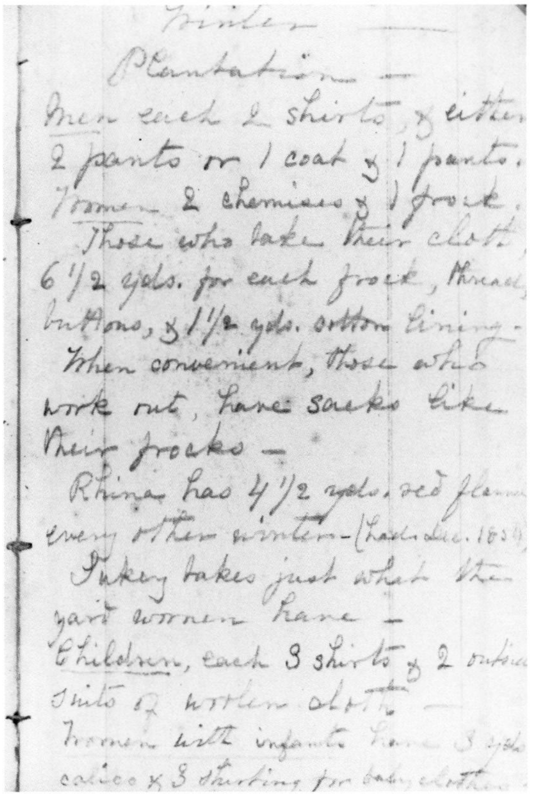

Fig. 56.
Each year planters supplied their slaves with either seasonal changes of inexpensive manufactured clothing or the cloth with which to make their own garments, in addition to a pair of shoes and one blanket. A Georgia cotton planter was unusually generous, providing for each of his male slaves "2 shirts, & either 2 pants or 1 coat & 1 pants," and for the women at least "2 chemises & 1 frock."

gangs of slaves. Each member of one gang drew a stalk of cane from a stack and cut off its top. The second gang planted the stalks. The third gang used hoes to cover the planted stalks with some three inches of dirt. Within four weeks the cane sprouted and began to grow rapidly. Until early August it required careful hoeing. In mid-September the slaves harvested and stacked the seed cane. The general harvest began in October. "Cutting cane was an employment that suited me," Solomon Northup wrote, "and for three years I held the lead row" on a Louisiana sugar plantation, "leading a gang of from fifty to an hundred hands." Wielding cane knives with very sharp fifteen-inch blades, the slaves sheared the tops from the stalks down as far as the stalks were green. It was important to keep the green part of the stalk from the ripe, for the juice of green cane soured the molasses. Then the slaves chopped the stalks off at the root and threw them into a cart bound for the sugarhouse.[12]

At the sugarhouse slave children unloaded the carts and placed the stalks on conveyer belts. The belts ran between two iron rollers that crushed the stalks. The juice fell beneath the rollers into a conductor that channeled the liquid through five filters before boiling in an iron pan. The molten syrup crystallized as it passed over coolers with fine sieve bottoms. The molasses fell through the sieves into a cistern below. The remaining sugar the slaves then packed in hogsheads for shipment to market. The molasses they refined by another process into brown sugar. In January, the slaves began again, preparing for planting another crop.[13]

But many jobs besides field work had to be done on the slave plantations of the Old South. A large corps of slave craftsmen—blacksmiths, bricklayers, cabinetmakers, coopers, shoemakers, and spinners—was necessary for the efficient operation of the plantations. Jacob Stroyer's African-born father was a hostler. He took care of his master's many horses and mules. Jacob's mother was a field hand. But she came from a family of slave craftsmen and house servants.

Some slaves were drivers. A slave with authority, a driver had direct responsibility for the slaves' day-to-day work. The driver, more than any other person, determined the plantation's success or failure. Jacob Stroyer's Uncle Esau was a driver on his plantation. The master, according to Jacob, thought more of Uncle Esau than he did of his overseer. The driver also meted out punishments—usually whippings—for offenses against plantation rules. Jacob considered his Uncle Esau to be "more cruel than any white man master ever had on his plantation."[14]

On rainy days female slaves went to the "loom room," where they worked at spinning, weaving, and dyeing cloth. There was a heavy emphasis in slave clothing on durability. In some districts slave women made all the workers' clothing on the plantations. Although each slave woman was expected to make most of her own family's clothes, across the South there was also a great market for coarse clothing made in New England mills. In ceremonies arranged by the master or mistress, each slave received one set each of winter and summer clothing. Large plantations with one hundred or more slaves could save money by having a cobbler who did nothing but make shoes for the slaves. The condition of the slaves' clothing on her husband's plantation shocked Fanny Kemble. Many of the slaves went barefoot even in midwinter. Each slave annually received two pairs of shoes, a certain number of yards of flannel, and a small allocation of a rough, uncomfortable cloth called "plains."[15]

The men's clothing consisted of pants, shirts, and coats. Children wore long-tailed shirts, and no undergarments. Lou Smith remembered his Oklahoma mistress, "she said us kids didn't need to wear any clothes and one day she told us we could jest take 'em off as it cost too much to clothe us."[16] Women's clothes, however, were not entirely devoid of ornament and fashion. A Mississippi slave recalled that his mother had a blue dress with pictures of gourds on it. According to Clara Walker, her Arkansas mistress "was good to me. She gave me lots of good clothes." Nannie Bradfield, an Alabama ex-slave, recalled that "Miss gave me a brown dress and hat." John Matthews remembered that "De white wimen wore hoops skirts but I neber seed a black woman wid one on. Dey jes' starched deir petticoats an' made deir dresses stand out like hoop under dem."[17] In this small way, slave women not only expressed a desire to be stylish, they also refused to accept complete defeminization.

Day-to-day, household slaves were in more frequent contact with the plantation mistress than field hands. Working in such close proximity to their mistress, house servants experienced both some of the best and some of the worst conditions of slavery. They received greater attention from the whites due to their greater contact, but that attention was not necessarily a positive influence on their situation. It is true that slaves in the big house had the advantage of obtaining better food, clothing, and furniture, but their working hours were irregular and they were always under the careful scrutiny of the whites. A plantation mistress discovered that one little girl, barely five years old, had been taught to knit by her mother. She at once took the child away from her mother and put her in a room in the big house. Plantation mistresses considered such actions as a generous opportunity for the child. They did not always recognize that it simultaneously broke up a slave family.[18]

A few house servants seem to have identified less with the slave families in the quarters than with the master's family in the big house. "When I was a small child and lived in the house with the white folks," said Ann May, of Mississippi, "I despised for anyone to call me a 'nigger'—that would make me fighting mad. No I don't want them to call me that yet. I am black, but I was raised with white folks and got no nigger ways." A few such house servants even earned reputations among the slave community as spies for the masters. For example, a slave named Frances worked by day as a maid on Pharoah Carter's Mississippi plantation. But by night she spied on the cabins.[19]

Despite their different situations, black slaves and white mistresses who lived and worked together occasionally forged bonds of genuine friendship and mutual dependency across the color bar. Sometimes slaves and mistresses worked

Fig. 57.
Unlike the field hand, a household slave lived in close contact with whites. While domestic servants probably benefited materially from this association—receiving better food and better clothes—their lives were under much closer scrutiny. They were at the beck and call of their owners at every hour. "We wan't 'lowed to sit down," one maid recollected. "We had to be doing something all day."

Fig. 58.
Shared work routines, living spaces, and cultural traditions together created a community among distinct groups of slaves. In 1862 Henry P. Moore photographed African-Americans on James Hopkinson's plantation on Edisto Island, South Carolina.

so closely with each other that such friendship turned to real affection between owner and owned. But there were also relationships of another type. Sarah Colbert remembered that her mistress "was very mean to the slaves, whipped them regularly every morning to start the day right."[20]

For slaves in such situations, everything they learned about the plantation mistress's strengths and weaknesses gave them leverage in the close and continuing relationships of the big house. House servants often gained their mistresses' confidence by playing the part of surrogate mothers and sisters. With each of the mistress's secrets they carried, the slaves felt a little freer. Esther Easter took revenge on a cruel mistress by revealing to her master that his wife was having an affair. "I is young then," she recalled many years later, "but I knows enough." "The Mistress didn't know I knows her secret, and I'm fixing to even up for some of them whippings she put off on me."[21]

Slaves were introduced to work almost as soon as they passed infancy. Children did much of the herding. Boys and girls carried water to the adults in the field, kindled fires, swept the yard, and completed other minor tasks that would have cost a field hand valuable time. By their early teens, slaves had been socialized into culturally defined gender roles. A few years later they joined a work gang for their initiation into what were often overwhelmingly male or female worlds.

Women often worked in groups apart from men—hoeing, spinning, weaving, sewing, or quilting. In female company most of the day, they spent much of their nonworking hours sharing joys, concerns, and heartbreaks with one another as well. They learned to depend upon one another for midwifery, medical care, and child care. The elderly ones enjoyed high status as nurses, midwives, and caretakers of the community's children. But aged women received less care and attention from their masters than from their friends and relatives. Some slaveholders

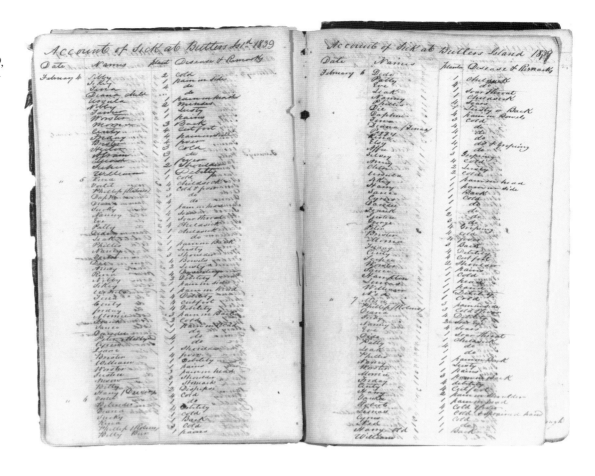

Fig. 59.
On one single day of operation, 6 February 1839, the hospital at Butler's Island, Georgia, treated thirty-nine slaves for physical conditions and illnesses ranging from childbirth to headaches. The plantation mistress, Fanny Kemble, deplored the "dirt, noise, [and] stench" of the facility.

simply freed slaves too old to work rather than assume the responsibility for their food, clothing, and housing.

Sickness often visited the slave plantations. Masters hired doctors to care for their expensive property, but the slaves placed little confidence in them. Some large plantations had infirmaries. Fanny Kemble found the infirmary at her husband's Georgia plantation "a wretched abode of wretchedness." In a vivid description in her journal, she wrote that there

> lay women expecting every hour the terror and agonies of childbirth, others who had just brought their doomed offspring into the world, others who were groaning under the anguish and bitter disappointment of miscarriages—here lay some burning with fever, others chilled with cold and aching with rheumatism, upon the hard cold ground, the draughts and damp of the atmosphere increasing their sufferings, and dirt, noise, stench, and every aggravation of which sickness is capable combined in their condition.

Her heart went out spontaneously to those whom she described as

these poor wretches [who] lay prostrate on the earth, without bedstead, bed, mattress, or pillow, with no covering but the clothes they had on and some filthy rags of blanket in which they endeavored to wrap themselves as they lay literally strewing the floor, so that there was hardly room to pass between them.[22]

Preserving the health and well-being of slaves was normally considered the responsibility of the plantation mistress. She took it upon herself to prescribe medicines for the slaves' illnesses and summoned physicians only if her cures did not work. Alabama's Anthony Abercrombie recollected that his mistress "was jes' as good to me as she could be. She useta dose me up wid castor oil, jimson root, and dogwood tea when I'd be feelin' po'ly." Carrie Davis recalled her Alabama mistress's healing the wounds of slaves after beatings: "Our Ol' Mistus had put salve on aheap of backs so dey could git deir shirts off. De shirts'd stick, you see." It was also the mistress's responsibility to ensure that valuable slave infants were brought to term by improving their mothers' diet and reducing their work load. Some dedicated mistresses made daily rounds to the cabins of sick slaves or to the infirmaries set aside for the sick, the invalid, and the infant members of the slave community.

Another former slave, Irene Poole, recalled that her Alabama mistress "used to go 'roun' de quarters eve'y mornin' to see 'bout her sick niggers. She always had a little basket wid oil, teppentine an' number six in it. Number six was strong medicine." Alabama slave Mary Rice remembered, "Once when I was awful sick, Mistis' Ma'y Jene had me brung in de Big House an put me in a room dat sot on de 'tother side of the kitchen so she could take kere of me herself 'cause it was a right fur piece to de quahter and I had to be nussed day and night."[23]

Other slaves had to make do with their own resources. According to Mississippi slave Smitty Hodges, "When slaves was sick, dey went to de woods and got roots an' herbs ter doctor 'em wid." Old slave women made "teas" for various ailments. Slaves used red-oak bark to combat dysentery, and tried other remedies to reduce menstrual problems. Slaves also wore herbs in pouches as a preventative. South Carolinian Silvia Durant recalled one popular charm, a dime worn around the ankle or elsewhere to ward off sickness or worms in children. Sarah Colbert added that slaves sometimes "went to one of the witchcrafters for a charm" against cruel owners.[24]

Most slave births were performed by slave midwives. Arkansas midwife Clara Walker recalled being hired out to other plantations to deliver white as well as black babies: "I made a lot of money for Ol' miss." According to Alabamian Ank Bishop, "all de women on Lady Liza's place had to go to de fiel' ev'y day an' dem what had suckerlin' babies would come in 'bout nine o'clock in de mawnin' an' when de bell ring at twelve an' suckerlin' em." Hannah Jones recalled of her Mississippi grandmother, "Three days after her first baby was born dey made her git up and make twelve stiff-front, tucked white shirts for her old mistress' boy who be goin' off to college and she was so sick and weak, some of de stitches was crooked. Old Miss ordered de overseer to take her out and beat her 'bout it."[25]

Few slaves in the antebellum South could reasonably expect to find a partner for a stable marriage on their own plantation. The possibility of finding a husband or wife was as much affected by a plantation's sex and age structure as by its size. The number of potential partners from which one could select a mate was very limited even on very large plantations. If a slave had extensive kinship ties, the pool of eligible mates might be even further reduced. Nevertheless, in spite of the limited choices they confronted, slaves seem to have been able to find partners. Moreover, by courting slaves who lived on other plantations they increased their number of possible partners. During her parents' courtship, Laura Montgomery's father brought gifts to her mother on a nearby plantation. "Some time he would brung er bucket of 'lasses, an' some time a water melon an' one time he brung some apples," Laura recalled.[26]

Masters were not above promoting slave marriages by buying and matching couples together. "Jacob," said one Mississippi master, "I brung you a good woman, take her an' live wid her."[27] But forced unions could cause as great a strain within the slave community as forced separations. Sometimes a husband or wife had to be purchased from his or her owner in order to facilitate a marriage. Some slaves were able to purchase title to their wives or other members of their families. One master allowed the slaves in his Mississippi plantation to work a cotton patch that would yield a sixty-dollar bale for themselves. "Uncle Dollie did this for a number of years," Sam Anderson recalled, "until he had saved $500 and paed this money to Moster for a girl for his wife, Aunt Onie, and his Moster had him to build them a house out from the quarters as he set her free, but Uncle Dollie continued a slave."[28]

Slave marriages had no legal standing. Nevertheless, slaves, slaveholders, and preachers all per-

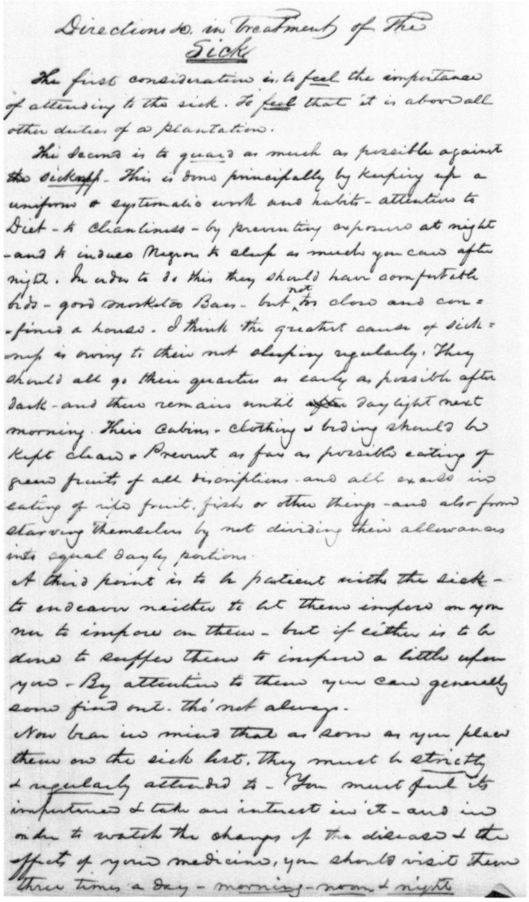

Directions &c. in treatment of the Sick

The first consideration is, to feel the importance of attending to the sick. To feel that it is above all other duties of a plantation.

The second is to guard as much as possible against the sickness. This is done principally by keeping up a uniform & systematic work and habits - attention to Diet - to cleanliness - by preventing exposure at night - and to induce Negroes to sleep as much you can after night. In order to do this they should have comfortable beds - good musketo Bars - but not too close and confined a house. I think the greatest cause of sickness is owing to their not sleeping regularly. They should all go their quarters as early as possible after dark - and there remain until ~~after~~ daylight next morning. Their Cabins - clothing & beding should be kept clean & Prevent as far as possible eating of green fruits of all discriptions - and all excess in eating of ripe fruit, fish or other things - and also from starving themselves by not dividing their allowances into equal dayly portions.

A third point is to be patient with the sick - to endeavor neither to let them impose on you nor to impose on them - but if either is to be done to suffer them to impose a little upon you - By attention to them you can generally soon find out. tho' not always.

Now bear in mind that as soon as you place them on the sick list, they must be strictly & regularly attended to - You must feel its importance & take an interest in it - and in order to watch the changes of the disease & the effects of your medicine, you should visit them three times a day - morning - noon & night

Fig. 60.
Paternalistic slaveholders made many attempts to control the lives of their slaves. Haller Nutt, considered a harsh master by his slaves, recommended to his overseer at Araby plantation in Louisiana that his slaves be confined to their quarters "until daylight next morning"—supposedly for health reasons.

formed rituals that signified the permanence of slave unions. "The marsters married the slaves without any papers," a North Carolina slave recollected. "All they did was to say perhaps to Jane and Frank, 'Frank, I pronounce you and Jane man and wife.' But the woman did not take the name of her husband, she kept the name of the family who owned her." Another North Carolina slave testified, "I reckon 'bout de funniest thing 'bout our plantation wuz de marryin'. A couple got married by sayin' dat dey wuz, but it couldn't last fer longer dan five years. Dat wuz so iffen one of 'em got too weakly ter have chilluns de other one could git him another wife or husban'."[29] Andrew Simms, a former Florida slave, said that on his plantation the slaves "just jumped the broomstick and goes to living with somebody else I reckon."[30] In Louisiana, as an ex-slave remembered, "De couple steps over de broom laid on de floor, dey's married den." And according to an Alabama ex-slave,

> De way dey done at weddings dem days, you picks out a girl and tells your boss. If she was from another plantation you had to git her bosses 'mission and den dey tells you to come up dat night and git hitched up. They says to de girl, "You's love dis man?" Dey says to de man, "You loves dis girl?" If you say you don't know, it's all off, but if you say yes, dey brings in de broom and holds it 'bout a foot off de floor and say to you to jump over. Den he says you's married. If either of you stumps you toe on de broom, dat mean you got trouble comin' 'tween you, so you sho' jumps high.[31]

"Jumping the broom" was nearly universal in the slave South as a wedding ritual.

Sometimes brides dressed in the castoff finery of the plantation mistress. According to Matilda Pugh, a former slave in Mississippi, "we wuz ma'ied in de parlor, an' I wo' a party dress of Miss Sara's." Alabamian Katherine Eppes recalled, "Ol Miss gin me my weddin' dress an' a long veil down to my foots." But not everyone was so favored. Another Alabama slave, Silvia Witherspoon, recollected, "I ma'ied dat ole nigger in a dirty work dress an' my feets was bare jus' lak dey is now."[32]

Slave marriages, based on complementary roles played by husband and wife, were surprisingly egalitarian. Since male slaves did not control property or other culturally valued subsistence goods, slave women were more independent of husbands than were southern white women. It was not easy, though, for slaves to preserve their marriages within the constraints of bondage, but

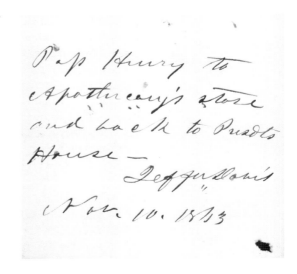

love and affection played important roles. Whether based on romance or on more pragmatic considerations, the family helped socialize slave children into familial roles and enabled them to create an identity beyond their condition of servitude.

The relationship between wives and husbands was ultimately superseded by that between mothers and children. Motherhood played a central role in the slave community. Slave marriages were fragile; at any time a husband or wife could be sold away. But the breakup of a slave family was experienced differently by women and men. Wives might lose husbands, but husbands typically lost both wives and children.

Child raising was largely communal due to the dictates of the master. This has led some to believe that the ties between slave children and their parents were not strong. On most planta-

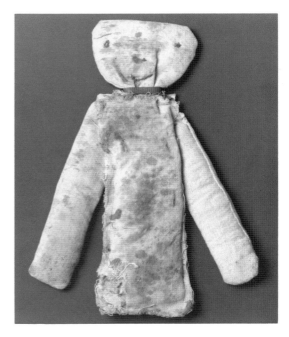

tions, mothers had to leave their children and resume work as soon as they were able. Nursing infants were commonly placed on a quilt beside the fields so that their mothers could feed them from time to time. Adelaide J. Vaughn recalled an Arkansas slave who was brought to the auction block without knowing that her master intended to sell her. When she realized that she was going to be separated from her child, "she broke away from her mistress and them and said, 'I can't go off and leave my baby.' And they had to git some men and throw her down and hold her to keep her from goin' back to the house. They sold her away from her baby boy."[33]

Older children or women too old to work watched the youngest children. They were fed from a trough or a pot filled with "pot likker" along with milk. When not engaged in small labors that helped ease them into the plantation work system, slave children played various games in the quarters, ranging from pastimes (running, jumping, skipping, jumping poles, walking on stilts, and riding stick horses, for example) to games of skill (jump rope, ball, marbles, or horseshoes). Often a master's children were playmates. Games of concealment, such as "I Spy," "Blindfold and Tag," "Peep Squirrel Peep," and "You Can't Catch Me" taught young slaves potentially useful skills. Sometimes they also made bows and arrows. According to a slave in the South Carolina upcountry, "some games children played was, hiding switches, marbles, and maybe others. Later on, some of de nigger boys started playing cards and got to gambling; some went to de woods to gamble." Former North Carolina slave Charlie Barbour recalled, "I 'minds me of de days when as a youngun' I played marbles an' hide an' seek. Dar wuzn't many games den, case nobody ain't had no time for 'em. De grown folkses had dances an' sometimes co'n shuckin's, an' de little niggers patted dere feets at de dances an' dey he'p ter shuck de co'n."[34]

During puberty, boys and girls became more interested in the opposite sex, and parents became more apprehensive. Female slaves experienced menarche around the age of fifteen but delayed childbearing for about two years. Giving birth was a life-affirming act that bolstered the status of slave women, but it made their workdays all the more exhausting. On the slave plantations as well as in Africa, motherhood was the most important rite of passage for black women. The slaves did not condemn what the white world called "illegitimacy." It was common for a slave woman to marry the father of her first child after its birth. This pattern reflected continuity with an ancient African custom that considered a marriage consummated only after a woman had demonstrated her ability to bear children.

The most dramatic threat to the well-being of the slave family was the auction block. It is clear that the settlement of the Lower South accompanied a widespread disruption of slave families in the East. Slaves in the Deep South's cotton lands, first opened in the 1820s and 1830s, came from many different states. Parvenu cotton planters acquired their labor forces on the auction blocks of the older slave states.

Slaves were not, however, sold only as stock for new plantations but also as gifts or parts of estate settlements. The auction block was one of the strongest forms of psychological control any slaveholder possessed. Henry Walker remembered his Arkansas mistress saying, "If you don't be good and mind we'll send yare off and sell you wid 'em." That threat, he recalled, frightened him more than any beating he ever received.[35]

Some former slaves disclaimed any knowledge of families being separated. North Carolina's Jane Arrington maintained that she "never saw a grown slave whupped or in chains and I never saw a slave sold." Her master "Jackson May would not sell a slave. He didn't think it right. He kept 'em together." But not all slaves escaped the horrors of being separated from family and friends. Viney Baker vividly remembered slavery days in North Carolina. "One night I lay down on de straw mattress wid my mammy," she said, "an' de nex' mo'nin' I woked up an' she wuz gone. When I axed 'bout her I fin's dat a speculator comed dar de night before an' wanted ter buy a 'oman. Dey had come an' got my mammy widout wakin' me up. I has always been glad somehow dat I wuz asleep."[36] It was not uncommon for a master to present his daughter with a slave as a wedding present. Such a gift might represent an act of kindness from father to daughter; in breaking up the slave's family it had a contrary effect. An Alabama slave contended that "Mistis never 'lowed no mistreatin' of de slaves, 'case dey was raisin' slaves for de market, an' it wouldn't be good bizness to mistreat 'em." Shipping slaves to market became so common in Virginia that the slaves made up a song about it—"Massa's Gwine Sell Us Tomorrow."[37]

Another major threat to the stability of the slave family was the sexual liberty taken by some white men with female slaves. If a slave family had an attractive daughter, she could be taken from her home and moved to "the big house where the young masters could have the run of her," as a former Virginia slave described it. In his memoirs, escaped slave Henry Clay Bruce wrote, "we would have been pure black, were it not that immoral

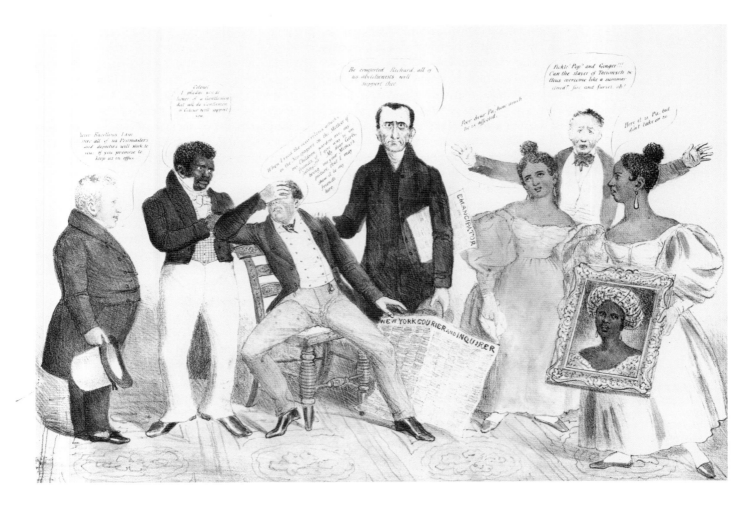

Fig. 63.
Few white fathers ever publicly acknowledged their black children. An 1836 political cartoon portrayed Richard Mentor Johnson, of Kentucky, elected vice president of the United States that same year, with his biracial daughters, Adaline and Imogene, whom he recognized.

white men, by force, injected their blood into our veins, to such an extent, that we now represent all colors from pure black to pure white, and almost entirely as a result of the licentiousness of white men." Another writer complained, "one of the reasons why wicked men in the South uphold slavery, is the facility which it affords for a licentious life. Negroes tell no tales in courts of law of the violation by white men of colored females." One who thus upheld slavery was South Carolina's leading man of letters, William Gilmore Simms. In his *Morals of Slavery* (1838), Simms characterized slavery as a beneficial institution because it protected the purity of white women by allowing slaveholders to vent their lust "harmlessly" upon slave women.[38]

House servants were perhaps more often at risk from sexual exploitation by their masters or his guests than were field hands. One of the Reverend Dr. Charles Colcock Jones's household slaves gave birth to a mulatto child. Jones, convinced that the father was a man who had been a visitor in his home, was outraged. He chastised the man for daring "to offer to me personally and to my family and to my neighbors so vile and so infamous an insult. You are the only man who has ever dared to debauch my family servants . . . and

to defile my dwelling with your adulterous and obscene pollutions."[39]

Overseers were also known to exploit slave women sexually. On Argyle Island, the twenty-four-year-old overseer was too familiar with the slaves to suit Louis Manigault, his employer. He sided with the slaves against their drivers, joined them in their prayer meetings, and fathered a mulatto son in the slave quarters. According to Fanny Kemble, both the father and son who successively managed her husband's plantations sexually abused the female slaves and fathered mulatto children by them. It would be hard to find "a more cruel and unscrupulous" man, she wrote of the younger, "even among the cruel and unscrupulous class to which he belonged."[40]

Mulatto children fathered by the master were rarely acknowledged on the slave plantations. According to Mary Boykin Chesnut, mistress of Mulberry plantation in South Carolina, a slaveholder's "wife and daughters in the might of their purity and innocence are supposed never to dream of what is as plain before their eyes as the sunlight, and they play their parts of unsuspecting angels to the letter."[41] The large numbers of plantation mulattoes contributed to the hostility felt by some mistresses toward their slaves. They considered black women promiscuous and directed their anger toward the slaves instead of toward their husbands. Under the slavery system, Mary Chesnut lamented, "we live surrounded by prostitutes." "God forgive us," she continued,

> but ours is a *monstrous* system and wrong and iniquity. Perhaps the rest of the world is as bad—this *only* I see. Like the patriarchs of old our men live all in one house with their wives and their concubines, and the mulattoes one sees in every family exactly resemble the white children—and every lady tells you who is the father of all the mulatto children in everybody's household, but those in her own she seems to think drop from the clouds, or pretends so to think.[42]

Mothers resented the young slaves who attracted their sons, and wives feared the female slaves who attracted their husbands. Such slaves threatened the position of the plantation mistress.

A few slaveholders flaunted their relations with slave women, risking condemnation by the public and by their own families. After his wife died, David Dickson, of Georgia, lived openly with his slave mistress and their children. Josias Grey scandalized Louisiana society when he took his mulatto children to public places. Governor Leroy Pope, of Alabama, consorted publicly with his mulatto mistress. The well-publicized relationship humiliated Pope's wife and set tongues wagging in his hometown. She became so angry that she forced him to send the slave to another plantation. Thereupon the governor spent most of his time at the other plantation, until social pressure compelled him to sell the woman.[43]

James Henry Hammond, former governor of South Carolina, was somewhat more clandestine about his relationships. Hammond took an eighteen-year-old slave to be his mistress. When her daughter reached the age of twelve, Hammond made her his mistress, too. When he brought his slave mistress into the big house, his wife moved out and refused to return until he sent the mistress away. The slave mistress moved out, and the wife returned. But soon the slave mistress returned as well.[44]

A classic example of the tensions inherent in such situations is the story told by Mary Reynolds, a former slave in Louisiana. Her master went to Baton Rouge "and brought back a yellow gal dressed in fine style. She was a seamster Nigger. He built her a house away from the quarters." The slaves had long known that their master "took a black woman as quick as he did a white and he took any on his place he wanted and he took them often." "This yaller gal," Reynolds remembered, "breeds so fast and gets a mess of white younguns. She teaches them fine manners and combs out they hair." One day two of the children "goes down the hill through the back gate into the yard by the doll house," where the planter's white children were playing. But before they could reach the toy, one of the white children said, "You cant go in the doll house 'cause that is for white chillun, Nigger chillun don't have no doll house. The little Nigger chile says, But I ain't no Nigger, we ain't no Niggers 'cause we got the same dada you got"—one who "comes

Fig. 64, Fig. 65. Religious instruction was a regular feature of life on many plantations. Some owners even built churches to accommodate religious services for the entire community. Probably slave-made, the small pew and pulpit are from the Salem Chapel on the Fairntosh plantation, near Durham, North Carolina.

to see us every day."

As the children quarrelled, the plantation mistress heard their conversation from her bedroom window. Mary Reynolds recollected vividly what happened later that day.

The tales from the house is that when Marster comes home that evenin' that his wife says howdy to him but she dont say it so nice—or just like he thinks she ought to. He axes her what the matter and she tells him, Since you axes me, I'm studying in my mind about them white younguns of that yellow Nigger wench from Baton Rouge. He says, Now, Honey, I fotch that gal just for you 'cause she is such a fine seamster. She says, It looks kinda funny that they got the same kind of hair and eyes as my chillun and they got a nose that looks like yours. He says, Honey you is just payin' 'tention to the talk of little chillun that ain't got no mind to what they say. She said, Over in Mississippi I got a home and plenty with my dada and I got that in my mind.

Missus didn't never leave and the Marster bought her a fine new span of surrey horses. But she don't never have no more chillun and since that time ain't so cordial with the Marster. Margaret that yellow gal had more white younguns but they don't go down the hill no more to the big house.[45]

It was difficult for wives to get out of such marriages in the Old South. In North Carolina, Samuel Hansley's wife sued him for divorce because of his relationship with his slave Lucy. The Hanover County Superior Court granted the decree in 1845, but the North Carolina Supreme Court reversed it in 1849.

The position of a plantation mistress involved in such a triangle was a difficult one. Sometimes a master's infidelity prompted a mistress's cruel and unfair behavior toward the slaves. For example, former slave Sarah Wilson recalled, "When I was eight years old old Mistress died, and Grandmammy told me why old mistress picked on me so. She told me about me being half Mister Ned's blood."[46] Henry Ferry told of a childless Virginia plantation mistress whose husband had fathered a son by one of his slaves.

Ole Marse John ain't never had no chillun by his wife. His wife was pow'ful jealous of Martha an' never let her come near de big house, but she didn't need to 'cause Marsa was always goin' down to the shacks where she lived. Marse John used to treat Martha's boy, Jim, jus' like his own son, which he was.

Him used to run all over de big house, an' Missus didn't like it, but she didn't dare put him out. One day de Parson come to call. He knew Marse John but didn't know Missus Mamie. He come to de house an' Jim come runnin' down de stairs to meet him. He took de little boy up in his arms an' rubbed his haid, an' when Missus come, tol' her how much de boy look like his father and mother. "Course it favor its father most," de preacher say, tryin' to be polite, "but in de eyes, de lookin' glass of de soul, I kin see dat he's his mother's boy."[47]

The mistress did not let on to the preacher that the boy was not hers, but she never again let the child come in the house.

Some slave women may have given their sexual favors more or less willingly in an effort to gain special treatment, or perhaps even manumission. As one woman slave remarked, "some did it because they wanted to."[48] Solomon Northup described a vain and beautiful young slave, Maria, who told her companions in the slave pen that she was willing to be a concubine but she had no desire to be a field hand on some plantation. She had no doubt that as soon as they were put on the auction block in New Orleans, she would be immediately purchased by some wealthy and unmarried gentleman.[49]

Whether they were willing or not, slave women had little recourse. "Any man with money can buy a beautiful and virtuous girl, and force her to live with him in a criminal connection," former slave William Craft wrote in his 1860 memoir, "and as the law says a slave shall have no higher appeal than the mere will of the master, she cannot escape unless it be by flight or death."[50] Others were forced to submit through coercion and violence. In Edgefield District, South Carolina, Charlotte's lecherous master tried to force her into a sexual relationship. She resisted, but he stripped her and forced her to sit naked upon a pile of manure until she finally submitted. Later, after she had borne him a child, he passed her on to his cousin, to whom she bore another child.[51]

Slave women fought back and so did their families. Robert Elliott recalled that on the Virginia plantation where he had lived a white man tried to molest his sister one day. When his father realized what was happening, he "jumped him and grabbed him in the chest. He pointed at the big house and said, 'If you don't git in that house right how, I'll kill you with my bare hands.'"[52] In this instance, the white man backed off and left the girl and her father alone. But other efforts to deter white sexual aggression were less successful.

(continued on page 73)

Plate 7.
Domestic slaves enjoyed better food and clothing as well as other advantages derived from
their close association with whites. Artist Christian Mayr's scene of a kitchen ball at White
Sulphur Springs, Virginia, in 1838 portrays the resort's fashionably dressed domestics cel-
ebrating the marriage of an African-American couple, dressed in white.

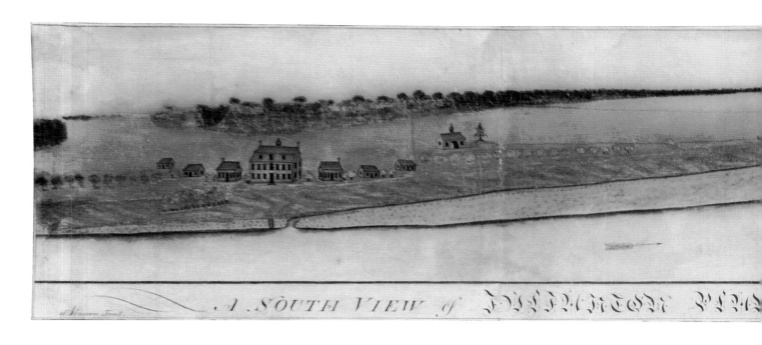

A SOUTH VIEW of JULIANTON PLAN

Plate 8.
In the late eighteenth century, surveyor John McKinnon completed a detailed landscape of Julianton, a Sea Island cotton plantation near Darien, Georgia. Most of Julianton's two hundred slaves lived near the fields in a long row of twenty-three cabins situated at some distance from the main house and the plantation's service buildings.

Plate 9.
At a Lynchburg, Virginia, dance in 1853, artist Lewis Miller observed African-Americans playing instruments of European origin, such as the fiddle, as well as others with African antecedents, such as the bones and banjo. "'Bout dat dancin'," a former slave recalled, "Honey, I could sho cut dem corners. Dancin' is one thing I more'n did lak to do, and I wish I could hear dat old dance song again."

Plate 10 (far right).
Historians estimate that during the antebellum period slave traders and owners "sold south" as much as 10 percent of the Upper South's slave population to supply labor for the Deep South's cotton and sugar plantations. Dealers transported large groups of African-Americans, including small children and infants, on foot in coffles, or caravans of slaves chained together. Lewis Miller observed one such group marching from Staunton, Virginia, to Tennessee in 1853.

O carry me back, O carry me back, to old Virginia Shore, home Spun, and humani block, & Corn, this very valuable grain in Virginia and much is raised.

Lynchburg—negro dance, August 18th 1853,

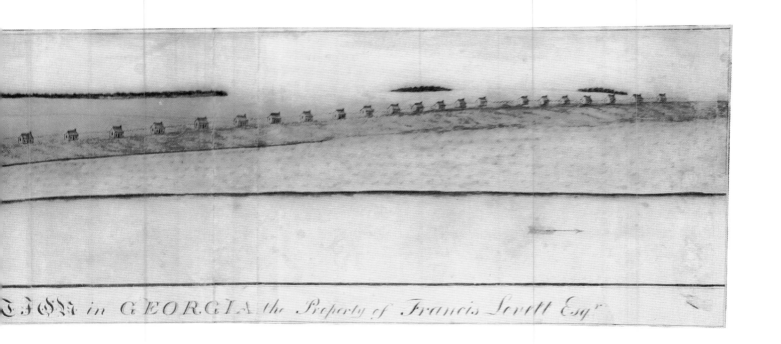

in GEORGIA the Property of Francis Levett Esq.

Arise! Arise! and weep no more
dry up your tears, we shall part
no more. Come rose we go to
Tennessee,
that happy Shore. to old virginia
never — never — return. —

Plate 11.
A uniquely southern furniture form used to store wine and liquor, this cellarette is attributed to a highly skilled slave carpenter, Peter Lee, of John Collins's Rodney Plantation, Marengo (now Hale) County, in the Alabama Black Belt.

Plate 12.
Elevated wooden blocks, such as the example from New Orleans, were standard fixtures in slave marts throughout the South. "I 'members when they put me on the auction block," former slave Lu Perkins reflected. "They pulled my dress down over my back to my waist, to show I ain't gashed and slashed up. That's to show you ain't a mean nigger."

Plate 13.
Archaeological excavations at the Bennehan-Cameron plantation complex near Durham, North Carolina, yielded several objects suggesting that African beliefs persisted among the resident slave population. Archaeologists speculate that a slave conjurer deliberately placed a cane between the walls of a 1799 addition and the earlier Bennehan main house.

Plate 14.
Africans taken as slaves brought the banza, or banjo, directly to the Americas. In 1794, Nicholas Creswell reported of Maryland African-Americans that on Sundays "they generally meet together and amuse themselves with Dancing to the Banjo. This musical instrument (if it may be so called) is made of a Gourd something in the imitation of a Guitar, with only four strings and played with the fingers in the same manner." The smaller gourd fiddle is an example of a related instrument also made and played by slaves.

Plate 15.
The South Carolina maker of this colonoware teapot attempted to shape it into a distinctly European—and atypical—form.

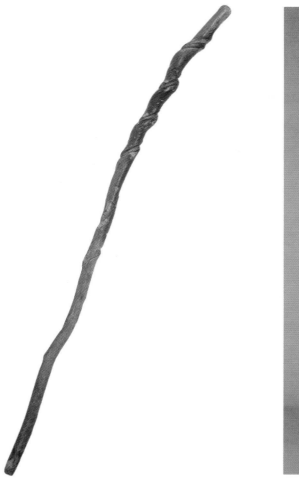

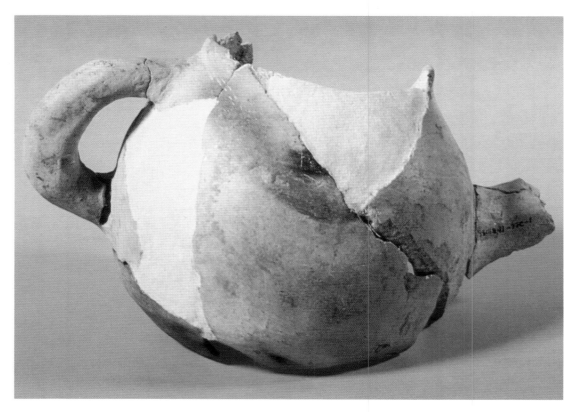

Plate 16.
A rare surviving example of a tignon from the collections of the Louisiana State Museum in New Orleans

Plate 17.
According to family tradition, slave artisans on the John Burry plantation near Shreveport, Louisiana, during the Civil War fashioned a suit made of sheep's wool dyed with hickory nuts.

Plate 18.
Within limits prescribed by whites, antebellum African-Americans found economic opportunities in southern cities. Service-related occupations open to blacks included catering, barbering, laundering, dressmaking, and tailoring; blacks also entered the building trades. Benjamin Henry Latrobe sketched several black barbers at work in Norfolk, Virginia, in 1797.

Plate 19.
Black soldiers, predominantly former slaves, guarded captured Confederates at Point Lookout, a large Federal prison camp in southern Maryland. In a telling sketch, one of a large group attributed to John J. Omenhausser, a prisoner there in 1863, a sentry warns a defiant prisoner that "De Bottom rails on top now."

PLANTATION SLAVES

Plate 20.
The rituals of life and death held particular significance for the slave community. In 1860 artist John Antrobus captured an evening burial service conducted by an African-American preacher and attended by slave mourners. Excluded from the gathering were the white owners (far right) and the plantation overseer (left).

(continued from page 64)

In one case, a cruel master lusted after a woman in the slave quarters. Regularly he would come to her cabin, wake her family, and tell her husband to leave the house while he used the wife for his sexual gratification. One night the husband waited outside for the white man. When the master had finished with the woman and was leaving the cabin, the slave husband strangled him. For this "crime," the husband was swiftly executed.[53]

Masters were sometimes inclined to sell their mulatto children in order to protect them from the abuse of their white stepmothers, half brothers, and half sisters. Frederick Douglass noted, "As cruel as the deed may strike anyone to be, for a man to sell his own children to human flesh-mongers, it is often the dictate of humanity for him to do so: for unless he does this, he must not only whip them himself, but must stand by and see the white son tie up his brother, of but a few shades darker complexion than himself, and ply the gory lash to his naked back."[54]

The white slave owners' slave kin, if they were not sold, were quite often made personal slaves in the big house. In many cases the body servants of the young people were their half brothers or half sisters. In rare instances such brothers and sisters developed close bonds. Ed Domino said, "my Mudder 'n' my mistus claim half-sisters. My mistus wouldn' 'low nobuddy t' touch me 'r' my mudder."[55]

There were also instances in which mulatto children grew up with the love and affection of the white family. Dora Franks, who had been a slave in Choctaw County, Mississippi, recollected, "My daddy was my young Marster. His name was Marster George Brewer and my mammy always told me dat I was his'n. I knew dat dere was some difference 'tween me and de rest o' chillen, 'cause dey was all coal black, and I was even lighter dan I is now. Lord, it's been to my sorrow many a time, 'cause de chillen used to chase me round and holler at me, 'Old yellow nigger.'" But she recalled her mistress with affection: "I stayed in de house most o' de time with Miss Emmaline." "I loved her 'cause she was so good to me." Her master and his wife had no young children left, and they loved her and treated her as a grand-daughter. "She and Marse Bill had about eight chillen, but most of 'em was grown when I come along. Dey was all mighty good to me and wouldn't allow nobody to hurt me." On one occasion she asked an old slave cook for a piece of white bread such as the whites ate. "She haul off and slap me down and call me all kind o' names dat I didn't know what dey meant. My nose bled and ruint de nice dress I had on. When Mistis come back Marse George was with her. She asked me what on earth happen to me and I told her. Dey call Caroline in de room and asked her if what I say was de truth. She tell em it was, and dey sent her away. I har tell day dey whip her so hard dat she couldn't walk no more."[56]

Occasionally a master's slave offspring were reared as though free. James Calhart James recalled that his father gave him money and good clothes and bought him toys and games. He was educated with his half brothers and half sisters, and he was allowed to attend the white church with the other children of the household. Lizzie Williams, who had been a slave near Selma, Alabama, told of a similar case: "Emily, she look lik' a white gal. She was treated jes like she white. Her daddy was a white man. . . . But de missy she was good to her. She never stay in de quarters, she stay in de house with de white fokes. But Emily had de saddes' look on her yaller face cas' de other niggahs whisper 'bout her pappy."[57]

Such status was never secure in a slave society. In his 1876 memoirs, Levi Coffin told of a child born to a white slave owner and a quadroon slave. When the boy was three years old, the master had family problems and sent him away from the plantation. He was given a good education and grew up as a free man, never knowing that he was a slave until his father died and his white relatives sold him to a slave dealer.[58]

Being victimized by the master's lust was only part of the sexual exploitation visited upon slave women. After legal slave importations were ended in 1807, the reproductive capacity of almost all slave women was manipulated for the slaveholders' profit. Male slavery rested on the work that men were required to perform. Female slavery was based not only on their work, but also on their bearing and rearing children to replenish their masters' labor force.

As early as 1831 the Reverend Dr. Charles Colcock Jones delivered an eloquent sermon urging slaveholders to instruct their slaves in the principles of the Christian religion. Not only would religious instruction save the slaves' souls, he said, it would also create "a greater subordination" among the slaves and teach them "respect and obedience [to] all those whom God in His providence has placed in authority over them."[59] Pastor of Savannah's First Presbyterian Church, the Reverend Dr. Jones was also master of three rice plantations and more than one hundred slaves in coastal Georgia. As a pastor, his concern for the salvation of his slaves' souls was genuine. But as a master he also consciously and deliberately used Christianity as an instrument of discipline and control. After all, he believed a faithful servant was more profitable than an unfaithful servant.

So he tailored the Christianity he taught his slaves to serve his desire to keep slaves reconciled to their bondage.

Some slaveholders were simply indifferent to the religious education of their slaves. At Cannon's Point plantation on Saint Simons Island, Georgia, Swedish visitor Fredrika Bremer tried to teach a gathering of slave children to recite the Lord's Prayer. "The children grinned, laughed, showed their white teeth," she said, "and evinced very plainly that none of them knew what that wonderful prayer meant nor that they had a Father in heaven."[60]

Other slaveholders actively opposed efforts to Christianize the slaves. Such slave owners maintained that the slaves were not fully human creatures. Thus they were not capable of reasoning and learning the truths of the Christian religion. The slaveholders especially feared the intense emotionalism the slaves preferred as the appropriate way to worship God. The whole enterprise seemed to them as pernicious as it was useless. The Reverend Dr. Jones and slaveholders of similar inclinations wanted their slaves delivered from what they considered the savage heathenism of Africa to the true light of the Christian gospel, preferably of the Episcopal or Presbyterian variety. Ultimately those of the evangelistic persuasion were able to prove to their more dubious brethrens' satisfaction that they favored only quiet and sedate worship services.

The kind of Christianity slaveholders wanted for their slaves is revealed in the incessant references to their spiritual welfare in the Jones family correspondence. "I trust you are holding on in your high profession of the Gospel of our Lord and Saviour Jesus Christ at all times, and constantly watch and pray," the Reverend Dr. Jones wrote his head slave carpenter, Sandy Maybank. "You know our life and health are in His hands," Jones constantly counseled his driver Cato, "and it is a great comfort to me to have a good hope that you love Him, and do put all your trust in our Lord and Saviour Jesus Christ, who is a precious Saviour to us in life and death." And he was very pleased when another driver, Andrew, sent back such replies as "it is no light thing to be a christian, for we may play with the lightning and the rattle snake, but dont trifle with Almighty God 'least he tear you to pieces in his anger and then be never to deliver you.'"[61]

The slaves' religious indoctrination began early on most plantations. "There was Sabbath School each Sunday afternoon, under the big live oaks," a planter's daughter recalled. "My father would read from the Bible and we would tell simple stories to the children and many grownups, who came with them." According to former slave Mattie Logan, "All the slaves who wanted religion was allowed to join the Methodist church because that was the Mistress' church." An Alabama slave said, "Miss Dell was a good Mistis an' she useter hab Sunday School ebber' Sund'y mornin' at de Big House an' all us l'il niggers went up dar for her to teach us 'bout de Bible an' Jesus." Hattie Clayton remembered, "Ol' Mistus useter take all de little scamps dat was too little for church an' read de Book to dem under de big oak tree in de front yahd." Another mistress "useter read de Bible to us niggers. She would talk to us 'bout de Good Book an' have prayer meetin' wid us." Emma Jones recalled that "at night some of de house niggers would gather 'roun' de fire, an' mistis would read us de scriptures, an' de white chilluns git tired an' slip out de do' but us little niggers couldn't ford to do dat; us hadda stay dere whether us liked it or not."[62]

Slaveholders were quite selective in the Christianity they taught their slaves. They often attempted to use religion as a means of asserting control. In the master's church the most important thing preached to them "was how to serve their master and mistiss," an Arkansas slave recalled. "Dey read the Bible and told us to obey our marster," according to North Carolinian Hannah Crasson, "for de Bible said obey your marster."[63]

Most slaves belonged to Baptist or Methodist churches. Despite their masters' fears, the slaves' style of worship was emotional. As Lewis Jefferson explained, "Ebery time I feel de Spirit move me I jes' gibe him de reigns an' I tells de wurld I is happy. When I is happy in de Lord dar is no shuttin' my mouf. I tells de whole wurld. I is gwine to Heaben when I die."[64]

Immanent in slave religion was the gaining of freedom, and not merely freedom from sin:

O, Lord, cum free dis nigger,
O, Lord, cum free dis nigger,
O, Lord, cum free dis nigger
Fur I cany wurk all de day.[65]

Slaves had prayer meetings out in the quarters, being careful to keep the residents of the big house from hearing them, so they could sing and pray to their hearts' content. Or they gathered secretly in wooded areas, away from the plantations and patrols. Charlie Van Dyke, a former Alabama slave, recalled that slaves often heard white preachers exhort them to be "good." "Church was what they called it," he said, "but all that preacher talked about was for us slaves to obey our masters and not to lie and steal. Nothing about Jesus, was ever said."[66]

Fig. 66.
Some masters saw Christianity as an effective tool with which to impart obedience and docility to their slaves. The tactic, however, fooled few slaves. In countless chapels, such as this cotton plantation's, "the preacher came and . . . He'd just say, 'Serve your masters. Don't steal your master's turkey. Don't steal your master's chickens. . . . Do whatsomever your master tells you to do.' Same old thing all the time."

In their secret meetings, the slaves prayed for deliverance from bondage. "I remember one old song we use to sing when we meet down in the woods back of the barn. My mother she sing an' pray to the Lord to deliver is out o' slavery," recalled W. L. Bost, of North Carolina.

Oh, mother lets go down, lets go down,
  lets go down, lets go down.
Oh, mother lets go down, down in the valley
  to pray.
As I went down in the valley to pray
Studyin' about that good ole way
Who shall wear that starry crown,
Good Lord show me the way.[67]

Slave Christians often looked for freedom through some heavenly decree. If they put all their faith in the Lord, He would deliver them from bondage just as in the Bible He had delivered the Hebrew children from Egypt. Broder Coteney, a slave preacher, likened his flock of slave Christians to a flock of sheep:

An dem buckra dat beat dem nigger onjestly an onmusefully, jes kase de po nigger cant help e self, dems de meanest buckra ob all, an berry much like de sheep-killin dog dat cowud to take sumpn dat cant help e self. Dat berry ting dat de nigger cant fend e self an helpless, mek de gentleman buckra berry pashunt an slow to punish dem nigger. An de berry fack dat de Lawd sheep is po help-less ting, mek de Lawd pity an lub we mo, an mek we pen pun Him an cry fur Him in de time ob trouble an danejur. An dat wha de Lawd want, fur we feel we own weakness an trust in Him strenk. De mudder lub de morest de chile dats de weakest an dat need um de morest, and so we wed de Sabeyur an e lettle wuns dat pend only pun Him.[68]

Nevertheless, expressing even such mild sentiments could be dangerous. Who could tell when slaves might begin to ask the Lord not merely to deliver them in the next world, but to aid their own efforts to cast off the shackles of those who claimed to own them in this one? Some slaveholders, like Mississippi's Pharoah Carter, forbade prayer meetings entirely. A house servant named Frances betrayed such a secret prayer meeting to Carter, who had the slave worshippers savagely beaten.[69]

Slave religious services were especially marked by music. Whether they slipped away into the woods on Sunday evenings or had general prayer meetings on Wednesday nights at slave chapels, the slaves would often "turn pots down and tubs to keep the sound from going out." Then they "would have a good time shouting, singing, and praying just like we pleased." At baptizings they sang appropriate spirituals such as "Roll, Jordan, Roll" or "Going to the Water." After evening services, slaves sang on the way home. "As the wagon be creeping along in the late hours of moonlight," someone would raise a tune. "Then the air soon be filled with the sweetest tune as us rid on home and sung all the old hymns that us loved." As they rode through the quarters, slaves who had not been to church would "come out to the cabin door and jine in the refrain. From that we'd swing on into all the old spirituals that us love so well and that us knowed how to sing."[70]

Some slaveholders continued to oppose teaching slaves about Christianity, believing that it was not safe to teach any religion to the slaves. Candus Richardson said that his master allowed no Bible on the plantation; it meant a beating or "a killing if you'd be caught with one." But "I lived to see both of him and Miss Elizabeth die a hard death. They both hated to die, although they belonged to church. Thank God for his mercy." With or without the blessings of their "earthly masters," slave Christians found ways to worship. As a North Carolina slave put it, "I reckon somethin' inside jes told us about God and that there was a better place hereafter. We would sneak off and have prayer meetin'."[71]

Supernatural beliefs, combining African and European folk religions, remained embedded in slave religion. There was considerable continuity with African patterns of folk belief on the slave plantations of the New World. Ghosts or haunts— the spirits of the dead—returned to trouble the living. "I knows dere is ghosts, 'cause when I was a little boy my mammy come in from de field and laid across de bed and I was sittin' in front of de fireplace and a big somethin' like a cow without no head come in de door," recalled an Alabama slave. Another time, he said, "dis spirit like an angel come to my mammy and told her to tell de white lady to read de Bible backwards three times."[72] A Mississippi ex-slave, Gabe Butler, recollected that "w'en I wus a chile I wus skeered uf ha'nts. W'en ebber I went by dat grave yard on de hill I cud hear dem callin' me en den I cud feel deir breath blowin' hot on me en den I wud run en no body cud kotch me. Yes dey did git atter me. I niver seed 'em but I kno'd dey wus dar close ter me. Dar sho' is spirits, I kno' case I out run dem."[73] Jane Smith, of Spartanburg, South Carolina, recalled hearing a ghost once. The night after her master had killed himself, she heard doors being shut, windows slamming, and chairs rocking on the front porch when there was no wind.[74] The slaves used various charms to ward off such spirits' unwelcome visits.

Slaves incorporated African spirit beliefs into their Christianity, but voodoo (or hoodoo) continued outside of and as a belief hostile to Christian tradition. Slave folk beliefs included many signs—if "a scheech owl lit on your chimney and hollered," it signified that "somebody in dat house was goin' to die." Certain practices were designed to ward off misfortune. Burning salt could prevent the death predicted by the screech owl. A rabbit's foot might bring good luck and guard against magic. Many slaves also planted their gardens by the phases of the moon to insure a good crop.[75]

Slaves also took their problems to plantation conjurers. The conjurers, assisted by various substances they believed to be magical, cast spells upon enemies and protected against "ruin or

Fig. 67.
Following African customs, slaves decorated graves with bits of shell, china, and other items representing or belonging to the deceased. In coastal South Carolina, Georgia, and other areas of the South, these practices continue to be observed.

Fig. 68.
Omar ibn Said, or "Uncle Moro," was a Moslem slave. Brought to South Carolina as a young man, Said fled his cruel master but was later apprehended in North Carolina. In jail, "having attracted attention by writing on the walls in Arabic," Said was purchased by a more benevolent individual. He spent the rest of his life in North Carolina.

wrote that sometimes less care was "taken of their dead bodies than if they were dumb beasts." But residents of the slave quarters would more commonly sing and pray through the night after a death. Slave Christians would "thank God that brother Charles, or brother Ned or sister Betsy, is at last free, and gone to heaven where bondage is never known. Some who are left behind, cry and grieve that they, too, cannot die and throw off their yoke of slavery, and join the company of the brother and sister who has just gone."[78] When a slave died, the other slaves would "go to the overseer, and obtain leave to sit up all night with their dead, and sing and pray. This is a very solemn season. First, one sings and another prays, and this they continue every night until the dead body is buried." A northern teacher working in Louisiana wrote in her diary, "This evening a negro . . . died suddenly—about 9 ocl'k. . . . Heard a sound of distant music. It was a lament for the dead. . . . The negroes assemble and spend a great deal of the night praying and singing."[79]

On some plantations all work was suspended until the dead were buried. Slaves from adjoining plantations received passes to come. On others, according to a traveler's account of a funeral in Virginia, "when a slave dies, the master gives the rest day, of their own choosing, to celebrate the funeral. This perhaps a month after the corpse is interred, is a jovial day with them; they sing and dance and drink the dead to his new home, which some believe to be in old Guinea." A Georgia slave recalled, "The mourners beat the drum while on the way to the cemetery; after arriving they marched around the grave in a ring and beat the drum and shouted."[80]

In 1833 northern traveler Frederick Law Olmsted witnessed a slave funeral in Virginia. "An old negro," he wrote, "raised a hymn, which soon became a confused chant—the leader singing a few words alone, and the company then either repeating them after him or making a response to them, in the manner of sailors heaving at a windlass."[81] Fanny Kemble described in her journal a slave funeral on Saint Simons Island in which she had participated during the winter of 1838.

> Yesterday evening the burial of the poor man Shadrach took place. . . . The coffin was laid on trestles in front of the cooper's cottage, and a large assemblage of the people had gathered round, many of the men carrying pine-wood torches. . . . Presently the whole congregation uplifted their voices in a hymn, the first high wailing notes of which—sung all in unison, in the midst of these unwonted surroundings—sent a thrill through all my nerves.[82]

cripplin' or dry up de blood." Conjurers enjoyed a considerable reputation among the slaves who sought their aid in all sorts of matters. They mixed hair, nails, thimbles, and needles in a "conjure bag," or "a li'l bottle and have roots and water in it and sulphur." On the Sea Islands of South Carolina, conjurers were known to "put bad mouth on you." Not all slaves believed in conjure. "Dem conjure-folks can't hurt you lessen you believe in 'em," one slave contended. Another said, "Ma told us chillen voodoo was a no 'count doin' of de devil, and Christians was never to pay it no attention." But others took no chances. "I been a good Christian ever since I was baptized," an Oklahoma slave said, "but I keep a little charm here on my neck anyways."[76]

"Funeral services," the Reverend Dr. Charles Colcock Jones once observed, "are much esteemed by the Negroes."[77] For the slaves on southern plantations, as for their African ancestors, funerals were more than merely esteemed. The funeral was, in fact, life's true climax. At once a religious ritual, a major social event, and a community pageant, the slave funeral drew upon cherished African tradition.

On some plantations, however, little care was given to the deceased. Escaped slave Henry Bibb

Fig. 69 (left), Fig. 70 (top), Fig. 71 (bottom), Fig. 72 (overleaf).
In late 1861 Union forces captured the Sea Islands coastal area near Beaufort, South Carolina. While the white Southerners, many of them only seasonal residents, fled the approaching army, their slaves and other self-emancipated African-Americans who joined them stayed behind. To prepare the nearly sixteen thousand former slaves living there for freedom, the army and a group of Northern missionaries attempted to sustain a reformed version of the plantation system. The so-called Port Royal experiment is one of the most fascinating stories of the war. Photographer Timothy O'Sullivan took four images outside Beaufort in April 1862 on J. J. Smith's plantation, occupied as a campsite by the 1st South Carolina Volunteers, a black unit led by Colonel Thomas Wentworth Higginson. O'Sullivan's depictions of slaves outside the plantation's cotton gin and in their quarter as well as his portrait of one family's five generations (overleaf) were the first photographs ever exhibited of slave life in the South. The images were among the Civil War scenes displayed at Alexander Gardner's gallery in Washington, D.C., in September 1863.

PLANTATION SLAVES

Grave decoration followed cherished African tradition. "Negro graves were always decorated with the last article used by the departed," according to a Georgia planter's daughter, "and broken pitchers and broken bits of colored glass were considered even more appropriate than the white shells from the beach nearby. Sometimes they carved rude wooden figures like images of idols, and sometimes a patchwork quilt was laid upon the grave."[83]

Not all the slaves in the antebellum South embraced Christianity. There was a considerable Islamic presence on the South Carolina and Georgia coasts. Moslem slaves deliberately sought Moslem marriage partners in the second generation. "On Sapelo Island near Darien," a Georgia rice planter's daughter recalled, "I used to know a family of Negroes who worshipped Mahomet. They were all tall and well-formed, with good features. They conversed with us in English, but in talking among themselves they used a foreign tongue that no one else understood. The head of the tribe was a very old man called Bi-la-li. He always wore a cap than resembled a Turkish fez. These Negroes held themselves aloof from the others as if they were conscious of their own superiority."[84]

The old man was Bilali Mohomet. Shadrach Hall, his great-grandson, remembered him as being "coal black." A devout Moslem, he said his prayers three times a day facing Mecca while kneeling on his sheepskin prayer rug. Bilali and other Moslem slaves carefully observed Moslem fasts and feast days. When he died, he was buried with his prayer rug and his Koran. Belali Mohomet and his wife prayed at sunrise, when the sun was directly overhead, and at sunset, according to Katie Brown, his great-granddaughter. Shad Hall recalled that when they prayed they bowed to the sun while kneeling on a prayer rug. They had beads on a long string. According to his descendants, Belali would pull the beads while saying, "Belambi, Hakabara, Mahamadu." His wife Phoebe would say, "Ameen, Ameen." Many former slaves on the Georgia coast remembered their ancestors praying in that fashion.[85]

The slaves' lives were controlled from dawn to dusk, but from dusk to dawn the slave community created its own social and cultural life. People got together to socialize—to converse, to sing, to dance, and to enjoy one another's company. Most plantations gave the slaves Saturday afternoons and Sundays off. The slaves divided the time tending their gardens, patching clothes, and completing other household chores, or hunting and fishing. One popular pastime was visiting other plantations, whether or not one could get a pass. Ben Horry dodged the patrols to visit his first girlfriend, Teena, on a neighboring rice plantation in the South Carolina low country. If he had been caught without a pass, he would have received a severe beating. But he said she was worth it. An Alabama slave, Sylvester Brooks, recollected the "patterrollers" all too clearly, "'cause dey whip me every time dey cotches me without my pass. Dat de way dey make us stay home at night."[86]

As in peasant cultures around the world, the slaves alternated long days of toil in the cotton, tobacco, sugar, and rice fields with periods of ritual festivity. Harvesttime was one such occasion. "After the cotton was picked dey would eat barbecue, and dance, and have a big time," a Georgia slave remembered. In addition, there were corn shuckings, wedding parties, and celebrations on various holidays. Midge Burnett recalled that on her plantation, "We had square dances dat las' all night on holidays an' we had a Christmas tree an' a Easter egg hunt an' all dat, case Marse William intended ter make us a civilized bunch of blacks." In the South Carolina upcountry, slaves went to barbecues on the Fourth of July after they finished their chores. Some Virginia slaves had a Whitsun holiday. "On dem days we would play ring plays, jump rope an' dance. Then nights we'd dance juba." Whitsun holidays appear to have been rare, but slaves typically celebrated Christmas and Easter.[87]

Christmas was the most important holiday in the plantation's annual cycle. On many plantations, the slaves gathered early on Christmas morning at the big house to receive greetings and small presents from the masters and extra rations of pork, beef, molasses, and tobacco. In Georgia,

Christmas am the day for the big time. A tree am fix, and some present for everyone. The white preacher talk 'bout Christ. Us have singing and 'joyment all day. Then at night, the big fire builded, and all us sot round it. There am 'bout hundred hog bladders save from hog killing. So, on Christmas night, the children takes them and puts them on the stick. First they is all blowed full of air and tied tight and dry. Then the children holds the bladder in the fire and pretty soon, "BANG!" they goes. That am the fireworks.[88]

A Missouri slave's report seems scarcely credible: "During Christmas time and de whole month of January, it was de rulin' to give de slaves a holiday in our part of de country. A whole month, to go and come as much as we pleased and go for miles as far as we wanted to, but we had better be back by de first of February."[89] Whatever the situation in Missouri, Christmas for most slaves meant two or three days of released time for celebration.

Slaves eagerly looked forward to Christmas not only because the occasion meant days off from work but also gifts of food, candies, and alcoholic beverages from the master. On many plantations there were dances at night during the holiday season. The patrols were eased up as masters allowed greater freedom of movement than usual. In North Carolina, as in Jamaica, the John Canoe festival was an exotic part of the annual Christmas celebration in which bands of dancers—keeping time to the beat of the "gumbo box," triangles, and jawbones—begged donations from spectators. Most slave drinking was confined to such holidays and dances. Masters, for example, gave out liquor rations at Christmas. A number of ex-slaves recalled drinking during dances. A Louisiana slave reported, "The men would save money out of the crops to buy their Christmas whiskey. It was all right for the slaves to get drunk on Christmas and New Year's Day; no one was whipped for getting drunk on those days." Frederick Douglass believed slaveholders deliberately got slaves drunk "to disgust the slaves with freedom, by plunging them into the lowest depths of dissipation." Such holidays, he believed, were "among the most effective means in the hands of the slaveholders in keeping down the spirit of insurrection."[90]

Corn shuckings were also festive occasions. George Woods recalled that in the South Carolina upcountry both whites and blacks gathered to shuck corn and have a good time. Once the crop was shucked, the slaves chased the master until they caught him. Then they hoisted him upon their shoulders and carried him around the house, laughing and singing all the while. Finally they took him inside the big house, placed him in a chair, combed his hair, crossed his knees, removed his hat, and threw it in the fire. According to tradition, the master had to have a new hat for a new crop. After a day of shucking corn, everyone gathered for a large meal, followed by a dance. Some slaves remembered that the reel was the most popular dance.[91]

Singing, dancing, and making music were especially significant folk performances on the slave plantations. The slaves sang on the way to the fields in the morning, sang while they plowed and hoed under the broiling sun, and came in singing from the fields. Some slaveholders did not approve of their slaves' singing. "Dey didn't allow us to sing on our plantation," an Alabama slave remembered, "'cause if we did we just sing ourselves happy and get to shouting and dat would settle de work."[92] But most slaveholders liked for their slaves to sing while working, and few could prevent it in any case. After the day's work was done, slaves entertained their children with play songs and at night sang them to sleep with lullabies.

Fanny Kemble found the melodies of the slaves' rowing songs on the Georgia coast "extraordinarily wild and unaccountable." She believed slaves had a natural gift of music. She was especially interested in what she considered the unusual structures of the slave songs: "The way in which the chorus strikes in with the burden, between each phrase of the melody chanted by a single voice, is very curious and effective, especially with the rhythm of the rowlocks for accompaniment."[93]

Some of the slave songs commented directly and satirically on the world of the plantation. Ebenezer Brown, who had been a slave in Mississippi, recollected a song the slaves sang as they worked in the cotton fields:

Howdy, my brethren, Howdy yo' do,
Since I bin in de lan'
I do mi'ty well, an' I thank de Lord, too,
Since I bin in de lan'
O yes, O yes, since I bin in de lan'
O yes, O yes, since I bin in de lan'
I do mi'ty well an' I thank de Lord too,
Since I bin in de lan'.[94]

Laura Montgomery, another ex-slave from the same Mississippi county, had learned a somewhat different version,

Howdy my brethren, How d' yer do,
Since I'se bin in de lan',
I do mighty po', but I thank de Lord sho'
Since I'se bin in de lan'.
O, yes! O, yes! Since I'se bin in de lan'.[95]

These two versions of the same song reflect the complexities of the slaves' cultural response to slavery in the American South. One song was sung by people hard at work when out in the fields under white supervision. The other was learned by the narrator in the privacy of the slave quarters, out of white earshot, where slaves felt freer to express their true feelings.

On Saturday nights, from Virginia and the Carolinas, through Alabama and Mississippi, to Louisiana and Texas, the slaves held dances and frolics. Talented slave "musicianers" played such old-time songs as "Arkansas Traveller," "Black Eyed Susie," "Jimmy Long Josey," "Soldier's Joy," and "Old Dan Tucker." According to a Mississippi slave, when the fiddler played the old reels, "you couldn't keep your foots still." A North Carolina slave exclaimed, "Oh, Lord, that fiddle could almost talk."[96] Slave dances, like white dances of the age, centered upon fiddle music. In Mississippi, dances called the "back step" and the "pigeon-wing" were popular. In coastal Georgia, the slaves danced an old African dance called the "buzzard lope."

Some masters had slaves dance to amuse their white guests, who were as amazed at the slaves' strange moves as at their great enthusiasm for dancing. A northern visitor condescendingly described one such musical gathering on a South Carolina rice plantation: "The little nigs, only four or five years old, would rush into the ring and shuffle away at the breakdowns till I feared their short legs would come off; while all the darkies joined in the songs, till the branches of the old pines above shook as if they too had caught the spirit of the music."[97] Slave music and dance served an important function on the plantations—especially as a temporary release from the soul-crushing burdens of bondage.

The daily speech of the slaves included a wide variety of folk linguistic phenomena, ranging from lexical, syntactical, or phonological variations from standard speech to full-blown Creole languages such as Gullah. The slaves' folk expressions made colorful and explicit comments on the experience of slavery. The slaves worked "from can to can't."

They had to "root like a pig er die." The master "didn' give me 'sweat off de black cat's eye.'" But slavery made the slaves tough; the "turkey buzzard lay me an' de sun hatch me."[98] A significant element of slave folk speech involved onomastics, or naming patterns. Not only were African day names still found among slaves as late as the 1860s, but African *patterns* of naming persisted to an even greater extent. Kin names were passed on within families, and surnames (or "titles") were in wide use within the slave community before the 1860s.

The African penchant for proverbial ways of speaking—that is, speaking by indirection—is reflected in slave proverbs, which served as metaphors of social experience. Some African proverbs survived almost unchanged: the Hausa "chattering doesn't cook the rice" continued in the South Carolina low country as "promisin' talk don' cook rice." But others underwent local changes. The Bantu "every beast roars in its own den" became the Gullah "every frog praise its own pond [even] if it dry." Some spoke directly to the experience of the slave plantation: "Ol' Massa take keer o' himself, but de niggah got to go ter God." Others took on heightened meaning in the context of slavery: "Dere's a fambly coolness twixt de mule an' de singletree" could be employed as a comment on master-slave relations. "Yuh mought as well die wid de chills ez wid de feber" could be employed as a comment on the relative merits of trying to escape or remaining in bondage.

Across the South, slaves narrated legends (folk narratives set in historical time that are told *as though* true) of "Ole Nat" (Nat Turner), "Moses" (Harriet Tubman), Frederick Douglass, John Brown, and Abraham Lincoln. According to one such legend, "I was looking right in Lincoln's mouth when he said, 'The colored man is turned loose without anything. I am going to give a dollar a day to every Negro born before Emancipation until his death—a pension of a dollar a day.' That's the reason they killed him."[99]

Another form of legend purported to explain how things came to be. Many such legends persisted as humorous stories (or etiological tales) even after any semblance of belief had eroded. Slaves in Winnsboro, South Carolina, told a story of the biblical Nicodemus, the publican.

In the days of the disciples there was a small colored man named Niggerdemos, that was a Republican and run a eating-house in Jerusalem. He done his own cooking and serving at the tables. He heard the tramp, tramp, tramp of the multitudes a-coming, and he asked: "What that going on out-

Fig. 73.
Slaves supplemented their diet by growing food and other crops in garden plots and earned income by selling the surplus to their owner or to neighboring communities. At Cornhill plantation, near Sumter, South Carolina, the planter set aside twelve acres for the slaves' use.

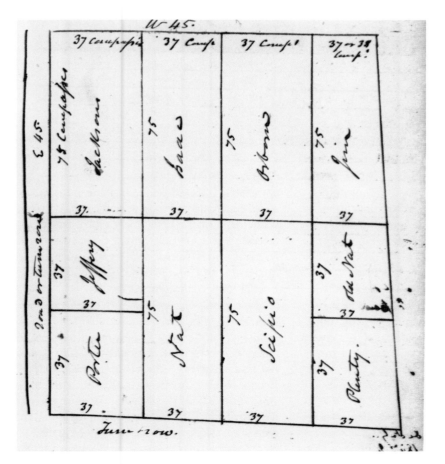

Fig. 74.
Antebellum plantation owners came under increasing pressure from reformers to build single-family housing for their slaves and to implement the planters' own standards of cleanliness and neatness in the workers' quarters. The slave housing on James S. Perryclear's three-hundred-acre plantation near Beaufort, South Carolina, consisted of one-room, wooden, white-washed cabins arranged in a row.

side?" They told him the disciples done borrowed a colt and was having a parade over the city. Niggerdemos thought the good Lord would cure him of the lumbago in his back. Hearing folks a-shouting, he throwed down his dishrag, jerked off his apron, and run to see all that was gwine on, but having short legs he couldn't see nothing. A big sycamore tree stood in the line of the parade, so Niggerdemos climbed up it, going high enough for to see all. The Savior tell him: "Come down; we gwine to eat at your house, Niggerdemos." Niggerdemos come down so fast, when he hear that, he scrape the bark off the tree in many places. Niggerdemos was sure cured of the lumbago, but sycamores been blistered ever since. Next time you pass a sycamore tree, look how it is blistered![100]

The folktales of the slaves included tall tales (or improvements on reality, with smart slaves smarter, bad weather worse, and big crops bigger), outra-

geous falsehoods narrated with a straight face in the sober tones of truth. "One day I was walking past a forty-acre patch of corn," one begins,

and the corn was so high and thick, I decide to ramble through it. 'Bout halfway over, I hears a commotion. I walks on and peeps. There stands a four-ox wagon backed up to the edge of the field, and two niggers was sawing down a stalk. Finally they drag it on the wagon and drive off. I seen one of them, in a day or two, and asks 'bout it. He say: "We shelled 356 bushels of corn from that one ear, and then we saw 800 feet of lumber from the cob."[101]

Trickster tales, with their theme of the struggle for mastery between the trickster (usually a small but sly, weak but wily, animal such as Bruh, or Brer, Rabbit) and his bigger and more powerful adversary, were the most popular tales on the plantations. Robert Pinckney, of Wilmington Island off the Georgia coast, told stories of the trickster defeating his rival by outwitting him. One of the tales, the story of the magic hoe, was widespread in Africa and especially well known in Hausa and Ashanti folklore.

Bruh Rabbit and Bruh Wolf wuz alluz tryin tuh git duh bes uh one anudduh. Now Bruh Wolf he own a hoe an it wuk fuh crop all by itsef. Bruh Wolf jis say "Swish," tuh it. Den he sit down in duh fiel an duh hoe do all duh wuk.

Bruh Rabbit he wahn dat hoe. He hide behine bush an watch how duh wolf make it wuk. One day wen deuh wolf way, Bruh Rabbit he steal duh hoe. He go tuh he own fiel an he stan duh hoe up an he say, "Swish." Duh hoe staht tuh wuk. It wuk and it wuk. Fo long duh crop is done finish. Den rabbit want hoe tuh stop, an he call out an he call out but hoe keep right on wukin. Bruh Rabbit dohn know wut wud tuh say tuh stop it. Pretty soon duh hoe cut down all Bruh Rabbit wintuh crop an still it keep on wukkin an wukkin. Bruh Rabbit wring he hans. Ebryting he had is gone. Jis den Bruh Wolf come long an he laugh out loud wen he see how Bruh Rabbit he keep callin out, "Swish, swish," an duh hoe go fastuhn fastuh. Wen he see Bruh Wolf, he ax um tuh make duh hoe stop. Bruh Wolf wohn say nuttn uhtall cuz he mad dat Bruh Rabbit steal he hoe. Den attuh a time he say, "Slow, boy," an duh hoe he stop wukkin. Den Bruh Wolf he pick up he hoe an carry um home.[102]

The slaves also narrated a cycle of human trickster stories featuring the slave John and his never-ending contest with his master. In one, John killed one of his master's shoats, or hogs,

and he catch him and when he ask him, "What's that you got there?" the nigger said, "A possum." The master said, "Let me see." He looked and seen it was a shoat. The nigger said, "Master, it may be a shoat now, but it sure was a possum while ago when I put 'im in this sack."[103]

In such tales as these, as in other elements of their rich folk culture, the slaves used language as symbolic action. By manipulating the words that defined their world, they verbally rearranged it and turned it symbolically upside down.

Folk cultural expression was also exemplified in slave foodways. At sunset in the slave quarters one could smell the aromas of cornbread, peas and rice, pork or fish, cooking over wood fires. Rations were given out on Saturdays and usually included corn meal, lard, meat, molasses, peas, greens, and flour and soda on occasion. William Ballard, of upcountry South Carolina, recalled that "we was allowed three pounds o' meat, one quart o' molasses, grits and other things each week—plenty for us to eat." Another slave re-

Fig. 75.
Perpetuating traditional African crafts, slaves made baskets of all sizes for storing and transporting items on the plantation.

Fig. 76.
Skilled African-American carpenters and joiners built furniture on many plantations. Slaves on the Organ plantation near Bastrop, Texas, made this sophisticated, yet simple, ca. 1840 corner cabinet.

Fig. 77.
In 1786, nearly one-third of the 216 slaves living at Mount Vernon were artisans. This brass harness ornament, part of George Washington's family crest, was found in the excavations of the blacksmith's shop.

largely unsatisfactory. But slave gardens, hunting, and fishing added variety to the cuisine. Hunting was one way in which slaves were allowed to supplement their rations. Mississippi slave Jim Martin used to sing,

> 'Cum 'long boys an' lets go er huntin',
> Cum long boys an' lets go er huntin',
> Come 'long boys an' lets go er huntin',
> Fur I heered de dogs bark,
> An' I knowd dey treed sumptin'.[107]

The slaves raised most of the plantation provisions. They herded livestock, raised foodstuffs, and helped slaughter and dress meat. Children did much of the herding. Most slave families also cultivated gardens in their off time, raising potatoes, pumpkins, watermelons, and other fruits and vegetables. Typically, each family had its own garden plot from which the members supplemented their weekly allocation of rations.

On some plantations, slaves who ran out of food before the end of the week could get a little more. For the most part, however, if the weekly ration proved insufficient, slaves had to find other sources of nourishment. Food theft became so common on the plantations that slaves had a song about it.

> Some folks say dat a nigger wont steal,
> I caught two in my corn field,
> one had a bushel,
> one had a peck,
> an' one had rosenears [roasting corn ears]
> strung 'round his neck.[108]

Biscuits were a rare delicacy for most slaves. An Alabama slave described them as the plantation mistress's Sunday treat. "I remembers ebery Sunday mawnin'," he said, "dat she'd make de older slaves bring all de little niggers up to de big house, so she could read de Bible to 'em and den she give us plenty of dem good biscuits and taters. . . . I really thought Mistis was an angel!" A Mississippi slave recalled that when he was a child and his mistress planned to punish him, she first lured him out of hiding with a biscuit.[109]

Even rarer were alcoholic beverages, although on some plantations slaves "always made least one barrel of peach brandy and one of cider. That would be vinegar 'nough by spring. 'Simmon beer was good in the cold freezing weather too. We make much as we have barrels if we could get the persimmons."[110] Slaves ate the foodstuffs of the plantation environment and remembered recipes and ancestral tastes. They thus not only maintained cultural continuity with African foodways but also creatively adapted African tra-

ported that "we were given plenty of milk and sometimes butter. We were permitted to have a fowl-house for chickens, separate from the white folks."[104]

"Each slave cabin had a stone fireplace in the end," a former slave remembered, where "over the flames at daybreak was prepared the morning meal. That was the only meal the field negroes had to cook. All the other meals," he added,

> were fixed up by an old man and woman who was too old for field trucking. The peas, the beans, the turnips, the potatoes, all seasoned up with fat meats and sometimes a ham bone, was cooked in a big iron kettle and when meal time come they all gathered around the pot for a-plenty of helpings! Corn bread and buttermilk made up the rest of the meal.[105]

Fanny Kemble, told that her husband's slaves had "sufficient" food, found that it was prepared by elderly cooks in the cookhouse. For lunch, cooked and eaten during breaks from field work, they doled out grits and occasionally rice that was unfit for market. For supper, six hours later, they sometimes varied the menu with crabs, oysters, and freshwater fish, which they spooned into the slaves' small cedar vessels. The slaves mostly ate with crude wooden spoons or by using their fingers, as the children did. They had neither knives nor forks, nor tables and chairs.[106]

For many slaves, however, their diet remained

ditions to the New World.[111]

Folk architecture was strikingly exemplified in the slave cabins, varying from slave quarters built of stone reported in Kentucky to "old ragged huts made out of poles" in Alabama. On one Mississippi plantation, slaves lived in large wooden houses with brick chimneys and up to six rooms. Such elaborate housing, however, was unique to its county. It marked the slaveholder's great wealth and generous paternalism. On another, "about three hundred negro families living in box-type cabins made it seem like a small town. Built in rows, the cabins were kept whitewashed, neat and orderly, for the Master was strict about such things." Ex-slaves described some slave cabins as "good houses, weatherboarden with cypress and had brick chimneys." A Georgia slave recalled, "We lived in weatherboard houses. Our parents had corded-up beds with ropes and we chillun slept on the floor the most part or in a hole bored in a log. Our house had one window jest big enough to stick your head out of, and one door, and this one door faced the Big House which was your master's house. This was so you couldn't git out 'less somebody seen you."[112]

More common slave dwellings were built of logs. Sometimes the logs were covered with slabs and sometimes cabins were large. A Missouri slave reported that "de hewed log house we lived in was very big, about five or six rooms." Far more typical was the one- or two-room cabin in which as many as a dozen people might sleep on "an old pile o' rags in de corner." One former slave said he had lived in a "little one room log cabin, chinked and daubed." A Tennessee slave reported, "We lived in one-room log huts. There was a long string of them huts. We slept on the floor like hogs. Girls and boys slept together— jest everybody slept every whar." A Mississippi slave reported, "we live in log huts, and when I left home grown, I left my folks living in the same log huts." But to others, log cabins would have seemed a luxury. A Georgia ex-slave recalled having lived in "old ragged huts made out of poles and some of the cracks chinked up with mud and moss and some of them wasn't." On some plantations, "dey wasn't fitten for nobody to live in. We just had to put up with 'em." The cracks between the logs were chinked with mud or clay, not always successfully. A Texas slave reported that "the cold winds in the winter go through the logs like the walls were somewhere else." Some cabins had plank floors, but others did not. A Georgia slave recollected, "Dey no floor in dem

Fig. 78.
Former slaves recalled blacks being bound to this tree for flogging on the Frogmore plantation, Saint Helena Island, South Carolina.

houses, 'cept what God put in dem." According to a Mississippi slave, "My ma never would have no board floor like de rest of 'em, on 'count she was a African." Furniture was simple and hand-made. Beds were often made with a post or two and a mattress of moss or straw. A more elaborate bed had ropes plaited to form a support for a feather mattress. Other furniture consisted of simple benches and chairs. The chimneys were usually built of sticks, clay, and mud, and with a coat of clay daubed over them. All too often the chimneys caught fire. "Many the time we have to get up at midnight and push the chimney away from the house to keep the house from burnin' up."[113]

Talented slave artisans created beautiful arts and crafts. On the rice plantations of the South Carolina low country, slaves made wide, shallow fanner baskets with low sloping sides after the African method of coiled basketry. In Georgia, slave basket makers made plaited baskets and mats. Throughout the South slave women made quilts—often in strip patterns—both to keep their families warm and to provide beautiful objects in their cabins. A North Carolina slave described how "the womenfolks carded and spun and wove cloth, then they dyed it and made clothes. And we knit all the stockings we wore." Slave black-smiths not only shod horses and other livestock but also made the striking wrought-iron gates and grilles that were especially well known in South Carolina and Louisiana. And slave crafts-men were adept at making musical instruments that were beautiful both to see and to hear. There were fiddles made from gourds, banjos made from sheep hides, "bones" made from beef ribs, and quills made from willow stalks: "Yous takes de stick and pounds de bark loose and slips it off, den split de wood in one end and down one side, puts holes in de bark and put it back on de stick. De quill plays like de flute."[114]

Most slaves never had an opportunity to learn to read and write. Both law and custom in the Old South conspired to keep the slaves illiterate or to prevent them from attaining positions closer to equality or to their masters. "De white folks didn't teach us to read or write," said Lindy Patton, a former slave in Alabama who testified in the 1930s. According to Sam T. Stewart, of North Carolina, his owners "never taught me to read and write; and most slaves who got any reading and writing certainly stole it. There were rules against slaves having books." Those rules were sometimes ruthlessly enforced. Former slave Elijah Green, of South Carolina, said, "An' do for Gods sake don' let a slave be catch with pencil an' paper. That was a major crime. You might as well

had kill your master or missus." Henry Brown, another Charleston ex-slave, added that for such an offense "durin' slavery he would be whip' 'til not a skin was lef' on his body."[115]

But despite legal prohibitions against slave lit-eracy, many masters and more mistresses taught at least some of their slaves to read and write. An ex-slave reported, with a touch of envy, that a fellow slave had been educated because "Miss Jane Alice was very fond of little Bob, and taught him to read and write." Some slaves, such as Prince, coachman on a South Carolina rice plan-tation, even acquired a reputation for being somewhat "bookish." And former slave Filmore Ramsey recalled that Mary Stewart, his mistress in Mississippi, had taught him to read, write, and recite poems and speeches.[116]

The mixture of kindness and cruelty so preva-lent throughout slave society is evident in slaveholders' efforts to teach slaves to read and write. According to Harriett Robinson, "Mistress Julia used to drill her chillun in spelling any words. At every word them chillun missed, she gave me a lick 'cross the head for it. Meanest woman I ever seen in my life."[117] Some other slaves learned to read and write from the white children rather than from the mistress. "When the white children studied their lessons," according to John Bectom in North Carolina, "I studied with them. When they wrote in the sand I wrote in the sand too. The white children, and not the marster or mistress, is where I got started in learnin' to read and write."[118]

Later, after emancipation, the importance of literacy became obvious to all. Mary Vereen Magill, wife of a South Carolina rice planter with a repu-tation for cruelty, taught one of her slaves, young Bruce Williams, to read and write. After eman-cipation he became a minister, founded Bethel A.M.E. Church in Georgetown, and served as a senator in the South Carolina legislature from 1876 to 1902. For those slaves who had been denied literacy in slavery, freedom only set in motion an unequal contest between former slave and former master. Ben Horry expressed the dilemma very well: "You had the learning in you head! Give me that pencil to catch up dem thing. I couldn't to save my life."[119]

Former slaves often described those who had claimed to own them in three basic categories— those considered "good masters," those consid-ered "temperamental masters," and those considered "mean masters." A Virginia slave re-called, "good masters had good slaves 'cause they treated 'em good, an' bad masters had lyin' thievin' slaves 'cause they made 'em that way."[120]

A "good" master tempered the physical pun-

Fig. 79.
Slaves used their unsupervised time, principally evenings, for meetings and visits to the neighborhood—occasionally leaving without their owners' permission. Throughout the South, white patrols attempted to prevent the slaves' illicit activities. Those the patrollers caught without a pass, "dey'd beat 'em an' run 'em back home."

ishments dealt out to the slaves. A Mississippi slave, Gabe Butler, said his master was "de best white man who ebber liv'd. He low'd no overseer to beat his darkies." According to another Mississippi slave, his master "wus a good man. He never 'lowed his slaves to be brutalized. He made dem wurk, but he never 'lowed the driver to strip the women folks en whip dem. En ernuther thing he never 'lowed a woman who wus breedin' to be whip'ed." But, as former North Carolina slave Sam T. Stewart remembered, "When a slave owner treated his slaves unusually good some other slave owner would tell him that he was raising slaves who would rise against him."[121]

The testimonies of ex-slaves characterizing the former masters as "good" while simultaneously describing the brutal punishments meted out must be approached with caution. "I ain't a'complainin'," Frank Adamson remarked, choosing his words carefully. "He was a good master, bestest in de land, but he just had to have a whippin' post, 'cause you'll find a whole passle of bad niggers when you gits a thousand of them in one flock." A similar variation on the "good master" theme was gingerly put forward by Victoria Adams: "De massa an' messus was good to me," she said, "but sometime I was so bad they had to whip me. I 'members she used to whip me every time she tell me to do something and I take too long to move 'long and do it."[122]

"Temperamental" masters were "good" except when angered. As Laura Montgomery noted of her masters, "Dey was all fine folks 'ceptin old Marse Bill when he got mad he wus mighty bad." "Mean" masters punished often and cruelly, and they made their slaves work very hard. Victoria Perry recalled her master as cruel and frightening. When he got mad at any slave he whipped them all. And he got mad often. He tied them to a post or tree, stripped their clothes to the waist, and whipped them until he grew tired. She said she had seen her mother whipped in such a manner until she bled. More than one slave in the Old South described his or her master as the meanest white man who ever lived. A Mississippi master was said to have urged his overseer to whip slaves even harder: "dat will loosen up deir hides so dey ken wurk better."[123]

If masters and overseers were inhumane, slaves went to the plantation mistress for help, for protection, for justice. And "Ole Miss" did frequently convince masters and overseers to be more lenient with their punishments. According to Ben Horry, when slaves on his South Carolina rice plantation broke into the barn and stole more rice, his mistress made the overseers give them additional rice rather than punish them for trying to steal it. "Anybody steal rice and they beat them, Miss Bessie cry and say, 'Let 'em have rice! My rice—my nigger!'"[124]

But plantation mistresses were not always successful in such efforts. Fanny Kemble, an English actress married to Georgia slaveholder Pierce Butler, was particularly incensed at the driver's harsh treatments of women. In her journal, she described how on one occasion several slave women were

> fastened by their wrists to a beam or a branch of a tree, their feet barely touching the ground, so as to allow them no purchase for resistance or evasion of the lash, their clothes turned over their heads, and their backs scored with a leather thong.

Hearing the story, "I turned sick, and my blood curdled." She complained to her husband of

> the brutal inhumanity of allowing a man to strip and lash a woman, the mother of ten children; to exact from her, toil, which was to maintain in luxury two idle young men, the owners of the plantation.

But her complaint was to no avail. Such punishments continued on the Butler plantations.[125]

One Alabama mistress was so angry about the treatment of a house servant that she rebuked her husband. "You know I don't allow you to tech my house servants," she exclaimed. "I druther see dem marks on my own shoulders dan to see 'em on Mammy's." Jane Montgomery, an Oklahoma ex-slave, recalled that her "Mistress never whip us and iffen master would start mistress would git a gun and make him stop." Former slave Lindy Patton remembered an occasion on her Alabama plantation when the master was going to whip one of the slaves. "De Misstis tol' him to leave de ole fool alone, said it warn't worth the trouble." But the mistress was not always aware of beatings that took place on the plantation. Alabamian Henry Cheatam recalled, "A heap of times ole Miss didn't know nuthin' 'bout it, an' de slaves better not tell her, 'caze dat oberseer whup 'em iffen he finds out dat dey done gone an' tol."[126]

But masters were not necessarily "good" or "bad" consistently. Even the "best" masters were sometimes cruel. Georgia slave Charles Ball wrote that his master, "when left to pursue his own inclinations, was kind and humane in his temper, and conduct towards his people." If it had not been for his master's wife, he said, "I should have had a tolerable time of my servitude with him; and should, in all probability, have been a slave in Georgia until this day." His mistress, however, "gave us a specimen of her character, on the first morning after her arrival amongst us, by beating severely, with a raw cow-hide, the black girl who nursed the infant, because the child cried, and could not be kept silent. When enraged," according to Ball, "she would find some victim to pour her fury upon, without regard to justice or mercy."[127]

The plantation mistress could be as cruel as the master. According to Sarah Wilson, who had been a slave in Oklahoma, "Old Mistress just as bad, and she took most of her wrath out hitting us children all the time." In fact, in some cases it was the master who restrained his wife. Another Oklahoma slave recalled, "When young Master was there he made her treat us good but when he was gone she made our lives a misery to us." Frank Cooper testified that his back was broken when "three white women beat me from angah because they had no butter for their biscuits and cornbread. Miss Burton used a heavy board while the missus used a whip. While I was on my knees beggin' them to quit, Miss Burton hit the small of mah back with the heavy board." According to Jacob Branch, his mistress in Texas punished another slave simply because he had never received a whipping before. "Missy think he gettin' it too good, 'cause he ain't never been whipped.

$150 REWARD.

RAN AWAY FROM THE SUBSCRIBER, ON THE NIGHT OF THE 27TH OCTOBER,

A Negro Man named Ben,

Calling himself BEN. THOMAS.—On the day he absconded, by means of false keys, he opened a desk and took therefrom about two hundred Dollars in specie, 20 Dollars of which was in gold half Eagles, and nearly the whole of the balance in American half Dollars. In addition to this, it is believed that he has not less than 100 Dollars, making about 300 Dollars in the whole.

Said Negro is about 30 years old, 5 feet 7 or 8 inches high, remarkably stout built and unusually broad across the shoulders; his weight about 180 pounds. He is uncommonly black, with tolerably good features, and wore whiskers when he went away. He did not take with him much clothing, and none of it particularly recollected, except a new dark fur-coloured hat. This he has probably changed, and cut off his whiskers. He was raised near Washington City, by Col. Hebb, and is well acquainted with that place. He is an excellent house and body servant, and a good gardener. He is shrewd and artful, and can affect great humility when it answers his purposes, and is capable of telling a very plausible story. He sometimes gets drunk, and when in that situation, is extremely quarrelsome and vicious. He has made some progress in learning to spell, and has for eight or nine months past pretended to be a Methodist, and may perhaps attempt to impose himself on that society for a member of their body.

The above reward of 150 Dollars and half the money of which he may be in possession when apprehended, will be given for Ben. if taken out of the State of Kentucky and delivered to me in Frankfort; or 75 Dollars and one half of the money of which he may be in possession, if taken within this State.

Frankfort, Kentucky, November 5th, 1827.   JOSEPH DESHA.

Fig. 80.
Although few slaves escaped bondage, running away was the most significant form of resistance to slavery. Listing the desires of all the different runaways he had known, Edward Lycurgas found one common characteristic: "But, one and all, dey had a good strong notion to see what it was like to own your own body."

She climb over de fence and start down de row with de cowhide."[128]

But physical assaults upon male slaves by white women were infrequent. Cruel plantation mistresses more often turned their ire upon female slaves. The cruelties a mistress inflicted were often prompted by a slave's failure to perform some task to the mistress's satisfaction. For example, Oklahoman Ida Henry remembered that "when passing around de potatoes, Old Mistress felt of one and as hit wasn't soft done, she exclaimed to de cook, 'What you bring these raw potatoes out here for?' and grab a fork and stuck it in her eye and put hit out." George G. King recalled seeing the mistress "pull his mammy's clothes over her head so's the lash would reach the skin." While his mother writhed in pain, "the Mistress walk away laughing."[129]

Slaves were frequently punished for circumstances beyond their control. As Texan Jacob Branch remembered, "My pore mama! Every washday old Missy give her de beatin'. She couldn't keep de flies from speckin' de clothes overnight." Delia Garlic recollected vividly the temper of her Arkansas mistress: "she pick up a stick of stovewood an' flails it ag'in' my head. I didn't know nothin' more 'till I come to, lyin' on de floor. I heard de mistus say to one of de girls: 'I thought her thick skull and cap of wool could take it better than that.'" But the mistress's temper led her to more horrible punishments. "One day I was playin' wid de baby. It hurts its li'l han' an' commenced to cry, an' she whirl on me, pick up a hot iron an' run it all down my arm an' han'. It took off de flesh when she done it."[130]

The worst punishments were reserved for slaves who attempted to emancipate themselves by flight. Jack Frowers was captured during an escape attempt near Aiken, South Carolina.

Just as soon as Master Holley got me home, he set the dogs to worry and bite me, and the scars on my legs and arms are what they did with their teeth. After he got tired of that fun, he took me to a blacksmith, who put a ring around my ankle, bending the ends in when it was red hot.[131]

Even slaveholders who were otherwise considered "good" masters meted out harsh reprisals against runaways to serve as examples to the other slaves. South Carolina rice planter Plowden C. J. Weston, for example, routinely sold recaptured runaways far away from their wives and children.

Slaves might pretend to be satisfied with their lot around whites, but it is untrue that the slaves accepted their condition because they had no concept of freedom. As a former slave put it, "De white folks had ebery thing fine an' ebery thing dey wanted, an' cud cum an' go wid out de patroller gittin' dem, but de slaves wanted to do de same thing; dat is de reason dey all wanted to be sot free." To see the advantages that whites possessed but they lacked was to perceive all too clearly the differences between freedom and slavery.[132]

Slaves did not always accept their situation passively. Their response took many forms. They pretended to be sick, slowed their pace of work, fought back, committed suicide or homicide, and emancipated themselves by flight. Whatever its form, slave resistance created a problem of discipline for slaveholders. Whether mild and sporadic or bold and persistent, acts of resistance threatened property or threatened safety. Acts of resistance also had the ultimate potential to weaken or even destroy an institution that held human beings in bondage.[133]

At the center of the slave community was a communications network known as the "grapevine," a crucial element of slave resistance. "We used to carry news from one plantation to the other I reckon, 'cause mammy would tell about things going on some other plantation and I know she never been there," recalled former slave Phyllis Petite. How did slaves learn what was going on in the larger world? According to Benjamin Russell, who had been a slave in South Carolina, "many plantations were strict about this, but the greater the precaution the alerter became the slaves, the wider they opened their ears and the more eager they became for outside information. The sources were: Girls that waited on the tables, ladies' maids and the drivers; they would pick up everything they heard and pass it on to the other slaves." Slaves also used "field calls and other kinds of whoops and hollers, what had a meanin' to 'em."[134]

Malingering—pretending to be sick in order to get out of work—was one way that slaves engaged in day-to-day resistance. A Georgia slave reported that his father had "beat ol' marster out 'o 'bout fifteen years work. When he didn't feel like workin' he would play like he wus sick an' ol' marster would git de doctor for him."[135] The slave narratives suggest that women were more likely than men to feign sickness as a form of passive resistance. But women may also have been more susceptible to genuine illness, especially disorders associated with the menstrual cycle and with childbirth.

As a more subtle method of resistance, slaves performed assigned work poorly, sabotaging the system through intentional failure. Texas slaves even had a song for this form of slave resistance:

Fool my master seven years.
Going to fool him seven more.
Hey diddle, de diddle, de diddle, de do.

One Virginia slaveholder told Frederick Law Olmsted that his slaves "never do more than just enough to save themselves from being punished, and no amount of punishment will prevent their working carelessly and indifferently." Moreover, "it always seems on the plantation as if they took great pains to break all the tools and spoil all the cattle that they possibly can, even when they know they'll be directly punished for it."[136]

One of the most prominent methods by which slaves resisted was stealing. By theft a slave could simultaneously take revenge upon oppressors and supplement a family's meager food supply. Few acts of slave resistance irritated the masters more. Food was the primary object of slave theft. Children began at an early age to take food from pantries and henhouses. Sometimes older slaves punished the children for such deeds, but they rarely informed on them to the masters.

Slave thieves were not always as successful as Bruh Rabbit, and the punishment was often more severe than the briar patch. A Mississippi slaveholder caught "Uncle Irwin," an elderly slave, pulling apart the boards of the plantation smokehouse in order to get in. The master had him whipped. Later, the slaveholder noticed that his corn supply was going down faster than he had expected. He set a trap to ensnare the corn culprit and apprehended the old man again. This time the master forced him to dance as he was whipped.[137]

Literacy was used as one form of slave resistance. Learning how to read and write was of great advantage to the slaves for sabotage and day-to-day resistance. Frederick Douglass's master forbade his wife to teach the young slave to read and write. The master said it would make him "unfit to be a slave." Douglass concluded that "the pathway from slavery to freedom" was literacy. An Alabama slave came to the same conclusion. "Ole Miss taught de niggers how to read an' write an' some of 'em got to be too good at it, 'case dey learned how to write too many passes so's de pattyrollers wouldn't cotch 'em."[138]

Slaves moving about after dark, whether visiting wives or sweethearts on other plantations or making an escape attempt, were subject to capture and punishment by slave patrols with dogs, horses, and whips. Each of the slave states required men—whether they owned slaves or not—to serve on the patrols as a means of controlling unauthorized slave movements, especially at night. The slave community's dread of the patrols, or "pattyrollers," is reflected in the lines of a song sung by a Mississippi slave:

Run nigger run, de patroller git yo'
Run nigger run, it is almost day.[139]

The slaves considered the "pattyrollers" the most virulent elements of white society.

Sometimes slaves fought back. One especially effective method was arson. Arson was a more obviously rebellious act than stealing. A patroller who had been harassing slaves might suddenly awake at night to find his barn aflame. Puzzled for several years at the number of structures on his plantation that mysteriously burned to the ground, Edmund Ruffin eventually came to realize that his slaves were torching the buildings as retaliation against a cruel overseer.[140]

Some slaves took their own lives rather than continue to submit. Former slave Adeline Marshall told of a Texas slave who had "hung hisself to 'scape his misery." But others turned violence upon their oppressors rather than upon themselves. The overseer on a Mississippi plantation attempted to beat a slave named Mose. Pulling up the stakes intended to hold him down, Mose attacked the overseer with one of the stakes before being clubbed unconscious. Mose's master, however, abandoned his effort to break the slave and auctioned him off.[141]

Women resisted slavery as fervently as men. The mistress, according to John Rudd, "had a long whip hid under her apron and began whippin' Mama across the shoulders, 'thout tellin' her why. Mama wheeled around from whar she was slicin' ham and started runnin' after old Missus Jane. Ole Missus run so fas' Mama couldn't catch up wif her so she throwed the butcher knife and stuck it in the wall up to the hilt." She was sold. Mary Armstrong, a former slave in Texas, recalled her master and mistress as "the meanest two white folks whatever live, cause they was always beatin' on their slaves." Her mistress, "Old Polly, she was a Polly devil if there ever was one," once "whipped my little sister what was only nine months old, and just a baby, to death. She come and took the diaper offen my little sister and whipped till the blood just ran—just 'cause she cry like all babies do, and it kilt my sister." Mary Armstrong never forgave her mistress, and eventually she had an opportunity to take revenge on her. "You see, I'se 'bout ten year old and I belongs to Miss Olivia, what was that old Polly's daughter, and one day Old Polly devil comes to where Miss Olivia lives after she marries, and tries to give me a lick out in the yard, and I picks up a rock about as big as half your fist and hits her right in the eye and busted the eyeball, and tells her that's for whippin' my baby sister to death. You could hear her holler for five miles." Seven decades after emancipation, Mary Armstrong had still not forgiven her mistress: "But that Old Polly was mean like her husband, Old Cleveland, till she die, and I hopes they is burnin' in torment now." Not even age prevented slaves from fighting back. After her young master whipped her, an elderly Mississippi mammy took a pole from her

loom and beat him "nearly to death," shouting with each stroke, "I'm goin' to kill you. These black tittles sucked you, and then you come out here to beat me!"[142]

Sometimes the slaves' revenge was even more forceful. "Accidents" were a means of taking revenge without necessarily having to take blame. An Alabama ex-slave told

> 'bout a mean man who whupped a cullid women near 'bout to death. She got so mad at him dat she tuk his baby chile whut was playin' roun' de yard and grab him up an' th'owed it in a pot of lye dat she was usin' to wash wid. His wife come a-hollerin' an' run her arms down in de boilin' lye to git de chile out, an' she near 'bout burnt her arms off, but it didn't do no good 'caze when she jerked de chile out he was daid.[143]

An Oklahoma slave, unwilling to endure the indignities of slavery any longer, suddenly turned upon her tormentors and "just killed all of 'em he could."[144]

Running away was perhaps the most important form of protest against human bondage. Those who sought permanent freedom naturally tried to get out of the South altogether. According to a former slave in South Carolina, "I 'member seein' one big black man, who tried to steal a boat ride from Charleston. He stole away one night from Master Mobley's place and got to Charleston, befo' he was caught up with. He tell

Fig. 81.
Before their capture, Nat Turner and his followers killed fifty-five white Virginians in 1831 with far-reaching consequences. In response to white fears, southern politicians swiftly tightened the laws governing the activities of both free blacks and slaves.

Fig. 82.
An African-American who fled slavery described his life as a slave to Harriet Tubman: "I'd been here for seventy-three years, working for my master without even a dime wages. I'd worked rain-wet sun-dry. I'd worked with my mouth full of dust, but could not stop to get a drink of water. I'd been whipped, and starved, and I was always praying, 'Oh! Lord, come and deliver us!'"

the overseer who questioned him after he was brought back: 'Sho', I try to git away from this sort of thing. I was goin' to Massachusetts, and hire out 'til I git 'nough to carry me to my home in Africa.'" To attempt self-emancipation was to undertake a perilous flight for freedom in the dead of night along dangerous and unfamiliar paths. "Ever once on a while slaves would run away to de North," recalled an Alabama slave. "Mos' times dey was caught an' brought back. Sometimes dey would git desp'rit an' would kill demse'ves 'fore dey would stand to be brought back."[145]

Those who pondered escape from slavery had to consider that their chances of success were poor and the penalty for failure was dire. Usually a flight for freedom ended in failure. Punishment was certain. Except for slaves in border states, self-emancipation seemed totally impractical. The North and freedom were all but unattainable for the great majority of slaves. Instead of striking out in quest of freedom against all odds, many chose the less rewarding but more practical approach of stealing away from the plantation and hiding out in the woods for a time. An escapee from a South Carolina plantation dug a hillside cave and took up residence in the woods, slipping

out at night to obtain food. When the slave catchers apprehended him five months later, he had in his possession a hog, two geese, some chickens, and some dressed meat apparently stolen from a smokehouse.[146]

Simon, a slave of Virginia's Colonel Landon Carter, ran away in 1766. After a month he was spotted and shot in the leg and foot. Eleven days later he was apprehended by the foreman. The other slaves, however, tried to make it appear to Carter that Simon had come in on his own. Despite Simon's having been shot, Carter believed his limp was faked and had him punished for shamming. Bart, another Carter slave, returned a week later after having been "out" about four months. He had run away after having been accused of bringing in only one load of wood. He contended he had brought in two. According to Carter, "he is the most incorrigible villian I believe alive, and has deserved hanging." Bart was tied and locked up but escaped once again.[147]

Often slave resistance was prompted by clear personal grievances or directed at individual offenses. Perhaps most slaves ran away for reasons other than seeking permanent freedom. Cruelty was certainly one reason, although slaves of kindly masters sought freedom as eagerly as those of

94

cruel ones. A former slave in the South Carolina upcountry reported seeing a slave turn on a cruel white overseer and beat him. "Once a nigger whipped the overseer," William Ballard explained, he "had to run away in the woods and live so he wouldn't get caught."[148]

But slaves did not necessarily have to be prodded by any specific punishment or incident to take flight. Sharper and Stepney, two slaves in the Abbeville District of South Carolina, slipped away from their plantation in 1862. Their bemused overseer informed the slaveholder that "I was uncertain whether they had run away or were only absenting themselves from work and particularly as they had not reason for leaving no fault being found with them or punishment inflicted."[149]

Young Harriet Jacobs, who inherited her father's sense of self-worth and rebellion, was determined to emancipate herself or die trying. To gain her freedom she enacted desperate and complicated schemes with the aid of fellow blacks who were willing to risk everything. A free black who helped Jacobs to escape told her, "I don't forget that your father was my best friend, and I will be a friend to his children as long as God lets me live."[150]

Slave women were less likely than men to run away, not because they loved freedom less, but because their mobility—crucial to a successful escape—was limited by their responsibility for the care of their children. Fugitive slaves typically were between fifteen and thirty-five years of age. Most slave women in this age group were pregnant, nursing an infant, or were caring for a small child. When slave women did resort to flight, it was more often in response to immediate personal grievances than to an effort to emancipate themselves. For instance, Martha Bradley, an Alabama slave, was "workin' in de field and de overseer he come 'round and say sumptin' to me he had no bizness say. I took my hoe and knocked him plum down. I knowed I'se done sumpin' bad so I run to de bushes." Her escape was short-lived, however. "Marster Lucas come and got me and started whoopin' me. I say to Marster Lucas whut dat overseer sez to me and Marster Lucas didn' hit me no more."[151]

But slave women were often intimately involved in planning and aiding the escape attempts of others. Even trusted house servants were co-conspirators in runaway efforts. Mary, a "highly favored servant . . . in charge of the house with the keys" on a South Carolina rice plantation, helped many of her family to escape in 1864. Not only did her sons run off, but also her daughter and her daughter's family and her brother and all of his family. Ultimately her mistress became

suspicious. There were, she wrote a friend, "too many instances in her family for me to suppose she is ignorant of their plans and designs."[152]

Aiding and abetting fugitive slaves could be as dangerous as an escape attempt itself. Harriet Miller's grandfather ran away from his master's Mississippi plantation to escape an overseer's brutality. He hid out nearby, and his family secretly supplied him with food and information. But the overseer came to the man's cabin and questioned his family about his whereabouts. When the man's daughter refused to answer, the overseer beat her to death.[153]

When slave catchers attempted to apprehend them, runaways rarely surrendered peacefully. Fugitives, facing severe punishment and perhaps death if returned to slavery, often elected to stand and fight. Occasionally the slaves had the better of the battle. "Lots of times when de patterollers would git after de slaves dey would have de worse fight," an Alabama slave remarked, "an' sometimes de patterollers would git killed."[154] But more often freedom seekers fell to overwhelming odds. A slave catcher in South Carolina sued for damages caused by the slave he had attempted to apprehend.

> A runaway slave named George, the property of a Gentleman of Chester District, stole two horses, broke open several houses and committed other offenses in Richland District for which a warrant was issued against him but it was found impossible to arrest him. He was at length taken in Columbia on the 4 July last but broke from custody. A hue and cry was immediately raised and your petitioner joined in the pursuit and first overtook the fellone where a contest ensued between them in which the slave cut out your petitioner's eye with a razor blade— The fellone has since been tried, convicted, and executed.[155]

A slave attempting to escape from North Carolina was attacked by patrollers. "He say he tried standin' so many beatin's, he jes can't stan' no mo." He tried to fight the patrollers. But there were too many for him, and he was killed.[156]

Some runaways formed armed maroon bands, hiding out in the woods or in the swamps and raiding storehouses for arms and food. One such group was reported in South Carolina during the Civil War. On 3 February 1863, Thomas G. Allen reported that

> On monday I commenced hunting down Cosawhatchie Swamp, during the afternoon the dogs struck a warm trail which we fol-

Fig. 83.
Working as cooks, laundresses, hospital workers, and nurses, impressed slaves, free blacks, and former slaves found employment—at little or no pay and under poor conditions—in both the Union and the Confederacy. A number of African-Americans worked in this Union army hospital in Nashville.

lowed about one mile into the swamp through water and bog sometimes swimming and sometimes bog down when the dogs trailed a negro boy; belonging to the Est. of Harry Youmans, who has been out since August last. the said boy stated that there was two others with him that day and four at the camp seven or eight miles below— all armed with guns and pistols. . . . On the 1st of Feby a gentleman from St. Luke's Parish who lives on the Swamp came to this camp and reported that the day before some runaways had broken into a house in his neighborhood and stole all the ammunition

and some provisions—I believe it is a part of the same gang.[157]

The most drastic form of slave resistance was insurrection. At least five major insurrectionary plots disturbed the consciousness of the slave South before emancipation: the Stono rebellion in South Carolina in 1739, Samba's conspiracy in Louisiana in 1763, the Gabriel Prosser uprising in Virginia in 1800, the great Louisiana slave revolt of 1811, the Denmark Vesey plot in South Carolina in 1822, and the Nat Turner insurrection in Virginia in 1831.

There were also numerous smaller uprisings.

Since most of them were aborted, their full dimensions remain unknown. Among them was one in French Louisiana in July 1776. In 1802, there was one involving sixteen slaves in Bertie County, North Carolina, and another of undetermined strength in Georgetown County, South Carolina. There was a second in Georgetown County in 1810, sufficient to cause a hasty mobilization of the militia. At least three slaves were executed for their part in a third slave uprising in Georgetown County in 1829. And there is evidence of a slave conspiracy in Adams County, Mississippi, in 1861.[158]

The most important rebellion was that led by Nat Turner. According to escaped slave Henry Clay Bruce, it caused "no little sensation amongst the slaveholders."[159] Stories of "Old Nat" lived in oral tradition among Virginia slaves. Allen Crawford, a Virginia ex-slave, described the rebellion vividly.

> It started out on a Sunday night. Fust place he got to was his mistress' house. Said God 'dained him to start the fust war with forty men. When he got to his mistress' house he commence to grab him missus' baby and he took hit up, slung hit back and fo'h three times. Said hit was so hard for him to kill dis baby 'cause hit had bin so playful setting on his knee and dat chile sho did love him. So third sling he went quick 'bout hit—killing baby at dis rap.

The insurrectionists then went to another house, according to Crawford, and "went through orchard, going to the house—met a school mistress—killed her."[160]

Another Virginia slave well recalled the fear of the white folks. According to Fannie Berry, "I can remember my mistress, Miss Sara Ann, coming to de window an' hollering, 'De niggers is arisin', De niggers is arisin', De niggers is killin' all de white folks—killin' all de babies in de cradle.'"[161] Harriet Jacobs wrote in her memoirs, *Incidents in the Life of a Slave Girl*, that she thought it strange that the whites should be so frightened "when their slaves were so 'contended and happy'!"[162]

The following day the militia was mustered to search the quarters of all slaves and free blacks. Harriet Jacobs said the militia planted false evidence to implicate some slaves in the rebellion: "In some cases the searchers scattered powder and shot among their clothes, and then sent other parties to find them, and bring them forward as proof that they were plotting insurrection."[163] Allen Crawford recalled that

The next day Blues and Reds—names of

soldiers—met at a place called Cross Keys, right down here at Newsome's Depot. Dat's whar they had log fires made and every one dat was Nat's man was taken bodily by two men who catch you and hold yer bare feet to dis blazing fire 'til you tole all you know'd 'bout dis killing.[164]

In the wake of the Turner insurrection, Henry Box Brown wrote in his memoirs, many slaves were "half-hung, as it was termed—that is, they were suspended from some tree with a rope about their necks, so adjusted as not quite to strangle them—and then they were pelted by men and boys with rotten eggs." The air was filled with shrieks and shouts. Harriet Jacobs said she "saw a mob dragging along a number of colored people, each white man, with his musket upraised, threatening instant death if they did not stop their shrieks." Jacobs could not contain her indignation: "What a spectacle was that for a civilized country! A rabble, staggering under intoxication, assuming to be the administrators of justice!"[165]

According to Crawford, "Ole Nat was captured at Black Head Sign Post, near Cortland, Virginia—Indian town. He got away. So after a little Nat found dem on his trail so he went back near to the Travis place whar he fust started killing and he built a cave and made shoes in this cave. He came out night fur food dat slaves would give him from his own mistress' plantation." After about a month Nat Turner's hiding place was discovered and he was taken into custody. Turner's captors, Crawford said, "brought him to Peter Edward's farm. 'Twas at this farm whar I was born. Grandma ran out and struck Nat in the mouth, knocking the blood out and asked him, 'Why did you take my son away?' In reply Nat said, 'Your son was as willing to go as I was.' It was my Uncle Henry dat they was talking about." Then, Crawford said, Virginia "passed a law to give the rest of the niggers a fair trial and Nat, my Uncle Henry, and others dat was caught was hanged."[166]

The shock of Nat Turner's revolt was followed by the appearance of a new and militant abolitionist newspaper, William Lloyd Garrison's *The Liberator*. Slaves took heart. White southerners concentrated their energies on trying to defend slavery against the criticism of a critical and unfriendly world. The institution that many white southerners had once considered an evil destined for eventual elimination was now praised by the South as a positive good, the secret of the region's fancied perfection. Southerners staked everything—their fortunes, their honor, the lives of their sons—on its defense. Unlike slaveholders anywhere else, they went to war to preserve their "peculiar institution."

When the Civil War finally erupted, most slaves had been expecting it for some time. They heard their masters boast of quick victory, and watched the women wave their men off to war. Confederate officers, as gentlemen, of course required body servants. Like many other slaves, James Cornelius followed his master into war. By the 1930s he was living on a pension from the state of Mississippi. "I'se proud I'se a old sojer," he said.[167]

During the war, plantation families keenly felt the absence or loss of family members. Sometimes they expressed their frustration by taking out their anger on their bondsmen. Harriet Robinson's mistress blamed the war on the slaves. "She say 'Your Master's out fighting and losing blood trying to save you from them Yankees, so you kin git your'n here.' Miss Julia would take me by my ears and butt my head against the wall." Hearing slaves mention the prospects of freedom often enraged plantation whites. When Sam McAllum's Mississippi mistress "hear'd de Niggers talkin' 'bout bein' free, she wore 'em out wid a cowhide."[168] An Alabama slave was caught praying for freedom. After a severe beating he slipped away and joined the Union army.

The slaves watched as masters and sons returned home from the front, some in boxes, some with crutches or empty sleeves, some to die of wounds and illness. "De Massa had three boys to go to war," a Georgia slave remembered, "but dere wuzn't one to come home. All the chillun he had wuz killed. Massa, he los' all his money and de house soon begin droppin' away to nothin'. Us niggers one by one lef' de ole place and de las' time I seed de home plantation I wuz a standin' on a hill. I looked back on it for de las' time through a patch of scrub pines and it look' so lonely."[169]

The slaves learned from the whites of the advance of Union forces and felt the approach of freedom. A North Carolina slave recalled vividly the coming of the Union troops: "I remember the Yankees. I will remember seein' them til I die. I will never forget it. I thought it was the last of me. The white folks had told me the Yankees would kill me or carry me off."[170]

But most slaves were thrilled at the coming of the Yankees, even if their owners were not. When Anna Williamson was impressed by the brass buttons on the Yankee uniforms, "my old mistress slapped me till my eye was red cause one day I says 'Ain't them men pretty?'"[171] Midge Burnett recalled that her master had not shared the slaves' enthusiasm about the coming of the Union troops.

"Marse William ain't eber hit one of us a single lick till de day when we heard dat de Yankees wus a-comin'. One big nigger jumps up an' squalls, 'Lawd bless de Yankees.' Marse yells back, 'God damn de Yankees,' an' slaps big Mose a sumerset right outen de do'." After that, "nobody else dasen't say Yankees ter de marster."[172]

When William T. Sherman's troops marched through South Carolina and many masters fled their plantations for safer ground, slaves sang

Master gone away
But darkies stay at home,
The year of jubilee is come
And freedom will begun.[173]

A Mississippi slave recalled that the Yankees "come ridin' up on fine hosses. Dey was all dressed in blue coats an' all had guns. I thought dey was comin' to sot us free." They had not come to free the slaves, however. They had come to confiscate food supplies and to burn cotton gins.[174] "De Yankees come in and dey pulled de fruit off de trees and et it," according to Alabama slave William Colbert. "Dey et de hams and cawn, but dey neber burned de houses. Seem to me lak dey jes' stay aroun' long enough to git plenty somp'n t'eat, kaze dey lef in two or three days, an' we neber seed 'em since."[175] Another Mississippi slave said, "I 'member de time of de Civil Wah' . . . an de Yankee sojers comes marchin' to town and smashed in sto' doahs' an' windows, an' all us lil' chillun' sho' did have a fine time 'cause we got pies an' candy an sech lak—much as we could eat. We wished de Yankees would come every day!"[176]

Some slaves struck out for the Union lines in pursuit of freedom. Zias, a slave on the McDowell plantation in Mississippi, took off with a pony. Zias came back in a blue uniform with the promise of forty acres and a mule. But he came back on foot. The Yankees had taken the pony.[177]

As defeated masters dragged themselves back to their plantations, the slaves could sense the war was over. Nelson Dickerson's master called his former slaves together and announced that they were free. He offered wages if they would stay.[178] Many ex-slaves remained on the plantations when the war was over, feeling that they had no better place to go. But some slaveholders never bothered to tell their slaves they were free. Amanda Oliver recollected that her "old mistress didn't tell us when we was free, but another white woman told my mother and I remembuh one day old mistress told my mother to git to that wheel and git to work, and my mother said, 'I ain't gwinter, I'm jest as free as you air.'"[179] Pharoah Carter did not tell his slaves, but they learned from freedmen on other plantations.

Fig. 84.
In 1863 the 1st Louisiana Native Guards, composed entirely of free blacks, distinguished itself in its first engagements against the Confederacy at Port Hudson and then at Milliken's Bend in Louisiana. The unit was one of the very few commanded by black officers.

Carter had a slave woman arrested on trumped-up charges of having stolen a bail of cotton. Her husband came to the jail with a group of white men and freed her. Such a bold move by any black man would have been unthinkable a year earlier.[180]

Freedom did not always live up to expectations. Gabe Butler, a Mississippi slave, recalled that "sum of de slaves sed when dey wud be sot free dey wud git forty acres uf land frum Mr. Lincoln an' sum said dey wud git plenty uf good things to eat an' sum sed dey wudn't have to wurk any more, kaze Mr. Lincoln wud give dem everything."[181] It did not work out that way. For many former slaves life scarcely changed. Katie

Darling said, "missy whip me after the war jist like she did 'fore. She has a hun'erd lashes up for me now."[182] One resentful mistress rued the day that slaves had been taught religion. According to a former slave, the mistress "claimed that it was his prayers and a whole lot of other slaves that cause you young folks to be free today."[183] Whatever his mistress thought, he was pleased to have done what he could. However circumscribed freedom might be, however limited the opportunities available to former slaves, his children would be born free. Never again in the United States would human beings be bought and sold at auction into slavery. □

FEMALE SLAVES IN THE PLANTATION SOUTH

Deborah Gray White

Fig. 85.
A Louisiana nursemaid and her young charge are captured in this ca. 1850 daguerreotype.

When Sojourner Truth moved to the podium at the Akron, Ohio, women's rights convention, the audience greeted her with boos and hisses. As a former slave, a black, and a woman, she made many people uncomfortable. The year was 1851, and to many people the emerging women's movement was part of the growing antislavery crusade. Issues concerning slavery and black and female status were tearing the nation apart, and some in the audience could not look at, much less listen to, Sojourner Truth without being reminded of the nation's problems.[1] Her supporters had secured her a place on the program, and her very first sentences served notice that she would talk about both women's and blacks' rights:

> Well, chilern, whar dar is so much racket der must be something out of kilter. I tink dat 'twixt de niggers of de Souf and de women at de Norf all a talkin' 'bout rights, de white men will be in a fix pretty soon.[2]

Having given her audience a hint of what was to follow, Truth then drew on her own experiences as a slave to demonstrate how slavery and racism mocked the logic upon which sex discrimination was based:

> Dat man ober dar say dat woman needs to be lifted ober ditches, and to have de best place every whar. Nobody eber helped me into carriages, or ober mud puddles, or gives me any best place and ar'n't I a woman? Look at me! Look at my arm! I have plowed, and planted, and gathered into barns, and no man could head me—and ar'n't I a woman? I could work as much and eat as much as a man (when I could get it), and bear de lash as well—and ar'n't I a woman? I have borne thirteen chilern and seen em mos' all sold off into slavery, and when I cried out with a mother's grief, none but Jesus heard—and ar'n't I a woman?[3]

Although the audience did not respond, Sojourner Truth knew the answer that millions of slave women received every day—a resounding "no." Black women stood beyond the bounds of womanhood as defined by nineteenth-century America. They were exploited sexually with impunity, stripped and whipped with a lash, and worked like oxen. In a society seemingly preoccupied with protecting and keeping women in the home, only slave women remained totally unprotected by men or by law.

The slave woman's naked exposure to the ugly, the crude, the base nature of southern society forced her to redefine womanhood. As suggested by Sojourner Truth, slave women invented a concept neither grounded in female frailty and meekness, nor founded upon women's inferiority to men.

"Slavery is terrible for men: but it is far more terrible for women," lamented Harriet Jacobs, one of the few slave women to write a narrative of her experiences. "Superadded to the burden common to all, they have wrongs, and sufferings, and mortifications peculiarly their own."[4] Despite their common bondage, men and women did not experience slavery in the same way. Slave women alone experienced sexual exploitation, childbearing and motherhood, and the slaveholders' sexism, each structuring her work and everyday existence.

The sexual exploitation of female slaves was rooted in the stereotypes surrounding black women. Unlike white women, who were thought to be prudish, pious, and domestic (an equally erroneous stereotype), black women seemed sensual and promiscuous, a notion formed when Englishmen first met Africans. Early European travelers associated Africa's hot climate and the relative nakedness of its people with sensuality. William Bosman, an Englishman who traveled extensively in West Africa, wrote in 1705 that the women of Guinea were "fiery," "warm," and "so much hotter than the men."[5]

As slave traders transported their human cargo across the Atlantic, so the ideas were transported, too. In 1736 the *South Carolina Gazette* published stories about "African Ladies" of "strong robust constitution" who were "not easily jaded out," but able to serve their lovers "by Night as well as Day."[6] In the Chesapeake, such ideas were equally strong. Suggesting that black women mated with orangutans, Thomas Jefferson was certain that the animal preferred "the black woman over those of his own species."[7]

The conditions under which slave women lived

Fig. 86.
Throughout her life, one former slave remembered her mother's legacy of self-reliance and independence: "'I'll kill you, gal, if you don't stand up for yourself,' she would say. 'Fight, and if you can't fight, kick; if you can't kick, then bite.'"

and worked only confirmed these stereotypes. In America, slavery depended upon natural reproduction rather than continual transatlantic importations. This put the burden of slave increase squarely on the slave woman's shoulders. Yet, since causal correlations were drawn between sensuality and fertility, any increase in the slave population served as evidence of the slave woman's lust. An Alabama slave owner associated reproduction with promiscuity when he linked the high birthrate of slaves on his plantation to the fact that he "did not know more than one negro woman that he could suppose to be chaste."[8]

Clearly, most slave women were chaste, but the circumstances of their condition suggested otherwise. Black women's bodies just did not command respect. On the auction block, slave buyers occasionally kneaded women's stomachs to determine their capacity for childbearing.[9] And unlike southern white women adorned in layers of cloth, women on rice plantations, for instance, by the very nature of their work sometimes worked with their dresses "reefed up" around their hips to keep the hems out of the water. In the fields, women worked with their skirts pinned up to keep them out of dirt and mud, and house servants pulled up their skirts to wash and polish floors.[10] Then again, women's bodies were ex-

Fig. 87.
In November 1841, Charles Henry, of Mobile, Alabama, manumitted, or freed, "a certain mulato woman named Francoise aged about thirty six years —and her three children." Quite possibly the children were his as well.

posed during whippings. An escaped slave remembered that when his mother was whipped she was stripped completely naked: "Dey didn't care nothing 'bout it. Let everybody look on at it."[11] Indeed, some whippings had sexual overtones. Few utterances are as revealing as those of ex-slave Henry Bibb's master who declared that "he had rather paddle a female than eat when he was hungry."[12]

Alone, these circumstances tell only a partial story and do not differentiate female from male slave experiences. Black men were also perceived as oversexed and their bodies exposed during work and whippings. What differed were the consequences. Since black women were thought to be promiscuous, they could be raped, forced by their owners into illicit relationships with masters, overseers, and other slaves, and then be blamed for their own sexual exploitation. There were few alternatives for the slave woman who had to choose between sex, or a whipping, or sale—or harm to her loved ones. Generally slave women did what their masters forced them to do, and then shouldered the burden of guilt and blame by themselves.

A number of their stories are left to us. Patsey, a slave on a Louisiana plantation was a spry, intelligent, quick-witted young woman until her masochistic master began sexually abusing her. His "brute passion" left her sullen and depressed.[13] Cynthia, a friend of ex-slave William Wells Brown, was given a choice: if she would accept a slave trader's proposals, he would take her back to Saint Louis as his housekeeper. But if she rejected him, he would sell her as a field hand to the worst plantation on the Mississippi River. Cynthia became the trader's housekeeper and mistress.[14] A similarly desperate choice faced Malinda Bibb. She tried to escape with her husband Henry but both were caught. While imprisoned, Malinda somehow managed alone to fight off a lecherous slave trader. Eventually she and her husband were sold to different masters. He later escaped to the North, while she became the concubine of her new owner. Henry Bibb was bitter when, years later, he learned of her situation. He reasoned that she undoubtedly "became reconciled to it . . . [and] was much better treated than she had ever been before."[15]

It was not unusual for women such as Malinda

Fig. 88.
Hard manual labor— plowing, hoeing, shoveling, and picking cotton— dominated the workaday world of many female slaves. As a former slave, Abbie Lindsay, described it, "They worked, in a manner of speaking, from can to can't, from the time they could see until the time couldn't." Henry P. Moore in 1862 photographed a woman drying cotton on the Century plantation, Edisto Island, South Carolina.

Bibb, Cynthia, or Patsey to be used sexually and then further abused despite promises of good treatment. In the southern slave pens, such women were often distinguishable by their dress and manners. Fredrika Bremer, a Swedish visitor, was amazed to find a well-dressed woman in a Washington, D.C., slave market. Bremer learned from the slave keeper that she was "brought up in all respects 'like a lady'" who "could embroider and play on the piano, and dress like a lady, and read, and write, and dance." The keeper went on to explain that the woman was sold by the white who raised her because "her mind had grown too high for her; she had become proud, and now, to humble her, they had brought her here to be sold."[16] Although some slave women were freed by their white lovers, many more were sold to plantations where they shared the misery of all slaves. Sometimes they were sold when white men married and settled into family life with white women. Sometimes a jealous wife put an end to a husband's illicit visits to a slave's cabin by forcing the sale of a particular female. Whatever the case, there was little comfort for the slave woman doubly abused.

Based in part on the prevailing stereotype of the immoral black women, and in part on the rationale that white women were spared abuse because of the slave women's availability, several of the South's leading statesmen justified the degradation of black females. Among them was William Harper, chancellor of the University of South Carolina. Harper, like most southerners, felt neither guilt nor empathy for the sexually exploited slave woman. "She is not," he commented,

> a less useful member of society than before. If shame be attached to her conduct, it is such shame as would be elsewhere felt for a venial impropriety. She has not impaired her means of support or materially impaired her character, or lowered her station in society; she has done no great injury to herself, to any other human being. Her offspring is not a burden but an acquisition to her owner; his support is provided for, and he is brought up to usefulness.[17]

Harper's defense reveals not only how little a slaveholder cared about a slave woman's feelings but also how much an owner valued a black woman's ability to reproduce the slave labor force.

In the one hundred years after 1750 the American black population, 90 percent of which was enslaved, was notable for, among other things, its fertility. In the pre–Civil War era black women were very prolific: each year more than one-fifth of those between age fifteen and forty-four bore a child.[18] This fact strikingly illuminates a major functional difference between male and female bondage. The male slave's life centered around the work he did for whites. Female slaves had much work to do also, but to it were added the tasks of birthing, nourishing, and rearing children. The extent to which the slave owner consciously emphasized one or the other—work or childbearing—ultimately depended on his needs, needs often determined by the region in which he lived. For example, the lower rates of black fertility in antebellum Alabama, Mississippi, Louisiana, and Texas probably indicate that there female labor in the fields was more important. The more recently settled regions needed as many hands as possible to establish the newer plantations. Yet, in both the Upper and Lower South, slave owners attended to the proverbial bottom line by striving to maximize profits. Since few ignored the important role that natural increase played in that goal, women's lives were to a great extent structured by their responsibility to replenish the slave labor force.[19]

It was no accident of nature that the average slave woman began motherhood two years before the average southern white woman. Slaveholders used every form of manipulation to get black women to have children early and frequently. There was often verbal prodding. The mistress of the Burleigh plantation in Georgia met Harriet, one of her just-married house slaves, with the greeting: "I wish you joy, and every year a son or daughter."[20] Usually, as reported by a North Carolina ex-slave, when two people declared their intention to live together all the master said was "don't forget to bring me a little one or two for next year."[21]

Besides the verbal proddings to reproduce, there were incentives built into the plantation system itself. For instance, pregnant women received more attention and food than nonpregnant women, usually did less work, and were sometimes even excused from work. One plantation manual advised that "women with six children alive at any one time are allowed all Saturday to themselves."[22] On plantations where the work load was exhausting and backbreaking, a lighter work assignment was frequently an incentive to become pregnant as often as possible. According to Frances Kemble, such was the case on her husband's Georgia plantation: "on the birth of a child certain additions of clothing and an additional weekly ration are bestowed on the family, and these matters, as small as they may seem, act as powerful inducements."[23]

Such an outright award system was frequently effective. Each time a baby was born on one of

Major Wallon's plantations, the mother received a calico dress and a "bright, shiny silver dollar."[24] B. Talbert, a Virginia planter, took the form of exploitation to its extreme. In 1792 he bought a woman named Jenny and promised her that if she bore a child for every one of his own five children, he would set her free. In eleven years Jenny had six children. In 1803, she and her youngest child were emancipated.[25]

When rewards failed to make the desired impression, owners resorted to punitive measures. Rose Williams, a Texas slave, told a harrowing tale of how her master forced her, on threat of sale, to live with a slave named Rufus. Master Hawkins bluntly told her, then age sixteen, that he had paid "big money" for her, and that her duty was to "bring forth portly children." Rose, like countless other slave women, found herself in a pitiable position. Helpless, she had no choice: "What am I's to do? . . . I yields."[26] No doubt, Rose Williams knew that most other slave women gave in, too. Those who failed to have children were sold; those incapable of childbearing were treated no better than barren sows and passed from one unsuspecting buyer to another.

The threat of sale put untold pressure on slave women of all ages. To avoid the auction block they had to have children early, and continue to have them through their childbearing years. With all the rewards and punishments, slaveholders had no need for "breeding farms" per se, and there is little evidence that such existed. The built-in manipulation served the slaveholder well and slaves knew it. The most repeated comment made by ex-slaves interviewed after emancipation was that during slavery "women wasn't anything but cattle."[27]

Although many slaveholders increased an expectant mother's food allotment and decreased her work load, the care given pregnant women was woefully inadequate. But even if pregnant women had received meticulous care, they would have suffered nevertheless. Early obstetric practices had advanced little beyond traditional midwifery. All women, black and white, had much to fear from doctors and midwives—especially as so

Fig. 89.
Whether toiling in the fields or at the "big house," slave women also took on the primary responsibility for rearing their children and for performing household chores such as cooking and cleaning for their own families.

many women died in childbirth. Yet black women were particularly neglected because of the common assumptions that they were less fragile, gave birth more easily, and, therefore, needed less care than white women. A planter along the Mississippi River told the northerner Frederick Law Olmsted that black women "were not subject to the difficulty, danger and pain which attended women of the better classes in giving birth to their offspring." He, therefore, seldom employed a physician.[28]

Some masters used slave midwives instead of doctors in order to reduce plantation expenses. Although midwives were often relatively competent, some of their techniques, such as placing an ax under the delivery mattress to "cut" the pain of childbirth, were based more on superstition than on proven medical science. Of course, they could do little for women with severe complications, or for women who suffered from illnesses resulting from the brutality and callousness of masters and overseers. Women who had been whipped or forced to perform heavy tasks during pregnancy had an especially hard time, as did those who were sent back to the fields too soon after delivery.[29]

Moreover, the planter manipulated a woman's life as much after as before childbirth. As outlined by Clayborn Gantling, women on the Terrell County, Georgia, plantation of Judge Williams faced a hard existence: "Women with little babies would have to go to work in de mornings with the rest, come back, nurse their children and go back to the field, stay two or three hours, then go back and eat dinner; after dinner dey would have to go to de field and stay two or three more hours and go and nurse the chillun again, go back to the field and stay till night."[30] This Georgia plantation had a nursery, but where there were none, women had to take their children to the fields and either work with them on their backs or put them down somewhere. They risked a whipping if they attended to them too often. The same was true of women who worked in the house. Very often they were not allowed to keep their children with them, and they, too, ran back and forth to the quarters, trying to satisfy their children and the master at the same time.[31]

Caring for her children structured even the slave woman's pattern of resistance. Children kept women close to the plantation, and as a result most slave runaways were male. In eighteenth-century South Carolina, for instance, women never comprised more than 20 percent of the runaway population.[32] The same was true in eighteenth-century Williamsburg, Richmond, and Fredericksburg, Virginia.[33] The same pattern is evident in the years immediately prior to the Civil War. In antebellum Huntsville, Alabama, of the 562 fugitives listed in newspapers between 1820 and 1860, only 87 were female.[34] The same low figures persisted in North Carolina and New Orleans.[35]

Most runaways were between sixteen and thirty-five years old.[36] Most slave women that age were either pregnant, nursing an infant, or caring for at least one small child. All this limited their mobility. This is not to say that male runaways did not love their offspring, only that women were by necessity more involved with their children. A father, for example, could not provide for a nursing infant because, as an ex-slave noted, "in dem days no bottle was given to no baby under a year old."[37] Moreover, since women and small children were often sold as a group, a father was more likely to be sold away from his children.[38] If a mother did escape, sometimes her children were lucky enough to have an aunt or grandmother on the same or a nearby plantation, and sometimes a father or uncle took care of a child. But slave women knew that children without mothers could easily be neglected. A statistic tells the story: of the 151 fugitive women listed in the New Orleans newspapers for 1851, all ran away with their children.[39]

But escaping with children only made an already hazardous undertaking all the more risky. Josiah Henson successfully reached Cincinnati with his wife and children, but he had to carry his two stout toddlers most of the way and at night listen to their cries of hunger and exhaustion.[40] Henry Bibb also tried to escape with his family but was unsuccessful. Several patrollers aided by a pack of hounds captured Bibb, his wife Malinda, and their small child. For Bibb, the difficulties of escaping with a wife and child proved insurmountable, and, although he regretted his capture, he was actually relieved. Some time later he escaped, but without his family.[41]

If women in the company of men had so much trouble escaping, imagine the problems encountered by women and children escaping alone. William Still, leader of Philadelphia's Underground Railroad, was always nervous about transporting women with children since they stood a greater chance of being caught. "Females," he wrote, "undertook three times the risk of failure that males are liable to."[42] William Penn, who also worked for the Underground Railroad, expressed a similar apprehension. Speaking of two women, both of whom had two children, he noted: "none of these can walk so far or so fast as scores of *men* that are constantly leaving."[43]

Despite the unfavorable odds and the burdens that motherhood imposed, a few women escaped. Some escaped with men, and many left for the same reasons as men—cruel treatment or the fear of it, fear of sale or the sale of a loved one, or simply the desire to be free. For many women, though, it was the children, or rather the fear of losing them, that provided the incentive to flee. The desperation of some slave mothers is captured in Harriet Beecher Stowe's fictionalized account of Eliza Harris and her son's escape to freedom across the ice floes of the Ohio River.[44] Many regarded the heartrending tale as evidence of Stowe's imagination. In fact, Stowe in fiction described what was a real-life episode for several women. One, a Kentucky slave, feared that her two little girls were to be sold away from her. Surviving on only fruits and green corn, the three

managed to cross the Ohio River.[45] Even with no river to cross, the odds were formidable. For instance, in 1859 a Maryland slave named Maria with the help of the Underground Railroad escaped with her children—all *seven* of them.[46]

Many female fugitives were much less fortunate than Maria and had to leave their children behind. Louisa Bell, of Norfolk, Virginia, although she successfully fled slavery, was consumed by thoughts of her children and the knowledge that her six-year-old boy was "full old enough to feel deeply the loss of his mother, but without hope of ever seeing her again."[47] Another woman, a Maryland slave named Vina, had to choose which of her children would be free and which would remain enslaved. She took her two daughters with her, placing her two small sons, as she put it, "into the hands of God."[48]

We can only imagine the emotional trauma that such women as Vina experienced. But surely the psychological torment was great. At least that is what the record left by Linda Brent tells us. At age twenty-seven, fleeing to Pennsylvania to escape her master's sexual overtures, Brent made a decision similar to Vina's. She knew her grandmother would keep a watchful eye on her son and daughter, but she nevertheless feared her mistress would punish them severely. The advice she sought and received served only to confuse her. From her friend and accomplice, Betty, she received encouragement to escape: "Lors, chile! What's you crying 'bout? Dem young uns vil kill you dead. Don't be so chick'n hearted! If you does, you vil nebber git thro' dis world." But her grandmother, who unlike childless Betty had raised three generations of black children, admonished: "Stand by your own children, and suffer with them till death. Nobody respects a mother who forsakes her children; and if you leave them, you will never have a happy moment."[49] Such was the dilemma of the potential runaway slave mother.

Truancy seems to have been the way many slave women reconciled their desire to flee and their need to stay. Studies demonstrate that females made the most likely truants because they were more concerned about breaking family ties. Benjamin Johnson, of Georgia, remembered that "sometimes de women wouldn't take it an' would run away an' hide in de woods. Sometimes dey would come back after a short stay an' den again dey would have to put the hounds on dere trail to bring dem back home."[50] For many women, truancy became a way of life. Determined not to be beaten by the overseer, a Louisiana woman, Celeste, built a rude, camouflaged hut with dead branches and palmetto leaves on the edge of a swamp near her master's residence. Every evening she returned to the plantation for food, thereby

Fig. 90.
In despair over the sale of her children, an African-American woman—arriving in Washington, D.C., in 1815 as part of a slave coffle, or procession of slaves chained together—attempted suicide by jumping from a tavern's second-story window, breaking her back and both arms.

Fig. 91.
In 1858 George Fuller sketched a gang of slave women hoeing within sight of the capitol building in Montgomery, Alabama.

Fig. 92, Fig. 93. Surviving examples of clothing produced by household slaves for their owners include a finely made nightshirt sewn for Andrew Jackson by a slave, Gracey, and a rough, homespun suit manufactured on a Louisiana plantation.

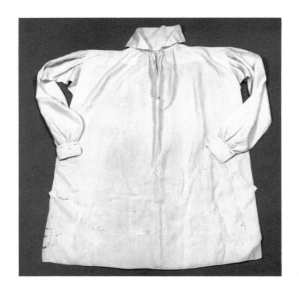

hiding for the better part of a summer.[51]

Childbearing and motherhood made female slavery different from male slavery but so, too, did the slaveholders' sexism. That their sexism played so large a part in the female slave's work load and day-to-day existence is somewhat ironic since the same masters so often treated black women like men. There is no question that slave women worked as hard as their male counterparts. Bonded women cut down trees to clear lands for cultivation. They hauled logs by leather straps fastened around their shoulders. They plowed using mule and ox teams, and hoed, sometimes with the heaviest implements available. They dug ditches, spread manure fertilizer, and piled coarse fodder with their bare hands. They built and cleaned southern roads, helped construct railroads, and, of course, cut cane and tobacco and picked cotton. In short, what fugitive slave Williamson Pease said regretfully of slave women was borne out in fact: "Women who do outdoor work are used as bad as men."[52] Almost a century later when Green Wilbanks remembered his Grandma Rose, he implied that her work had something of a neutering effect. Grandma Rose was a woman who could do any kind of work a man could do, a woman who "was some worker, a regular man-woman."[53]

Indeed, because so little deference was accorded black females, Sojourner Truth had to remind her audiences that she was a woman. Yet, when black women were concerned, slave owners were unable to overcome all their notions about women: while the plantation society denied black women most of the so-called "rewards" of womanhood, female slaves nevertheless suffered under all its restrictions and performed all the "woman's work." Given all the slave woman's backbreaking labor, it is easy to overlook the slave woman's additional responsibilities. On the Sea Islands, for instance, slave women sorted cotton lint according to color and fineness and removed cotton seeds that the gin had crushed into the cotton and lint, such was "woman's work." Men usually shelled corn, threshed peas, and cut potatoes for planting, and platted shucks. Grinding corn into meal or hominy, however, was for women, as were spinning, weaving, sewing, and washing.[54]

Such work made women's days particularly long, for they sometimes worked long after they returned from the fields—and long after men had retired. Frances Willingham, of Georgia, remembered that when slaves came in at night "woman's cleant up deir houses atter dey et, and den washed and got up early next mornin' to put de clothes out to dry." In contrast, men would "set 'round talkin' to other mens and den go to bed."[55] Women also sometimes sat up sewing. "When the work in the fields was finished women were required to come home and spin one cut a night," reported another Georgian. "Those who were not successful in completing this work were punished the next morning."[56] Women had to spin, weave, and sew in the evenings in part because slave owners bought few ready-made clothes, and when they did, the white family and single slave men were the most likely recipients. On one South Carolina plantation each male slave every autumn received an allotment of one cotton shirt, one pair of woolen pants, and one woolen jacket. In the spring each man got one shirt and two pairs of cotton pants. Slave women, on the other hand, in a year received six yards of woolen cloth,

Fig. 94.
Slave mothers often had little choice but to take their babies into the fields. Charles Ball observed that women "laid their children at the side of the fence, or under the shade of the cotton plants, whilst they were at work; and when the rest of us went to get water, they would go to give suck to their children." One woman, he recalled, carried her baby in a cloth backpack.

Fig. 96.
Slave owners assigned many jobs, such as laundering, by gender, thereby coincidentally providing slave women the chance of working cooperatively and forming a community of their own.

slave woman's reproductive capacity. Yet slaveholders could never be sure that the woman who complained of uterine or menstrual aches and pains was not in danger of losing or impairing her ability to have children. A Virginia planter summed up the "problem" when he complained of the "liability of women, especially to disorders and irregularities which cannot be detected by exterior symptoms, but which may be easily aggravated into serious complaints." He further explained that women were rendered "nearly valueless" for work because of the ease with which they could impose upon their owners.[67]

Given the poor medical care that slave women received, the economic incentives to work slaves for long hours, and the increased work load that other slaves had to assume when another slave was absent, it is hardly likely that it was so easy to fake an illness. Moreover, slave owners did not always acquiesce. James Mercer, for one, never allowed a woman to "lay up" unless she had a fever.[68] Other masters had women examined before they allowed them to skip a day's work.[69] Nevertheless, in the eighteenth and nineteenth centuries women's diseases were still shrouded in mystery. Slaveholders depended on women to reproduce the labor force and therefore could ill afford to take unnecessary risks. All things considered, as long as she did not overdo it, the clever and shrewd woman could feign illness and get away with it.

These forms of resistance suggest that female slaves were resourceful, self-reliant women. There are few other ways to describe how such powerless individuals used both force and wit to get their way. One must be careful, however, not to assume that every woman was a Sojourner Truth or a Harriet Tubman. Self-reliance and strength did not come naturally but had to be learned. On southern plantations women who worked together learned these traits from each other. They also learned how to cooperate and depend on one another. Self-reliance and self-sufficiency, therefore, must be viewed within the context of what the individual slave woman did for herself, and of what slave women as a group were able to do for one another.

Because we are accustomed to the notion that women were worked like men, we usually overlook the cooperative female community. Yet, in the nineteenth century, and especially on plantations with ten or more women, women often worked in exclusively or predominantly female gangs. One common work group was known as the "trash gang" and was assigned such tasks as raking stubble, pulling weeds, or doing "light" hoeing. At harvesttime they picked or cut the plantation's principal crop.[70] This mostly female gang was distinct from others because it was made up of pregnant women, women with nursing infants, young teenagers, and old slaves. Women entered and left the group regularly but more often than not, on plantations with large work forces, they exited the "trash gang" only to join another female gang that was hoeing, piling fodder, or doing some form of heavy labor. Domestic work was also done in female groups. Usually women spun thread, wove cloth, sewed, and quilted together apart from men. On Saturday afternoons women usually gathered together to do laundry. Thus women were put in one another's company for most of the day, every day. This meant that those with whom they ate meals, sang work songs, and commiserated during the workday were people with the same responsibilities and problems. It also meant that slave women developed a way of doing things, and a way of assigning value, that flowed from their communal perspective on southern plantation life.

Unlike southern white women who lived separated from each other on individual farms and plantations, the close slave quarters and the organization of female slave life allowed black women to develop a cooperative mentality. Pregnant women, for instance, often depended on the company of their peers during delivery and convalescence. The midwife, or "doctor woman," as the woman who assisted in plantation medical care was sometimes called, was usually an older or elderly slave.[71] Other women were assigned by slave owners to sit with the woman giving birth. After delivery and through the childhood of the offspring, a mother could count on both the medical and herb knowledge of the midwife whose know-how extended far beyond birthing. Midwives and "doctor women" made any number of teas and broths from the leaves and barks of plants and trees to treat ailments such as whoop-ing cough, diarrhea, toothaches, colds, head-aches, and backaches.[72]

Slave women also depended on these health-care providers to help them through difficult times. It was not unusual for a master or overseer to ask a midwife to confirm the illness of a woman who missed work. In such cases the midwife could either expose a malingerer or corroborate her story. Such women also performed abortions or, in rare cases, assisted in infanticide. On Charles Colcock Jones's Georgia plantation a midwife was suspected of the latter. A woman named Lucy had given birth in secret and then denied that she had ever been pregnant. Although a midwife attended her, she too claimed not to have delivered a child, as did Lucy's mother. Jones had a physician examine Lucy, and the doctor confirmed what Jones had suspected, that Lucy had indeed given birth. Twelve days later, the decomposing body of a full-term infant was found. The women then admitted to Lucy's delivery, but claimed the child had been stillborn. Jones believed otherwise, but he could not break the three women's collective defense.[73]

Women had many reasons to have abortions. Not the least of them was the slaves' hatred of a system that attached a monetary value to their children and made them chattel. Another was the

Fig. 97.
For slave women, mothering and child care were collaborative efforts. During the day, older female slaves frequently took care of young children until they were old enough to work.

Fig. 98.
Childbearing benefited both slave and master: "The masters were very careful about a good breedin' woman. If she had five or six children she was rarely sold." Edwin Forbes in 1864 sketched a group of African-Americans drying laundry in their Virginia cabin.

need to hide infidelity or adolescent pregnancy. Whatever the reason, childbirth, health care, and abortion were areas that were essentially female, and women cooperated to keep it that way. Indeed, it was almost impossible for slaveholders to penetrate the private world of female slaves, particularly when discovery meant certain punishment.

Women came to each other's aid not only for health care, but also for child care. The slave woman's long and grinding day has already been noted. In order to survive the dual responsibilities of laborer and mother, slave women needed help. On small farms or new plantations women had to take their children to the fields with them and attend to them during scheduled breaks. Often, however, there were one or more elderly females who looked after children while their mothers labored in the fields. These women usually took their responsibilities seriously because they spent as much time, if not more, with a child than the child's biological parent. As remembered by Robert Shepherd, of Georgia, "Aunt Viney . . . had a big old horn what she blowed when it was time for us to eat, and us knowed better dan to git so fur off us couldn't hear dat horn, for Aunt Viney would sho' tear us up."[74] Along with providing discipline, old women cooked for and counseled plantation children.

According to Josephine Bristow, Mary Novlin, the nursery keeper on Ferdinand Gibson's South Carolina plantation, "looked after every blessed thing for us all day long en cooked for us right along wid de mindin'."[75]

Nursery superintendents also ministered to the hurts and illnesses of infants and children.[76] It was not at all uncommon for the children's weekly rations to be given to the "grannies" rather than to the children's parents.[77] Apparently neither slave owners nor slaves expected a child's biological mother to fulfill a youngster's every need. Given the circumstances, the responsibilities of motherhood had to be shared, and this required close female cooperation.

Such communal practice helped slaves hurdle one of the most difficult of predicaments—determining who would provide maternal care for a child whose mother was either sold or deceased. Fathers sometimes doubled as mothers, but when slaves, as opposed to the master, determined child care they usually chose a woman as a child's surrogate mother. Most often that woman was a relative, usually an aunt or a sister, but in the absence of female relatives, non-kin women assumed the task.[78] Sometimes, as in the case of Georgian Mollie Malone, the nursery superintendent became the girl's substitute mother.[79] Sometimes friends did. After a slave killed her mother, Texan Julia Malone, then just a small child, was raised by the woman with whom her mother shared a cabin.[80] On southern plantations, the female community made sure no child was truly motherless.

Because black women on a given plantation spent so much time together they inevitably developed an appreciation of one another's skills and talents. This intimacy enabled them to establish criteria with which to rank and order themselves. Masters and mistresses could give a particular woman an edge, for instance, by teaching her to read, or giving her a coveted job. Black women knew who among them was a leader, who had a specific gift, who was exceptionally selfless. They could thus give each other prestige and status, even when it was not forthcoming from the master.

There were many women who achieved higher than ordinary status. Good cooks and seamstresses were admired as were, of course, midwives and "doctor women." On most farms and plantations the overseers, managers, foremen, and drivers were men, either black or white, but occasionally women were put in charge of female work gangs. If these female gang leaders were not admired, they were at least respected. The same may be said of women thought to be witches. Along with respect there was probably fear. Old women, though, were in a class apart. The female slave community could claim, as did Frederick Douglass in remarks about members of the slave community at large, that "there is not to be found, among any people, a more rigid enforcement of the law of respect to elders, than they maintain."[81] Absolute age was important, but a woman's age also indicated the number of children one had and one's stage in the childbearing cycle. Women called "Aunt" or "Granny" were middle-aged or elderly, but odds were that they had also had children. A "Granny" might be past childbearing. By virtue of their greater experience, wisdom, and number of children, old women commanded the respect of the young.

To consider the cooperative aspect of female slave life, to realize that the woman's community existed at all, is to understand one of the ways that black women provided a buffer against the depersonalizing regimen of plantation work and the general dehumanizing nature of slavery. The importance of the community of women cannot be overemphasized. Men were more likely to be sold than were women who could have children. Add to this that women were much more confined to the plantation than men, that some women had husbands who were able to visit only once or twice a week, and the fact that slave women generally outlived men by at least two

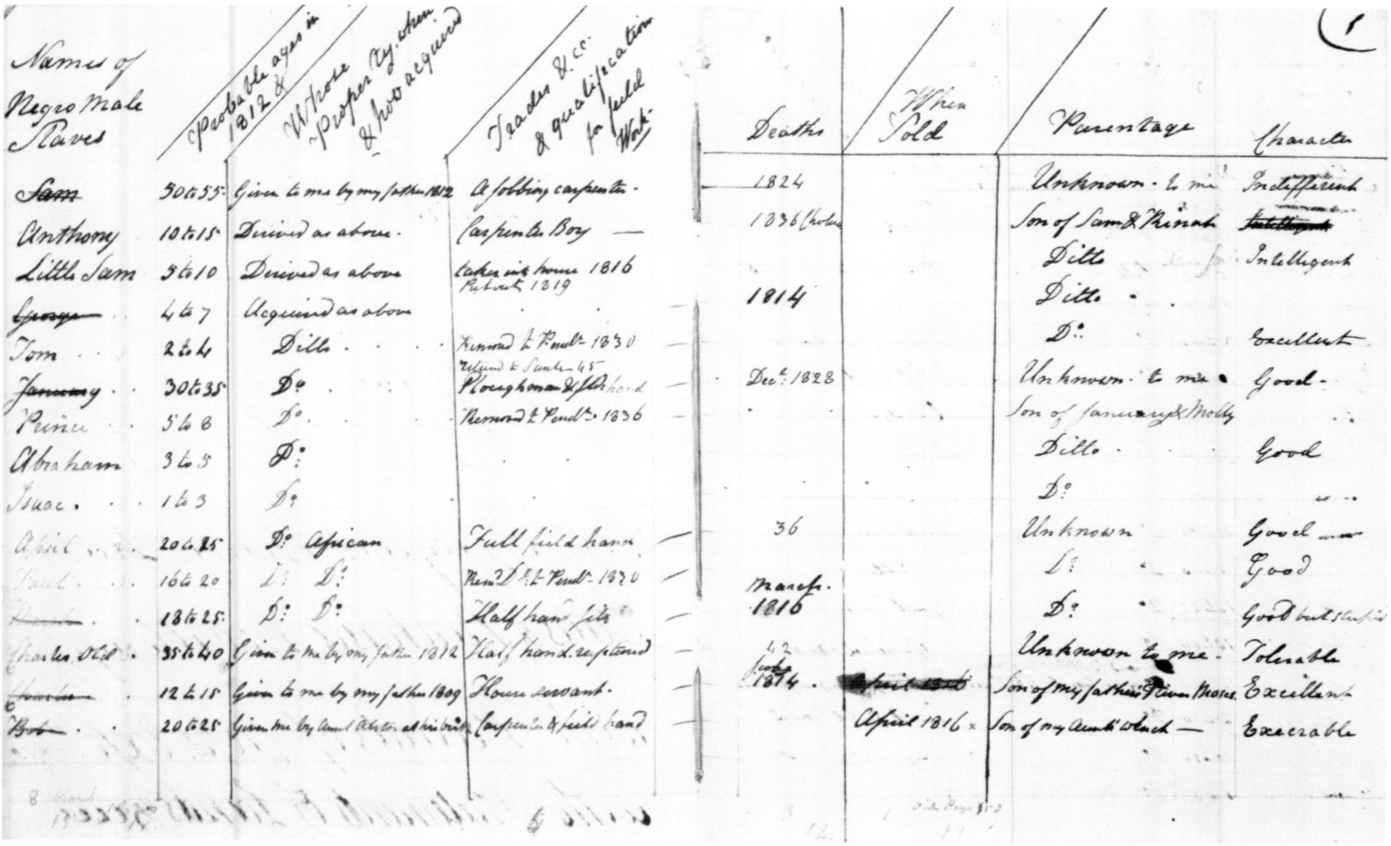

Names of Negro Male Slaves	Probable ages in 1812 &	Whose property when & how acquired	Trades &c. & qualification for field Work	Deaths	When Sold	Parentage	Character
Sam	50 to 55	Given to me by my father 1812	A jobbing carpenter	1824		Unknown to me	Indifferent
Anthony	10 to 15	Derived as above	Carpenter Boy	1836 [illegible]		Son of Sam & Rinah	[illegible]
Little Sam	5 to 10	Derived as above	taken into house 1816 Return 1819			Ditto	Intelligent
George	4 to 7	Acquired as above		1814		Ditto	
Tom	2 to 4	Ditto	Removed to Pendl. 1830 Returned to Santee 45			D°.	Excellent
January	30 to 35	D°	Ploughman & field hand	Decr. 1828		Unknown to me	Good
Prince	5 to 8	D°.	Removed to Pendl. 1836			Son of January & Molly	
Abraham	3 to 5	D°				Ditto	Good
Isaac	1 to 3	D°				D°	
April	20 to 25	D° African	Full field hand	36		Unknown	Good
Paul	16 to 20	D° D°	Rem. to Pendl. 1830			D°	Good
[illegible]	18 to 25	D° D°	Half hand [illegible]	March 1816		D°	Good but [illegible]
Charles Old	35 to 40	Given to me by my father 1812	Half hand & [illegible]	42 July 1814		Unknown to me	Tolerable
[illegible]	12 to 15	Given to me by my father 1809	House servant		[illegible]	Son of my father's [illegible]	Excellent
Bob	20 to 25	Given me by my Aunt [illegible]	Carpenter & field hand		April 1816	Son of my Aunt's [illegible]	Execrable

Fig. 99.
Although the owner frequently encouraged, and even arranged, specific and often involuntary pairings, many slave marriages resulted in long-term partnerships that contributed substantially to the stability of the family. In his inventory of male slaves, South Carolina's Charles Cotesworth Pinckney listed, among others, the four sons of Sam and Rinah and the three sons of January and Molly.

BY

HEWLETT & BRIGHT.

SALE OF

VALUABLE

SLAVES,

(On account of departure)

The Owner of the following named and valuable Slaves, being on the eve of departure for Europe, will cause the same to be offered for sale, at the NEW EXCHANGE, corner of St. Louis and Chartres streets, on *Saturday,* May 16, at Twelve o'Clock, *viz.*

1. SARAH, a mulatress, aged 45 years, a good cook and accustomed to house work in general, is an excellent and faithful nurse for sick persons, and in every respect a first rate character.

2. DENNIS, her son, a mulatto, aged 24 years, a first rate cook and steward for a vessel, having been in that capacity for many years on board one of the Mobile packets; is strictly honest, temperate, and a first rate subject.

3. CHOLE, a mulatress, aged 36 years, she is, without execption, one of the most competent servants in the country, a first rate washer and ironer, does up lace, a good cook, and for a bachelor who wishes a house-keeper she would be invaluable; she is also a good ladies' maid, having travelled to the North in that capacity.

4. FANNY, her daughter, a mulatress, aged 16 years, speaks French and English, is a superior hair-dresser, (pupil of Guilliac,) a good seamstress and ladies' maid, is smart, intelligent, and a first rate character.

5. DANDRIDGE, a mulatoo, aged 26 years, a first rate dining-room servant, a good painter and rough carpenter, and has but few equals for honesty and sobriety.

6. NANCY, his wife, aged about 24 years, a confidential house servant, good seamstress, mantuamaker and tailoress, a good cook, washer and ironer, etc.

7. MARY ANN, her child, a creole, aged 7 years, speaks French and English, is smart, active and intelligent.

8. FANNY or FRANCES, a mulatress, aged 22 years, is a first rate washer and ironer, good cook and house servant, and has an excellent character.

9. EMMA, an orphan, aged 10 or 11 years, speaks French and English, has been in the country 7 years, has been accustomed to waiting on table, sewing etc.; is intelligent and active.

10. FRANK, a mulatto, aged about 32 years speaks French and English, is a first rate hostler and coachman, understands perfectly well the management of horses, and is, in every respect, a first rate character, with the exception that he will occasionally drink, though not an habitual drunkard.

☞ All the above named Slaves are acclimated and excellent subjects; they were purchased by their present vendor many years ago, and will, therefore, be severally warranted against all vices and maladies prescribed by law, save and except FRANK, who is fully guaranteed in every other respect but the one above mentioned.

TERMS:—One-half Cash, and the other half in notes at Six months, drawn and endorsed to the satisfaction of the Vendor, with special mortgage on the Slaves until final payment. The Acts of Sale to be passed before WILLIAM BOSWELL, *Notary Public,* at the expense of the Purchaser.

New-Orleans, May 13, 1835.

PRINTED BY BENJAMIN LEVY.

years, and we find that on a given plantation the male's presence was more tenuous than the female's and that, outside of their forced dependence on whites for food and shelter, women were more dependent on each other than they were on men. This is not to say that male-female relationships were unfulfilling or of no consequence, or that women always got along with one another and never fought or disagreed, only that male-female relationships were fraught with more uncertainty about the future than solely female ones. It is to say also that the female slave community existed apart from whites who exploited and hurt black women in every way. This community schooled its members in survival, helped and protected them when possible, but most of all gave its women the opportunity to forge independent ideas about womanhood.

No doubt the most important lesson they taught was that their central role was one of motherhood. Clearly, masters and slave women perceived motherhood differently. Masters were primarily concerned with their selfish economic needs. The slave woman's concerns were more personal, more emotional. Motherhood was important for kinship reasons. Although African-American slaves did not, as did some of their African forebears, trace lineage through the maternal family, they, like their ancestors, did revere motherhood. Mothers were those least likely to be separated from their children, and mothers formed the crucial link between a child and his or her separated father.

In addition, in the antebellum South the security that so often accompanied motherhood served to reinforce its importance. Since non-prolific women were sold, childbearing was a way to anchor oneself to a plantation for an extended period of time, and thus maintain enduring relationships with family and friends. Childbirth to a degree also secured the nuclear family against breakup by sale because stable, childbearing families were an asset to slaveholders. Beyond all this, giving birth was a life-affirming action. It was, ironically, an act of defiance, a signal to the slave owner that no matter how cruel and inhumane his actions, African-Americans would not be utterly subjugated or destroyed. For these reasons, motherhood was a black girl's most important rite of passage. It is not surprising that the slave community resisted the system's attempt to turn every female into a "brood mare."

Indeed, slave masters confronted slave community mores that cautioned girls to step into motherhood slowly and reverently. Slaves courted but "courtin' wasn't fast," noted one male ex-slave.[82] Mothers watched their daughters vigilantly, not only to help them avoid white men,

but slave men and boys. They also kept them fairly ignorant of matters concerning sex, including the mechanics of childbirth. "People was very particular in them days," said a former slave. "They wouldn't let children know anything."[83] Frances Fluker, of Mississippi, was among the many who confirmed this assessment. She claimed: "I come a woman 'for I knowed what it was. . . . They didn't tell me nothin'."[84]

Although this was one way mothers conspired to resist a slave owner's pressure, they could not forever shelter daughters from his manipulative tactics, or even slave courtship rituals. More than likely, though, it was the slave community's counterpressure that made child mothers a rarity. Recent data suggest that the average slave woman was capable of childbearing at age seventeen. That most black women had their first child at nineteen proves that vigilance and resistance paid off. Since, however, the average white woman did not begin childbirth until age twenty-one, it seems that slaveholder pressure was not entirely overcome.

The slave owner's pressure is also manifested in child spacing, marriage patterns, and social mores. Slave women usually had their first child at approximately age nineteen, waited a while before having their second child, and after the second had subsequent children at two-and-a-half-year intervals.[85] Most bonded women married the father of their first child, but many established a more enduring relationship with a second male and went on to marry and have the rest of their children with him. This pattern suggests an accommodation to the slaveholders' practice of selling non-prolific women. The first child proved a woman's fertility. The consummation of an early or fleeting relationship, this child nevertheless anchored its mother to the plantation. The lasting nature of the bond between a woman and the father of her second child suggests that such relationships were of more consequence and not aimed at satisfying a master's demands.

Like child spacing and marriage patterns, attitudes about illegitimacy show a reconciliation between the system's demands and the slave community's needs. Slaves knew what pressures confronted young adult women, and they also knew that parenthood and kinship gave them roles outside slavery. So central was motherhood to womanhood that unmarried mothers were not stigmatized, neither were their children deemed illegitimate. What we know about female runaways, the system's dependence on natural increase, the custom of keeping secret the mechanics of sex and childbirth, the cooperative aspect of slave motherhood, and the attitudes about illegitimacy and kinship all point to motherhood, more than marriage, as defining the slave woman's most crucial obligations.

Of course, this did not mean that male-female relationships were of no importance. As noted above, they were fraught with many uncertainties. They were varied and unpredictable, much as one would expect any male-female interaction to be. But unlike ordinary relationships, they were subject to the slave owner's interference. Because whites could and did make unsettling and life-threatening decisions, they shaped not only the nature of any male-female slave relationship but also the role women assumed in their

families. As expected, the role, and the kind of womanhood it demanded, were different from that known to the vast majority of white women.

Slave women had few opportunities to flaunt their femininity. Their work hours were too long and their work clothes too tattered and dirty. Only on Sundays, religious holidays, and other festive occasions could they dress in their finest, usually one dress laid aside and worn sparingly. There were also customs familiar to any society. Female slaves used sweet-smelling flowers and herbs as perfume and often kept their good dresses packed in them so that the clothing absorbed the

Fig. 101.
Sold at age fourteen, Louisa Picquet as she was being taken away heard "some one cryin', and prayin' the Lord to go with her only daughter, and protect me.... Mother was right on her knees, with her hands up, prayin' to the Lord for me. She didn't care who saw her: the people all lookin' at her. I often thought her prayers followed me, for I never could forget her."

fragrance. Hoops were made of grapevines and worn to make the dress fall away from the body. A brightly colored hat or head wrap made for the finishing touch. On average, house servants dressed better than field hands since they had access to castoffs from the master's family, but all slaves tried to dress up for religious services and parties.[86] According to former slave Gus Feaster, "the gals come out in the starch dresses. . . . They took their hair down outen the strings" and "pulled off the head rags."[87]

Slave women wanted to look attractive not just for themselves but for slave men. Courtship was one of the few bright spots in an otherwise oppressive environment. Slave owners did not discourage courting because it ultimately ended in marriage and childbirth, both of which benefited slave masters. In particular, men became more manageable because their wives could be held hostage for their husband's misbehavior. Women gave birth to children that kept females from running away, and that profited the slave master doubly. Although slaves knew how courtship aided the planter, and mothers kept watchful eyes on their daughters, the sexes could not be kept apart. South Carolinian Gus Feaster recollected that "De gals charmed us wid honeysuckle and rose petals hid in dere bosoms. . . . Dey dried chennyberries and painted dem and wo'em on a string around dere necks."[88]

Men responded to such flattery, often initiating their own courtship encounters. Henry Bibb twice consulted conjurers on how to turn a girl's head.[89] A Georgia house servant named Abraham risked the whip when without permission he wore his master's shoes to a party so as to attract female attention.[90] While not regular events, parties did provide occasions for some of the more humorous aspects of the courtship ritual. A case in point involved Sam, a Louisiana slave, and a woman, Miss Lively, for whom he had an ardent passion. At a Christmas party Sam tried to impress Lively with his dancing talents, and she cooperated by giving him the honor of her first dance. While his rivals sat crestfallen, Sam rose to demonstrate his worthiness. His movements tested the strength of his every muscle and ligament until exhaustion got the better of him. Tireless, Miss Lively continued to dance with every male suitor there. In the end, she outdanced them all, proving that her reputation, as well as her name, were well deserved.[91]

Many women looked forward to courtship, many also anticipated enjoying wholesome relationships with their husbands. And for their part, slave men were as solicitous as they could be toward their women. There were men like Charles, a slave belonging to President Polk, who was suspected of running from his master's Mississippi plantation to be with his wife on Polk's Tennessee estate.[92] There were men like Sam, Debby's husband, who eternally teased yet delighted his wife.[93] There were men like the slave of William Black, who when put on the auction block pleaded with prospective buyers to purchase him, his wife, and his daughter as a family.[94] And there were men like Anderson, Romeo, Pete, Archy, and Gery who took their wives with them when, in 1864, they fled the Bayside plantation in Louisiana for the Federal lines.[95] To these must be added free black men who purchased their wives and children from slavery, and those who tried but found their spouse's owner unwilling.

Slave women, too, did their part to make slave relationships endure. When separated from their spouses, they took it just as hard as did the men. Susan and Ersey, slaves belonging to the proslavery novelist Nathaniel Tucker, were devastated when they heard they might be forced to leave their mates in Saint Louis, Missouri, for a plantation in Texas. They begged Tucker to reconsider, claiming that "to be separated from our husbands forever in this world would make us unhappy for life."[96] Similarly, in a Richmond slave market a bondwoman who had just been taken from her husband told Frederick Olmsted that "my heart was a'most broke."[97]

These examples make it impossible to ignore the oppressive hand of whites in black life. Notwithstanding the traditional nature of courtship, as well as recent historical studies showing that slave marriages often lasted anywhere from five to fourteen years, there is no denying that slavery's everyday workings influenced male-female relationships and the role women played in slave families.

Slavery made it impossible for women to be overly dependent on their husbands. Husbands were sometimes sold away and were in any case unable to protect wives from the whip, hard work, or rape by white males. Women married to men on other plantations were particularly self-sufficient. In her husband's absence, a wife developed methods of dealing with domestic responsibilities and crises. Usually wives living apart from their spouses got along without outside help, or they relied on relatives and females with similar problems and needs. When women depended mostly on other women, female solidarity usually increased while husbands and other men lost much of their control over the women involved.

Many bondwomen supplemented their food allotment. Male slaves did this, too, but since women could not be overly dependent on the

Fig. 102.
At the conclusion of the
Civil War, and intending
to begin new lives together
as free men and women,
many African-American
couples married legally, as
did this Vicksburg, Mississippi pair. As one indi-
vidual put it, "My hus-
band and I have lived
together fifteen years and
we wants to be married
over agin now."

male, both men and women scavenged for additional food. Female house servants, cooks, and
nurses had access to food and hence an advantage. Molly, Mary Chesnut's maid, made no secret of the fact she fed her children and others' in
the midst of her mistress's Confederate household. "Dey gets a little of all dat's going," she
told Mrs. Chesnut.[98] Field workers were less fortunate but they had their sources. Frederick
Douglass remembered that his grandmother
caught fish.[99] Ex-slave Betty Brown explained that
her mother hunted; "she'd have 'coon hides n'
deer n' mink, n' beavers, lawd."[100] Still other
women stole provisions. Eliza Overton, of Missouri, admitted that her mother took hogs from
the plantation and cooked them in the woods
over boiling water.[101] Many others also used their
wits and skill to supplement their diets. When
men did this, too, the slave family benefited
doubly. Women, however, did not, could not,
leave this activity up to their husbands.

In some cases women were paired with abusive
husbands. But the female slave's restraints in
matters of "divorce" were quite different from
the free woman's. Although slave owners and
overseers, for example, demanded orderly conduct, they also encouraged those couples who

quarreled incessantly to find new partners. On
George Noble Jones's Florida plantation a slave,
Rose, initiated a separation from her husband,
Renty, because of his infidelity. The two argued
so much that the overseer gladly granted the
request.[102] Such separations were not unusual,
and antebellum slave sources do not indicate any
overbearing pressures from the slave community
forcing incompatible couples to remain together.
In fact, women left their husbands for a variety of
reasons. One left because her husband "drawed
back to hit her with a chair."[103] A religious
woman left her spouse because he preferred parties to prayer meetings.[104] Still another woman
who changed mates declared, "I didn't like him,
and I neber did."[105] Her first husband may well
have been thrust upon her by her master. Beyond
this, slave owners wanted women to have children;
women knew this and undoubtedly sometimes
chose mates hurriedly. Yet, ironically, women
thereby found some small measure of freedom in
that they could later change mates, something
that eluded most southern white women.

All this says something about female slave
identity and about slave families. Slave women
were not sheltered from life's ugliness nor dependent upon men for food or protection. Although

men played important roles as lovers and as fathers, slave women within southern society had to take their own initiative in the quest for survival. They depended on men, as they did on female friends, for companionship. Slave women brought to a marriage relationship about as much as men and, by virtue of their unique contributions to the family, women had as much influence and support. And as slave owners made few decisions affecting her everyday marital life, a woman in many cases exercised considerable autonomy within her marriage. This does not mean that she was the dominant figure, but that her relationship with a lover or husband was as an equal partner.

Slave families, therefore, were unusually egalitarian. Equality, however, was not based on sameness because, while men and women often had the same tasks, many jobs and responsibilities still belonged by definition to one sex or the other. This suggests instead that equality within the slave family was based on complementary roles, roles that were different yet so critical to survival that they were of equal necessity.

In comparing the roles of wife and mother, it is evident, though, that the mother-child relationship superceded that of husband-wife. It could be no other way. Slaveholder practices encouraged the primacy of the former, and in the mores of the slave community motherhood ranked above marriage. In fact, women in their role as mothers were central figures in the nuclear slave family. Mothers by having and nurturing children earned for their families some security against sale and separation. Mothers helped supplement the family diet. And mothers served as the critical information link when fathers were sold away or ran away. By itself, the fact that slave society did not condemn "illegitimacy" indicates the mother's central role, a role presumed to be independent of the father's or husband's.

The picture of slave women is thus in stark contrast to the life of most nineteenth-century white women in America. Black women were victims of both racism and sexism. They were dragged from Africa because they were black. Because they were black and slave, they lost their rights and, under penalty of the whip and even death, worked for someone else's profit. As black women they were used sexually; they shouldered the dangerous burden of childbirth and the laborious chores of child care and domestic work. They were also tied to the plantation with less chance than men for escape or just a change of environment. They survived these conditions debilitating to body and mind all the while inventing a womanhood with meaning to them—one wherein they could be charmed by and pleasing to men, but one also grounded in sexual equality. It allowed love and marriage, but encouraged a peculiar dependence: dependence on women as much as men, dependence above all on oneself. Most important, womanhood was defined by motherhood, a role as exalted by black women and their slave community as it was debased by the slave system. Resistance was the cornerstone. Slave women resisted the brutal system, and they resisted white America's contempt. Of all the women in America, they best could give an affirmative answer to Sojourner Truth's question: "ar'n't I a woman?" □

BLACK LIFE IN OLD SOUTH CITIES

David R. Goldfield

Fig. 103.
"A city slave is almost a freeman, compared with a slave on the plantation," reflected Frederick Douglass. *"He is much better fed and clothed, and enjoys privileges altogether unknown to the slave on the plantation."*

he clock struck four. It was still dark when Emmanuel Quivers rose from bed. Wagons already rumbled in the street, voices called, a whistle shrieked in the distance. The workday in the city had begun. Soon, Quivers left behind his wife and children and took the short walk across the James River and Kanawha Canal to the Tredegar Iron Works, just beside the James River. Quivers's step was more purposeful that day. By nightfall, he and his family were to leave Richmond, accompanied by the blessings of Tredegar's owner, Joseph Reid Anderson, and clutching documents declaring the Quivers family free. Quivers recalled when he came to work for Anderson a decade earlier as a hired slave among dozens of other hired slaves in Tredegar's hot furnace room. By the early 1850s, Quivers had established himself as a hard and reliable worker, earning as much as $120 a year through bonuses and overtime. As a reward, Anderson negotiated a loan for Quivers, enabling the slave to purchase his freedom. Anderson then promoted Quivers to facilitate the repayment of the loan. By 1857, Quivers was earning as much as eight to twelve dollars a week and had secured a second loan from Anderson to purchase his family and migrate to the West. The ironworker soon paid off the loan and planned to move his family to California.[1]

Andrew Marshall drove a dray through the streets of Savannah, but his thoughts were on serving the Lord. Marshall had purchased his freedom with a two-hundred-dollar advance from his owner, Savannah merchant Richard Richardson. Using the contacts he had made while serving Richardson as a coachman, Marshall began a dray business and, by 1824, was probably the wealthiest free black in Savannah. He owned several parcels of real estate, a slave, and a coach.

By this time, however, Marshall, then in his sixties, felt another calling. Financially secure, he began to minister to the slaves and free blacks who attended the First African Baptist Church in the city. Marshall organized the one-thousand-member congregation into an institutional church, establishing a benevolent society, a missionary group, and a Sunday school. By the time he died in 1856 at the age of one hundred, Marshall had established a legendary reputation among both Savannah's white and black populace.[2]

William Wells Brown played an important role in the New Orleans slave trade. The Crescent City was the most active slave market in the South, with slaves and accompanying speculators converging on the city, coming down the Mississippi, up from the Gulf of Mexico, or overland from the Southeast. On any winter weekday, planters seeking hands for the sugar or cotton plantations along the lower Mississippi, or local residents hoping to find domestic workers or laborers, visited the auction blocks at the foot of Canal Street or tried the more opulent atmosphere of the Saint Charles Hotel. Slave trading was a big business in the urban South, rivaling staple crops in profitability. Brown's role in the business was to prepare slaves for sale. A slave himself, Brown empathized with the unfortunate men and women, many of whom had already been separated from their families, and most of whom had doubtless heard stories of the rigors of plantation labor in the Deep South. It was a task Brown loathed, but nevertheless performed well. As he recalled several years later from the vantage point of freedom in the North, "Before the slaves were exhibited for sale, they were dressed and drawn out into the yard. Some were set to dancing, some to jumping, some to singing, and some to playing cards. This was done to make them appear cheerful and happy. My business was to

A SLAVE-PEN AT NEW ORLEANS—BEFORE THE AUCTION. A SKETCH OF THE PAST.

Fig. 104.
Auctioneers customarily groomed slaves before a sale. An ex-slave recalled, "When selling time came we had to wash up and comb our hair so as to look as good as we could as to demand a high price. Oh yes, we had to dress up and parade before the white folks until they picked the ones they wanted."

Fig. 105.
William Taylor, a Baltimore resident, sold his "Excellent Waiter & good House Servant" because the man was a habitual runaway.

To Be Sold out of Jail

A Mulatto Man about 25 Years of age, active & healthy — is an Excellent Waiter & good House Servant. and Sold for no fault But an Idle Trick of Running away.

For Information apply to the Printers.

Baltimore October 13. 1797.

761 D1f Continue this advertisement untill countermanded when it [illegible] be paid for and on enquiry upon W.m Taylor no. 8 Bankstreet—

see that they were placed in those situations before the arrival of the purchasers, and I have often set them to dancing when their cheeks were wet with tears."[3]

These were extraordinary men. Blacks in the cities of the Old South were typically not as successful as these three, nor did they leave much trace of their existence. Their lives, slave or free, were typically mundane: they scratched out an existence from work and fellowship, all the while aware that their status and their lives could be changed dramatically by the actions of individual whites or the larger society. Despite their unique positions in antebellum southern urban society, the lives of Quivers, Marshall, and Brown highlight a number of features common to the lives of all blacks then living and working in southern cities.

Although slaves and free blacks invariably occupied the lowest rungs of the urban occupational ladder, there were considerably more opportunities to learn skills and apply business acumen in the city than in the countryside. Plantation slaves knew this and sought as often as possible to visit the city to market their produce, visit friends and relatives, or to accomplish more drastic objectives—such as running away. Second, most successful slaves and free blacks owed a great deal to white benefactors or supporters. This client relationship filtered through all levels of urban black society. Masters and employers offered some protection for slaves, and influential customers or neighbors vouched for free blacks. From getting work to getting out of legal difficulties, blacks understood the value of white support. Third, black life in the urban South belied basic white, southern beliefs about blacks. Urban slaves were not content with slavery, as their masters assumed; given a sliver of hope, they would invariably choose freedom. Blacks also had allegedly limited intellectual abilities. Yet, the presence of respected black preachers, the thirst

for knowledge represented by the scattering of clandestine schools in the city, and the good business sense evidenced by the black elite all challenged claims of inferiority.

Finally, whatever the possibilities inherent in urban life for antebellum black southerners, reminders of their subservient and precarious position were frequent. The presence of the slave trade was only the harshest of many reminders that blacks, particularly slaves, had limited control over their own lives. Every southern city had ordinances, supported by custom, that restricted movement, employment, education, worship, and recreation. Though enforcement of these provi-

sions was notoriously lax, on occasion white authorities swept down on blacks, capriciously and cruelly. A constant tug-of-war raged in the cities of the Old South. Slaves sought to expand their freedoms, while whites wanted to limit them; free blacks strove to protect their anomalous position in a society that identified blacks with slavery, while whites sought to reduce their position to virtual bondage. Yet, even in this tense and often hostile environment, black southerners carved out lives within the community. Only in the 1850s did these lives seem threatened by forces within and beyond the urban South.

The history of black life in the antebellum

urban South may be interesting, but is it important? After all, only one out of ten slaves lived in cities, and while free black urban residents comprised one-third to one-half of all free black southerners, less than 5 percent of the South's black inhabitants were free. Not many white southerners lived in cities either—less than one in eight. And, except for New Orleans, antebellum southern cities were modest affairs, typically with fewer than thirty thousand inhabitants by 1850. New York, Philadelphia, Saint Louis, Chicago, Boston, Baltimore, and Cincinnati each had well over a hundred thousand residents by that date. New Orleans was the only southern city among the ten most populous urban centers in the United States in 1850.

But numbers are not necessarily reflective of importance and impact. Antebellum southern cities were the South's outlet to the wider commercial world, conduits for information, manufactured goods, staple crops, and labor resources. Planters maintained close connections with urban merchants, slave traders, family members, and, in capital cities, legislators. Plantation slaves also visited cities as often as possible to market their garden crops, sell some cotton or tobacco, visit friends and relatives, and attend church. The

boundary between city and country was permeable. What occurred in the city invariably had an impact on the countryside and, therefore, on the South as a whole. The flexibility that slavery demonstrated in an urban setting and the economic assertiveness of free blacks affected the slavery debate, race relations, and, perhaps most important, life in the postwar South. Urban slaves and free blacks often assumed leadership positions after the Civil War. The institutions they formed in the antebellum era, especially the black churches, served as community focal points in the years after emancipation. Moreover, the class, color, and status divisions that marked urban black communities before the war persisted to some degree after the war. Finally, the mechanisms whites employed to maintain order in the Old South cities—segregation, the leasing of convict labor, and black codes—became the foundation for white supremacy in the postwar era. The story of black life in the antebellum urban South, in other words, not only helps us to understand more fully the history of the Old South but the origins of the New South as well.

Many visitors to Old South cities came away with at least one misimpression, judging by their

Fig. 107.
By 1860 there were 17,146 free and enslaved African-Americans in Charleston, South Carolina, alone.

126

written travel accounts. An English visitor to New Orleans in the early 1850s wrote, "The vast proportion of blacks in the street soon struck me. I should think they were five to one of the white population."[4] Swedish traveler Fredrika Bremer recorded a similar impression of Charleston in 1850, where "Negroes swarm the streets. Two-thirds of the people one sees in town are negroes."[5] And a visitor to Richmond a few years later observed that the city was "literally swarming with negroes."[6]

Such observations were, for the most part, wildly inaccurate. New Orleans's alleged five to one ratio of blacks to whites was almost directly the opposite. Bremer's perception of Charleston was closer to reality, but still considerably off the mark, as less than half of the city's population was black. Though Richmond's chronicler offered no figures, the impression he left was that of a heavily black city. Yet, less than 40 percent of Richmond's residents were black. What accounts for these discrepancies?

A simple answer is that compared with the northern cities these travelers had visited, the urban South was by comparison essentially dark-complexioned. New Haven, Connecticut, had the highest percentage of blacks—4.9 percent—of any northern city in 1850. Every southern city easily exceeded that figure. But even without the shock of comparison, it was understandable how newcomers misinterpreted the black population of the urban South. Blacks were prominent in the urban work force, on the streets, in the shops, along the wharves, and in the factories. The early-morning city, the city of Emmanuel Quivers, was a black city, with workers trudging off to factories, docks, and terminals, domestic servants marketing for their masters and mistresses, black-driven drays clamoring over the streets, and black laborers digging culverts or repairing streets. "Now go down to the markets," the *Richmond Daily Dispatch* invited its readers in 1853, "and you will hear the voices of hundreds, wrangling, chaffering, buying and selling, till you would imagine yourself in Babel, but for the reason that the tongues are almost all of one kind, those of colored people."[7]

The contributions of black labor to the urban antebellum South were indeed significant. Slaves, for example, accounted for more than 70 percent of the unskilled labor in Richmond and Charleston, 50 percent in Mobile, and over 40 percent in Nashville. But these figures barely indicate the versatility and importance of slave labor in the urban South. In cities such as Louisville and Richmond in the Upper South, slave labor provided most of the industrial work force. The tobacco factories used slaves almost exclusively.

In Richmond, more than one-half of all male slaves living in the city in 1860 worked in tobacco factories. These were typically unskilled operatives whom factory owners had either purchased or leased from agents. Visitors often commented on the spectacle of tobacco-factory slaves "stripped to the waist" on summer days, "tugging and heaving at long iron arms, which turned screws, accompanying each push and pull by deep-drawn groans."[8] Hours were long—fourteen a day in summer, as high as sixteen in the winter—and working conditions were difficult. But the slaves often set their own pace, occasionally pacing their work to songs much as field hands often set the cadence of their picking or sowing. Iron foundries also employed slave labor. The Tredegar Iron Works in Richmond, soon to be the arsenal of the Confederacy, employed a large slave force on the eve of the Civil War.

Industries were scarcer in the Lower South, reflecting the predominance of women among urban slaves in such cities as Charleston, Augusta, Savannah, Mobile, and New Orleans. Yet, when entrepreneurs promoted industrial enterprise in these places, they often touted the benefits of slave labor in the bargain. "The South can manufacture cheaper than any part of the world," a writer in the *New Orleans Times-Picayune* boasted in 1859, a feat made possible, he added, "with slave labor that, under all circumstances and at all times, is absolutely reliable."[9] In 1827, the *Macon Telegraph*, promoting the establishment of textile factories, observed that "slaves are most profitable of all operatives. . . . They are more docile, more constant, and cheaper than free men."[10] By the 1840s, several textile mills in Macon employed slave labor, a fact of great concern to some white laboring men who sought to block such competition. But a resolution of cotton planters in 1851, and a strong editorial that same year, defended the use of slave labor in much the same terms as had the editorial nearly twenty-five years earlier.

Southern railroad companies headquartered in cities held large numbers of bondsmen for railway repair and construction work. The South Carolina Railway in Charleston owned 103 slaves in 1860. Three railroads in Richmond owned nearly six hundred bondsmen between them. While many of these slaves worked in the countryside, they lived in and contributed to the life of the city.

Although slave labor was important to the South's nascent industrial and corporate activities, most urban slaves toiled as domestic servants. The vast majority of urban slaveholdings were small (two or fewer slaves), reflecting the dominance of domestic labor. These slaves, primarily

Fig. 108.
A child's nurse and a waiter, typical occupations for household slaves in a prosperous urban setting, are included in a ca. 1858 portrait of a Chattanooga, Tennessee, family.

women, performed the usual tasks associated with domestic service in the plantation big house: cleaning, cooking, and assisting with child rearing. In cities, domestic slaves took on additional responsibilities such as marketing. As a New Orleans resident noted, "almost the whole of the purchasing and selling of edible articles for domestic consumption [is] transacted by colored persons."[11] The smaller proportion of male domestic servants often assisted their masters' businesses as general laborers or as assistants to butchers, carpenters, wagon makers, and shoemakers.

The working conditions of domestic slaves were scarcely better than those encountered by workers in tobacco factories. They, too, rose before dawn and went to bed as late as ten o'clock at night. Unlike the tobacco operatives, domestic servants were on call twenty-four hours a day, seven days a week. They often lived in cramped quarters attached to the main house, so they enjoyed privacy less than did the factory workers who generally lived off the premises. The saving element in their work lives was that their duties frequently required domestic slaves to be out and

about the city, driving a dray for a master (as Andrew Marshall had done), delivering packages or messages, or shopping at the food market. It was here, in the moil of the city, that the domestic slave could take his or her respite, visit with friends or family, dawdle awhile over the array of goods at the market, or (if a male slave) step into one of the numerous groceries or grog shops for something to eat or drink.

Skill levels among urban slaves were generally low. If an economic ladder existed for urban slaves, it was one with very few rungs. In the late eighteenth century, urban slaves possessed artisanal skills. By the late 1840s, however, immigrants, native-born whites, and free blacks dominated the skilled trades—competitors who (with the exception of native-born whites) were much less evident a half-century earlier. Also, manumission laws were generally lenient in the post–Revolutionary era, which meant that skilled slaves were then able to purchase their freedom and remain in their communities. This reduced the pool of skilled slave labor. Subsequent legislation limiting the ability of urban slaves to learn a trade further eroded slave skills. This is not to say that some

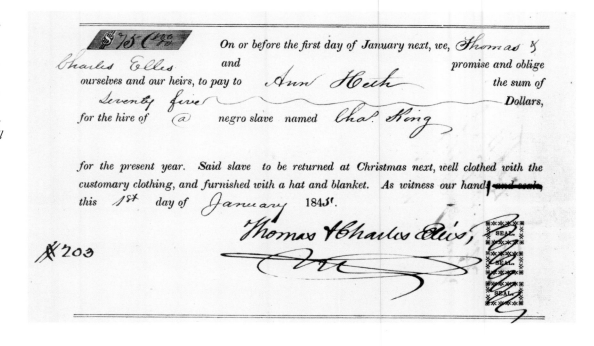

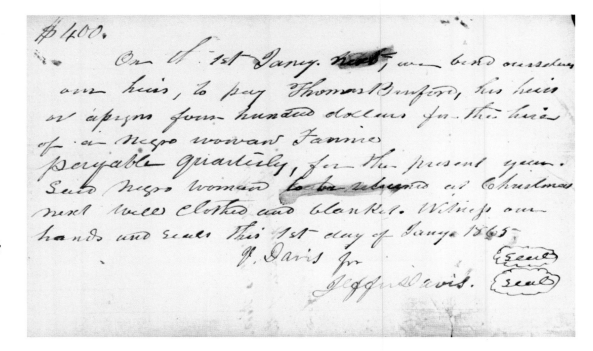

southern cities did not depend on some skilled slave labor. An 1848 census in Charleston revealed that nearly one out of five male slaves had artisanal skills, concentrated primarily in the building and shipping trades. But Charleston was an exception. In most southern cities either a majority or a substantial minority of urban slaves possessed few skills.

Although urban slaves possessed few more skills than a plantation field hand, the nature of urban work often required different types of work arrangements than existed on plantations. The cul-tivation of cotton, rice, tobacco, and sugar was a year-round activity. There were also numerous odd jobs plantation slaves were required to fill, from fence-mending to hauling logs. Urban businesses, on the other hand, often had seasonal variations; merchants, for example, were busiest from October to April, and textile mills frequently shut down during the summer months. Moreover, urban enterprises required significant capital investments in machinery and physical plants so that additional outlays for a labor force were not possible. Also, most businesses in the urban

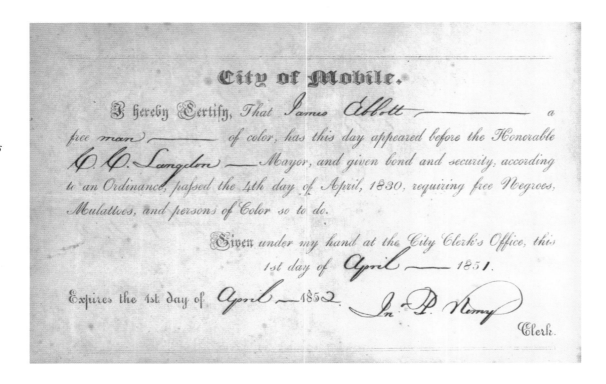

South were small in scale, rarely requiring more than one or two additional workers besides family members. Purchasing a slave or two could be difficult for a struggling new enterprise, and the money could be better spent on equipment, rent, or shipping.

A system of slave hiring evolved to meet such particular urban requirements. Actually, urban slave hiring probably appeared simultaneously with the growth of southern colonial towns. In 1712, the South Carolina legislature made disapproving note of slaves who hired out their own time in Charleston. During the nineteenth century, especially during the last two antebellum decades when urban economies expanded across the South, slave hiring became a prominent method of utilizing slave labor in cities. For large enterprises, such as manufacturing establishments, slave hiring replaced outright ownership by the 1850s. Virginia cities such as Danville, Lynchburg, and Richmond, where manufacturing played a significant role in the urban economy, resorted extensively to slave hiring. More than one-third of the slaves working during the 1850s in Lynchburg and Richmond, for example, were hired. The percentage of slaves working under hiring contracts was considerably less in cities of the Lower South, usually under 15 percent, as most of those cities lacked the large-scale enterprises that most favored hiring over ownership. Throughout the South, roughly 5 percent of the slaves worked in a hiring relationship, indicating that the system was primarily an urban labor form.

Typically, slaves worked with a fixed term of hire, six months or one year, with the employer providing appropriate clothing, food, lodging, and medical care in addition to a hiring fee paid to the owner. Slaves and employers got together in several ways. Sometimes an urban slave owner heard that a neighbor or local businessman was looking for a slave to perform domestic or other labor and thus concluded an agreement; on other occasions, slaveholders, either in the city or on farms in adjacent counties, sent slaves to brokers who then found suitable employment; and slaves, usually with the consent of their masters, sometimes took the initiative and found an employer. By the 1840s, slave hiring had become so commonplace in the urban South that hiring brokers proliferated to handle the volume. Every December their advertisements crowded newspapers. A typical notice, this one appearing in a Louisville newspaper, read: "An experience of many years business with the citizens of Louisville and vicinity renders us competent of judging and picking good homes and masters for your negroes."[12] Slave owners generally paid a commission of from 5 to 8 percent to the brokerages.

Not all slave hiring was so formalized. The nature of the urban economy required short-term weekly, daily, or even hourly work. For these purposes, slave owners and potential employers usually dealt directly with each other or were brought together by an enterprising slave. Cities hired slaves for short-term work on roads, trash collection, sewer construction, and bridge building. Owners typically received up to fifty cents a day. New Orleans authorities, for example, expended about thirty thousand dollars annually in slave-hiring fees. By the 1850s, nearly one-third of the slaves hired in Richmond and Savannah were hired for a period of less than one year. The work undertaken by most hired slaves indicated that males dominated the hiring system. Urban slave owners generally did not release their female domestic slaves for hired work.

The essence of slave hiring was its flexibility, its ability to adjust to an expanding and seasonal urban economy. For some white southerners, slave hiring was too flexible, particularly the practice of slaves' hiring their own time. The idea of slaves negotiating with employers for the best "arrangements"—housing, bonuses, treatment, and food—irked some who believed that such behavior created an independence and attitude that might prove ultimately subversive to the institution of slavery. As early as 1712, the South Carolina legislature attacked self-hire in Charleston as allowing slaves "to maintain themselves, and other slaves their companions, in drunken-

ness and other evil courses."[13] Cities sought to regulate self-hiring by outlawing it entirely (though unsuccessfully) or by requiring slaves who wished to work in a hire arrangement to purchase badges at stiff prices, ranging up to seven dollars annually in Charleston—although slave owners often purchased the badges for their slaves thus nullifying the intent of the law. Frustrated editors and petitioners surfaced periodically decrying the practice. Hired slaves, some complained, were without benefit of the master–slave relationship and "its controlling and ameliorating influences." Essentially, some alleged, the system allowed the slave to "choose his master," one, the slave hoped, who "will grant him the largest license." The upshot was to render the slave "insubordinate and vicious," resulting in a general "deterioration in morals, in habits, and in health."[14]

Slaves who hired their own time had a different perspective. Former slave Frederick Douglass recalled the exhilaration he felt the first time he hired out on his own: "After learning to calk, I sought my own employment, made my own contracts, and collected my own earnings; giving Master Hugh no trouble in any part of the transactions to which I was a party." Douglass added that "some slaves have made enough, in this way, to purchase their freedom."[15] A few slaves became entrepreneurs in their own right, employing other slaves and hiring out as teams for construction work.

Despite the pique of some whites, self-hire persisted and probably grew in the late antebellum decades. As Douglass indicated, a master could merely set a specified fee with his slave and leave it to the bondsman to secure a hiring contract to fulfill that agreement. In the meantime, the slave could obtain a hire that not only paid his master, but in the bargain left some money for himself. The latitude allowed the slave also reflected the urban labor market that, during periods of prosperity, was chronically short of labor. At these times, especially during the prosperous 1850s, calls to reopen the African slave trade or to import workers from Europe were heard most often. Usually, flush times in the city coincided with a prosperous farm economy and both city and farm competed for available labor. Purchase prices increased, putting slave ownership out of the reach of some city residents; unskilled slaves from the countryside went back to the farms; and some urban slaveholders took advantage of the higher prices and sold their slaves to farmers. The result was a smaller, more skilled urban slave-labor pool, too expensive to purchase, but reasonable enough to hire. Merchants, city administrators, factory owners, and just plain householders

JON—JON

Jones, Rachel, widow, 39 German
   Mahler, cabinet maker, Gillingham's al.
   Elisha, fisherman, Cross *f h*
   †Matilda, laundress, Honey al. near Hanover st. *f h*
   †Isaac, grain measurer, s. end of s. Howard
   †Jacob, stage driver, Harford extended *o t*
   †James, potter, Harford extended *o t*
   †Andrew, shoe black, cor. of Goodman st. and Sugar al.
   †Sarah, laundress, N. Calvert near Centre
   William, pilot, 57 Alisanna *f p*
   Barnard, ship carpenter, Fleet between Washington st. and Castle al. *f p*
   Owen, rigger, Wilk opposite the Methodist Church
   John, rigger, Argyle al. near Shakespeare *f p*
   †Thomas, laborer, Strawberry al. near German st. *f p*
   †George, laborer, Strawberry alley N. of Gough st *f p*
   †Joseph, cheese man, 17 George *f p*
   †Noah, carter, Union lane s. of Lexington st.
   †James, barber, N. Eutaw s. of Franklin
   †Isaac, laborer, Larew's al.
   †Rebecca, laundress, 2 German lane
   Margaret, widow, boarding house, 66 Cumberland row
   William, constable, 67 Harrison
   Ann, widow, 7 Conewago
   Lewis, boot and shoe maker, Cowpen al. near Liberty st.
   Henry, sawyer, French al.
   Margaret, binder, 20 Primrose al.

Fig. 112.
By the Civil War, the busy commercial port of Baltimore included a significant free-black population of more than 25,000, far outnumbering the city's 2,218 slaves. Baltimore's 1819 city directory included dagger symbols to distinguish African-Americans from white citizens. Note the residences of free blacks among whites and the variety of occupations.

Fig. 113.
Free blacks dominated
personal-service trades in
many cities. Henry Lee, an
African-American, used a
personalized perfume
bottle in his Vicksburg,
Mississippi, business.

immediately after the American Revolution when manumissions were easier. In fewer cases, some (such as Emmanuel Quivers and Andrew Marshall) had purchased their freedom. While there were free blacks in Lower South cities who attained their freedom in these ways, many were mixed-blood offspring of black slave women and prominent white men who had set the woman (and, therefore, her child) free, often teaching the child a trade or providing some financial support. This was especially the case in the former French ports of New Orleans and Mobile, but it was also evident in such southeastern cities as Savannah and Charleston. The free blacks of the Lower South, therefore, tended to be lighter-skinned, more affluent, higher-skilled, and perceived themselves as being more distinct from slaves than their counterparts in the cities of the Upper South. These distinctions were reflected in the respective urban labor markets.

Generally, the skill levels and occupational status of free blacks tended to increase the farther south one traveled; free black occupational status was lowest in New England cities, for example, and highest in New Orleans. In New Orleans, free people of color (as they were called) even occupied some white-collar positions in professional, managerial, and scientific occupations. They accounted for 5 percent of the total work force in these activities, easily outdistancing their counterparts in every other city in the nation. The affluence of the Crescent City's free people of color also exceeded other cities', with nearly one-third of free-black household heads in the city owning property in the 1830s. The percentage of free-black property holders in Upper South cities at that time was typically under 10 percent.

But New Orleans was not the only Lower South city where free blacks lived in relative prosperity. In Charleston, three out of four free black men worked at skilled trades. They accounted for 25 percent of the city's carpenters, 40 percent of its tailors, and 75 percent of the millwrights, even though they comprised only 15 percent of the work force. Occasionally, free blacks were among the wealthiest citizens in southern communities. William Johnson, of Natchez, Mississippi, a free-black barber, owned several properties in town, a plantation, and numerous slaves.[16] Andrew Marshall, mentioned earlier, was among Savannah's leading landholders in the 1820s.[17] Solomon Humphries, a free black in Macon, owned a grocery store and a textile mill.

Free blacks clustered in certain occupations that whites perceived as "nigger work." Despite the prejudicial nature of such perceptions, they enabled free blacks to carve out a narrow but significant niche in the skilled labor market of

were not likely to be finicky about whether they received their help via a broker, slave owner, or through inquiries from the slaves themselves.

The limited success of employment restrictions and the eagerness with which blacks took advantage of the exigencies of the urban labor market is even clearer with respect to urban free blacks. Free blacks were the most urbanized group in the Old South, with roughly one-third residing in antebellum southern cities. The attractions of the city were obvious. Unless free blacks owned property, their status in the countryside as farm laborers was only slightly better than the slaves'. Other economic opportunities were limited or nonexistent in rural areas. Also, a free black out and about in the countryside risked confrontation with patrols or individual whites who presumed he was a slave. Anonymity was easier in the city. It was not startling that fugitive slaves sometimes did not go north, but went to the nearest city. Most important perhaps, there was the possibility of making a living in the urban South.

The character of the free-black population differed markedly between cities in the Upper and Lower South. Free blacks in Upper South cities had usually gained their freedom in the period

*Fig. 114.
Although the available occupations were often menial, urban life nevertheless offered economic opportunities for both slaves and free blacks. In Richmond, Virginia, for example, African-American women hawked food to travelers arriving by rail.*

southern cities. Barbering, for example, was the quintessential "nigger work." Though few free-black barbers amassed the fortunes of William Johnson, barbering provided a comfortable living and good connections to prominent whites. Free blacks also monopolized catering, carting, and stable services in some cities. The definition of "nigger work" varied from city to city. Tailoring was a prominent free-black occupation in Charleston, but not in Richmond, for instance. In the former city, 45 percent of skilled free blacks were clustered in either tailoring or carpentry work. In Richmond, the building trades, shoemaking, and barbering accounted for 80 percent of skilled free-black labor.

The typical free black, however, whether in New Orleans or Richmond, worked in menial occupations. Their wages were generally lower

than comparable white laborers, and their willingness to work for less and their perceived tractability (especially when compared with Irish workers) generally guaranteed them some employment. They often worked alongside hired slaves in factories, on city work crews, or along the wharves. Skilled free-black women were rare. The vast majority worked in domestic service as cooks, laundresses, and housekeepers. Occasionally, a few might peddle some handicrafts or garden produce at the market.

Demographics eventually conspired to challenge slave and free-black labor in the urban South by the 1830s. Except in a few industrial cities, females predominated among the urban black population. The skewed sex ratios limited natural increase. At the same time, immigrants from Europe began to filter into southern cities, frequently by way of northern urban centers. Also, the white farm population, attracted by opportunities in the city and the lack of the same chance in the countryside, continued their steady migration to the urban South. As result, southern cities became whiter, and the work force

whiter still since many of the white newcomers were of prime working age.

By 1850, immigrants comprised more than 20 percent of Charleston's population, 25 percent of Savannah's, and more than 33 percent of Mobile's. But their representation in the work force was much greater: two-thirds of free workingmen in Mobile, and half in Charleston. In Richmond and Nashville, foreign-born workers counted for more than 40 percent of the free work force. While immigrants soon picked up the racial customs of the South, their ambivalence was reflected in their frequent fraternization with urban blacks and at the same time their willingness to engage in fierce and occasionally violent labor competition with them.

The success of immigrants in challenging urban black labor varied from city to city. In Charleston, for example, hired slaves and free blacks dominated the drayage business until the 1840s; by 1860, Irish workingmen accounted for two-thirds of the city's teamsters. Slaves were the primary victims of the displacement, indicating that the demand for slaves in the countryside, rather than preference for white teamsters, accounted for most of the shift. In other cities, the rising cost of hiring slaves, even for the most menial work, actually made immigrant labor cheaper. On the other hand, immigrants were less successful in Charleston in dislodging slaves and free blacks from artisanal work. Blacks had built up a loyal white clientele who did not switch regardless of racial preferences. In Richmond, slaves and free blacks continued to dominate the tobacco and iron industries. The general wisdom among Richmond businessmen was that slave labor was more efficient than comparable immigrant labor.

Immigrants were sometimes more successful in driving out free blacks. They were less concerned than native-born whites about the stigma of "nigger work," and they began to intrude on such venerable free-black occupations as barbering and drayage. In Norfolk, prior to 1850, free blacks dominated shipping-related artisanal trades. By 1860, these trades were shifting to immigrant labor. In New Orleans, however, free blacks persisted in the dock trades, but lost ground to immigrants in drayage and hotel service. Whether or not free blacks remained in traditional black occupations varied widely from place to place, depending on local customs, the skills of immigrants, and the degree of prosperity and hence labor demand in a particular city. Generally, though, the free blacks' occupational status tended to decline after 1840. Immigrant workers were willing to underbid free-black labor, accounting for the anomaly in the 1850s of an expanding economy and declining wages in unskilled and semi-skilled occupations.

Charleston was an exception to free-black occupational erosion, if for no other reason than that the locals resisted economic and social changes more than residents of most other cities. During the 1830s, the city experienced a significant influx of Irish immigrants from the glutted labor market of New York. Although they were successful in challenging hired slaves for some of the drayage business, they were unable to dislodge free blacks from artisanal work. By 1860, free blacks still dominated the tailoring, butchering, bricklaying, shoemaking, and painting trades.

Immigrants were not the only competitors whom blacks, slave and free, confronted in the urban labor market. Native-born whites also threatened the occupational status of slaves and free blacks, especially in skilled positions.[18] Although they generally disdained to compete for "nigger work," native-born whites guarded the traditionally white artisanal crafts fiercely, even resorting to violence on occasion. Frederick Douglass recalled the severe beating he received when he hired out as a caulker in Baltimore in 1836. Yet he understood the animosity he encountered: "The white laboring man was robbed by the slave system of the just results of his labor, because he was flung into competition with a class of laborers who worked without wages."[19] Employers often used slaves as strikebreakers, a tactic not likely to reduce tensions between black and white workers. While such individual encounters may have been numerous in the urban South, none of the mass racial rioting that plagued Boston, Philadelphia, and Cincinnati from the 1820s through the 1840s occurred in southern cities.

White workers in the urban South sought rather to eliminate or control the presence of blacks in the work force through legislative prohibitions.

As early as 1783, white carpenters and bricklayers in Charleston demanded protection from black artisans who undercut their wages. The authorities declined to act. In 1822, white butchers in Savannah petitioned the city council "to prevent slaves from butchering and selling meats in the Market on their own account and for their individual benefit," allegedly because these meats were "unfairly acquired."[20] Evidently the council tabled the petition since a similar request from the same group appeared before it twenty years later. In 1847, a group of skilled iron puddlers at Richmond's Tredegar Iron Works went out on strike to protest the presence of slaves alongside them. Tredegar's owner, Joseph Reid Anderson, promptly fired the white workers and replaced them with blacks. The Richmond newspapers backed Anderson completely, as the protestors' action "strikes at the root of all the rights and privileges of the master, and if acknowledged, or permitted to gain foothold, will soon wholly destroy the value of slave property."[21]

Not all white workers' efforts to limit or eliminate black competition failed. Occasionally, under the guise of security or enforcement of existing legislation, white workers sought to eliminate black competition. White workers in Natchez initiated an "inquisition" against free blacks in 1841, ostensibly to investigate their conduct. According to an 1831 law in Mississippi, any free black convicted of even a minor violation was to be removed from the state. The workers succeeded in frightening a good number of free blacks into leaving Natchez, though more prominent individuals, such as William Johnson, rode out the storm. Elsewhere, white workers persuaded city administrations in the 1830s and 1840s to pass minimum-wage laws under the theory that if wages were set high enough, slaves or free blacks could not undercut white workers. The impact was marginal, however. City administrations, again responding to pressure from white workers, barred blacks from certain skilled trades as early as the 1780s. Cities also experimented with legislation restricting or prohibiting self-hire and requiring slaves to purchase badges if they were to be hired out. As noted earlier, these constraints failed to reduce black labor competition.

Why were white workers so unsuccessful (at least prior to 1850) in limiting job competition from urban free blacks and slaves? Visitors noted that the occupational status of blacks in the urban South was often higher than that of blacks in northern cities. As one student of the subject concluded, "Certainly there was no lack of racial prejudice in the South, but it does appear that this prejudice did not make itself felt in the form of discrimination in employment to the degree that was common in northern cities."[22] There are several reasons for this seeming anomaly. First, when white workers attacked slave labor, they indirectly attacked slave owners, a powerful group in southern society. To limit slave hiring or reduce the presence of slaves in certain occupations affected the masters' profits. When Joseph Reid Anderson dismissed the striking white workers, the *Richmond Enquirer* defended the action by noting that had Anderson not acted accordingly, it would "render slave property utterly valueless and place employers in the power of their employed."[23]

From the perspective of the white employer or customer, blacks performed valuable services in cities where labor, especially skilled labor, was often in short supply. When Richmond acceded to a demand to ban blacks from the drayage business in 1810, merchants besieged officials, complaining that "there is at present a great want of waggons, drays and carts for transporting articles from one quarter of the City to another (a sufficient number of white drivers not having yet engaged in the business)."[24] The city temporarily lifted the ban but, even then, only extended it until forty white drivers could be found. A South Carolina legislative committee in the 1840s, investigating the lax enforcement of self-hire restrictions in Charleston, acknowledged the evils of the system, but added that without it, it "would be impossible to have [the] sort of labor" in cities necessary to advance the urban economy. "Until you can change the direction of the public prejudice, presuppositions & habit, you can never enforce a law which conflicts with them."[25]

Finally, when immigrants comprised the protest group, white authorities had even less sympathy with their demands. The loyalty of immigrants to the institution of slavery was open to question. As a delegate to Kentucky's 1849 constitutional convention observed, Louisville's immigrants were "hostile to slavery and its continuance." A writer in the *Southern Quarterly Review* that same year was equally pessimistic about the growing numbers of immigrants in Charleston and other cities: "Every city is destined to be the seat of free-soilism. It is unconsciously making its appearance in Charleston, and it is destined to increase with every fresh arrival of European immigrants. Whites are driving our slaves from their old employments all fostered by the cities."[26] There was also concern that, despite competition, immigrants and blacks might eventually recognize a common cause—a prospect not only threatening to peaceful labor relations, but to the institution of slavery itself. As Fanny Kemble wrote in the late 1830s about the influx of Irish workers to Georgia, "there is no saying

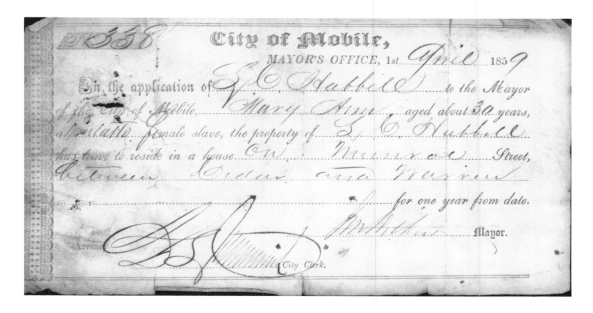

Fig. 117.
Some owners permitted their urban slaves to reside outside the master's home. In 1859, L. C. Hubbell paid a fee so that his slave Mary Ann could live on her own in Mobile, Alabama.

but what they might actually take to sympathy with the slaves, and I leave you to judge of the possible consequences."[27] And, whatever racial solidarity existed, immigrants probably forfeited it by competing directly with slaves and free blacks for work and wages.

So slaves and free blacks clung precariously to their niche in the urban labor market. Slaves sought to advance their autonomy within the context of urban work, and free blacks hoped to maintain their economic and hence personal freedom despite their anomalous position in southern society. The relative success of both slaves and free blacks in fulfilling these objectives enabled each group not only to draw a modicum of satisfaction and identity from work, but also to enhance their lives away from work.

Black family life, just as did work in the city, reflected both the constraints and the promise of urban life. The slave family was a significant yet often unstable institution on the plantation. The sale of family members, whites' sexual and labor demands, escapes, and death all tore at the fabric of plantation family life. Similar pressures existed in the city for both slave and free-black families, yet both privacy and opportunities were greater in the urban areas.

Fathers and husbands on the plantation and in the city, for example, had limited authority in the family. The master controlled the work, discipline, and eventual sale of family members. On the other hand, the urban male slave might have command over his own work, an opportunity not available on the plantation. The self-hire system and the chance to earn money placed male slaves closer to the role of family breadwinner.

Urban slaves also might have the opportunity

of living elsewhere, or living out, as it was called. Despite restrictions against this practice, hired slaves could, with the master's permission (and sometimes without), establish a household away from the owner's domicile. It is difficult to know the percentage of urban slaves who did so, but, based on newspaper accounts and local census records, one out of six slave households was living out by the late 1840s. Many masters preferred the system because it meant that they did not have to provide housing for their slaves or worry about feeding them. Some large slaveholders, such as manufacturers, provided their hired slaves with a housing allowance. A few cities, such as Athens and Mobile, required slave owners to remit a fee to enable their slaves to live elsewhere (although such was contrary to both Georgia and Alabama law).

While living out was a privilege for urban slaves, it was hardly a luxury. Most accommodations were spartan at best and wretched at worst. A mid-nineteenth-century traveler, Charles G. Parsons, noted of Savannah that while "many of the dwelling houses are spacious and elegant" and the stores both "large and well filled," there were other areas filled with "low, dingy, dirty, squalid, cheerless negro huts."[28] Slaves who lived out resided on the margins of the law and their residences were often even worse than what Parsons described. Slaves lived in jerry-built shacks, warehouses, and even the hallways of hotels. A visitor to a Charleston hotel found "the male servants of the house . . . already laid down for the night in the passages with their clothes on. They had neither beds nor bedding, and you may kick them or tread upon them (as you come in) with impunity." In New Orleans, the traveler added, "they had no beds . . . to sleep on,—all lying, like

Fig. 118.
Slave traders in the Upper South cities of Baltimore, Alexandria, Richmond, and Norfolk were the chief sources of slaves for the largest market, New Orleans. In Alexandria, the widely known firm of Price, Birch & Company collected slaves in crowded pens before they were "sold south."

controlled by fire codes that prohibited the erection of flimsy wooden structures. As early as 1838, for example, the Neck area north of Charleston "rapidly filled with small cheap wooden houses" erected by slaves working in the city.[32] This residential concentration by race was unusual in the antebellum urban South as blacks, slave and free, typically resided in all parts of the city. In any case, the ability to live out, regardless of the quality of dwelling, allowed slave husbands and wives to remain together even if they were owned by separate masters—a practice almost impossible in the countryside.

The majority lived, though, with their masters since most urban slaves worked in domestic service and in one- or two-slave households. Sometimes husband and wife worked and lived together with the same master; more often, they visited each other in their separate domiciles. When slaves did reside with their masters, they occupied a room that was either in the house or part of a modest slave quarters attached to the main house. The slave quarters that characterized life on large plantations were obviously not possible in cities, given the cost of urban land and the generally small slaveholdings. Occasionally, modest slave quarters emerged near factories, but since these dwellings were more similar to male dormitories than permanent living quarters (factory work forces were overwhelmingly male), there was little opportunity for family life to flourish. A typical arrangement of slave quarters in Charleston for slaveholdings of more than four was a two-story building attached to the owner's house. The first floor was reserved for a kitchen, storage, and a stable. Above were two or more rooms, usually measuring no more than ten by fifteen feet. These rooms were more often than not crowded, certainly poorly ventilated, and, considering their proximity to the main house, offered little privacy. The casual coming and going, the entertaining of friends (and even of fugitive slaves), or the rearing of children apart from a master's dominion were all considerably more difficult under these living conditions than in living-out arrangements.

While living out was conducive to a more private life for a slave family, the ability of individual slaves to form families in cities was more limited than on the plantation. Female slaves generally outnumbered male slaves in most southern cities, reflecting the dominance of domestic work. In Mobile, for example, slave women outnumbered men by a two to one ratio. Industrial cities of the Upper South, however, relied more heavily on male labor. In these cities, men dominated the slave population. Both Louisville and Richmond had more than one-and-a-half

dogs, in the passages of the house."[29]

Some slaves were able to rent out houses, however modest, for themselves and their family. Henry Box Brown, who hired out in a Richmond tobacco factory, paid seventy-two dollars a year for a house; at that, his family had never "been so pleasantly situated before."[30] A British traveler to Richmond noted that "the dwellings occupied by the lower classes of coloured people are of a miserable kind, resembling the worst brick-houses in the back-lanes of English manufacturing towns."[31] Such houses were often located on the urban periphery, outside of areas

Fig. 119.
The considerable contrast between the lives of slaves and some "free persons of color" was particularly apparent in New Orleans. Wearing chains and a slave collar, a gang of one female and three male slaves clean and repair city streets while a well-dressed free black crosses the street in this 1828 lithograph of New Orleans.

times as many male as female slaves in the 1840s and 1850s.

Even if the gender ratios were relatively close, the precarious nature of the male slave's residence in the city rendered stable family life difficult. Unskilled slaves were vulnerable to sale to the countryside, especially during periods of agricultural prosperity. Urban slave populations tended to decline or stabilize during the early 1830s and through most of the 1850s, primarily due to high demand in the plantation South. The rapid expansion of the Cotton Kingdom through the lower Mississippi Valley accounted for the first wave of urban sales, and continued expansion into Texas as well as relatively high prices for cotton contributed to the boom in the 1850s. It is, though, difficult to tell how many slaves who were sold in southern cities were actually urban-based rather than brought in from the countryside. Historians have calculated that a southern slave was likely sold at least once in his or her lifetime. The chances for urban slaves were much greater. One historian has estimated that one in five urban slaves was sold annually in New Orleans. Since the majority of those sold were probably adult males, the threat if not the reality of sale to the countryside was always present for male slaves. One such individual, Peter Randolph, later wrote that "the city slave (whose lot is thought to be so easy) suddenly finds himself

upon the auction-block, knocked down to the highest bidder, and carried far and forever from those dearer to him than life . . . by a fate worse than death."[33] Sometimes a mother and her child or children were sold together, but rarely was an entire family placed on the block in one unit. In the event of sale, in other words, it was unlikely that urban slave families remained intact.

The urban slave trade was extensive even during the winter months, especially in places such as Richmond, Charleston, and New Orleans. Newspapers were filled with advertisements from slave traders; auction blocks and slave pens were often within or on the edge of the major business streets; and coffles (gangs of slaves chained together) paraded into town—each offering the urban slaves a grisly spectacle of what might become their fate. Aside from the visual reinforcement, the thought of field work generated considerable anxiety. William Wells Brown recalled the time he was sold from the city: "As I had been some time out of the field, and not accustomed to work in the burning sun, it was very hard."[34] Not surprisingly, masters and employers found the threat of sale an effective disciplinary tool.

Family life for urban free blacks was relatively more stable than slave family life, though free blacks suffered from similar obstacles. Females predominated among the urban free-black population, especially in the cities of the Deep South such as Mobile and New Orleans where manumission patterns favored women. Still, even in Upper South cities such as Petersburg, free-black women outnumbered men by a three to two ratio. And, in an era when female heads of household were relatively rare, free-black women in Petersburg accounted for more than half of the free-black household heads. In other cities, free-black women comprised a majority or at least a strong minority of household heads.

The prevalence of free-black women as household heads may not, however, have implied that the free-black family structure was weak. In a society that attributed both slavery and freedom to race, the free black was always in a precarious position, none more so than the free-black male, who conjured up all sorts of fears among whites. Given the presence of fugitive slaves (mostly male) in the city, as well as the chance that restrictive laws could be applied arbitrarily, urban free-black males sought to maintain low profiles. Announcing his presence to the census taker, frequently a local white resident, may not have been the wisest course. In some instances, the male in the household may have posed as a slave. Urban free blacks held slaves, of course, but many if not most held those slaves for reasons other than labor exploitation. Slaves held relatives in bondage for the purpose of freeing them, or because ever-tightening manumission laws required such arrangements. In other words, assessing the extent and stability of free-black families is a difficult task.

Unlike slaves, urban free blacks had the opportunity to establish households in relative freedom, though they generally followed similar residential patterns. Urban free blacks, because of limited income, restrictions on movement, and the desire to remain as anonymous as possible, also sought out the alley dwellings, the shacks outside of town, or the stables and warehouses in various parts of the city. Since free blacks had attained a higher occupational status and greater relative acceptance in Deep South cities, residential patterns tended to be more exclusive, though nothing approaching the growing black ghettos of northern cities such as "Nigger Hill" in Boston or "Hayti" in Pittsburgh. In Charleston, for example, Coming Street was the residential heart of the free-black community. In Savannah, little more than half of the free-black population by the 1850s lived in the Oglethorpe ward. Workshops, warehouses, and a railroad depot dominated that neighborhood, making its location least desirable for residential dwellings, but most affordable for free blacks. The ward had few brick dwellings and unlike the city's other wards, contained no public square. These and other free-black districts, though lacking in aesthetics and service amenities, provided the opportunity for fellowship in recreation, religion, and mutual support. It was from these small and tenuous communities that post–Civil War black leadership emerged.

It is more proper to speak of a black community rather than of separate slave and free-black communities in the antebellum urban South. Free blacks and slaves came together in family situations, leisure activities, and in churches. They shared race, a most significant standard of Old South life; they shared living accommodations, work, resistance against and experiences of oppressions real and potential, and the capriciousness of a society unsure of, yet dependent upon, its black population. The interaction was greatest in the cities of the Upper South, where skin color, their own recent life as slaves, small numbers, and a harsh prejudice against free blacks combined to push the free into close association with the enslaved. It was precisely these relationships (many of which, ironically, were occasioned by the hostility and exclusion of white society) that raised alarms among some whites concerned that fraternization would plant destructive thoughts in the mind of slaves.

These concerns were often well founded. Whites often mentioned the Denmark Vesey conspiracy in Charleston in 1822 as an example of the adverse influence free blacks might exercise over slaves. Vesey was a blacksmith who had purchased his freedom in 1800. According to the testimony of other free blacks and slaves, Vesey had planned to rally blacks inside and around the city to gather at strategic points on the night of 16 June, seize the guardhouse and arsenal, and proceed to murder the whites, plunder the city, and escape to the Caribbean. The conspirators never had an opportunity to carry out their plot due to the timely intervention of a slave, Peter Devany Prioleau, who, on the advice of his friend, William Pencil, a free black, informed his master who in turn notified white authorities. Once the hysteria had subsided by the late summer and thirty-five blacks executed for their alleged role in the plot, the Vesey conspiracy became a symbol of the dangers posed by free blacks, and especially by free black-slave associations (ignoring the fact that just such a relationship uncovered the plot).[35]

Whites did not require proof of murderous conspiracies to doubt the wisdom of free black-slave connections. In 1858, the *New Orleans Times-Picayune* claimed the existence of an organization of slaves and free blacks that transferred freedom papers from ex-slaves living in the North to slaves in New Orleans. There were also peri-

140

Fig. 120.
In an illustration bordering on caricature, fashionably dressed African-Americans enjoy themselves at a Vicksburg, Mississippi, dance. A Richmond woman complained in 1857 that "when we see [African-Americans] thronging the streets and stores, well cloaked, cravated, and crinolined . . . there is not much of slavery in their appearance."

odic complaints in port cities that free-black pilots or seamen passed information and literature on to slaves or, worse, helped to hide fugitives. Some cities passed ordinances prohibiting free blacks from entering the water-transport trades for these reasons, but as with most legislation restraining occupations or work relationships, they were of limited effectiveness.

Despite the perceived dangers of such relationships, free blacks and slaves consorted often and even openly in antebellum southern society. After work especially, there were numerous opportunities for camaraderie between the two. All southern cities possessed taverns, grog shops, and grocery stores that served food and drink to patrons at reasonable prices. Many of these establishments were concentrated in the least desirable parts of town typically inhabited by blacks and working-class whites. They were the poor men's social clubs of the era. Although it was illegal to serve liquor to slaves throughout the urban South, the shops' proprietors (who were typically white) rarely bothered to distinguish between slave and free customers and only occasionally were they hauled before the authorities to answer for their conduct. The problem was less the sale of alcohol to slaves than the alleged plots that might be hatched in such a convivial and heady atmosphere. As one New Orleans journalist observed, the shops were "places of temptation to the lower classes, where intoxication can be cheaply purchased, where mobs and caucuses of our Slaves nightly assemble at their orgies, to inflame the brains with copious libations, and preach rebellions against their white masters."[36]

Still, it was nearly impossible for city authorities to stop the illicit traffic, or the assemblages of free blacks and slaves on these premises. The frustrated mayor of Mobile, who had vowed to clean up such dens, complained that "for the convenience of [black] guests side and back doors are provided sufficiently numerous to assist a spiriting of the 'spirits' out of sight when *necessary*." Even when caught, proprietors often escaped punishment. To the charge that they were serving brandy to blacks, "the keeper of the cabaret and his employees . . . swore positively that it was sasparilla and water." Case dismissed. A South Carolina legislative committee, investigating the situation in Charleston grog shops, blamed "the combinations which are formed by the Army of Retailers for defeating and eluding the vigilance of the strictest police."[37] The ineffectiveness of the legal constraints against the liquor trade not only underscores the sovereignty of free enterprise in the urban South, but also indirectly demonstrates the extent to which slaves and free blacks were allowed to consort with each other during leisure hours.

A more sedate, but equally common, means of getting together was visiting. Since free blacks and slaves who lived out often resided in close proximity to each other, if not in the same household, visiting must have occurred regularly. Given the inherent instability of black family life in the city and the constraints on black life in general,

visiting enabled blacks to develop an informal support network as well as to fulfill social needs. In each other's dwellings, they could discuss such taboo subjects as the sectional crisis, emancipation, and escape; they could vent frustration and anger at whites; they could pass down stories of family and past generations; and they could share neighborhood gossip. Similar interactions occurred in the evenings on the plantation, but urban blacks had more mobility and less direct white surveillance. There were no overseers and few masters in black urban districts.

Perhaps the most open and extensive fellowship between urban free blacks and slaves occurred on Sundays. Sunday provided the chance to break from the world of work and regimentation. They expressed this limited freedom by frequenting the grog shops (which were open on Sundays), visiting, dressing up, and going to church. The first two were also weekday activities; dressing up, however, was usually reserved for Sundays and provided an opportunity for self-expression in a society that frowned on black individuality.

Visitors frequently commented on such Sabbath finery, a sharp contrast to the drab costumes of the workweek. Marianne Finch, an English visitor to Richmond, noted that a black person "only appears in full-bloom on a Sunday, and then he is a very striking object; whether male, or female, whether in silks and muslins; or beaver and broadcloth."[38] Frederick Law Olmsted admired the black women he saw in Richmond:

"Many of the coloured ladies were dressed not only expensively, but with good taste and effect, after the latest Parisian mode. Some of them were very attractive in appearance, and would have produced a decided sensation in any European drawing-room."[39]

Others were more shocked than impressed by such displays. Antebellum southern society placed considerable emphasis on show; a fine house, expensive appointments, and fashionable clothes helped to define the status of a lady or gentleman. Clothing, in other words, was a reflection of an individual's place in society. It was inconceivable and irritating to some that those with the least status—African-Americans—should presume to be something they were not—full and equal citizens of southern urban society. A writer to a Charleston newspaper in 1832 expressed this view, relating that he saw a man walking in front of him whose manner and dress reminded him of a friend. "I therefore quickened my pace, came up, and slapt him on the shoulders, but, to my no small surprize . . . a sable Dandy stared me in the face." The chagrined writer complained, "how shall I distinguish our coloured Dandies and Dandresses from a Gentleman or Lady?"[40] Coming in the wake of the Vesey conspiracy, such violations of etiquette were difficult to swallow. Soon, a Charleston grand jury proposed requiring blacks to dress "only in coarse stuffs" because "every distinction should be created between the whites and the negroes, calculated to make the latter feel the superiority of the former."[41] The proposal went nowhere, although dress codes for blacks continued to be a contentious issue among some white southerners. In 1859, a Charleston free black was mobbed by whites, ostensibly because of his flashy attire.

Sunday was a day not just for drinking, visiting, or dressing up; in fact, for many, these activities were extraneous to the day's major function as the Sabbath. If clothing represented a rare public expression of individuality, the black urban church was the ultimate private expression of the African-American spirit.

Black urban churches owed their origins to the wave of black religious conversions that occurred during and after the Great Awakening in the 1740s. The evangelical sects—Baptist, Methodist, and Presbyterian—were especially eager for slave conversions. At the same time, the antislavery stance of some of these groups and their emphasis on God's rather than man's law were attractive to blacks. Some whites also found the egalitarian message of the new religious enthusiasm alluring. Though the vast majority of southern blacks and whites remained outside any church whatsoever, the Baptists and Methodists were gaining adherents. The evangelicals impressed on the masters the importance of religious training for their slaves, even while denouncing the institution of slavery. In 1785, the General Committee of the Virginia Baptist Church stated succinctly that "hereditary slavery [is] contrary to the Word of God."[42] By 1800, however, economic realities as well as the desire for increased membership and respectability muted or silenced the evangelicals' antislavery rhetoric.

Their basic tenets, however, remained attractive to southern blacks. Their presence in interracial evangelical congregations was less often an example of coercion by white masters eager to impart lessons of obedience (though such occurred, of course) than because black southerners were eager to hear the Gospel and express their joy at God's work. Frederick Douglass's conversion to evangelical Christianity in the 1820s was doubtless repeated many times. As he recalled it,

weeks I was a poor, broken-hearted mourner traveling through doubts and fears, I finally found my burden lightened, and my heart relieved. I loved all mankind, slaveholders not excepted. . . . I saw the world in a new light, and my great concern was to have everybody converted.[43]

While most southern blacks, Douglass included, typically worshiped in interracial churches (though they were segregated by seating), they increasingly founded their own churches, especially in cities where there was a sufficient number of blacks close enough to one another and at least some black capital to support a church building and its activities. Independent black churches began to emerge in southern cities as early as the 1770s. Black Baptists established churches in Williamsburg, Augusta, and Savannah during the revolutionary era. In Savannah, the First African Baptist Church grew so quickly that by 1803 two new black Baptist churches appeared in the city. All three had free-black ministers.

Whites were of two minds on the creation of separate black churches. On the one hand, worship services were preferable to the more secular and raucous diversions possible in southern cities. Also, some whites took seriously the evangelical clergy's admonition that masters had a duty to convert slaves to Christianity. The growth of black churches was gratifying proof that genuine conversion was occurring. There was also the simple matter of logistics. The popularity of evangelical

Fig. 122.
Founded in 1841 as an autonomous black congregation, Richmond's First African Baptist Church counted both slaves and free blacks among its members. First African's important community activities included church-sponsored benevolent societies that paid for burials and cared for the old and sick.

I was not more than thirteen years old, when, in my loneliness and destitution, I longed for some one to whom I could go, as to a father and protector. The preaching of a white Methodist minister . . . was the means of causing me to feel that in God I had such a friend. He thought that all men, great and small, bond and free, were sinners in the sight of God; that they were by nature rebels against [H]is government; and that they must repent of their sins, and be reconciled to God through Christ. . . . Though for

theology among blacks filled interracial churches to more than capacity—the alternative was to build new and bigger churches or let blacks organize their own. Considering the price of urban lots and construction, the latter was easier. Sometimes the black congregation existed as an adjunct of a white church, with a white minister overseeing the services, though usually in a perfunctory manner. More often, blacks went off with the white congregation's blessing; the whites were relieved to be spared any additional expense as well as the spectacle of the emotional and demonstrative worship patterns of black congregants.

Whites were concerned, though, about unsupervised assemblages, especially under the leadership of free-black preachers. They were well aware that the gospel was open to varying interpretations and that religion might not be the only topic at services. The leadership opportunities that churches provided, the possibility that Sunday schools were employed for teaching reading and writing, and the independence blacks might feel with their own building, minister, and worship style all ran counter to prevailing notions of the black's place in southern society. As a group of white Charlestonians noted in 1847, independent black churches gave blacks such a "plentitude of freedom of thought, word and action" that they might get "excited by the privileges they enjoy, as a separate and to some extent independent society."[44]

Charleston whites may have been especially sensitive to this issue since they believed that the black churches fomented the Vesey conspiracy. After authorities uncovered the plot, a mob destroyed the city's black Methodist church and officials began an harassment of black congregations that lasted the remainder of the antebellum period. Yet, despite these views, there were an estimated six thousand black Methodists in Charleston during the 1850s and, even as tolerance plummeted late in the decade, the Presbyterians erected a new twenty-five-thousand-dollar church exclusively for a thousand-member slave and free-black congregation.

White ambivalence notwithstanding, urban blacks continued to establish churches, especially after the early 1840s when another evangelical wave swept the South. Also, black urban populations had by then increased to a point that many congregations had outgrown their buildings or been split by theological or personal disagreements. Equally important was the splitting of national evangelical church organizations. Baptists, Methodists, and Presbyterians purged their ranks of antislavery remnants while redoubling their efforts to bring the gospel to slaves. Blacks

thus took the opportunity to found new churches, even in smaller communities. In Macon, Georgia, for example, blacks between 1845 and 1860 formed separate Baptist, Methodist, and Presbyterian churches.

Urban blacks were active in other religious denominations as well. An Episcopal church in Charleston, occupied by free blacks and slaves, was the target of mob wrath in 1849, though police dispersed the crowd before any damage occurred. Worshipping in interracial churches, black Catholics existed throughout the South, with a heavy concentration in New Orleans. But the predominantly Irish clergy had little understanding or appreciation of black Catholics. In New Orleans, white Catholics forced the Holy Family nuns to abandon their mission to the city's blacks. Affluent free people of color, however, were able to isolate themselves from the Irish clergy, preferring to maintain ties to their French heritage. They were also active in establishing charities directed at needy black families, though they never attempted to establish a separate black Catholic church. In fact, there were no black Catholic churches anywhere in antebellum America. It is not surprising, then, that after the Civil War black Catholics often converted to one of the evangelical denominations or to the African Methodist Episcopal (A.M.E.) or African Methodist Episcopal Zion (A.M.E. Zion) churches.

Formed from interracial Methodist churches, the A.M.E. church was born of the 1816 merger of a black church in Baltimore and another in Philadelphia; in 1822 another Philadelphia congregation joined with a New York congregation to form the A.M.E. Zion church. Both churches recruited actively in the South, but with difficulty and little success—though in Charleston as many as fourteen hundred blacks (mostly slaves) were members of the A.M.E. church in the early 1820s, only to be routed in the wake of the Vesey conspiracy. Whites closed down a New Orleans congregation a decade later, enforcing an ordinance banning any black organization not under the control of whites. The fact that blacks typically included the word *African* in the name of their church underscores the close connection between religion and ethnic identity. There were an estimated twenty-two black churches, headed by black ministers, in the eleven largest southern cities by 1860. And there were countless other congregations that met secretly or as adjuncts to white churches.

White visitors often noticed the contrast between the blacks' services and their own—a difference born of the African-Americans' distinctive experience and cultural heritage. Some visitors

were shocked. Frederick Law Olmsted saw the service as "a delusive clothing of Christian forms and phrases" added to "the original vague superstition of the African savage." Clapping, singing, shouting, and even dancing punctuated the minister's sermon. Yet Olmsted was not unmoved by the scene. He described an old black man responding to the preacher: "Oh, yes! That's it, that's it! Yes, yes—glory—yes!" Soon the congregation erupted into "shouts, and groans, terrific shrieks, and indescribable expressions of ecstasy—of pleasure or agony—and even stamping, jumping, and clapping of hands." Olmsted found "my own muscles all stretched, as if ready for a struggle —my face glowing, and my feet stamping."[45] A more sympathetic white observer from New England left this account of a black service in antebellum Louisville:

The meeting commences with singing,

through the congregation. Loud and louder still, were their devotions—and oh! what music, what devotion, what streaming eyes, and throbbing hearts; my blood runs quick in my veins, and quicker still, as they proceed and warm up in this part of the exercises. It seems as though the roof would rise from the walls, and some of them go up, soul and body both.[46]

Though some southern whites disapproved, they did not interfere. They believed that the service offered a release of energy and emotion otherwise prohibited in antebellum southern society. They also believed the sermons could reinforce prevailing notions of race. When white ministers officiated over black churches that was sometimes the case, but when blacks assumed the pulpits the opposite often occurred. Some black ministers avoided contemporary and racial issues entirely, preferring to move their congregations with lurid sermons of sin and damnation. Others, however, succeeded in weaving more worldly themes into their remarks, even if indirectly. Visiting a Baptist church in Savannah, Fredrika Bremer described such a minister recollecting the visit of the president of the United States to a local wealthy resident. Blacks and other poor residents had been cordoned off, while members of the local elite entered the house to pay their respects. "Now, did Christ come in this way? No! Blessed be the Lord! He came to the poor! He came to us, and for our sakes," the preacher cried. Bremer recalled that cries of "'Amen! Hallelujah!' resounded through the chapel for a good minute or two; and the people stamped with their feet, and laughed and cried, with countenances beaming with joy."[47]

An important member of his community, the black preacher alone could openly, if indirectly, express the conditions and aspirations of slave and free black alike. Since most professions were closed to free blacks, talented black men went into the ministry. They often held other positions during the week, however, as congregations composed primarily of slaves could offer only a pittance of a salary. Once in the pulpit, ministers had to satisfy both their congregation and those whites who might visit occasionally. Successful ministers learned to be circumspect without being obsequious and exercised their leadership outside the pulpit in educational and social matters quietly but effectively.

Andrew Marshall, noted earlier, was one such minister. He served as pastor of the First African Baptist Church in Savannah for over thirty years, organizing benevolent societies to aid elderly free blacks and providing pensions to widows and children of deceased members. Free-black women in his congregation performed missionary work among the city's black poor. In 1826, Marshall initiated a Sunday school for two hundred members, mostly slaves. The school at first operated under the guidance of a white Presbyterian church but in 1835 passed to his parish's control. Marshall's caution served him and his congregation well; white Baptist churches invited him to preach, whites worshipped in his church, and he became the first black minister to address the Georgia legislature. When he began in the early 1820s, First African had a thousand members; by the mid-1830s the church had grown to nearly twenty-five hundred slaves and free blacks.[48]

Like Marshall, black ministers led their congregations in matters transcending religion. But whereas a good deal of associational life in the black urban community emanated from the black church, formal educational institutions for blacks were rare. And if they existed at all, they periodically met with strong opposition, even violence. Francis Pinckney Holloway, a prominent free black in Charleston, opened a private school solely for free blacks, but eventually had to flee the city in the face of threats against his school and person. Free blacks in Richmond opened a night school for freedmen and slaves in 1811 only to see it soon destroyed by angry whites. Henry Morehead recalled attending a clandestine night school in Louisville. "My owners used to object to my going to school," he later recalled, "saying that I could learn rascality enough without it." Their response "dampened my feeling for getting learning, somewhat, but I went to a night school, at my own expense of course, to learn to spell and to read. My owners found it out, and set policemen to break the school up." Such "put an end to my schooling—that was all the schooling I ever had."[49]

There was no legitimate, institutionalized way that urban blacks, especially slaves, could obtain an education in the Old South. When southern cities established rudimentary public education during the 1850s, only Mobile provided for black education at public expense. (In fact, Mobile merely subsidized an already existing program for free-black Creoles.) Some blacks learned by picking up newspapers or pamphlets, or through the benevolence of a master or mistress, or a white colleague at work. But many learned to read and write from ministers in Sunday school classes or in secret sessions in the church basement on weeknights. Although it is not possible to venture a guess at the degree of black literacy in the antebellum urban South, visitors who were aware of the laws against learning were astonished by what they saw. As one traveler to several southern cities observed, "many slaves have learned to read in spite of all prohibitions." In Richmond, for example, "I am informed, almost every slave-child is learning to read."[50] Though obviously an exaggeration, the black church played an important role in eliciting that impression.

Church membership also provided the basis for mutual aid and benevolent societies that pooled the resources of one or several congregations. Aside from promoting black fellowship and welfare, these associations underscored the very real differences between black life on a plantation and in the city. Seldom did plantation blacks have a chance to form their own churches; even rarer were the instances of black rural organizations. Although not as extensive as similar black groups in the North, the southern versions offered a modest amount of support, especially for free blacks.

The extent of black benevolent societies is

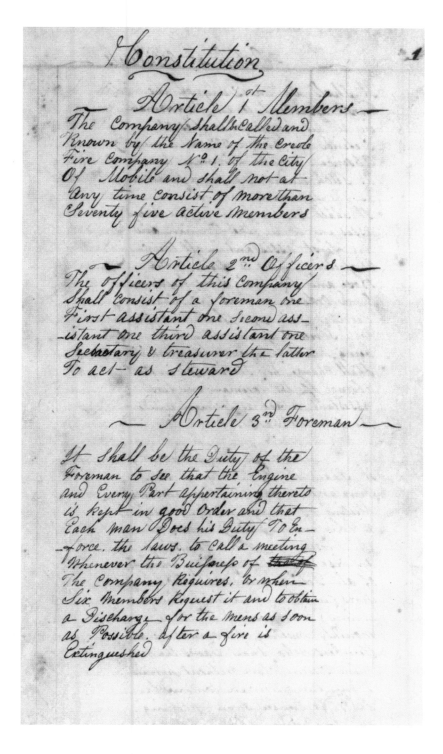

Fig. 124.
Formed in 1819 in Mobile, Alabama, the Creole Fire Company was typical of the frater-nal societies formed by elite, urban free blacks. Among other regulations, the detailed consti-tution stipulated that any member "found guilty of conduct unbecoming a gentleman" was to be fined and reprimanded.

unknown because few African-Americans applied for state charters, as did their white counterparts, who were in any case uncomfortable with any assemblage of blacks. Benevolent societies dispensed donations from affluent blacks to the black poor, while mutual aid societies collected funds to support any members who were unemployed, ill, or unable to afford a decent burial. As early as 1783, free blacks in New Orleans organized the Perseverance Benevolence and Mutual Aid Association; in 1790, elite free blacks in Charleston founded the Brown Fellowship Society as a mutual-aid association. The Minors Moralist Society, of Charleston, composed of affluent free blacks, funded the education of poor and orphaned free-black children. Free-black women also organized societies such as the New Orleans Colored Female Benevolent Society, founded in 1846, dedicated to the "suppression of vice and inculcation of virtue among the colored class," and formed "to relieve the sick and bury the dead."[51] Free blacks also joined national fraternal organizations such as the Masons.

A common feature of these groups was the insistence on proper burial for blacks. In a society that afforded African-Americans little dignity, funerals took on significance as distinctive cultural expressions. They were also another way to escape white surveillance, which accounts in great part for why blacks lingered so long at funeral services and embellished them with music and song. As one historian noted, "the funeral became one of the most important occasions in the social life of many black communities."[52] It was a high social occasion, a time to dress in the uniform of the mutual-aid or fraternal organization, an opportunity for eloquence, and a good excuse for socializing. Whites, though, complained about these events. According to one Charleston resident, "Three or Four, sometimes every evening in the week, there are Funerals of Negroes, accompanied by processions of 3, 4, and 5 hundred Negroes and a tumultuous crowd of other slaves who disturb all the inhabitants around the burying Ground."[53] Although whites complained as they did about any gathering of blacks, they nevertheless generally respected the black way of death, as funerals were sacred to them as well.

Some of these organizations were separate from churches, but nearly all were infused with religious principles and drew their members from the various congregations. And while they helped to create both the sense and reality of an African-American urban community, the blacks' associational life also reflected the fissures within that society. Whites often feared that free blacks and slaves would make common purpose, but commonality was often difficult, especially in Lower

South cities with lengthy traditions of affluent free-black populations. It is not surprising that whites in these cities were less frequently concerned about the free blacks' machinations against institutions or white society in general. But even in other parts of the South, divisions existed in black communities that made concerted action within the constraints of a biracial society less probable.

Legal status provided the obvious basis of distinction within the antebellum urban-black community. Despite or perhaps because of the efforts of white society to compress the two groups into a caste of color, free blacks not only sought to protect their legal differences from slaves but also maintain their distance as well. These efforts were especially evident in Deep South cities where color, status, and ethnic differences between free blacks and slaves were most apparent. In these cities, light skin was a badge of freedom, though dark-skinned free blacks existed. Among the Deep South's heavily urbanized free-black population, more than 75 percent was mulatto, compared with a region-wide figure of 10 percent. Free blacks were also likely to be relatively well-off, have ties to the white community (Louisiana law, for example, required every free black to have a white guardian), and, in New Orleans and Mobile at least, have French ancestry.

The divisions between free blacks and slaves in the Deep South's cities were more complex than skin color, however. The ethnic dimension was especially important in the Gulf Coast cities, even transcending legal status. The key distinction in New Orleans was between "Latin Negroes" and "American Negroes." The former resided in the French quarter, the latter in the American district. Theaters in the Crescent City provided separate seating for the "free people of color," apart from both white and black patrons. In Mobile, Creole free blacks (those with French or Spanish ancestry) were distinguished by law from other free blacks and from slaves. There were religious differences as well, with Creole blacks (slave and free) more often belonging to the Catholic church. In both cities, Creole blacks sent their children to French- and Spanish-language schools.

Class divisions also separated free blacks from each other and from slaves, too. Elite free blacks (never more than 10 percent of the free-black population in a given city) such as Natchez barber William Johnson identified with white society, held slaves, and looked with condescension toward their less-well-off brethren, both slave and free. They were likely to have white protectors or benefactors and generally escaped the periodic crackdowns on free-black privileges. In Charleston, the free-black elite established their own association, the Brown Fellowship Society, intermarried, attended the Episcopal church, concentrated in certain occupations such as tailoring, and had close ties with white elites.

Ironically, the black church, perhaps the single most unifying element in the antebellum black community, also reflected the divisions within that same community. In the early 1800s, an interracial Methodist church in Norfolk had integrated seating for blacks and whites, but free blacks seated themselves separately from slaves. Free-black elites typically attended interracial churches rather than independent African ones. The interracial churches were likely to be Episcopalian or Presbyterian where the service was more sedate than in the African-Methodist or African-Baptist churches with their poorer free blacks and slaves. In the Gulf Coast cities, it was not unusual for Creole free blacks to purchase pews in the cathedral.

Divisions within black urban communities paled in the 1850s as white society, for a variety of reasons, sought to compress black society. The heightening sectional controversy, the changing nature of southern cities, the increasing political and economic power of the urban white working class, and the white elite's anxieties about all these trends created a decade of uncertainty and turmoil for southern urban blacks. In many respects, the 1850s presaged the post–Civil War years in terms of white attempts to limit black freedoms and in terms of blacks, especially free blacks, seeking to counter those threats.

Southern cities in the 1850s were generally whiter than they had been at any other time in the nineteenth century. A combination of increased white migration, both from abroad and from the countryside, the selling or return of slaves to the booming agricultural economy, and growing restrictions on the presence, livelihoods, and mobility of free blacks together accounted for the trend. Although urban slave populations demonstrated a cyclical pattern throughout the antebellum period, the relative decline was especially significant during the 1850s. Slave populations declined absolutely in Charleston, Louisville, New Orleans, and Norfolk, while they increased at a slower rate than in previous decades in Mobile, Richmond, and Savannah. Smaller cities, where white migration was less significant, were less sensitive to the attractions of a prosperous agricultural economy. Baton Rouge, Little Rock, Macon, and Natchez experienced strong increases in their respective slave populations during the 1850s. On the other hand, during the same period the free-black population increased (though at lower rates than before) in

Fig. 125.
Charleston's use of badges gave whites some measure of control over the labor performed by African-Americans. Although the regulations were at first restricted to slaves and not closely enforced, in 1848 the city instituted further regulations that required free blacks as well as slaves to register their names and occupations and to wear the distinctive tags.

all the major southern cities except Charleston. The great boom occurred in the foreign-born population, continuing a trend begun in the 1840s. By 1860, 44.5 percent of the white inhabitants in New Orleans were foreign-born, while Savannah, Mobile, Louisville, and Memphis registered one-third of the population as foreign-born. As noted earlier, the percentage of these newcomers in the work force was even higher, since the vast majority were young adults.

While southern cities were becoming more pluralistic, they were also becoming more complex. The urban South experienced its greatest decade of growth in the 1850s, sharing a national trend. New areas of the cities opened to accommodate their populations. City services, previously perfunctory, now became more routinized as local government expanded its responsibilities. Police and fire services, street numbering, public health measures, street paving and repair, and welfare services were initiated or measurably expanded. There were also additional pressures on local officials as several states expanded their suffrage rights to include all adult white males. The Democratic party in particular sought to integrate the newcomers into the political process, a tactic that both heightened government accountability and raised nativist concerns. The southern city became more fragmented, more separated into different racial, ethnic, and status groups. As southern society pulled together to encounter a common enemy, the North, and, more particularly, the Republican party, the demography of the urban South posed a potential threat to southern unity. The dilemma for local leaders was how to order the increasingly disparate urban environment and yet retain both its economic vitality and political orthodoxy.

Local leaders faced other pressures as well. As

the sectional crisis worsened, white southerners feared that the growing economic dominance of the Northeast would eventually result in the political subjugation of their region. The concern increased as an avowedly sectional party—the Republican party—emerged in the mid-1850s. In an attempt to compete with northeastern cities and reduce financial dependence on northern merchants and brokers, leaders of the urban South launched programs to build railroads, extend international trade, and develop indigenous industry. The attempt, which fell short of its objectives, served further to heighten anxieties and sectional tensions, especially when it appeared that the Republican party would gain control of both the White House and the Congress in 1860. These three factors—changes in the South's urban population, the role of its cities in the national economy, and increasing sectionalism—formed the context within which the racial policies of the 1850s were formulated and implemented.

Southern cities and states legislated new restrictions against slaves and free blacks and renewed enforcement of old legislation that had temporarily lapsed. Given the context of the 1850s, the reasons for these measures included a desire to maximize the efficiency of a limited supply of labor, a response to pressures from increasingly influential white workingmen, anxieties over internal security, and concern about the future of slavery. Policies bore most heavily on the free blacks. Slaves had "built-in" protectors in their masters; free blacks also had white supporters, but the financial link was much weaker. Free blacks, in other words, were more vulnerable to the shifting trends.

Fig. 126.
Only two antebellum free-black tags survive from Charleston, South Carolina, both ironically decorated with the liberty cap.

The general direction of legislation and re-enforcement during the 1850s was to reduce the distinction between free black and slave. Especially late in the decade, after the Panic of 1857, after John Brown's raid on Harpers Ferry in 1859, and after the rise to prominence of the Republican party, white southerners—particularly working-class whites—sought to eliminate or reduce drastically this anomalous class. Many agreed with the *Mobile Register*'s statement in 1859 that "We can have a healthy State of society with but two classes—white and slave."[54] This was not a new crusade. Limits on manumission and free-black civil rights had existed since the late eighteenth century. Also, after the Gabriel conspiracy in Richmond in 1800, the Denmark Vesey conspiracy in Charleston in 1822, and the Nat Turner rebellion in southside Virginia in 1831, southern states and cities levied harsh new laws against free blacks, though their enforcement was deferred.

The changes in manumission legislation reflected both these trends and the worsening racial climate of the 1850s. After chipping away at individuals' ability to manumit slaves, southern states finally closed the door to freedom during the 1830s, permitting manumission only by judicial or legislative decree. By the late 1850s, most southern states had locked the door, prohibiting manumission altogether. Although these were statewide measures, they affected southern cities most directly since, after 1830, while manumissions had declined in the countryside, they increased in the city despite the need to obtain outside permission.

Urban masters were also more resourceful in getting around restrictions on liberation. Unable directly to manumit a slave, they executed a deed of trust, that is they "sold" a slave to a friend, or even to a free-black relative, for a nominal sum (usually one dollar), stipulating, as a Charleston mistress did, that "Kitty and Mary shall enjoy free and undisturbed liberty as if they had been regularly emancipated."[55] These "slaves," then, had virtual freedom. The practice of evading state law was so common in Mobile, for example, that city census takers established the category of "quasi-free people of color." Free blacks, after the 1830s, secured the freedom of many of their kin in this way, designating a white guardian in a deed of trust.

In the eyes of the law, however, they were still slaves, and their offspring were slaves as well. During the 1850s, authorities in South Carolina decided to enforce the 1822 state law prohibiting manumissions. Therefore, any black unable to prove manumission prior to that date was a slave, regardless of any deed of trust or other arrangement. The crackdown was especially hard on

Charleston's free blacks since, as one white observed in 1848, there were "evasions [of the 1822 law] without number."[56] In connection with the renewed enforcement of an 1820s law requiring slaves to wear badges in order to obtain work, the strictures posed a dilemma for the city's blacks. To work without a badge one had to prove freedom—either the black or his mother or grandmother (since freedom descended from the mother's line) had to have been manumitted prior to 1822 and possess the papers to prove it. If the authorities arrested a black without a badge and the individual could not prove his or her freedom, the penalty was typically appropriation of the black and the black's property by the city. But to buy a badge was an admission that one was not, in fact, a free black, but a slave. Charleston's officials swooped into action during the spring of 1860, a time of heightened sectional tension and growing political power among white workingmen (1860 was the first time in the city's history that census takers had recorded a white majority). Arrests of "slaves" working without badges increased from zero in March to twenty-seven in April and up to ninety-three in August. In a sense, the sweep was an attempt to re-enslave free blacks.

The implications of the new restrictions and re-enforcements were perhaps the most tragic, but not the only example, of increased racial tensions during the 1850s. The cities also fashioned extensive black codes that prescribed slave and free-black behavior and served as prototypes for the codes used during Reconstruction. The regulations were usually more restrictive in the cities of the Upper South, where free blacks and slaves mingled more often, than in some of the Gulf Coast cities where free blacks often stood apart from slaves and where whites were content to stress the differences between the two black groups. Richmond authorities, for example, passed a new code in 1857 that proved typical. The regulation banned self-hiring by slaves; it drastically reduced the ability of blacks to assemble without white supervision; it required a slave or free black to obtain a pass from his master or employer designating "the particular place or places" where he could go; it excluded blacks altogether from certain parts of the city unless to "attend to a white person"; the code also specified street etiquette, prohibiting smoking, carrying a cane, standing on the sidewalk, or using "provoking language."[57] The law also assigned fines for whites who helped blacks to evade any of these provisions. Such provisions had been discussed and some even implemented in numerous southern cities prior to the 1850s. But only in that decade were all of these measures codified

Fig. 127.
Working-class whites deeply resented the economic opportunities and privileges accorded to urban slaves and free blacks—and wanted such concessions removed. In a petition published in a Charleston, South Carolina, newspaper in 1860, white protestors asked, "Is it not a public evil which compels the citizen . . . to place himself in competition and rivalry upon an apparently equal footing with the service or colored race?"

——o——

PETITION OF THE MECHANICS, ARTIZANS, AND OTHERS, of the City of Charleston, praying the enactment of a law to prevent free negros or persons of color from carrying on any trade, calling, or occupation, in their own name or the name of others.

To the Honorable the Senate and House of Representatives of South Carolina, now met sitting in General Assembly.

The petition of the undersigned Mechanics, Artizans, and others, of the City of Charleston, respectfully showeth unto your Honorable Body,

That it is a prevailing and common practice, in the City of Charleston, for free negros and persons of color to carry on and conduct mechanical and other pursuits, as contractors and masters.

That it is also common for slaves to do the same thing, sometimes, and not unfrequently, in their own names, and sometimes in the names and under the nominal, and merely nominal, cover and protection of white or free persons of color.

Your petitioners show to your Honorable Body that these are serious public evils, and a great grievance to your petitioners especially.

That the existing state of the law operates to produce, and does produce and encourage, these evils and grievances.

The existence of the facts which your petitioners charge will not be denied or doubted—that they are public evils; that they are special grievances, operating peculiarly upon your petitioners; and that they are encouraged by the conditions of the law, which, as it now stands, is unjust and unfair to your petitioners, and draws, practically, a degrading distinction between them and their pursuits, and other classes and their pursuits, they will endeavor briefly to show. They think it can be shown, if it is admitted, and they hope it will be, that the mechanic or artisan who understands, and is capable of conducting, his business, must be endowed with intellectual powers above what are necessary for mere manual labor.

The propositions which your petitioners have stated, are supported by reasons which so run into one another, that they may be dealt with and brought to your view collectively, and in this way a desirable brevity may be attained in urging upon your honorable body your petitioners' claims to consideration and relief.

Under the existing state of the law, every other pursuit, except such as your petitioners are engaged in, where skill and intelligence are required, above what is necessary to the mere laborer, is carefully protected by stringent enactments of law against the intrusion of the colored and slave races.

The merchant is not allowed to employ his slave, or a free negro or colored person, as his clerk; so, too, is it of the wharfinger, of the lawyer, of the doctor, the tradesman, and the shop-keeper; all these avocations, and all others, whatever they may be, are, as your petitioners understand it, protected by law from the intrusion of the colored race. The law does not allow them the chance of an equality, and it makes it a penal offence for those who attempt it in any other pursuit, except in the mechanic arts. This is unjust and unfair. It might be enough to say that all laws which are unjust and unfair, are public evils.

But your petitioners further show, as a fact, that under the operation of these laws, the colored races, excluded from other pursuits, have been tempted—in fact, driven—to become mechanics, and have taken the place, to a large extent, of the intelligent white youths, who, in former times, selected such pursuits as avocations for life, by which they could hope to rise in position, respectability and independence among their fellow-citizens. The reason of this effect of the operation of the law is manifest. It is because they are placed upon a footing of unequal rivalry with the colored race; and this the white race among us will not, and ought not to be expected to consent to.

Is not that a public evil which compels the citizen, or any one of the dominant race, to abandon the pursuit of his choice, or to place himself in competition and rivalry upon an apparently equal footing with the servile or colored race? —a rivalry, too, where the chances of success are unequal, unless he will reduce his manner of living, his deportment, and personal bearing, to the level of a menial.

Is there any one so hardy as to say that it is good policy to reduce any portion of our white population, or to elevate any portion of our colored population to equal condition and standing? The suggestion itself carries with it to intelligent and thinking minds instant conviction of the unwise and unfair condition of things, encouraged, if not created, by the law itself.

The parent who, from necessity, or from the high consideration "that labor is honorable," seeks employment for the child, in which he can rise to eminence, will turn from that which is accessible to negros as competitors, and seek for him that which is not. All others are open to him, and from all others the negro race is excluded as competitors. Will he seek the Mechanic Arts? Assuredly not. The effect, the inevitable effect of this is to degrade the Mechanics, and to drive away from their homes those active and enterprising young men who may not be able to find employment in the over-crowded pursuits not subject to this evil; depopulating our cities and towns, and sending from us those who might and would be a pride and blessing in any well regulated community.

——o——

together into a comprehensive code.

Other city ordinances reflected both the changing nature of the southern city and the growing racial tensions. Segregation, evident in churches and theaters since the late eighteenth century, spread as southern cities developed new institutions and technologies. Cities began to segregate jails, hospitals, and public burial grounds as they became local responsibilities after the 1830s. When horse-drawn railways appeared in the 1850s, some cities such as New Orleans and Richmond kept separate cars for blacks. Segregation went further in New Orleans—given the three-caste system of slaves, free blacks, and whites—as authorities provided for three separate graveyards. The city also insisted on segregated brothels, though in this instance the categories were reduced to two, black and white. Segregated seating prevailed in interracial churches, though both whites and blacks continued to prefer separate churches for each race. This preference clashed, however, with the new restraints on black gatherings. A "solution" was for black churches, increasingly harassed, to affiliate formally with a white church. In 1859, for instance, all four black congregations in New Orleans placed themselves under a white Baptist church. Their slave ministers then worked with the direction of a white minister.

In some cases, blacks were not only segregated, they were excluded. The rise of the public school in southern cities during the 1850s is a case in point. Exclusion from certain employment is another. Charleston, for example, prohibited teaching slaves artisanal crafts. Blacks were also excluded (except as staff or as assistants to white masters) from hotels and restaurants.

Many of these new restrictions (and their enforcement) limited the role of blacks in the urban economy. The limitation was not coincidental; white workingmen supported and, in numerous instances, initiated such legislation or clamored for enforcement of existing measures. They had protested before, of course, but their growing political power, increasing economic importance (as unskilled slaves left for the countryside), and the anxieties generated by the free-black population helped white workers win new adherents among local leaders.

Ethnic politics also emerged during the 1850s. Charleston's white elite added Irish and German candidates to their citywide tickets; in Savannah, police harassment of immigrant shopkeepers became an important municipal issue. Native-born politicians, especially Democrats, courted immigrant votes. Thomas Avery, a successful congressional candidate whose district included an Irish neighborhood in Memphis, felt concerned about taking his three daughters to a labor-union party at which the young Irish men would expect them to dance. Avery expressed his appreciation to the girls for what had been distasteful both to himself and to them: "You have done splendidly. I know how you feel, but luckily I don't think those fellows know. You made them think you were having the time of your life. It will make them feel kindly toward me."[58]

Workingmen's clubs and unions grew in the 1850s along both ethnic and craft lines—such as, for example, the Irish union that Avery visited or the New Orleans Typographical Society, made up of native-born craftsmen. Under these new circumstances, it is not surprising that the measures white workers had been advocating so unsuccessfully for decades became law in the 1850s. Since the 1820s, for instance, white butchers in Savannah had tried to eliminate competition from black butchers. In 1854 they succeeded in getting an ordinance passed to that effect. Perhaps the most concerted efforts occurred in Charleston, where the new majority white population clashed with free-black artisans. A new political coalition of upcountry lawmakers and Charleston's white workingmen caused slaveholders and the free blacks' white allies to pause before actively opposing new racial restraints.

The assaults of Charleston's white workers accelerated in the 1850s and climaxed in 1859 and 1860. They elected their champion, Charles Macbeth, as mayor and although the city council refused to give in to their demands to prohibit all slave hiring, it did agree to enforce existing laws to the letter. The re-enforcement of the badge and manumission laws was a direct result. And from the perspective of a white workingman, the pressure had effect. As James M. Johnson, a prominent Charleston free black, wrote to his brother-in-law in August 1860, "it [the crackdown] must prove the Death of many & the loss of earthly goods, the hard earnings of a life time, to others." He reported at least one beneficiary to this policy: "Col. Seymour stood in front of our House speaking to an Irish carter on the subject & pointed to No 7 & 9 as being for sale."[59]

Encouraged, white workingmen pressed their case further with the state legislature. They elected two of their own in 1859, James M. Eason and Henry T. Peake. In 1860, they introduced a bill to prevent free blacks from engaging in any artisanal occupations, a measure sure to deal a severe blow to Charleston's free-black population. The bill failed, but the two mechanics were undeterred and introduced an even more damaging bill to enslave all free blacks living within the state by 1 January 1862. The objective was to induce free blacks to leave the state—thereby eliminating a work force competitor. That bill also failed. Soon thereafter, the firing on Fort Sumter and the war overcame efforts to remove blacks from the labor force.

Not all whites had united against blacks in the 1850s. As in the past, the harshest measures failed because white elites, motivated by both economic self-interest, conscience, and class prerogatives (especially strong in the class-conscious Carolina low country) refused to support them. Frustrated white workers thus soon recognized that blacks were not their only enemies. In 1858, the South Carolina Mechanics Association, of Charleston, unsuccessfully petitioned the legislature for a law to subject "to indictment both the hirer as well as the owner of any slave hiring out time."[60] Besides elites, other whites were put off by the immigrants' competing with slaves for "nigger work." And finally, as the South's urban economy became increasingly complex, skilled slave labor performed an essential role that whites could hardly ignore.

Free blacks also received support, though belated in the case of Charleston, from white benefactors. The ownership of property, personal probity, and hard work were all concepts that mid-nineteenth-century Americans valued; defenders of free blacks stressed these very traits. Implicit in the defense was the absence of such characteristics among white workingmen. When a group of Richmonders attacked free blacks as a criminal element, an editor replied, "On the contrary, they number among them men of the highest character and respectability—men of piety—men of substance—men of considerable intelligence."[61] The argument is interesting not only for its defense of free blacks, but also because it contradicted an increasingly prevalent assumption of the late antebellum era that blacks were inherently inferior and incapable of making their own way in the world. After the Civil War, when white supremacy became even more the guiding tenet of southern society, such defenses grew yet fewer. Before the war, some whites were less conscious of the contradiction. Others did not especially subscribe to the conventional racial wisdom, but dared not challenge it directly.

Consider the arguments advanced by John Harleston Read, Jr., a low country legislator who led the fight against the enslavement bill in 1860. He testified that free blacks were "good citizens, and [exhibited] patterns of industry, sobriety and irreproachable conduct." "They are the owners," he added, "of a vast amount of property, both real and personal." Read also reminded his colleagues that, aside from the economic consequences of such a law, its moral foundation was extremely weak: "Whilst we are battling for our rights, liberties, and institutions, can we expect the smiles and countenance [sic] of the Arbiter of all events when we make war upon the impotent and unprotected, enslave them against all justice?"[62]

Although direct protest by urban blacks was obviously limited during the 1850s, they did not entirely leave their defense to wavering white protectors or owners. When Richmond authorities passed the comprehensive black code of 1857, the city's free blacks hired a white lawyer to contest (unsuccessfully) the statutes. As the Charleston debacle unfolded in 1859 and 1860, free blacks there resorted to several tactics. They challenged police sent to enforce regulations (and, from at least one account, the police retreated), and they lobbied influential whites, particularly their customers who depended upon their labor. After these strategies proved of limited effectiveness, many chose another option—migration, even though for some that meant the forced sale of property. They left for the North, Philadelphia or Boston, for example, some for Haiti and some to other cities in the South where they had friends or relatives. A few stayed. Between August and November 1860, more than seven hundred free blacks left Charleston. The Philadelphia correspondent of the *New York Tribune* filed the following report:

All have been driven suddenly out of employments by which they gained a living, and are now seeking, under great disadvantages, to begin life anew. Many had acquired real estate and other property, but in the haste to get away were compelled to sell at great loss, while of what they leave behind unsold, they fully expect to be cheated. Some leave relations behind them —an old mother, a decrepid [*sic*] father—whom they are unable to bring away. Some have brought with them their copper badges, which read thus: Charleston, 1860, Servant, 1243.[63]

This was obviously the most unsatisfactory option of all: leaving one's home, where one had lived and worked and had shared fellowship for generations. The new destination was not likely to afford better opportunities. To be black in America, regardless of latitude, meant to be less than free. This was only slightly more of an option than slaves faced during the 1850s, many of whom found themselves back on the farm or in a different part of the South entirely.

Yet the southern city had provided slave and free black alike with a life different from and, in many respects, better than life in the country. Work was more varied, and the opportunity for making a living and cash was greater. So was the ability to form a black community with fellowship and institutions. Although these advantages were precarious, they served as crucial foundations for building a black life after the Civil War. It was not surprising that the core of black leadership, protest, and intellect emerged from the urban South after 1865; nor was it surprising that the southern city would become the wellspring of the civil rights movement nearly a century later. This is the ultimate legacy of black life in the cities of the Old South. □

THE ARCHAEOLOGY OF SLAVE LIFE

Theresa A. Singleton

If I could do it, I'd do no writing at all here. It would be photographs; the rest would be fragments of cloth, bits of cotton, lumps of earth, records of speech, pieces of wood and iron, phials of odors, plates of food and of excrement.[1]

Fig. 128. Recently freed, a group of African-Americans posed for photographer Henry P. Moore in the spring of 1862 while on their way to the fields on the Hopkinson plantation, Edisto Island, South Carolina. Archaeological investigations of such sites associated with slavery can increase our knowledge of the living conditions, material possessions, foodways, and cultural traditions of antebellum African-Americans.

Excavations of slave cabins in the late 1960s marked the beginning of a new research field known as African-American archaeology. From the careful analysis of tangible material remains—broken pottery, mortar, food bone, tools, buttons, and beads, for example—archaeologists are able to piece together information on how African-Americans spent their daily lives, built their homes, prepared their food, and crafted household equipment and personal possessions. Ultimately, archaeologists using these varied materials are seeking answers to general questions about African-American life. How, for example, was an African heritage transplanted, replaced, or reinterpreted in America? In what ways are the artifacts recovered from African-American sites reflections of ethnic patterns or of social conditions such as poverty and the unequal access to material goods? How did African-Americans survive the rigors of everyday life? What are the material differences in the lives of slaves, free blacks, and tenant farmers, or between urban and rural communities?

In the southern United States, the primary concern of African-American archaeology is the investigation of former slave quarters. Archaeologists since the 1930s have excavated sites of the plantation big house, and have thereby supplied important information for the restoration of planters' houses later opened to the public. Inspired by the growing scholarly interest in America's diverse ethnic heritage and in the poor and powerless as well, archaeologists more recently have turned to the study of slaves and other people who left few written records. Archaeologists have thus in more recent years investigated slave sites in nearly every state of the former plantation South, from Maryland to Texas, including the plantation homes of George Washington and Thomas Jefferson.

But the archaeology of slave sites brings both opportunities and problems to the scholarship of slavery, the most studied topic of the African-American experience. As an opportunity, archaeology recovers a primary source of information that may well provide numerous reinterpretations of certain aspects of slave life. Many of the activities represented by excavated artifacts—vestiges of food collection and preparation, craft practices, personal possessions, and details of house construction, alteration, and repair—are infrequently described in written and oral sources about slavery. The study of these objects, however, offers even more. From the studies of excavated remains come suggestions for understanding the context of everyday plantation life, the African-American response to enslavement, and processes of change and exchange between masters and slaves.

The problems presented by archaeological data are also many. The archaeologist can only interpret abandoned, discarded, or lost objects preserved in buried deposits. This leaves out any cherished objects that may have been kept and handed down from generation to generation. As for organic materials—clothing, wood, and basketry, for example—most remain preserved underground in only the most exceptional circumstances. The preservation of deposits left by a site's former occupants is also affected by subsequent activities, whether deep plowing, dredging, or construction. Thus disturbed, such materials raise questions for archaeological inquiry. Archaeology is not, however, simply the study of the recovered objects alone—it is also the study

Fig. 129.
The large and diverse group of ceramics, glass, and personal objects recovered from Mount Vernon's "House for Families" suggests that George Washington's household slaves enjoyed an atypically high level of material comfort. Precisely how slaves acquired such goods is not known: the objects may represent gifts from the Washington family, discards rescued and reused by the servants, or perhaps purchases made by Mount Vernon blacks in the nearby seaport town of Alexandria.

of the context in which the object is found and how it relates to other excavated materials. Moreover, all the evidence that the archaeologist studies is indirect: artifacts provide the basis for inference on particular aspects of behavior, not direct evidence of behavior. The artifacts are, instead, the by-products of behavior. Therefore, the interpretation of slavery's archaeological record requires that archaeologists also incorporate historical and ethnographic descriptions of slave behavior derived from written sources and oral tradition.

Thus reinforced, archaeological studies of slavery have made significant contributions in, first, the identification of African-American ethnic patterns and, second, in providing information on slave living conditions.[2] These themes, however, represent only two of the primary ways that archaeologists view and interpret data to study plantation society.[3] The two themes are also somewhat arbitrary, as they form only part of a larger, integrated complex of human activities anthropologists traditionally define as *culture*. A deliberate attempt is made here, however, to distinguish between two aspects of culture, between what are termed *value culture* and *reality culture*. The former, as applied to slave life, refers

to customs, beliefs, and values presumably influenced by an African heritage. The latter includes those aspects of slave life largely influenced instead by external forces, especially social controls inherent within slave society.[4] Using this approach, objects can often be understood from both perspectives. For example, the study of slave foodways provides insights into African-American customs associated with food preparation and serving, an aspect of a value culture. However, the foods slaves consumed were determined to a large extent by a reality culture: slaves ate the foods supplied to them or foods they foraged for themselves.

Conclusions are, however, based upon preliminary research and thus necessarily speculative. Further, because the unit of analysis for most archaeological research is often a single site, to suggest that the archaeological findings characterize an entire southern region or the entire South is an as-yet untested assumption. That said, many of the generalizations offered here are, nevertheless, based upon findings uncovered at numerous sites and, in a few cases, at all the sites excavated to date.[5] Historical and ethnographic accounts also support many of the generalizations.

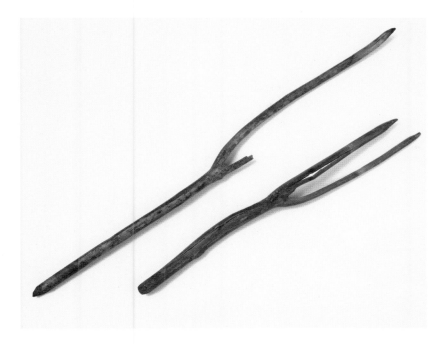

Fig. 130.
Two sticks, carefully peeled and trimmed at each end, were found between the inner and outer walls of a ca. 1850 slave cabin at Horton Grove quarter, part of the Stagville plantation complex outside Durham, North Carolina. According to several former slaves interviewed during the 1930s, antebellum African-Americans sometimes used forked sticks in various ways to ward off witches.

Fig. 131.
An interesting artifact of African origin, a cowrie shell from the Bennehan plantation's slave quarter near Durham, North Carolina, is one of several examples uncovered by archaeologists at different slave sites. Indigenous to the Pacific basin, the shells were used as a form of currency throughout Africa.

One of the initial objectives for excavating slave sites was to identify material elements of an African heritage. Several early studies in slave archaeology were undertaken on the cotton and, later, rice plantations along the coastal reaches of Georgia where a large slave population once lived in relative isolation from whites. Archaeologists became particularly interested in these coastal slave sites because scholars had discerned several cultural traditions in language, music, and material culture among modern-day descendants of the sites' slave communities.[6] What archaeologists had hoped to uncover were remnants of slave crafts that would shed light on the origin and develop-

ment of material culture traditions.[7] When archaeologists failed to uncover any identifiable African or African-styled artifacts, some assumed that such objects were likely made from only perishable materials that had long ago deteriorated and disappeared.[8] As a consequence, most of the subsequent research at Georgia slave sites addressed questions concerning slave living conditions.

Since the initial studies of slave sites on the Georgia coast, the search elsewhere for archaeological evidence of African-American ethnicity has been more successful. Although interpretations are tentative, the sites have supplied empirical data for the widely held view that enslaved Africans and their descendants nurtured and sustained a few aspects of an African heritage in spite of the oppressive and dehumanizing conditions of slavery. Archaeological evidence of African-American ethnicity is indicated from several sources: objects presumably brought from Africa, re-creations of African-styled or African-influenced objects, and mass-produced objects and other European-American materials reinterpreted by slaves for a special African-American meaning.

In light of the more recent archaeological evidence of African-American ethnicity recovered from other areas, reasons for the absence of ethnic objects from the Georgia sites are still unclear. Most of the artifacts recovered from Georgia slave sites date from the 1800s, when many slave owners supplied their slaves with mass-produced objects fashioned for European-American tastes rather than with slave-crafted objects. The availability of ready-made objects prompted by England's Industrial Revolution eventually resulted in the worldwide substitution of imported objects for items handcrafted locally. Therefore, handcrafted household objects preserved in the archaeological record are found more frequently at sites dating before rather than after 1800. Although fewer handmade objects are recovered from nineteenth-century sites, archaeologists have nevertheless been able to identify ethnic patterns from the careful study of both mass-produced and reworked European-American objects.

Although the vast majority of slaves brought few, if any, objects with them from Africa, several objects of presumed African origin have been recovered from slave sites. Cowrie shells, Indo-Pacific artifacts used widely in Africa as a medium of exchange, are one example. Only three cowrie shells have been uncovered in North America, one each at sites in Virginia, North Carolina, and Louisiana.[9] Perhaps the slaves who once owned these small objects were wearing the shells when captured in the slave trade. How slaves used these shells is unknown, although seven cowrie shells

Fig. 132.
Like the cowrie shell, rings
made of horn (left) and
ebony (right) found at the
Portici plantation in
Manassas, Virginia, possibly represent a cherished
link with a slave's African
past.

found in a slave burial site in Barbados suggest a possible answer. Along with European-made glass beads, drilled dog teeth, fish vertebrae, and a carnelian bead (a handcrafted product of Cambray in southern India), the seven shells formed part of an elaborate and striking necklace with African characteristics.[10]

Another object—an ebony-wood ring recovered from Portici plantation at Manassas National Battlefield Park, Virginia—is also believed to be African in origin. Made of a hard, heavy wood native to African and Asian tropical environments, this curious artifact was found with yet another ring, one made of animal horn. It, too, may be of African origin. Recovered from in and around the plantation's detached kitchen, both rings most likely belonged to domestic servants involved in preparing food for the main house.[11] Yet another two rings have been unearthed in Virginia: one, made of horn, at Monticello and another, made of bone, recovered from a slave pen in Alexandria.[12]

Although the origin, function, and significance of these objects remain a mystery, both the rings and cowrie shells document the presence and use of African objects by slaves. Such artifacts may have functioned as heirlooms—especially as some of these objects have been found within mid-

nineteenth-century contexts, when fewer African-born slaves were still alive.

Objects made on plantations also display African influences. Such re-creations of African motifs provide the most compelling archaeological evidence for the persistence of an African heritage. African influences are suggested in decorations, pottery making, foodways, building techniques, charms, and ritual objects.

The earliest manifestations of an African-American cultural expression may have been the African-influenced designs placed upon objects made in colonial Virginia. In his study of seventeenth-century tobacco pipes from the Chesapeake region, Matthew C. Emerson has suggested that slaves crafted the clay pipes' decorative work, especially the stamped and incised motifs highlighted in white. He has identified similar design elements within the same time period in the arts and crafts of Ghana, Nigeria, and Senegal-Mali. As the pipes are European in form and made of Chesapeake clays, Emerson believes the pipes reflect a combination of European form, native materials, and some African art. If his theory is correct, these pipe decorations may be the earliest physical evidence of an African-American expression of cultural identity in the southern United States.[13]

Fig. 133.
Archaeologists excavated
two rings and other objects
from the Portici planta-
tion kitchen (lowermost
foundation). From ap-
proximately 1820 to
1861, between twenty and
fifty slaves lived on Spen-
cer Ball's seven-hundred-
acre wheat-producing
plantation, now part of
the Manassas National
Battlefield Park.

Emerson's interpretation of slave-made pipes is, however, highly controversial. Early historical accounts as well as archaeological studies have provided evidence that Algonkian Indians also made clay pipes. Furthermore, British colonists apparently made clay pipes, too, particularly during periods of economic hardship when imported goods from England were scarce and expensive.[14] Yet the possibility that enslaved Africans may have influenced pipe-making practices can not be totally discounted. Seventeenth-century Chesapeake society offered social conditions and labor relationships that permitted an exchange of ideas, technology, and information among native Americans, Europeans, and Africans. The three groups often worked and resided together under circumstances that rarely occurred in later times. In this way, Chesapeake pipes may be an early material example of a three-way cultural exchange.

Incised decorations found on pewter spoons may be another example of enslaved Africans' applying an African aesthetic to enhance a European object. Vestiges of geometric designs found on spoons from the Garrison plantation in Maryland and the Kingsmill plantations in Virginia are remarkably similar to the spoon bowls and handles decorated today by Maroons (descendants of self-emancipated slaves) living in Surinam, South America.[15]

Ceramics, though, are the most frequently re-

COLONOWARE

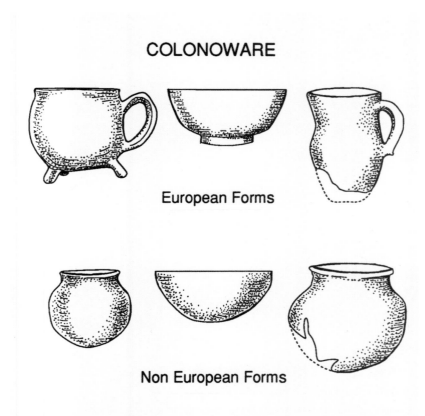

European Forms

Non European Forms

covered slave-produced artifacts. Used for preparing, serving, and storing food, slave-made ceramics are frequent finds at plantation sites in South Carolina, Virginia, and several islands in the Caribbean. Known as *colonoware* in the southern United States, such ceramics are a low-fired, unglazed earthenware apparently made by both native- and African-Americans.[16] Archaeologists once thought that only native Americans produced this pottery and that its presence at colonial sites was thus an indicator of European and native American cultural interaction. Native Americans indeed fashioned their colonoware pottery to suit the tastes of European settlers. In the British colonies, for example, they fashioned punch bowls, porringers, and drinking cups, as well as plates and bowls with the ringed feet that English settlers preferred. In Spanish Florida, their vessels sometimes replicated Spanish olive jar and majolica earthenware forms. Present-day native Americans—such as the Catawba, near Rock Hill, South Carolina—still produce pottery similar to colonoware. But, in recent years, scholars have agreed that African slaves also produced a variety of colonoware shaped into large and small globular pots and shallow bowls. These forms are found at sites once occupied by slaves

Fig. 134.
A low-fired earthenware, colonoware is attributed to both African-American and native-American makers. Found primarily at eighteenth-century plantation sites in South Carolina, the African-American pieces differ in form and function from the Indian examples. Slaves recreated the rounded forms of African pottery for their own food preparation and consumption purposes.

Fig. 135.
Archaeologists speculate that the eventual disappearance of slave-made colonoware during the antebellum period is an indication of cultural change and represents a period of marked assimilation for African-Americans. A shallow bowl dating between 1791 and 1841 recovered from the Pohoke site in Manassas, Virginia, provides a late example of African-American colonoware.

Fig. 136.
A small brass ornament decorated with a clenched fist is one of two charms recovered from the slave housing at the Hermitage, the home of Andrew Jackson outside Nashville, Tennessee. Such an amulet, one former slave recalled, is "what will keep de witches away."

long after the demise of Indians in the same area.

In South Carolina, several clues support the inference that slaves made pottery for their own use. Excavations at three plantations have yielded evidence of damaged vessels, lumps of fired clay, unfired pottery fragments, as well as clay pits—all signs that pottery was made on the plantation.[17] Colonoware, in fact, often comprises 80 to 90 percent of the ceramics found at sites occupied by slaves in the 1700s. Further research by Leland Ferguson, an historical archaeologist at the University of South Carolina, has suggested that some of the forms resemble pottery still made in parts of West Africa today. More recently, he has from a small sample of pottery identified markings similar to the cosmograms used in traditional rituals of the Kongo people from Africa's Congo-Angolan region.[18] To the Kongo, the icon—a cross enclosed within a circle—symbolizes the daily course of the sun and the continuity of life through birth, death, and rebirth.

Many archaeologists agree that slaves produced some colonoware, but the extent to which this pottery exhibits African origins is still uncertain. Matthew Hill, an archaeologist working in Africa at historic sites along the middle Gambia River, has identified vessel forms similar in shape to South Carolina examples. He observed, though, that African ceramics were far from plain, that they were in fact elaborately decorated, even ostentatious, whereas the South Carolina colono-

ware was in contrast undecorated. Hill's findings raise the possibility that while colonoware is a form of pottery from a distinctly non-European tradition, Africans produced the vessels under newly established conditions rather than in recreated and traditional African forms.[19]

Unlike in South Carolina, no direct evidence for slave-made pottery has been recovered from plantations in Virginia, although rounded vessels similar to those found in South Carolina have been identified at the Mount Vernon and Portici plantations. At Portici, the pottery fragments recovered from areas occupied by slaves date from the period between 1806 and 1863, several generations after the last indigenous native Americans resided in the area. This finding suggests that slaves made the pots.[20] Some archaeologists believe that slaves also produced colonoware that copied European forms. James Deetz, an archaeologist at the University of California, Berkeley, believes that on tidewater plantations along the James River slaves began making colonoware in English forms as a consequence of their contact with whites. Based on his work at Flowerdew Hundred, Deetz found that on sites dating prior to 1680, when black slaves and white indentured servants shared their living space with planters, no colonoware ceramics were present. After that date, planters increasingly turned to African slaves for labor and housed them separately from whites. Colonoware is found at such later sites. Deetz reasoned that enslaved blacks, when settled in segregated quarters without household utensils, produced pottery in forms they had previously used in the planter's household.[21]

Why is evidence of pottery making among enslaved African-Americans so important? The archaeological data on slave-made ceramics provides information on an African-American craft practice that was virtually unknown from other sources. More important, the use of this pottery suggests that enslaved African-Americans prepared food to suit their own tastes, perhaps incorporating aspects of traditional African cuisines. Thus, some African customs associated with preparing and serving food may have been maintained during slavery. Slaves also used these slave-made ceramics to prepare food for their masters. Colonoware accounts for a significant portion— sometimes more than half—of the ceramics used in planter households, thus suggesting that culinary techniques used by slaves influenced the local cuisine of southern whites as well. Gumbos, pilaus, and pilafs—all southern meals prepared in a single pot—are but a few examples of the present-day legacy of the African influence in culinary practices.[22]

Excavated food remains also point to the gen-

*Fig. 137.
Blue-colored glass beads found at the Portici plantation in Virginia are among the many such samples recovered by archaeologists at various slave sites. Female slaves probably wore the beads strung together as necklaces.*

*Fig. 138, Fig. 139.
Slaves found inventive new uses for their owners' castoffs. At Andrew Jackson's Hermitage plantation, an African-American converted a toothbrush handle into an awl (below), a sewing tool. Another slave fashioned a chisel from a horseshoe, later unearthed at Virginia's Portici plantation.*

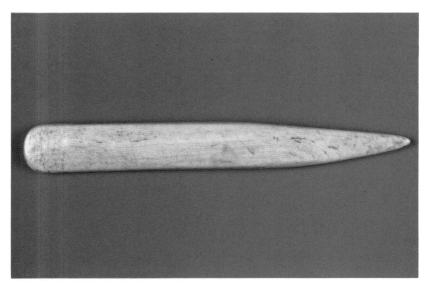

eral practice of cooking one-pot meals. Carcasses cut into small portions, highly fragmented bones, or bones from which the meat has apparently been sliced all suggest that meats were boiled, in stews or soups for example, rather than roasted.[23] The making of stews was perhaps a culinary preference, but it may also have been a creative way of using pieces of meat considered undesirable by slaveholders.[24]

The best documented evidence of enslaved Africans' influencing their material world is seen in numerous examples of architecture.[25] Excavations at the sites of Curriboo and Yaughan, two former indigo plantations in Berkeley County, South Carolina, have revealed the earliest archaeological evidence of African-styled slave housing identified on a southern plantation. These slave quarters made of mud walls and presumably covered with thatched palmetto leaves are similar to the thatch-roof houses found in many parts of Africa. Although no standing walls survive, archaeologists have found wall trenches containing a mortar-like clay. Presumably the entire structure was made of this material. The importance of clay as a primary material for both construction and pottery making is further suggested by the presence of numerous nearby clay pits.[26]

Slaves built the mud-wall houses at Curriboo and Yaughan plantations in approximately 1740 and lived in them until about 1790 when the houses were razed and replaced with frame structures occupied until the plantations closed in 1820. The change from mud-wall to frame dwellings also coincided with a decreasing use of colonoware ceramics at both plantations. These changes may well indicate that the slaves' opportunity to fashion domestic material as they desired was rapidly disappearing.

Nearly every slave site has at least one or two unexplained objects. Archaeologists in all subject areas have a tendency, however, to interpret such unexplained objects as charms or ritual items. Many of these interpretations are supported by historical and ethnographic documentation, whereas others are more speculative. Unfortunately, the purpose and meaning of some objects may always remain a mystery.

Two charms recovered from slave cabins at the Hermitage, the plantation home of Andrew Jackson outside Nashville, Tennessee, may be akin to charms used by slaves in both the antebellum South and in Latin America. Although stylistically different, both charms, made of stamped brass or another copper alloy, depict the same image—a clenched human hand. The image is believed to be quite similar to certain Latin American amulets, or *figas*, associated with African-oriented spiritualist cults and in widespread use since at

least the mid-1800s.[27] The charm may also be what was referred to as a "hand" to "keep de witches away." An ex-slave in Florida recollected that an

> Old witch doctor, he want ten dollars for a piece o' string, what he say some kinda charm words over. . . . I didn't have no ten dollar, so he say ifen I git up five dollar he make me a hand—you know, what collored folks calls a jack. Dat be a charm what will keep de witches away. I knowns how to make em, but day doan do no good thout de magic words, and I doan know dem.[28]

The best evidence of ritual paraphernalia comes from the Jordan plantation in Brazoria County, south of Houston, Texas. There archaeologist Kenneth Brown uncovered an assemblage of ar-

tifacts from a cabin apparently used in healing and divination rituals. The Jordan plantation operated with slave laborers from 1848 until emancipation and with wage laborers, most of whom were former slaves, until 1890 or 1891. Until forced to leave, the workers continuously occupied the now-excavated cabins and both written and archaeological records suggest that they maintained a cultural continuity from slavery to freedom. Brown believes that because of their forced abandonment of the site, the occupants hastily left behind objects not customarily found in the archaeological record. Excavations of the remains of several individual cabins revealed vestiges of specialized activities: the community evidently included a carpenter, seamstress, a cattle herder, or cowboy, and a *shamam*, or healer.

Ritual materials recovered from a restricted area of the shaman's cabin included several bases from cast-iron kettles, pieces of much-used chalk, bird skulls, fragments of a small weighing scale, an animal's paw, samples of medicine, seashells, bottles, parts of one or more dolls, spoons, nails, knives, and scrapers made from chert, a flintlike rock. Many of these objects were no doubt once used for a number of other purposes, but when taken together the artifacts suggest some form of ritual use. Support for Brown's interpretation comes from abundant ethnographic studies conducted in the Caribbean and parts of Africa that describe the use of wooden or metal trays, white chalk or powder, metal staffs, bird symbols, and other objects used in healing rituals.[29]

The assemblage of artifacts from the Jordan plantation presents an excellent example of how African-Americans reworked mass-produced and other objects to achieve a special African-American meaning. Colored glass beads, particularly blue beads found in slave sites from Virginia to Texas, provide another example of the slaves' reinterpretation of manufactured objects to meet their own cultural uses. William H. Adams, an archaeologist at Oregon State University, has recently suggested that the predominance of blue beads in the antebellum South may well be a vestige of the widespread belief within the Muslim world, including many parts of Africa, that a single blue bead worn or sown on clothing protected the bearer against "the evil eye."[30] Blue beads, in fact, often comprise as much as a third of all the beads found at slave sites.

Still other artifacts might have held a special meaning for slaves. Although archaeologists have yet to decipher what the objects meant to the people who used them, they have recovered coins, frequently of Spanish origin and pierced for hanging, from both Monticello and Harmony Hall plantation in Georgia as well as the smoothed and polished penis bone of a raccoon, unearthed at Mount Vernon. An incised line encircles one end of the bone, suggesting that the object was worn suspended from a string or thin chain. The type of bone suggests its use as a fertility symbol. Polygonal objects, resembling gaming pieces, and made primarily from pottery as well as glass and reworked wood, have been recovered from several plantations, including Thomas Jefferson's Poplar Forest and Monticello and the Portici plantation, all in Virginia, as well as the Garrison plantation near Baltimore, Maryland, and the Drax Hall plantation in Jamaica.[31]

It is possible that these artifacts may not be expressions of African-American ethnicity at all, but instead simply attempts by slaves to make adornments, gaming pieces, and other objects from what was available to them. The material poverty of slaves—the concept of "making do"—should not be overlooked as a potential explanation for the slaves' reworking of discarded materials to create something else.[32] Yet the African-American community's selection of certain objects, such as coins, as suggested by the testimony of ex-slaves, may indeed reflect some aspect of ethnic conjuring practices.[33] But because most of what became African-American is an amalgam of reinterpreted African culture and adopted European materials, identifying the excavated evidence of African-American ethnic patterns thus poses a continuing challenge to archaeologists.

Every archaeological study of a slave site contributes information on living conditions, whether or not the topic is an expressed goal of the research. The study of the slaves' material life also sheds light on how a particular plantation operated, especially how certain plantation resources were distributed, utilized, and recycled. Archaeology thereby supplies detailed information that can amplify other sources. For example, provision records, when available, are often incomplete and contain information on objects not generally found in the archaeological record, objects such as clothing, blankets, boneless meats, cornmeal, and vegetables, items long since disappeared. On the other hand, some items that do find their way into the archaeological record—purchased housewares, personal possessions, or the remains of wild foods collected by slaves—are virtually absent from these written records. The interpretation of these otherwise undocumented records

Fig. 141.
Hunting contributed substantially to the slaves' diet. Despite the various laws forbidding slaves to possess firearms, archaeologists have nevertheless recovered various fragments of guns, homemade weapons, and related tools. These knife-sharpening stones were found at the Hermitage outside Nashville, Tennessee.

Fig. 142.
Recent excavations at Mount Vernon's large dormitory slave-quarter have yielded one of the largest assemblages of artifacts and faunal remains yet discovered in the Chesapeake region. The large frame structure, called the "House for Families" by George Washington, was home to almost seventy household slaves between 1760 and 1793.

verbal descriptions, sketches, photographs, and standing structures to provide a wealth of information on the above-ground appearance of slave dwellings. In turn, archaeology contributes to the study of slave housing by providing structural details and evidence of how slaves lived in their cabins. Excavations yield information on materials and methods used to lay foundations and to make repairs and modifications, while the artifacts recovered from building trenches provide an approximate date of construction. Those artifacts found in and around houses also suggest the period of occupation and an approximate date for abandonment.

Colonial slave housing is, however, poorly understood from both historical and archaeological resources. Most scholars agree that early slave housing was makeshift and flimsy—with many slaves living in lofts, barns, kitchens, sheds, and in houses with communal arrangements. For the most part, the quartering of slaves in separate cabins became a widespread practice only in the nineteenth century. Thus archaeology can in time make a major contribution by providing details of early slave housing. Unfortunately, with few notable exceptions, most archaeological studies have furnished more data on the well documented housing of the 1800s. Traces of earlier slave houses were likely destroyed as slave owners expanded, rebuilt, and reorganized their plantations.

A few colonial slave quarters have, though, been excavated. At the Kingsmill plantations near Williamsburg, Virginia, archaeologists uncovered several buildings dating from 1705 to 1789 that presumably housed slaves. The structures included brick dependencies flanking the mansion and housing the kitchen, plantation office, and probably quarters for a number of slaves as well; a forty-by-eighteen-foot and a twenty-eight-by-twenty-foot communal slave quarter; and earthbound wooden houses of varying sizes.[36] At George Washington's Mount Vernon the cellar of a frame slave-quarter built upon a brick foundation has recently been excavated. Based upon a slave census compiled in 1786, this communal slave quarter known as the "House for Families" may have housed as many as fifty to sixty slaves from 1760 to 1793.[37] In the Lower South, the earliest excavated slave dwellings are the ca. 1740-1790 mud-wall structures at Yaughan and Curriboo. The African-styled houses functioned as individual cabins, each housing three to four slaves.[38] The practice of placing slaves in individual cabins apparently came early to the South Carolina low country.

Excavations of eighteenth-century slave quarters in Virginia have uncovered a distinctive but

of the slaves' material culture has often become the subject of archaeological debate.[34] Other archaeological resources supplement existing narrative descriptions of slave life and together reveal much of the slaves' housing, household equipment, personal possessions, diet, nutrition, and health.

Most archaeological studies of slave settlements are generally undertaken in and around slave dwellings and consequently yield information on the dwellings themselves. Slave housing varied over time and from place to place and was often dictated by the slaveholders' preferences. Studies conducted by architectural historians and folklorists have shown the development, regional styles, and variations in slave housing from the colonial to the antebellum period.[35] These studies utilize

Fig. 143.
"We done our cookin',
eatin', sleepin', and
ever'thin in dis little one-
room log house," recalled
a former slave. The single-
room cabin on Cockspur
Island, Georgia, is repre-
sentative of that type of
slave housing.

curious feature—earthen root-cellars. Ranging in size from two by three feet to five by eight feet and from two to four feet deep, the cellars were either unlined or, if lined, fashioned with brick, stone, or wood, and usually contained tools, locks, nails, ceramics, some glass, buttons, and discarded food remains. Archaeologist William M. Kelso excavated eighteen cellars from one large communal quarter at Kingsmill and ten more found within six cabins along Mulberry Row at Monticello.[39] Because the root cellars were slowly backfilled with artifacts and refuse, he believes that they were used not only for storing food but also for concealing pilfered goods. Kelso suggests

that "hiding tools might make a workday shorter, and that leftover bones from the theft of good quality meat could hardly go out in the yard to give the thief away."[40] Kelso's interpretation is supported by narratives of both masters and slaves describing just such activities. At Thomas Jefferson's plantation, Poplar Forest, the manager wrote that there the workers had been "razing eny kind of vegetable." But "the very moment your back is turned from thee place Nace takes every thing out of the garden and carries them to his cabin and burys them in the ground."[41] The slaves sometimes had good reason to put any food remains in the cellars, too. As Charles Grandy,

an ex-slave, later recalled,

> I got so hungry I stealed chickens off the roos'. Yessum, I did, chickens used roos' on de fense den, right out in de night. We would cook de chicken at night, eat him an' bu'n de feathers. Dat's what dey had dem ole paddyrollers [slave patrols] fer. Dey come roun' an' search de qua'ters fer to see what you bin stealin'. We always had a trap in de floor fo' de do' to hide dese chickens in.[42]

Apparently, the slow buildup of refuse in these root cellars eventually resulted in health hazards, which may in part explain their absence in many antebellum slave houses.

In many cases, owners prevented slaves from digging root cellars. In an analysis of antebellum housing in Virginia, Larry McKee proposes that while the stated purpose of the "reformed" or "improved" slave housing advocated in period agricultural journals was to promote healthy living conditions, the planters' implied goal was to control unauthorized behavior. The desire was most obviously expressed in the building of slave cabins upon foundation piers that raised wood-plank floors a foot and a half to two feet above ground. The raised floors did allow "healthy" air to circulate beneath the structure, but, more important, prevented the digging of any root cellars. The crawl space underneath the cabin was still used for storage but, unlike root cellars, could easily be checked by a plantation owner or manager. McKee further suggests that contemporary descriptions of the "filth" surrounding the slaves' cabins may have been the way African-Americans resisted the planters' desire for cleanliness, orderliness, and control of the quarters.[43] Archaeologists have excavated antebellum slave cabins raised above ground and without root cellars at the Willcox and Shirley plantations along Virginia's James River.[44] But period cabins with such cellars have also been identified, suggesting that the struggle between master and slave, over that issue at least, was not always won by the planter.

Although researchers generally believe that only a very small number of slaves ever lived in well-built housing, antebellum slave dwellings took many forms. Two distinct floor plans, however, such as identified at both Virginia plantations, seem to have predominated. At the Willcox plantation a single-family structure measured sixteen by twenty feet; at Shirley a double pen, or duplex, measured twenty by forty feet and housed two family units separated by a common wall. Slave houses of comparable dimensions and floor plans have been identified archaeologically in several localities.

Fig. 144. Plantation carpenters built the still remarkably well preserved two-story slave quarters at Horton Grove in the North Carolina piedmont. Divided into four units each, the houses served multiple families.

Fig. 145.
A rough concrete known as tabby *proved to be an extremely durable as well as fire- and weather-resistant material for the construction of slave housing. Examples of such slave quarters survive at the Kingsley plantation on Fort George Island, Florida.*

Fig. 146.
During the 1980s archaeologists from the University of Florida investigated several coastal plantation sites within the vicinity of Kings Bay, Camden County, Georgia. One of them, Harmony Hall, a small antebellum plantation on the west bank of the North River, was home to a slave work force of only six individuals.

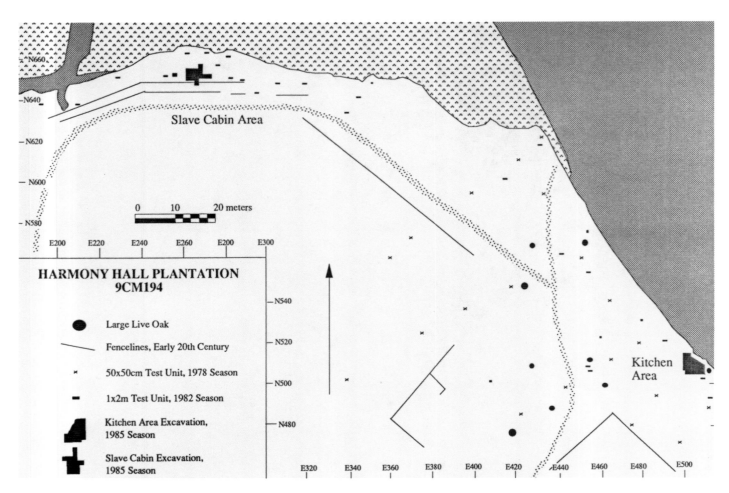

Slave Cabin Area

0   10   20 meters

E200   E220   E240   E260   E200   E300

HARMONY HALL PLANTATION
9CM194

●   Large Live Oak

—   Fencelines, Early 20th Century

×   50x50cm Test Unit, 1978 Season

▬   1x2m Test Unit, 1982 Season

◤   Kitchen Area Excavation, 1985 Season

✚   Slave Cabin Excavation, 1985 Season

N660
N640
N620
N600
N580

N540
N520
N500
N480

Kitchen Area

E320   E340   E360   E380   E400   E420   E440   E460   E480   E500

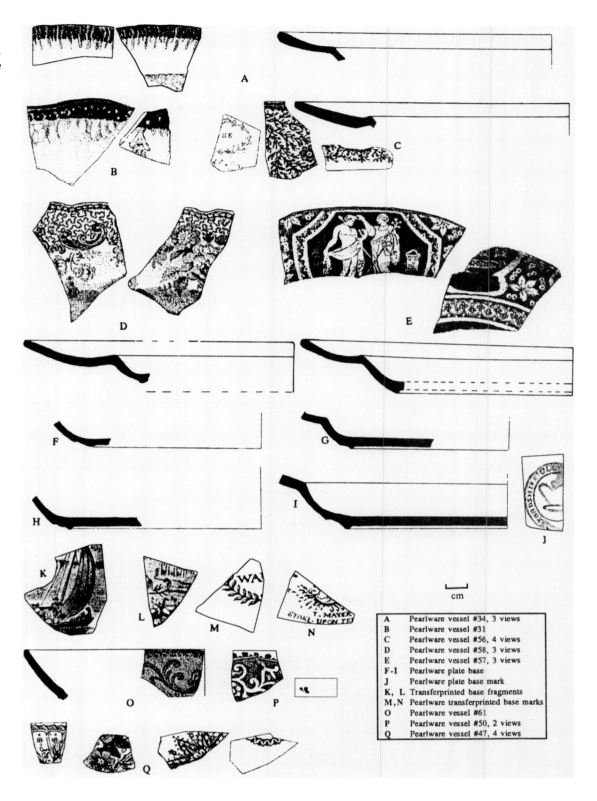

*Fig. 147.
Although archaeologists recovered imported ceramics such as pearlware from Georgia's Harmony Hall slave-cabin site, the examples were inexpensive and of relatively low status. For the slaves, the plantation's standard of living thus appears to have been lower than that found among larger slave populations, such as at Couper's Point on Saint Simons Island, Georgia.*

A	Pearlware vessel #34, 3 views
B	Pearlware vessel #31
C	Pearlware vessel #56, 4 views
D	Pearlware vessel #58, 3 views
E	Pearlware vessel #57, 3 views
F-I	Pearlware plate base
J	Pearlware plate base mark
K, L	Transferprinted base fragments
M, N	Pearlware transferprinted base marks
O	Pearlware vessel #61
P	Pearlware vessel #50, 2 views
Q	Pearlware vessel #47, 4 views

There were also larger structures housing three or more slave families. Though less common, several multifamily dwellings still stand or have been investigated archaeologically. Along Horton Grove, at the Stagville plantation outside Durham, North Carolina, slaves occupied a two-story quarter divided into four units. Similar two-story slave dwellings have been excavated at the Somerset plantation in Creswell, North Carolina.[45] At the Jordan plantation in Texas yet another variation has been identified. There archaeologists have uncovered eight long, barracks-like structures built in pairs. Archaeological evidence indicates that three to four individual living units were built within each building. After emancipation, when the plantation employed wage laborers, some of the barracks were reorganized to accommodate only two families, thus allowing the recently freed laborers to double their living space.[46]

A variety of materials were used to build slave quarters. Houses were generally log or frame and occasionally all brick. Along the southeastern coast, oyster shells offered a distinctive masonry material called *tabby*, a cement-like substance made of crushed shells, sand, and lime. Tabby could be molded into bricks for chimneys and foundations, or poured like modern-day cement to form walls and floors. It was also used as mortar. Excavations have revealed that crushed oyster shells also served as footings for building foundations and in making floors and pathways.[47] Slaves apparently collected oysters and deposited the discarded shells in and around their dwellings, a practice identified archaeologically at numerous slave sites along the Georgia coast. In the late 1830s Fanny Kemble commented on the shells' common occurrence when visiting her husband's Hampton plantation on Saint Simons Island, Georgia. As the oysters "are a considerable article of the people's diet," she wrote,

the shells are allowed to accumulate, as they are used in the composition of which their huts are built, and which is a sort of combination of mud and broken oyster shells, which forms an agglomeration of a kind very solid and durable for building purposes; but, instead of being all carried to some specified place out of the way, these great heaps of oyster shells are allowed to be piled up anywhere and everywhere, forming the most unsightly obstructions in every direction.[48]

In addition to documenting a structure's floor plan, building materials, or modifications, archaeology also provides tangible information on living conditions in the slave quarters. For example, unearthed evidence frequently indicates that houses rarely contained glass windows; that chinking, daub, and other materials were needed to insulate drafty walls; and that hearth fires were extremely hot, often causing chimneys made of mud and sticks to collapse. The heat was so intense that even brick chimneys sometimes show signs of buckling and an accompanying separation of the hearth from the outer chimney walls.[49] Other evidence indicates that rodent infestations were apparently common, and the vestiges of refuse found within and around the dwellings support some of the contemporary descriptions that cabins were dirty and unhealthy. On the other hand, archaeological evidence also shows that some dwellings were well built and regularly maintained.

Household and personal items recovered from slave quarters also provide information on the quality of life in cabins. Slaves possessed a few meager household possessions—generally coarse earthen- and stoneware vessels used to prepare and store food, cooking pots and kettles of colonoware or iron, and mismatched dishes, usually bowls and cups for consuming soups or stews. As so few spoons or forks have been recovered, either such utensils were seldom left behind or perhaps slaves used other objects or even their hands. Some evidence of furnishings—such as a drawer pull, an upholstery tack, a caster, or even a brass pulley from a clock—is occasionally recovered.[50] Recovered personal possessions vary from site to site. Some are associated with clothing and adornment—buttons, beads, jewelry, or combs—while others are related to the slaves' nonwork hours, items used in hunting and fishing, gardening, playing music and games, smoking, inbibing alcoholic beverages, perhaps even reading.

Fine china and tea sets have been uncovered from several slave cabins. Some archaeologists suggest that this may be another indicator that a few slaves, particularly artisans and drivers, occupied a higher status within the plantation community. Written records from specific plantations often refer to larger food rations and sometimes amenities such as tobacco awarded to specific slaves, usually skilled craftsmen or field laborers performing very difficult work. Nevertheless, there are no written references in plantation records to the provisioning of slaves with ceramics. Because it remains unclear how slaves received these items, archaeologists have offered three possible explanations. First, these objects were perhaps castoffs that slaves received as gifts from the planter's household. Second, slaves may have purchased them with cash they earned through "hiring out" their labor or by selling or trading produce, handicrafts, or livestock to acquire money for the items. And third, china was perhaps stolen from the big house. Although any of these possibilities may account for slaves' possessing chinaware, all three factors most likely occurred to varying degrees from time to time.

The recovery of objects associated with food preparation indicates that slaves prepared at least some of their meals in their cabins and not in a plantation's central kitchen. Although the presence of central kitchens is well documented in plantation records, no evidence of these kitchens has been recovered archaeologically. The conflicting information presented by written plantation records and archaeological discoveries raises several questions. Were some meals prepared in

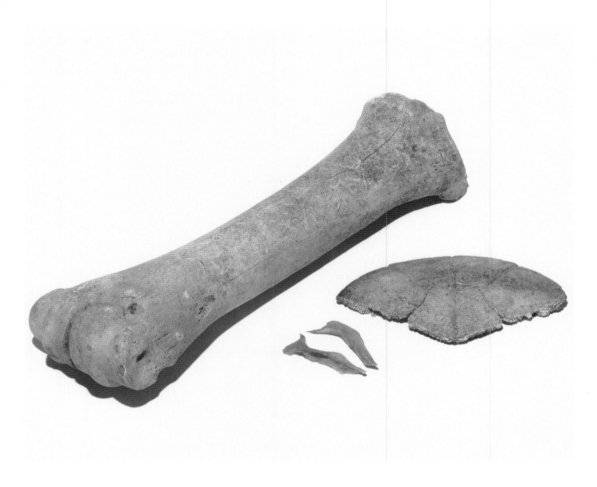

*Fig. 148.
Slaves at George
Washington's Mount
Vernon augmented their
diet with large amounts of
fish, such as perch, from
the nearby Potomac River
as well as game from the
surrounding woods.
Portions of a turtle shell
(right) and a cow leg (left)
are among the food
remains recovered by
archaeologists.*

plantation kitchens while others were in slave cabins? Do the cooking equipment and food remains recovered from cabins represent the preparation and consumption of regular meals or occasional efforts to satisfy hunger? When did central kitchens come into use for the preparation of slave meals? And why have archaeologists as yet been unable to identify central kitchens? Only future research can reconcile the conflicting information presented by the two sources of information.

There is also contradictory written and archaeological evidence as to slave literacy and the use of firearms. Excavated artifacts suggestive of literacy among slaves include graphite pencils, writing slates (some with words and numbers etched on the surface), even eyeglasses. Evidence of firearms includes buckshot, lead shot, gun plates, trigger guards, and flints. Initially, archaeologists were surprised to find such objects associated with activities often prohibited by law in many slave states.[51] But references found in plantation records, slave testimony, and other accounts indicate that some slaves acquired reading and writing skills and some had access to firearms for hunting. However, the frequency with which these objects turn up at archaeological sites suggests that more slaves had access to firearms and

possessed literacy and enumerative skills than previously thought from the study of written records alone.

The study of food remains has perhaps contributed more to the amplification of written records on slave living conditions than any other archaeological resource. Written records reveal that the plantation laborers' diet normally included preserved meats, cornmeal, and vegetables grown in provision gardens, foods that normally leave few, if any, archaeological remains. And yet extensive food traces, particularly of animal bones, have been found, indicating that slaves consumed other kinds of foods to supplement their normal plantation rations.[52]

Through *zooarchaeology*, the study of animal food-bone, many characteristics of the slaves' food habits can be determined: for example, the kinds and relative proportions of animal foods consumed, the cuts of meat, the amounts of consumable meat represented by the remains, and sometimes how these foods were prepared—whether, for example, slaves boiled or roasted the food. Most zooarchaeological studies indicate that domestic animals furnished the bulk of the animal protein in the slaves' diet. And although the remains of pork or beef are the most commonly found, at a few sites sheep and goats evidently were an important food source. Chickens, however, appear to have been a minor food item consumed only occasionally and perhaps valued more for their eggs. Slaves often received the less meaty and lower quality meat-portions of these domestic animals, likely livestock raised on the plantation. Some zooarchaeologists have interpreted the slaves' consumption of low-quality meats as an indicator of African-Americans' inferior social status within the plantation hierarchy. In fact, some skeletal elements (such as skulls, feet, and ribs) often found at slave sites may have been meat portions discarded as waste in the butchering of meat for the planter household.[53]

Evidence from several sites suggests that there were dietary variations among slaves of the same plantation. This is consistent with numerous provision records indicating that the amount of rations a slave received depended upon the worker's skill level or other factors. But the archaeological findings seem to point to differences not just in the quantity of rations but also in the quality of meat and methods of food preparation. For example, along Mulberry Row at Thomas Jefferson's Monticello, zooarchaeologist Diana Crader observed carving marks on pig-limb bones identical to the marks found on bones recovered from the plantation kitchen that serviced the mansion. Crader suggests that "the discovery of such carving marks on meaty limb bones suggests a higher quality of meat and a different method of meat preparation (roasts instead of stews) than would be expected in a slave dwelling."[54] Since the food remains recovered from the other cabins along Mulberry Row conform more to the usual patterns of slave diet, the different diet evident in building "o" (as designated in Jefferson's insurance records) is attributed to the higher status of certain African-Americans within Monticello's slave community. Similar evidence of dietary differences between house slaves and field hands has been identified at Portici plantation.[55]

Other zooarchaeologists question whether the recovery of "low-quality" meats is alone sufficient evidence of class differences either between planter and slaves or between members of the slave community.[56] In a study of nineteenth-century urban foodways, Joanne Bowen Gaynor found that wealthy households regularly consumed supposedly inferior parts of meat—such as heads, feet, and other forms of offal—as these foods were delicacies in many socially fashionable cuisines. She concludes that what constituted dietary variation along class lines appears to be much more complex than simply the consumption of low- versus high-quality meats. Also to be considered, she adds, are the "quantity and variety of food, the use of imported spices and speciality foods, characteristic dishes, their ingredients, and the way that they are combined, and rules guiding the presentation and consumption of food."[57]

The study of wild-food remains provides even more revealing evidence of slave food habits. At every slave site where food remains have been recovered and analyzed, there is evidence that African-Americans consumed at least some wild foods, often making use of every possible food resource within reach, taking "advantage of the woods, fields, rivers, and creeks surrounding the plantation."[58] This was particularly true on plantations located along the southeastern coast where wild-food resources abounded in the ocean, marshes, and tidal creeks as well as in the oak and hickory forests. It is estimated that wild foods may have comprised as much as 40 percent of the meat in the slaves' diet.[59] Coastal slaves apparently hunted and fished throughout the year, collecting crabs, clams, oysters, sea catfish, stingrays, sharks, mullet, turtles on both sea and land, opossum, raccoon, and rabbit. Zooarchaeologist Elizabeth Reitz and several colleagues suggest that many of these resources could be captured easily using nets or traps and with minimal expenditure of time or effort while attending to other chores.[60] Curious, though, is that deer, wild birds, and ducks were found to be insignificant food resources at these sites. But as these animals are often taken with guns, their absence may be more a sign of the slaves' restricted access to firearms or to specific game than a matter of taste preference.

At inland sites, the slaves' reliance upon wild-food resources differed from plantation to plantation. Wild foods comprised less than 5 percent of the animal species represented at Monticello, located in the Virginia piedmont.[61] But at the Hermitage, near Nashville, Tennessee, wild birds and small mammals were significant food resources that made up 60 percent of the animal species represented. The use of wild birds in particular suggests more active hunting than was required to obtain fish and turtles along the coast. Designated hunters may have been responsible for provisioning slaves with these foods.[62] The preliminary analysis of food remains at Mount Vernon suggests that fish were an important source of food for those slaves living in the "House for Families." Most of the fish were presumably caught from Washington's plantation fishery. The remains of non-riverine fish species imply that the slaves may have caught still others using hook and line.[63]

Food remains provide information on the kinds of animal food slaves consumed, but the quality and quantity of foods consumed can only be estimated.[64] To determine the diet's nutritional

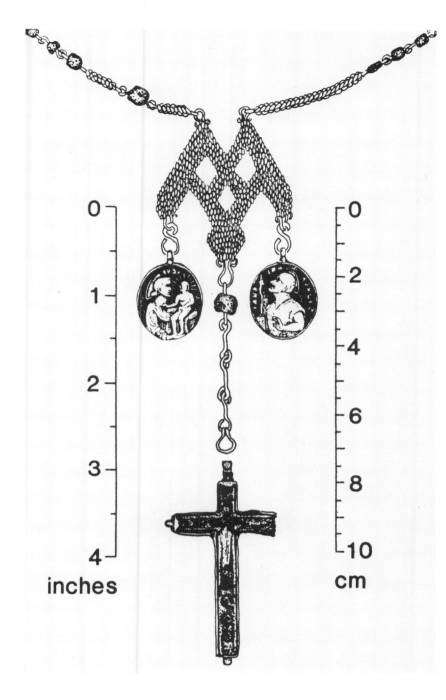

Fig. 149.
The study of human remains recovered during the archaeological investigation of a New Orleans cemetery revealed a marked increase in bone development as well as evidence of the physical effects of hard labor and corporal punishment on African-Americans. One of the burial sites contained a slave's rosary.

value requires an analysis of human remains. Such studies can yield information on diet, nutrition, disease, and general health, but due to legal, religious, and moral considerations, archaeologists generally avoid, whenever possible, excavating burial sites. However, in the search for other information, researchers sometimes inadvertently unearth abandoned and forgotten slave burial sites. Such finds are usually recovered from unmarked cemeteries, though human remains are sometimes found among domestic sites and work areas.[65] Cemeteries are, though, intentionally excavated when threatened by land redevelopment or environmental damage.[66]

While archaeologists generally analyze an excavated cemetery's artifacts and mortuary patterns, the technical analysis of human remains is the field of physical or biological anthropologists. Analyses of human bones and teeth can provide a wide range of information on biological and social factors affecting a population's health. Nutrition intake, metabolism, genetics, aging, hormonal interactions, biomechanical stress, diet, type and levels of activity, as well as a subject's reproductive history all affect the human skeleton.[67]

Researchers have unearthed fewer slave cemeteries than slave dwellings, but the African-American populations studied by physical anthropologists represent a broader cross section of slave society than archaeologists' studies of workers' quarters.[68] Archaeologists' excavations of particular settlements have been directed primarily toward the study of plantation slaves. Physical anthropologists, on the other hand, have also studied urban slaves in New Orleans and industrial slaves engaged in ironworking at the Catoctin Furnace in Maryland.[69] In spite of population differences, several general health problems were common to the three populations of rural, urban, and industrial workers. In each case slaves had diets very high in carbohydrates and sugar and low in protein; they withstood periods of malnutrition, particularly in childhood; they experienced high levels of tooth decay, tooth loss, and dental diseases; and they suffered from degenerative arthritic conditions resulting from physically strenuous lives.

Differences in health appear to be largely in the degree of occurrence. For example, some evidence of anemia—presumably both genetic (sickle cell) and acquired (iron-deficiency)—was found in all three populations. Anemia was, though, a major health problem among the industrial and plantation slave populations, only a minor condition in the urban African-American population.[70]

Similarly, evidence of physical stress resulting from occupational activities was more pronounced

Fig. 150.
Four medicine bottles
stored beneath the floor of
several slave cabins at
Andrew Jackson's Hermitage contained calomel or
mercurous chloride, commonly used during the
antebellum period to treat
various infections and
illnesses.

among industrial and plantation slaves than among urban slaves. Both males and females within the industrial and plantation populations showed arthritic conditions associated with the heavy work of lifting, digging, or pounding.[71] The skeletal remains of urban slaves displayed more variation in the degree of occupational stress: only some showed signs of pronounced patterns of such stress, probably attributable to manual labor on the docks of New Orleans or work on the canals and levees. Generally, though, the urban slaves' workday was not characterized by heavy occupational stress—perhaps reflecting the diversity of slave labor in an urban setting.[72] Each population showed signs of generalized infections, but chronic infection was particularly high among the plantation slaves. Written sources repeatedly point to infection as a major health problem on southern plantations, and this finding supports that condition. The combined effects of infective organ-

isms, diet, labor demands, and living conditions all played a role in the high infections among plantation slaves.[73]

Indications of how slaves were treated for health problems can also be discerned through archaeology. Collections of charms and other healing paraphernalia, such as uncovered at the Jordan plantation in Texas, suggest the kinds of folk medicine slaves sought. But excavations of slave quarters also provide indications of the kinds of medications slave owners administered to their workers. For example, excavations along the Georgia coast revealed that slaves regularly consumed patent medicines with high alcoholic content.[74] While some of this consumption reflects recreational imbibing, plantation records for the Butler plantation, visited by Fanny Kemble, also indicate that planters dispensed patent medicines and homemade rum to the slaves as a preventative for rheumatic diseases.[75] Future excavations of plantation infirmaries may possibly turn up medical instruments and other objects used to treat slaves.

The continuing archaeological study of slave living conditions will, therefore, provide detailed information on slave provisioning, whether slaves acquired or were given household and personal objects, what activities slaves pursued when not working, and the impact of unhealthy housing, a deficient diet, and strenuous labor upon the physical well-being of African-Americans. In short, these studies seek to document through tangible evidence the everyday lives of slaves.

Whereas slave sites have been the major focus of African-American archaeology in the South, sites occupied by antebellum free blacks and by emancipated men and women after the Civil War are receiving increased attention. Like those for slave sites, these studies have attempted to identify ethnic patterns and living conditions. But unlike the growing manifestations of ethnicity in ceramic production and use, architecture, and ritual objects found at slave sites, such archaeological evidence at sites occupied by nonslaves is considerably more subtle. For instance, no distinctly African-American crafts such as colonoware have been attributed to southern free blacks or ex-slaves.[76] On the other hand, these sites do provide information on the material world of African-Americans in other realms of southern society.

Free-black sites investigated thus far vary widely. They range from the frontier outpost of Gracia Real Santa Teresa de Mose, established just north of present-day Saint Augustine by self-emancipated slaves who fled from South Carolina to Spanish Florida in the early 1700s, to the homes of prominent individuals, such as Benjamin Banneker and Frederick Douglass. In general, few differences are found between the sites occupied by free blacks and by whites of comparable social and economic position.[77] The most extensive study of a free-black antebellum community conducted thus far examined ten sites in two Alexandria, Virginia, neighborhoods.[78] The major ethnic difference in the material world of white middle-class artisans and merchants and free-black Alexandrians was apparent in foodways. Black Alexandrians consumed more pork than did whites and displayed a particular preference for pigs' feet. In addition, the predominance of bowls suggests that free blacks, as did slaves, may have preferred soups, stews, and other single-dish meals. At present, foodways seem to be the most sensitive indicator of an African-American value culture. Even at post-Reconstruction sites, distinctive patterns of African-American foodways have been identified.[79] But the inequalities between black and white in antebellum Alexandria are also evident in the archaeological record. For example, the white middle class had access to private wells and by the 1850s even piped water. Black Alexandrians, however, had few wells and had "to walk several blocks to procure their water in buckets."[80]

Some slave sites often contain deposits that date after emancipation and demonstrate a considerable degree of cultural continuity from slavery to freedom. Such was again the case at the Jordan plantation in Texas. Two studies of communities established for the resettlement of former slaves have also been recently undertaken, one being at Mitchelville, part of the Union army's 1862 Port Royal experiment to settle black laborers on the South Carolina Sea Islands.[81] Located on Hilton Head Island and occupied until the early 1880s, the Mitchelville site has provided detailed information on a planned community of freedmen. Compared to those found at coastal slave sites, the artifacts and food remains at Mitchelville show marked differences. The freedmen and -women, for example, purchased expensive items such as furniture, stemware, silver utensils, and other tableware, as well as fancy jewelry. They also consumed more domestic meat (pork, beef, chicken, turkey, and goose) than did slaves. Emancipation for the freedmen at Mitchelville undoubtedly meant greater access to material goods than they had ever experienced before.[82]

What does the future hold for African-American archaeology? Certainly the immediate future seems bright, with new projects far too numerous to list here. Suffice it to say that investigations have thus far been initiated in at least thirty states, Canada, several Caribbean islands, and Central America. A few sites associated with the slave trade are currently being studied in Africa so as to examine systematically the trade's impact on both sides of the Atlantic. Moreover, there is much more to be learned from African-American archaeology than a community's ethnic patterns and living conditions. The archaeological record can be used to examine other kinds of questions for which material culture can serve as a primary source of information. For instance, future studies will explore questions of cultural change, power relationships between slave and master, even slave resistance. In time, yet other questions and problems will be added to the list, making archaeology an increasingly significant field of inquiry in the study of African-American life. □

Notes

SLAVERY IN THE AMERICAN EXPERIENCE
Drew Gilpin Faust

The author is grateful to Lee Cassanelli, Brian Crane, Richard S. Dunn, and Charles Rosenberg for assistance, comments, and criticism.

[1] Edmund S. Morgan, "Slavery and Freedom: The American Paradox," *Journal of American History* 59 (1972): 5–29.

[2] See I. M. Finley, *Ancient Slavery and Modern Ideology* (New York, 1980); Charles Verlinden, *The Beginnings of Modern Colonization* (Ithaca, 1970); Marc Bloch, *Slavery and Serfdom in the Middle Ages: Selected Essays*, trans. William Beer (Berkeley, 1975); William D. Phillips, Jr., *Slavery from Roman Times to the Early Transatlantic Trade* (Minneapolis, 1985).

[3] The debate over the volume of the slave trade has been long-lived and acrimonious. See Paul E. Lovejoy, "The Impact of the Atlantic Slave Trade on Africa: A Review of the Literature," *Journal of African History* 30 (1989): 365–94. The estimate of the internal death rate is based on Joseph C. Miller, *Way of Death: Merchant Capitalism and the Angolan Slave Trade, 1730–1830* (Madison, 1988).

[4] See for example Suzanne Miers and Igor Kopytoff, eds., *Slavery in Africa: Historical and Anthropological Perspectives* (Madison, 1977); Paul E. Lovejoy, *Transformations in Slavery: A History of Slavery in Africa* (New York, 1983).

[5] For an overview of Latin American slavery see Herbert S. Klein, *African Slavery in Latin America and the Caribbean* (New York, 1986).

[6] See Edmund S. Morgan, *American Slavery, American Freedom: The Ordeal of Colonial Virginia* (New York, 1975); Winthrop D. Jordan, *White Over Black: American Attitudes Toward the Negro, 1590–1812* (Chapel Hill, 1968); Allan Kulikoff, *Tobacco and Slaves: The Development of Southern Cultures in the Chesapeake, 1680–1800* (Chapel Hill, 1986).

[7] Russell Menard, "From Servants to Slaves: The Transformation of the Chesapeake Labor System," *Southern Studies* 16 (1977): 355–90; Richard S. Dunn, "Servants and Slaves," in *Colonial British America:*

Essays in the New History of the Early Modern Era, ed. Jack P. Greene and J. R. Pole (Baltimore, 1984), 157–94.

[8] Herbert S. Klein, *The Middle Passage: Comparative Studies in the Atlantic Slave Trade* (Princeton, 1978); James A. Rawley, *The Transatlantic Slave Trade: A History* (New York, 1981); Lovejoy, "The Impact of the Atlantic Slave Trade," 365–94.

[9] Peter H. Wood, *Black Majority: Negroes in Colonial South Carolina from 1670 through the Stono Rebellion* (New York, 1974); Ira Berlin, "The Slave Trade and the Development of Afro-American Society in English Mainland North America, 1619–1775," *Southern Studies* 20 (1981): 122–36.

[10] Allan Kulikoff, "The Beginnings of the Afro-American Family in Maryland," in *Law, Society and Politics in Early Maryland*, ed. Aubrey C. Land, Lois Green Carr, and Edward C. Papenfuse (Baltimore, 1977), 171–96; Allan Kulikoff, "The Origins of Afro-American Society in Tidewater Maryland and Virginia, 1700–1790," *William and Mary Quarterly*, 3d ser., 35 (1978): 226–59.

[11] Ulrich B. Phillips, *American Negro Slavery: A Survey of the Supply, Employment and Control of Negro Labor as Determined by the Plantation Regime* (New York, 1918).

[12] Kenneth M. Stampp, *The Peculiar Institution: Slavery in the Ante-Bellum South* (New York, 1956).

[13] Stanley M. Elkins, *Slavery: A Problem in American Institutional and Intellectual Life* (Chicago, 1959).

[14] See for example Ann J. Lane, ed., *The Debate Over Slavery: Stanley Elkins and His Critics* (Urbana, 1971).

[15] Elkins's interest in comparative slavery was informed by the work of Frank Tannenbaum, *Slave and Citizen: The Negro in the Americas* (New York, 1946).

[16] Quoted in Stanley M. Elkins, *Slavery: A Problem in American Institutional and Intellectual Life*, 3d ed., rev. (Chicago, 1976), 276.

[17] John W. Blassingame, *The Slave Community: Plantation Life in the Antebellum South* (New York, 1972); Herbert G. Gutman, *The Black Family in Slavery and Freedom, 1750–1925* (New York, 1976); Lawrence W. Levine, *Black Culture and Black Consciousness: Afro-*

American Folk Thought from Slavery to Freedom (New York, 1977); Eugene D. Genovese, *Roll, Jordan, Roll: The World the Slaves Made* (New York, 1974).

[18]Just as with the overall interpretation of slavery's impact, academic debate on this, too, is keen. Other historians regard the same statistic, that one in three couples was separated, quite differently and stress instead that a majority — two of three — was able to remain in long-lived unions. For an overview of the debate see for example Gutman, *The Black Family*; Michael Tadman, *Speculators and Slaves: Masters, Traders, and Slaves in the Old South* (Madison, 1989).

[19]Deborah Gray White, *Ar'n't I a Woman?: Female Slaves in the Plantation South* (New York, 1985); Elizabeth Fox-Genovese, *Within the Plantation Household: Black and White Women of the Old South* (Chapel Hill, 1988).

[20]See Albert J. Raboteau, *Slave Religion: The "Invisible Institution" in the Ante-bellum South* (New York, 1978); Mechal Sobel, *Trabelin' On: The Slave Journey to an Afro-Baptist Faith* (Westport, Conn., 1979); John B. Boles, *Black Southerners, 1619–1869* (Lexington, Ky., 1983); Genovese, *Roll, Jordan, Roll*.

[21]Eugene D. Genovese, *From Rebellion to Revolution: Afro-American Slave Revolts in the Making of the Modern World* (Baton Rouge, 1979); Gerald W. Mullin, *Flight and Rebellion: Slave Resistance in Eighteenth-Century Virginia* (New York, 1972); Herbert Aptheker, *American Negro Slave Revolts* (New York, 1943).

[22]Willie Lee Rose, "The Domestication of Domestic Slavery," in Rose, *Slavery and Freedom*, ed. William W. Freehling (New York, 1982), 25.

[23]Edward Spann Hammond summarizing his father James Henry Hammond's principles of management in Edward Spann Hammond, Plantation Manual 1857–1858, 11 July 1857, Edward Spann Hammond Papers, South Caroliniana Library, University of South Carolina, Columbia.

[24]For the most complete study of paternalism see Genovese, *Roll, Jordan, Roll*.

[25]Ira Berlin and Ronald Hoffman, eds., *Slavery and Freedom in the Age of the American Revolution* (Charlottesville, 1983); William W. Freehling, "The Founding Fathers and Slavery," *American Historical Review* 77 (1972): 81–93; Duncan J. MacLeod, *Slavery, Race, and the American Revolution* (Cambridge, 1974).

[26]Benjamin Quarles, *The Negro in the American Revolution* (Chapel Hill, 1961); Philip S. Foner, *Blacks in the American Revolution* (Westport, Conn., 1976).

[27]Edgar J. McManus, *Black Bondage in the North* (Syracuse, 1973); Arthur Zilversmit. *The First Emancipation: The Abolition of Slavery in the North* (Chicago, 1967); Jordan, *White Over Black*; see also Edgar J. McManus, *A History of Negro Slavery in New York* (Syracuse, 1966).

[28]David Brion Davis, *The Problem of Slavery in the Age of Revolution, 1770–1823* (Ithaca, 1975).

[29]U.S. Constitution, art. 1, sec. 2.

[30]Quoted in John Chester Miller, *The Wolf by the Ears: Thomas Jefferson and Slavery* (New York, 1977), 221.

[31]Quoted in Theodore Rosengarten, *Tombee: Portrait of a Cotton Planter* (New York, 1986), 139.

[32]For population statistics see Boles, *Black Southerners*, 75.

[33]Ibid., 75–76; Gavin Wright, *The Political Economy of the Cotton South: Households, Markets, and Wealth in the Nineteenth Century* (New York, 1978).

[34]Philip D. Morgan, "Task and Gang Systems: The Organization of Labor on New World Plantations," in *Work and Labor in Early America*, ed. Stephen Innes (Chapel Hill, 1988); Philip D. Morgan, "Work and Culture: The Task System and the World of Lowcountry Blacks, 1700 to 1880," *William and Mary Quarterly*, 3d ser., 39 (1982): 563–99.

[35]Robert S. Starobin, *Industrial Slavery in the Old South* (New York, 1970); Richard C. Wade, *Slavery in the Cities: The South, 1820–1860* (New York, 1964); Claudia Dale Goldin, *Urban Slavery in the American South, 1820–1860: A Quantitative History* (Chicago, 1976).

[36]Ira Berlin, *Slaves Without Masters: The Free Negro in the Antebellum South* (New York, 1974); Leonard P. Curry, *The Free Black in Urban America, 1800–1850: The Shadow of the Dream* (Chicago, 1981).

[37]Charles Wiltse, ed., *David Walker's Appeal, in Four Articles* (New York, 1965); John Lofton, *Insurrection in South Carolina: The Turbulent World of Denmark Vesey* (Yellow Springs, Ohio, 1964).

[38]For a comparative view see David W. Cohen and Jack P. Greene, eds., *Neither Slave Nor Free: The Freedmen of African Descent in the Slave Societies of the New World* (Baltimore, 1972).

[39]"Neither citizen nor slave," free blacks, historian Ira Berlin remarked, "dangled awkwardly in the middle of the southern caste system," sharing "some of the privileges of whites" and "many of the liabilities of slaves, yet they stood apart from both" (Berlin, *Slaves Without Masters*, 250).

[40]Benjamin Drew, *The Refugee: A North Side View of Slavery*, in *Four Fugitive Slave Narratives*, ed. R. W. Winks (Reading, Mass., 1969), 4.

[41]Bertram Wyatt-Brown, "The Mask of Obedience: Male Slave Psychology in the Old South," *American Historical Review* 93 (1988): 1230.

[42]Peter Kolchin, "Reevaluating the Antebellum Slave Community: A Comparative Perspective," *Journal of American History* 70 (1983): 581.

[43]Peter Kolchin, *Unfree Labor: American Slavery and Russian Serfdom* (Cambridge, 1987).

[44]C. Duncan Rice, *The Rise and Fall of Black Slavery* (New York, 1975); see also Larry E. Tise, *Proslavery: A History of the Defense of Slavery in America, 1701–1840* (Athens, 1987).

[45]Stanley W. Campbell, *The Slave Catchers: Enforcement of the Fugitive Slave Law, 1850–1860* (Chapel Hill, 1970).

[46]Robert Barnwell Rhett in Charleston *Mercury*, 31 Oct. 1859.

[47]See for example James H. Brewer, *The Confederate Negro: Virginia's Craftsmen and Military Laborers, 1861–1865* (Durham, 1969); Robert F. Durden, *The*

Gray and the Black: The Confederate Debate on Emancipation (Baton Rouge, 1972).

[48]Alexander Stephens in Atlanta *Southern Confederacy*, 13 Mar. 1861.

[49]Addie Harris to G. W. Randolph, 29 Oct. 1862, Letters Received, Confederate Secretary of War, Record Group 109, M437 R53 H1166, National Archives, Washington, D.C.

[50]See for example Bell I. Wiley, *Southern Negroes, 1861–1865* (1938; reprint, Baton Rouge, 1974); Clarence L. Mohr, *On the Threshold of Freedom: Masters and Slaves in Civil War Georgia* (Athens, 1986).

[51]Dudley T. Cornish, *The Sable Arm: Negro Troops in the Union Army, 1861–1865* (1956; reprint, Lawrence, Kans., 1987); Benjamin Quarles, *The Negro in the Civil War* (Boston, 1953); James M. McPherson, *The Negro's Civil War: How American Negroes Felt and Acted During the War for the Union* (New York, 1965).

[52]Quoted in Leon F. Litwack, *Been in the Storm So Long: The Aftermath of Slavery* (New York, 1979), 64.

[53]Joseph T. Glatthaar, *Forged in Battle: The Civil War Alliance of Black Soldiers and White Officers* (New York, 1990).

[54]For a recent overview of the incident see John Cimprich and Robert C. Mainfort, Jr., "The Fort Pillow Massacre: A Statistical Note," *Journal of American History* 76 (1989): 830–37.

[55]Quoted in Litwack, *Been in the Storm So Long*, 51.

[56]James L. Roark, *Masters Without Slaves: Southern Planters in the Civil War and Reconstruction* (New York, 1977).

[57]Quoted in Litwack, *Been in the Storm So Long*, 213.

PLANTATION LANDSCAPES OF THE
ANTEBELLUM SOUTH
John Michael Vlach

[1]Margaret Mitchell, *Gone With the Wind* (1936; reprint, New York, 1941), 94.

[2]For an overview of the growth of a southern mythology in film see Edward D. C. Campbell, Jr., *The Celluloid South: Hollywood and the Southern Myth* (Knoxville, 1981), 3–32.

[3]John Pendleton Kennedy, *Swallow Barn; or, A Sojourn in the Old Dominion* (1832; reprint, Baton Rouge, 1986), 28.

[4]Ritchie Devon Watson, *The Cavalier in Virginia Fiction* (Baton Rouge, 1985); Jack Temple Kirby, *Media-Made Dixie: The South in the American Imagination* (Baton Rouge, 1978), 64–78; Francis Pendleton Gaines, *The Southern Plantation: A Study in the Development and Accuracy of a Tradition* (1924; reprint, Gloucester, Mass., 1962), 62–94; Paul H. Buck, *The Road to Reunion, 1865–1900* (Boston, 1937), 196–235; Jay B. Hubbell, *Southern Life in Fiction* (Athens, 1960), 1–30; see also Virginia Museum of Fine Arts, *Painting in the South: 1564–1980* (Richmond, 1983); Jessie Poesch, *The Art of the South: Painting, Sculpture, Architecture and the Products of Craftsmen, 1560–1860* (New York, 1983).

[5]Frank L. Owsley, *Plain Folk in the Old South* (Baton Rouge, 1949), 2, 9.

[6]James C. Bonner, "Plantation Architecture of the Lower South on the Eve of the Civil War," *Journal of Southern History* 11 (1945): 371.

[7]Ibid.

[8]Ulrich B. Phillips, *Life and Labor in the Old South* (Boston, 1929), 389.

[9]John B. Boles, *Black Southerners, 1619–1869* (Lexington, 1983), 107.

[10]See Lawrence W. Levine, *Black Culture and Black Consciousness: Afro-American Folk Thought from Slavery to Freedom* (New York, 1977); John Michael Vlach, *The Afro-American Tradition in Decorative Arts* (Cleveland, 1978).

[11]Sam Bowers Hilliard, *Atlas of Antebellum Southern Agriculture* (Baton Rouge, 1984), 70.

[12]On the significance of landscape as a cultural concept see Donald W. Meinig, ed., *The Interpretation of Ordinary Landscapes: Geographical Essays* (New York, 1979).

[13]Gregory A. Stiverson and Patrick H. Butler III, eds., "Virginia in 1732: The Travel Journal of William Hugh Grove," *Virginia Magazine of History and Biography* 85 (1977): 26.

[14]The term *Quarter* refers to a section of a plantation estate; when lowercased, the word describes a dwelling house.

[15]Jack P. Greene, ed., *The Diary of Colonel Landon Carter of Sabine Hall, 1752–1778*, 2d ed. (Richmond, 1987), 2:856.

[16]See for example Thomas Anburey, *Travels Through the Interior Parts of America* (London, 1789), 2:381–82; Greene, ed., *The Diary of Colonel Landon Carter*, 2:1095.

[17]For a description of Mason's slave craftsmen see Gerald W. Mullin, *Flight and Rebellion: Slave Resistance in Eighteenth-Century Virginia* (New York, 1972), 12.

[18]Hunter Dickinson Farish, ed., *Journal and Letters of Philip Vickers Fithian, 1773–1774: A Plantation Tutor of the Old Dominion*, rev. ed. (Williamsburg, 1957), 80–81.

[19]Rhys Isaac, *The Transformation of Virginia, 1740–1790* (Chapel Hill, 1982), 39–40; see also Dell Upton, "White and Black Landscapes in Eighteenth-Century Virginia," *Places* 2 (1985):59–72.

[20]Phillips, *Life and Labor in the Old South*, 239.

[21]Herman Ginther, *Captain Staunton's River* (Richmond, 1968), 17–18; Green Hill, Campbell County, Va., Historic American Buildings Survey, Prints and Photographs Division, Library of Congress, cited hereafter as HABS; Robert A. Lancaster, Jr., *Historic Virginia Homes and Churches* (1915; reprint, Spartanburg, S.C., 1973), 422.

[22]For further discussion of the I-house see Henry Glassie, *Pattern in the Material Folk Culture of the Eastern United States* (Philadelphia, 1968), 66–67.

[23]Peter H. Wood, *Black Majority: Negroes in Colonial South Carolina from 1670 through the Stono Rebellion*

(New York, 1974), 35–62; Phillips, *Life and Labor in the Old South*, 116.

[24]Quoted in Wood, *Black Majority*, 132.

[25]Charles W. Joyner, *Down by the Riverside: A South Carolina Slave Community* (Urbana, 1984), 19–20.

[26]Ibid., 42.

[27]Daniel C. Littlefield, *Rice and Slaves: Ethnicity and the Slave Trade in Colonial South Carolina* (Baton Rouge, 1981), 74–114.

[28]Frederick Law Olmsted, *The Cotton Kingdom: A Traveller's Observations on Cotton and Slavery in the American Slave States*, ed. Arthur M. Schlesinger (New York, 1953), 181.

[29] David Doar, *Rice and Rice Planting in the South Carolina Low Country* (Charleston, 1936), 8.

[30]Malcolm Bell, Jr., *Major Butler's Legacy: Five Generations of a Slaveholding Family* (Athens, 1987), 122–24; see also Charles F. Kovacik and Robert E. Mason, "Changes in the South Carolina Sea Island Cotton Industry," *Southeastern Geographer* 25 (1985): 77–104.

[31]Ulrich B. Phillips, ed., *Plantation and Frontier, 1649–1863* (New York, 1969), 1:252.

[32]J. H. Easterby, *The South Carolina Rice Plantation as Revealed in the Papers of Robert F. W. Alston* (Chicago, 1945), 448.

[33]Zephaniah Kingsley Plantation, Fort George Island, Fla., HABS.

[34]Olmsted, *The Cotton Kingdom*, 181.

[35]Ibid., 181–82.

[36]Ibid., 184–85.

[37]For the development of African-American music in Georgia for example see Lydia Parrish, *Slave Songs of the Georgia Sea Islands* (New York, 1942).

[38]Julia Floyd Smith, *Slavery and Rice Culture in Low Country Georgia, 1750–1860* (Knoxville, 1985), 55–56.

[39]Joyner, *Down by the Riverside*, 49.

[40]Elias B. Bull, "Storm Towers of the Santee Delta," *South Carolina Historical Magazine* 8 (1980): 96.

[41]Sam Bowers Hillard, "The Tidewater Rice Plantation: An Ingenious Adaptation to Nature," *Geoscience and Man* 12 (1975): 57–66.

[42]Phillips, *Life and Labor in the Old South*, 94–95.

[43]Ibid., 212.

[44]George A. Davis and O. Fred Donaldson, *Blacks in the United States: A Geographical Perspective* (Boston, 1975), 15.

[45]Ulrich B. Phillips, *American Negro Slavery: A Survey of the Supply, Employment and Control of Negro Labor as Determined by the Plantation Regime* (1918; reprint, Baton Rouge, 1966), 226.

[46]Ibid., 218.

[47]Orville Vernon Burton, *In My Father's House Are Many Mansions: Family and Community in Edgefield, South Carolina* (Chapel Hill, 1985), 42.

[48]George P. Rawick, ed., *The American Slave: A Composite Autobiography* (Westport, Conn., 1972), S.C., 3: pt. 4, 177.

[49]Ibid., Ala., 6: pt. 1, 385–86.

[50]George P. Rawick, Jay Hillegas, and Ken Lawrence, eds., *The American Slave: A Composite Autobiography, Supplement, Series 1* (Westport, Conn., 1977), Miss., 9: pt. 4, 1857.

[51]Olmsted, *The Cotton Kingdom*, 280.

[52]Rawick, ed., *The American Slave*, N.C., 15: pt. 2, 364.

[53]For a portrait of a slaveholding farm see John Solomon Otto, "Slaveholding General Farmers in a Cotton County," *Agricultural History* 55 (1981): 167–79.

[54]Thornhill, Greene County, Ala., HABS.

[55]Eugene D. Genovese, *Roll, Jordan, Roll: The World the Slaves Made* (New York, 1974), 321.

[56]Weymouth T. Jordan, *Hugh Davis and His Alabama Plantation* (1948; reprint, Westport, Conn., 1974), 45, 104; for remarks on slave gardens see James O. Breeden, ed., *Advice Among Masters: The Ideal in Slave Management in the Old South* (Westport, Conn., 1980), 266–75.

[57]George P. Rawick, *From Sundown to Sunup: The Making of the Black Community* (Westport, Conn., 1972), 71.

[58]Abigail C. Holbrook, "A Glimpse of Life on Antebellum Slave Plantations in Texas," *Southwestern Historical Quarterly* 76 (1973): 380.

[59]J. Carlyle Sitterson, *Sugar Country: The Cane Sugar Industry in the South, 1753–1950* (Lexington, 1953), 5.

[60]Phillips, *Life and Labor in the Old South*, 120.

[61]Sitterson, *Sugar Country*, 45–46.

[62]Ibid., 46–47.

[63]Phillips, *American Negro Slavery*, 242–44.

[64]Olmsted, *The Cotton Kingdom*, 249.

[65]Sitterson, *Sugar Country*, 45.

[66]Terry G. Jordan, "Division of the Land," in *This Remarkable Continent: An Atlas of United States and Canadian Society and Cultures*, ed. John F. Rooney, Jr., Wilbur Zelinsky, and Dean R. Louder (College Station, Tex., 1982), 59, map 3–4.

[67]John B. Rehder, "Sugar Plantation Settlements of Southern Louisiana: A Cultural Geography" (Ph.D. diss., Louisiana State University, 1971), 84–93; John B. Rehder, "Diagnostic Landscape Traits of Sugar Plantations in Southern Louisiana," *Geoscience and Man* 19 (1978): 135–50; Roland C. McConnell, *Negro Troops of Antebellum Louisiana: A History of the Battalion of Free Men of Color* (Baton Rouge, 1968), 47; Phillips, *American Negro Slavery*, 165.

[68]Rehder, "Sugar Plantation Settlements," 98–109.

[69]Sitterson, *Sugar Country*, 66.

[70]Ibid., 118.

[71]Ibid., 135; W. E. Butler, *Down Among the Sugar Cane: The Story of Louisiana Sugar Plantations and Their Railroads* (Baton Rouge, 1980), 21–26.

[72]Sitterson, *Sugar Country*, 137–47, 152.

[73]Ibid., 30, 45 (quotation).

[74]Richard C. Wade, *Slavery in the Cities: The South, 1820–1860* (New York, 1964), 325–27.

[75]See for example J. L. Dawson and H. W. DeSaussure, *Census of Charleston for 1848* (Charleston, 1849), 31–36.

[76]See for example Roulhac Toledano et al., *Creole Faubourgs*, vol. 4 of *New Orleans Architecture* (Gretna, La., 1974), 74–77.

[77]Wade, *Slavery in the Cities*, 59.

[78]Moses Waring House, Mobile, Ala., HABS.

[79]Wade, *Slavery in the Cities*, 116.

[80]Ward House, Charleston, S.C., HABS.

[81]Mills Lane, *The Architecture of the Old South: South Carolina* (Savannah, 1984), 188; Alice R. Huger Smith and D. E. Huger Smith, *The Dwelling Houses of Charleston, South Carolina* (Philadelphia, 1917), 298; Robinson-Aiken House, Charleston, S.C., HABS.

[82]*List of Taxpayers of the City of Charleston for 1859* (Charleston, 1860).

[83]Herbert Anthony Keller, ed., *Solon Robinson, Pioneer and Agriculturist: Selected Writings, 1846–1851* (Indianapolis, 1936), 368.

[84]Isaac, *The Transformation of Virginia*, 16.

THE WORLD OF THE PLANTATION SLAVES
Charles Joyner

The author wrote a portion of this essay while an associate of the W. E. B. DuBois Institute for Afro-American Research at Harvard University. The support of the DuBois Institute is gratefully acknowledged.

[1]Jacob Stroyer, *My Life in the South*, 3d ed. (Salem, Mass., 1885), quoted in Willie Lee Rose, ed., *A Documentary History of Slavery in North America* (New York,1976), 401–5.

[2]Cato to Charles Colcock Jones, 3 Sept. 1852, quoted in Robert S. Starobin, ed., *Blacks in Bondage: Letters of American Slaves*, 2d ed. (New York, 1988), 49.

[3]George P. Rawick, Jan Hillegas, and Ken Lawrence, eds., *The American Slave: A Composite Autobiography, Supplement, Series 1* (Westport, Conn., 1977), Miss., 6: pt. 1, 243.

[4]Lydia Parrish, *Slave Songs of the Georgia Sea Islands* (New York, 1942), 245–47.

[5]Charles L. Perdue, Jr., Thomas E. Barden, and Robert K. Phillips, eds., *Weevils in the Wheat: Interviews With Virginia Ex-Slaves* (1976; reprint, Bloomington, Ind., 1980), 306.

[6]Ibid., 281.

[7]Ibid., 322.

[8]Ibid., 148 (Hunt), 224 (Perry).

[9]Evangeline W. Andrews, ed., *Journal of a Lady of Quality: Being the Narrative of a Journey from Scotland to the West Indies, North Carolina, and Portugal in the Years 1774 to 1776* (New Haven, 1922), 194.

[10]Parrish, *Slave Songs*, 225.

[11]Ibid., 236.

[12]Solomon Northup, *Twelve Years a Slave*, ed. Sue Eakin and Joseph Logsdon (Baton Rouge, 1968), 159–61.

[13]J. Carlyle Sitterson, *Sugar Country: The Cane Sugar Industry in the South, 1753–1950* (Lexington, 1953), 112–56.

[14]Quoted in Rose, ed., *A Documentary History of Slavery*, 400.

[15]Frances Anne Kemble, *Journal of a Residence on a Georgian Plantation in 1838–1839*, ed. John A. Scott (1961; reprint, Athens, 1984), 99–100.

[16]George P. Rawick, ed., *The American Slave: A Composite Autobiography* (Westport, Conn., 1972), Okla., 7:301.

[17]Ibid., Ark., 11: pt. 7, 22 (Walker); Ala., 6:45 (Bradfield); Rawick, Hillegas, and Lawrence, eds., *The American Slave, Supplement, Series 1*, Miss., 9: pt. 4, 1456 (Matthews).

[18]Rawick, ed., *The American Slave*, Ind., 6:189.

[19]Rawick, Hillegas, and Lawrence, eds., *The American Slave, Supplement, Series 1*, Miss., 9: pt. 4, 1465 (May); Miss., 8: pt. 3, 899 (Frances).

[20]Rawick, ed., *The American Slave*, Ind., 6:57.

[21]Ibid., Okla., 7:89.

[22]Kemble, *Journal of a Residence*, 256, 363–64.

[23]Rawick, ed., *The American Slave*, Ala., 6:7 (Abercrombie), 105 (Davis), 321 (Poole), 329 (Rice).

[24]Ibid., Miss., 7:69 (Hodges); S.C., 2: pt. 1, 346 (Durant); Ind., 6:59 (Colbert).

[25]Ibid., Ark., 11: pt. 7, 22 (Walker); Ala., 6:36 (Bishop); Mo., 11:215 (Jones).

[26]Rawick, Hillegas, and Lawrence, eds., *The American Slave, Supplement, Series 1*, Miss., 9: pt. 4, 1555.

[27]Ibid., Miss., 7: pt. 2, 601.

[28]Ibid., Okla., 12:5 (Anderson).

[29]Rawick, ed., *The American Slave*, N.C., 14: pt. 1, 95–96, 123–24.

[30]Ibid., Okla., 7:295.

[31]Ibid., Tex., 4: pt. 1, 158, 189.

[32]Ibid., Ala., 6:103 (Pugh), 120 (Eppes), 430 (Witherspoon).

[33]Ibid., Ark., 11: pt. 7, 9.

[34]Ibid., S.C., 2: pt. 1, 28; N.C., 14: pt. 1, 74 (Barbour).

[35]Ibid., Ark., 11: pt. 7, 29.

[36]Ibid., N.C., 14: pt. 1, 47 (Arrington), 71 (Baker).

[37]Ibid., Ala., 6:191; Norman R. Yetman, comp., *Life Under the "Peculiar Institution": Selections from the Slave Narrative Collection* (New York, 1970), 299.

[38]Perdue, Barden, and Phillips, eds., *Weevils in the Wheat*, 84; Stanley Feldstein, *Once a Slave: The Slaves' View of Slavery* (New York, 1971), 218–19 (Bruce quotation); Catherine Clinton, *The Plantation Mistress: Woman's World in the Old South* (New York, 1982), 204 (Simms quotation).

[39] Robert Manson Myers, ed., *The Children of Pride: A True Story of Georgia and the Civil War* (New Haven, 1972), 740–41.

[40] Kemble, *Journal of a Residence*, 207. After two such unsatisfactory experiences, Manigault at last secured the services of a suitable overseer, William Capers, in 1859. When Capers died in 1864, his employer wrote that his overseer "was a remarkable man in some respects, & knew more of the Negro Character and how to manage a Plantation than any of our former Overseers (William Kaufman Scarborough, *The Overseer: Plantation Management in the Old South* [Baton Rouge, 1966], 164–66).

[41] C. Vann Woodward, ed., *Mary Chesnut's Civil War* (New Haven, 1981), 169.

[42] Ibid., 29.

[43] Eugene D. Genovese, *Roll, Jordan, Roll: The World the Slaves Made* (New York, 1974), 417–18; Clinton, *The Plantation Mistress*, 211–12.

[44] Drew Gilpin Faust, *James Henry Hammond and the Old South: A Design for Mastery* (Baton Rouge, 1982), 86–88.

[45] George P. Rawick, ed., *The American Slave: A Composite Autobiography, Supplement, Series 2* (Westport, Conn., 1979), Tex., 8: pt. 7, 3292–94.

[46] Rawick, ed., *The American Slave*, Okla., 7:347.

[47] Perdue, Barden, and Phillips, eds., *Weevils in the Wheat*, 91.

[48] Social Science Institute, Fisk University, *Unwritten History of Slavery: Autobiographical Account of Negro Ex-Slaves* (Nashville, 1945), in Rawick, ed., *The American Slave*, 18:2.

[49] Northup, *Twelve Years a Slave*, 41.

[50] William Craft, *Running a Thousand Miles for Freedom; or, the Escape of William and Ellen Craft from Slavery* (London, 1860), quoted in Arna Wendell Bontemps, comp., *Great Slave Narratives* (Boston, 1969), 279.

[51] Orville Vernon Burton, *In My Father's House Are Many Mansions: Family and Community in Edgefield, South Carolina* (Chapel Hill, 1985), 185–86.

[52] Perdue, Barden, and Phillips, eds., *Weevils in the Wheat*, 84.

[53] Fisk University, *Unwritten History of Slavery*, in Rawick, ed., *The American Slave*, 18:2.

[54] Frederick Douglass, *Narrative of the Life of Frederick Douglass, an American Slave. Written by Himself* (Boston, 1845), 3–4.

[55] Rawick, ed., *The American Slave, Supplement, Series 2*, Tex., 4: pt. 3, 1218–19.

[56] Yetman, comp., *Life Under the "Peculiar Institution": Selections*, 127.

[57] Rawick, ed., *The American Slave*, Md., 16:34 (James); N.C., 15: pt. 2, 396–97 (Williams); for a variant transcription of the Williams quotation see Yetman, comp., *Life Under the "Peculiar Institution": Selections*, 317.

[58] Feldstein, *Once a Slave*, 222–23. Except for the gender of the protagonist, the incident is remarkably similar to the plot of Robert Penn Warren's 1955 novel, *Band of Angels*.

[59] Charles Colcock Jones, *Suggestions on the Religious Instruction of the Negroes in the Southern States* (1838; reprint, Philadelphia, 1947), quoted in Starobin, ed., *Blacks in Bondage*, 42.

[60] Fredrika Bremer, *The Homes of the New World; Impressions of America*, trans. Mary Howitt (1853; reprint, New York, 1868), 2:491.

[61] Quoted in Starobin, ed., *Blacks in Bondage*, 43, 52.

[62] Sarah Hodgson Torian, ed., "Ante-Bellum and War Memories of Mrs. Talfair Hodgson," *Georgia Historical Quarterly* 27 (1943): 351; Rawick, ed., *The American Slave*, Okla., 7:189 (Logan); Ala., 6:20, 77 (Clayton), 155, 237 (Jones).

[63] Rawick, ed., *The American Slave*, Ark., 11: pt. 7, 246; N.C., 14: pt. 1, 193 (Crasson).

[64] Rawick, Hillegas, and Lawrence, eds., *The American Slave, Supplement, Series 1*, Miss., 8: pt. 3, 1146.

[65] Ibid., Miss., 7: pt. 2, 716.

[66] Rawick, ed., *The American Slave*, Ind., 6:53; Ala., 6:398 (Van Dyke).

[67] Ibid., N.C., 14: pt. 1, 143.

[68] John G. Williams, *"De Ole Plantation"* (Charleston, 1895), 40.

[69] Rawick, Hillegas, and Lawrence, eds., *The American Slave, Supplement, Series 1*, Miss., 8: pt. 3, 899.

[70] Yetman, comp., *Life Under the "Peculiar Institution": Selections*, 167; Benjamin A. Botkin, ed., *Lay My Burden Down: A Folk History of Slavery* (1945; reprint, Athens, 1989), 145–46.

[71] Rawick, ed., *The American Slave*, Ind., 6:159 (Richardson), 161; N.C., 14: pt. 1, 143.

[72] Yetman, comp., *Life Under the "Peculiar Institution": Selections*, 57.

[73] Rawick, Hillegas, and Lawrence, eds., *The American Slave, Supplement, Series 1*, Miss., 6: pt. 1, 316.

[74] Rawick, ed., *The American Slave*, S.C., 3: pt. 4, 111.

[75] Yetman, comp., *Life Under the "Peculiar Institution": Selections*, 63.

[76] Ibid., 63, 115–16, 201, 251, 258.

[77] Jones, *Suggestions on the Religious Instruction of the Negroes*, 59.

[78] Feldstein, *Once a Slave*, 86.

[79] Peter Randolph, *Sketches of Slave Life: or, Illustrations of the "Peculiar Institution" by Peter Randolph, an Emancipated Slave*, 2d ed. (Boston, 1855), 49; James A. Padgett, ed., "A Yankee School Teacher in Louisiana, 1835–1837: The Diary of Caroline B. Poole," *Louisiana Historical Quarterly* 20 (1937): 677.

[80] Arthur Singleton [Henry Coggswell Knight], *Letters from the South and West* (Boston, 1824), 352; Savannah Unit, Georgia Writers' Project, Work Projects Administration, *Drums and Shadows: Survival Studies Among the Georgia Coastal Negroes* (1940; reprint, Athens, 1986), 62.

[81] Frederick Law Olmsted, *A Journey in the Seaboard Slave States in the Years 1853–1854, With Remarks on Their Economy* (1856; reprint, New York, 1904), 1:28–29.

[82]Kemble, *Journal of a Residence*, 146–47.

[83]Torian, ed., "Ante-Bellum and War Memories," 352.

[84]Georgia Bryan Conrad, "Reminiscences of a Southern Woman," *Southern Workman* 30 (1901): 13. The name is transcribed Bilali, Bi-la-li, Bu Allah, or Ben Ali in various sources.

[85]Savannah Unit, Georgia Writers' Project, *Drums and Shadows*, 161, 166.

[86]Rawick, ed., *The American Slave*, S.C., 2: pt. 2, 304 (Horry); Tex., 4: pt. 1, 149 (Brooks).

[87]Yetman, comp., *Life Under the "Peculiar Institution": Selections*, 63; Rawick, ed., *The American Slave*, N.C., 14: pt. 1, 157 (Burnett); Perdue, Barden, and Phillips, eds., *Weevils in the Wheat*, 97.

[88]Botkin, ed., *Lay My Burden Down*, 238.

[89]Yetman, comp., *Life Under the "Peculiar Institution": Selections*, 281.

[90]Rawick, ed., *The American Slave*, Ala., 6:111–12; Douglass, *Narrative of the Life*, 106–8.

[91]Rawick, ed., *The American Slave*, S.C., 3: pt. 4, 249.

[92]Yetman, comp., *Life Under the "Peculiar Institution": Selections*, 262.

[93]Kemble, *Journal of a Residence*, 141–42, 259–60.

[94]Rawick, Hillegas, and Lawrence, eds., *The American Slave, Supplement, Series 1*, Miss., 6: pt. 1, 244.

[95]Ibid., Miss., 9: pt. 4, 1554.

[96]Yetman, comp., *Life Under the "Peculiar Institution": Selections*, 190; Botkin, ed., *Lay My Burden Down*, 63.

[97]Edmund Kirke [James Robert Gilmore], *Among the Pines: Or, The South in Secession Time* (New York, 1862), 145–48.

[98]Yetman, comp., *Life Under the "Peculiar Institution": Selections*, 56; Perdue, Barden, and Phillips, eds., *Weevils in the Wheat*, 53, 108, 186.

[99]Botkin, ed., *Lay My Burden Down*, 18.

[100]Ibid., 13–14.

[101]Ibid., 10.

[102]Savannah Unit, Georgia Writers' Project, *Drums and Shadows*, 110–11. The plot is exactly like the Ashanti folk tale of the spider and the porcupine, in Robert Southerland Rattray, *Akan-Ashanti Folk-Tales* (Oxford, 1930), 43.

[103]Botkin, ed., *Lay My Burden Down*, 3–4.

[104]Rawick, ed., *The American Slave*, S.C., 2: pt. 1, 26 (Ballard); S.C. 3: pt. 4, 51.

[105]Ibid., Okla., 7:188.

[106]Kemble, *Journal of a Residence*, 99–100.

[107]Rawick, Hillegas, and Lawrence, eds., *The American Slave, Supplement, Series 1*, Miss., 9: pt. 4, 1442.

[108]Rawick, ed., *The American Slave*, N.C., 14: pt. 1, 424.

[109]Ibid., Ala. 6:190; Rawick, Hillegas, and Lawrence, eds., *The American Slave, Supplement, Series 1*, Miss., 9: pt. 4, 1455.

[110]Botkin, ed., *Lay My Burden Down*, 66.

[111]See for example Stacy Gibbons Moore, " 'Established and Well Cultivated': Afro-American Foodways in Early Virginia," *Virginia Cavalcade* 39 (1989): 70–83.

[112]Rawick, Hillegas, and Lawrence, eds., *The American Slave, Supplement, Series 1*, Miss., 10: pt. 5, 2200; Botkin, ed., *Lay My Burden Down*, 89; Rawick, ed., *The American Slave*, Okla., 7: 76, 233; Yetman, comp., *Life Under the "Peculiar Institution": Selections*, 336.

[113]Yetman, comp., *Life Under the "Peculiar Institution": Selections*, 52, 144, 151, 205, 282, 291; Rawick, ed., *The American Slave*, Okla., 7:145, 172, 207; Botkin, ed., *Lay My Burden Down*, 89.

[114]Botkin, ed., *Lay My Burden Down*, 63; Yetman, comp., *Life Under the "Peculiar Institution": Selections*, 170.

[115]Rawick, ed., *The American Slave*, Ala., 6:311 (Patton); N.C., 15: pt. 2, 320 (Stewart); S.C., 2: pt. 1, 125 (Brown), pt. 2, 197 (Green).

[116]Ibid., Ind., 6:131; Rawick, Hillegas, and Lawrence, eds., *The American Slave, Supplement, Series 1*, Miss., 9: pt. 4, 1792–93 (Ramsey).

[117]Rawick, ed., *The American Slave*, Okla., 7:271.

[118]Ibid., N.C., 14: pt. 1, 95.

[119]Work Projects Administration Mss., South Caroliniana Library, University of South Carolina, Columbia; Rawick, Hillegas, and Lawrence, eds., *The American Slave, Supplement, Series 1*, S.C., 11:194 (Horry).

[120]Perdue, Barden, and Phillips, eds., *Weevils in the Wheat*, 181.

[121]Rawick, Hillegas, and Lawrence, eds., *The American Slave, Supplement, Series 1*, Miss., 6: pt. 1, 314 (Butler); Miss., 10: pt. 5, 2199; Rawick, ed., *The American Slave*, N.C., 15: pt. 2, 318 (Stewart).

[122]Rawick, ed., *The American Slave*, S.C., 2: pt. 1, 11 (Adams), 15 (Adamson).

[123]Rawick, Hillegas, and Lawrence, eds., *The American Slave, Supplement, Series 1*, Miss., 9: pt. 4, 1550 (Montgomery); Rawick, ed., *The American Slave*, S.C., 3: pt. 3, 260 (Perry).

[124]Rawick, ed., *The American Slave*, S.C., 2: pt. 2, 317.

[125]Kemble, *Journal of a Residence*, 161 (second quotation), 215 (first quotation).

[126]Rawick, ed., *The American Slave*, Ala., 6:60 (Cheatam), 120 (Mistress), 311 (Patton); Okla., 7:228 (Montgomery).

[127]Charles Ball, *Slavery in the United States: A Narrative of the Life and Adventures of Charles Ball, a Black Man, Who Lived Forty Years in Maryland, South Carolina and Georgia, as a Slave* (1837; reprint, New York, 1937), 348–51.

[128]Rawick, ed., *The American Slave*, Okla., 7:301, 347 (Wilson); Ind., 6:62 (Cooper); Yetman, comp., *Life Under the "Peculiar Institution": Selections*, 40 (Branch).

[129]Rawick, ed., *The American Slave*, Okla., 7:135 (Henry), 166 (King).

[130]Yetman, comp., *Life Under the "Peculiar Institution": Selections*, 40 (Branch); Rawick, ed., *The American Slave*, Ala., 6:130 (Garlic).

[131]Langdon Cheves to Langdon Cheves, Jr., 2 May 1864, Cheves Family Papers, South Carolina Historical Society, Charleston.

[132]Rawick, Hillegas, and Lawrence, eds., *The American Slave, Supplement, Series 1*, Miss., 9: pt. 4, 1500–2; Miss., 8: pt. 3, 1132.

[133]Philip J. Schwarz, *Twice Condemned: Slaves and the Criminal Laws of Virginia, 1705–1865* (Baton Rouge, 1988), 3.

[134]Rawick, ed., *The American Slave*, Okla. 7:239 (Petite); S.C., 3: pt. 4, 52–53 (Russell); Tex., 4: pt. 1, 203.

[135]Ibid., Ga., 12: pt. 2, 59.

[136]Botkin, ed., *Lay My Burden Down*, 3; Olmsted, *A Journey in the Seaboard Slave States*, 1:116–17.

[137]Rawick, Hillegas, and Lawrence, eds., *The American Slave, Supplement, Series 1*, Miss., 6: pt. 1, 246.

[138]Douglass, *Narrative of the Life*, 40; Rawick, ed., *The American Slave*, Ala., 6:191.

[139]Rawick, Hillegas, and Lawrence, eds., *The American Slave, Supplement, Series 1*, Miss., 6: pt. 1, 47.

[140]Ruffin, in fact, dismissed three overseers in succession for cruelly mistreating his slaves (Betty Mitchell, *Edmund Ruffin: A Biography* [Bloomington, 1981], 30).

[141]Rawick, ed., *The American Slave, Supplement, Series 2*, Tex., 7: pt. 6, 2578 (Marshall); Rawick, Hillegas, and Lawrence, eds., *The American Slave, Supplement, Series 1*, Okla., 12:6 (Mose).

[142]Rawick, ed., *The American Slave*, Ind., 6:171 (Rudd); Ark., 8: pt. 2, 42; Yetman, comp., *Life Under the "Peculiar Institution": Selections*, 18–19 (Armstrong).

[143]Rawick, ed., *The American Slave*, Ala., 6:60.

[144]Ibid., Okla., 7:17.

[145]Ibid., S.C., 3: pt. 3, 130; Ala., 6:390.

[146]Ibid., S.C., 3: pt. 4, 113.

[147]Jack P. Greene, ed., *The Diary of Colonel Landon Carter of Sabine Hall, 1752–1778*, 2d ed. (Richmond, 1987), 1:286–92, 291 (quotation), 301.

[148]Rawick, ed., *The American Slave*, S.C., 2: pt. 1, 27.

[149]Charles T. Haskell to Langdon Cheves, 16 June 1862, Cheves Family Papers.

[150]Harriet A. Jacobs, *Incidents in the Life of a Slave Girl, Written by Herself*, ed. Jean Fagan Yellin (Cambridge, Mass., 1987), 129.

[151]Rawick, ed., *The American Slave*, Ala., 6:46.

[152]Adele Petigru Allston to Colonel Francis W. Herot, 31 May 1864, in J. H. Easterby, ed., *The South Carolina Rice Plantation as Revealed in the Papers of Robert F. W. Allston* (Chicago, 1945), 199.

[153]Rawick, Hillegas, and Lawrence, eds., *The American Slave, Supplement, Series 1*, Miss., 9: pt. 4, 1500–1.

[154]Rawick, ed., *The American Slave*, Ala., 6:418.

[155]Petition of John Rose, Richland District, 1831, Slavery Files, South Carolina Archives, Columbia.

[156]Rawick, ed., *The American Slave*, N.C., 15: pt. 2, 132.

[157]Thomas G. Allen to General Walker, 3 Feb. 1863, Francis W. Pickens and Milledge L. Bonham Papers, Library of Congress.

[158]For an overview of slave insurrections see Herbert Aptheker, *American Negro Slave Revolts*, 5th ed. (New York, 1983); Eugene D. Genovese, *From Rebellion to Revolution: Afro-American Slave Revolts in the Making of the Modern World* (Baton Rouge, 1979).

[159]Henry Clay Bruce, *The New Man: Twenty-Nine Years a Slave, Twenty-Nine Years a Free Man. Recollections of H. C. Bruce* (York, Pa., 1895), 25–26.

[160]Perdue, Barden, and Phillips, eds., *Weevils in the Wheat*, 75–76.

[161]Ibid., 35.

[162]Jacobs, *Incidents in the Life of a Slave Girl*, 63.

[163]Ibid., 64.

[164]Perdue, Barden, and Philips, eds., *Weevils in the Wheat*, 76.

[165]Henry Box Brown, *Narrative of the Life of Henry Box Brown, Written by Himself* (Boston, 1852), 19; Jacobs, *Incidents in the Life of a Slave Girl*, 66.

[166]Perdue, Barden, and Phillips, eds., *Weevils in the Wheat*, 76.

[167]Rawick, Hillegas, and Lawrence, eds., *The American Slave, Supplement, Series 1*, Miss., 7: pt. 2, 507.

[168]Rawick, ed., *The American Slave*, Okla., 7:271 (Robinson); Miss., 7:103 (McAllum).

[169]Ibid., Ala., 6:82.

[170]Ibid., N.C., 15: pt. 2, 346.

[171]Ibid., Ark., 11: pt. 7, 194.

[172]Ibid., N.C., 14: pt. 1, 157.

[173]Yetman, comp., *Life Under the "Peculiar Institution": Selections*, 149.

[174]Rawick, Hillegas, and Lawrence, eds., *The American Slave, Supplement, Series 1*, Miss., 9: pt. 4, 1556.

[175]Rawick, ed., *The American Slave*, Ala., 6:82.

[176]Rawick, Hillegas, and Lawrence, eds., *The American Slave, Supplement, Series 1*, Miss., 8: pt. 3, 1254.

[177]Ibid., Miss., 6: pt. 1, 250–51.

[178]Ibid., Miss., 7: pt. 2, 604.

[179]Rawick, ed., *The American Slave*, Okla., 7:231.

[180]Rawick, Hillegas, and Lawrence, eds., *The American Slave, Supplement, Series 1*, Miss., 8: pt. 3, 902.

[181]Ibid., Miss., 6: pt. 1, 324.

[182]Rawick, ed., *The American Slave*, Tex., 4: pt. 1, 280; for a variant transcription see Yetman, comp., *Life Under the "Peculiar Institution": Selections*, 70.

[183]Rawick, ed., *The American Slave*, Ind., 6:159.

FEMALE SLAVES IN THE PLANTATION SOUTH
Deborah Gray White

[1]Olive Gilbert, comp., *Narrative of Sojourner Truth, A Bondwoman of Olden Time* (1878; reprint, New York, 1968), 131–33.

[2]Ibid., 133.

[3]Ibid., 133–34. Truth's 1851 speech is widely quoted. Usually the word *ain't* is substituted for *ar'n't*; the latter appears in her 1878 narrative.

[4]Harriet A. Jacobs, *Incidents in the Life of a Slave Girl, Written by Herself*, ed. Jean Fagan Yellin (Cambridge, 1987), 77.

[5]William Bosman, *A New and Accurate Description of The Coast of Guinea* (1705; reprint, London, 1967), 208–11.

[6]*South Carolina Gazette*, 10 July 1736.

[7]Merrill D. Peterson, ed., *The Portable Thomas Jefferson* (New York, 1975), 187.

[8]Frederick Law Olmsted, *A Journey in the Back Country, 1853–1854* (New York, 1907), 113.

[9]George P. Rawick, ed., *The American Slave: A Composite Autobiography* (Westport, Conn., 1972), N.C., 15: pt. 2, 229.

[10]Johann David Schopf, *Travels in the Confederacy, 1783–1784* (Philadelphia, 1911), 1:147. See also Frances Anne Kemble, *Journal of a Residence on a Georgian Plantation in 1838–1839*, ed. John A. Scott (1961; reprint, Athens, 1984), 180, 227–28; Frederick Law Olmsted, *A Journey in the Seaboard Slave States* (New York, 1856), 391.

[11]Benjamin Drew, *The Refugee: A North–Side View of Slavery*, in *Four Fugitive Slave Narratives*, ed. R. W. Winks (Reading, Mass., 1969), 48–49, 92.

[12]Henry Bibb, *Narratives of the Life and Adventures of Henry Bibb, An American Slave*, in *Puttin' on Ole Massa: The Slave Narratives of Henry Bibb, William Wells Brown, and Solomon Northup*, ed. Gilbert Osofsky (New York, 1969), 120.

[13]Solomon Northup, *Twelve Years a Slave, Narrative of Solomon Northup*, in *Puttin' on Ole Massa*, 120.

[14]William Wells Brown, *Narrative of William Wells Brown, A Fugitive Slave*, in *Puttin' on Ole Massa*, 194–95.

[15]Bibb, *Narratives of the Life and Adventures*, 162–63.

[16]Fredrika Bremer, *The Homes of the New World; Impressions of America*, trans. Mary Howitt (1853; reprint, New York, 1868), 1:492–93.

[17]Chancellor [William] Harper, "Harper on Slavery," in *Cotton Is King and Pro-Slavery Arguments*, ed. E. N. Elliot (Augusta, Ga., 1860), 41–46.

[18]Reynolds Farley, *Growth of the Black Population, A Study of Demographic Trends* (Chicago, 1970), 21, 34. See also Reynolds Farley, "The Demographic Rates and Social Institutions of the Nineteenth-Century Negro Population: A Stable Population Analysis," *Demography* 2 (1965): 389, 390; Melvin Zelnick, "Fertility of the American Negro in 1830–1850," *Population Studies* 20 (1966): 82.

[19]The topic of slave fertility has stimulated heated debate and involved controversial issues, including the subject of interregional slave sales. Some historians have argued that the older southern states of Maryland, Delaware, Virginia, and North Carolina "bred" slaves for the "buyer" southwestern states and that slave fertility was, therefore, more important to slave owners in the older regions (Kenneth M. Stampp, *The Peculiar Institution: Slavery in the Ante-Bellum South* [New York, 1956], 245–58; Frederic Bancroft, *Slave Trading in the Old South* [1931; reprint, New York, 1969]). Others have found that slave owners in the older South realized a greater profit on slave women than slave men (Alfred Conrad and John R. Meyer, "The Economics of Slavery in the Ante-Bellum South," *Journal of Political Economy* 66 [April 1958]: 106–15). Richard Sutch concluded that "slave owners in the American South systematically bred slaves for sale." Slave breeders in the border and Atlantic-coast slave states held "disproportionally large numbers of women in the childbearing age group . . . , fostered polygamy and promiscuity among their slaves and then sold the products of the breeding operation in southwestern slave states" (Richard Sutch, "The Breeding of Slaves for Sale and Westward Expansion of Slavery 1830–1860," in *Race and Slavery in the Western Hemisphere: Quantitative Studies*, ed. Stanley Engerman and Eugene Genovese [Princeton, 1975], 173–210). Robert Fogel and Stanley Engerman argued instead that slave fertility was more highly valued in the newer than in the older regions. The interregional migration's higher proportion of single women without children than in the population that remained behind accounts, they claimed, for the higher fertility rate in the older southern states (Robert William Fogel and Stanley L. Engerman, *Time on the Cross: The Economics of American Negro Slavery* [Boston, 1974], 44–52, 78–84).

[20]Susan Dabney Smedes, *Memorials of a Southern Planter*, ed. Fletcher M. Green (New York, 1965), 42.

[21]Rawick, ed., *The American Slave*, N.C., 2:32; Ga., 12: pt. 1, 165.

[22]John Spencer Bassett, *The Southern Plantation Overseer as Revealed in His Letters* (Northampton, Mass., 1925), 32.

[23]Kemble, *Journal of a Residence*, 95.

[24]Rawick, ed., *The American Slave*, Ga., 13: pt. 4, 8.

[25]Helen T. Catterall, ed., *Judicial Cases Concerning American Slavery and the Negro* (Washington, D.C., 1936), 2:151–52.

[26]Benjamin A. Botkin, ed., *Lay My Burden Down: A Folk History of Slavery* (1945; reprint, Athens, 1989), 160–62.

[27]Social Science Institute, Fisk University, *Unwritten History of Slavery: Autobiographical Account of Negro Ex-Slaves* (Nashville, 1945), in Rawick, ed., *The American Slave*, 18:92.

[28]Catterall, ed., *Judicial Cases*, 3:503.

[29]Kemble, *Journal of a Residence*, 296; Rawick, ed., *The American Slave*, Ga., 12: pt. 2, 260–61; S.C., 2: pt. 2, 68; Fla., 17:213.

[30]Brown, *Narrative of William Wells Brown*, 187.

[31]Rawick, ed., *The American Slave*, N.C., 15: pt. 2, 144; Ga., 12: pt. 1, 64; Ronnie C. Tyler and Lawrence R. Murphy, eds., *The Slave Narratives of Texas* (Austin, 1974), 36; Louis Hughes, *Thirty Years a Slave* (Milwaukee, 1897), 85.

[32]Peter H. Wood, *Black Majority: Negroes in Colonial South Carolina from 1670 through the Stono Rebellion* (New York, 1974), 244.

[33]Gerald W. Mullin, *Flight and Rebellion: Slave Resistance in Eighteenth-Century Virginia* (New York, 1972), 40.

[34]James B. Sellers, *Slavery in Alabama* (University, Ala., 1950), 292.

[35]Eugene D. Genovese, *Roll, Jordan, Roll: The World the Slaves Made* (New York, 1974), 798; Judith Kelleher Schafer, "New Orleans Slavery in 1850 as Seen in Advertisements," *Journal of Southern History* 46 (1981): 43.

[36]Stampp, *The Peculiar Institution*, 110; Genovese, *Roll, Jordan, Roll*, 648; Joe Gray Taylor, *Negro Slavery in Louisiana* (Baton Rouge, 1963), 179; Lorenzo J. Greene, "The New England Negro as Seen in Advertisements for Runaway Slaves," *Journal of Negro History* 29 (1944): 131.

[37]Quoted in Deborah Gray White, *Ar'n't I A Woman?: Female Slaves in the Plantation South* (New York, 1985), 71. See also Kenneth F. Kipple and Virginia Himmelsteib King, *Another Dimension to the Black Diaspora: Diet, Disease, and Racism* (Cambridge, 1981), 97.

[38]Bancroft, *Slave Trading*, 186–87.

[39]Schafer, "New Orleans Slavery," 47.

[40]Josiah Henson, *An Autobiography of the Reverend Josiah Henson* in *Four Fugitive Slave Narratives*, 60.

[41]Bibb, *Narratives of the Life and Adventures*, 126–28.

[42]William Still, *The Underground Railroad, A Record of Facts, Authentic Narratives, Letters, etc.* (Philadelphia, 1872), 50.

[43]Ibid., 188.

[44]Harriet Beecher Stowe, *Uncle Tom's Cabin* (1852; reprint, New York, 1962), 74. See also Levi Coffin, *Reminiscences of Levi Coffin* (Cincinnati, 1898), 147–49; Marion Gleason McDougall, *Fugitive Slaves* (1891; reprint, New York, 1967), 47.

[45]Coffin, *Reminiscences*, 114.

[46]Still, *Underground Railroad*, 68, 264; Linda Brent, *Incidents in the Life of a Slave Girl*, ed. Lydia Maria Child (1861; reprint, New York, 1973), 151–64.

[47]Still, *Underground Railroad*, 264.

[48]Ibid., 158.

[49]Brent, *Incidents in the Life*, 93, 104. See also Rawick, ed., *The American Slave*, Ala., 6:73; Okla., 7:317.

[50]Rawick, ed., *The American Slave*, Ga., 12: pt. 2, 324.

[51]Northup, *Twelve Years a Slave*, 360–61. See also Rawick, ed., *The American Slave*, S.C., 2: pt. 2, 145; Bassett, *The Southern Plantation Overseer*, 129.

[52]Drew, *The Refugee*, 92.

[53]Rawick, ed., *The American Slave*, Ga., 13: pt. 4, 139.

[54]J. A. Turner, ed., *The Cotton Planters' Manual* (New York, 1865), 97–98; Guion B. Johnson, *A Social History of the Sea Islands* (Chapel Hill, 1930), 28–30; Jenkins Mikell, *Rumbling of the Chariot Wheels* (Columbia, S.C., 1923), 19–20; Stuart Bruchey, ed., *Cotton and the Growth of the American Economy: 1790–1860* (New York, 1967), 176–77, 179–80.

[55]Rawick, ed., *The American Slave*, Ga., 13: pt. 4, 157.

[56]Ibid., Ga., 13: pt. 3, 186.

[57]*Plantation Manual* (n.p., n.d.), 1, Southern Historical Collection, University of North Carolina, Chapel Hill (cited hereafter as SHC).

[58]Rawick, ed., *The American Slave*, Ark., 10: pt. 7, 193.

[59]J. W. Loguen, *The Rev. J. W. Loguen as a Slave and as a Free Man* (Syracuse, 1859), 20–21.

[60]Rawick, ed., *The American Slave*, S.C., 2: pt. 2, 65–66.

[61]Elizabeth Donnan, ed., *Documents Illustrative of the History of the Slave Trade to America* (Washington, D.C., 1930), 3:323.

[62]Joshua Coffin, ed., *An Account of Some of the Principal Slave Insurrections*, in *Slave Insurrections, Selected Documents*, ed. American Antislavery Society (1822–60; reprint, New York, 1968), 15; *South Carolina Gazette*, 1 Aug. 1769.

[63]C. Vann Woodward, ed., *Mary Chesnut's Civil War* (New Haven, 1981), 218–19.

[64]Smedes, *Memorials of a Southern Planter*, 180. Many eighteenth-century slaves exhibited resistant behavior. Whenever Landon Carter's spinners thought he was away they slacked off. One day he caught them by surprise and had them whipped. Suckey, one of Robert Carter's slave women, used Carter's absence to her advantage. When the overseer demanded that she report to work, she calmly sent word that Carter had excused her so she might wash clothes and "go to any meeting she pleased, any time in the weke." The overseer was thrown into a quandary and wrote Carter requesting that he separate Suckey from the rest of the slaves if she was to be given special privileges (Jack P. Greene, ed., *The Diary of Colonel Landon Carter of Sabine Hall, 1752–1778*, 2d ed. [Richmond, 1987], 2:762; Ulrich B. Phillips, *Plantation and Frontier: Documents, 1649–1863* [Cleveland, 1909], 1:325).

[65]Henson, *Autobiography of the Reverend Josiah Henson*, 116.

[66]Bassett, *The Southern Plantation Overseer*, 35, 59, 77, 119, 139, 142 (quotation), 144, 150, 151, 156, 157.

[67]Olmsted, *Journey in the Seaboard Slave States*, 190.

[68]Mullin, *Flight and Rebellion*, 55.

[69]Olmsted, *Journey in the Back Country*, 79.

[70]Rawick, ed., *The American Slave*, Ga., 13: pt. 3, 160; Mo., 10: pt. 7, 255; Hughes, *Thirty Years a Slave*, 41; Adwon Adams Davis, *Plantation Life in the Florida Parishes of Louisiana, 1836–1846, as Reflected in the Diary of Bennet H. Barrow* (New York, 1943), 127; Beth G. Crabtree and James W. Patton, eds., *"Journal of a Secesh Lady": The Diary of Catherine Devereux Edmondston, 1860–1866* (Raleigh, 1979), 46.

[71]Todd L. Savitt, *Medicine and Slavery: The Diseases and Health Care of Blacks in Antebellum Virginia* (Urbana, Ill., 1978), 180, 182.

[72]For examples of cures, see Rawick, ed., *The American Slave*, Ark., 10: pt. 5, 21, 125; Ala., 6:256, 318; Ga., 13: pt. 3, 106.

[73]Robert Manson Myers, ed., *The Children of Pride: A True Story of Georgia and the Civil War* (New Haven, 1972), 528, 532, 542, 544, 546.

[74]Rawick, ed., *The American Slave*, Ga., 13: pt. 3, 245.

[75]Ibid., S.C., 2: pt. 1, 99.

[76]Ibid., Ga., 12: pt. 2, 112; S.C., 2: pt. 2, 55; Fla., 17:174.

[77] See for example, Plantation Manual, 1, SHC.

[78] Rawick, ed., *The American Slave*, Ala., 6:73.

[79] Ibid., Ga., 13: pt. 3, 104.

[80] Ibid., Tex., 5: pt. 3, 43.

[81] Frederick Douglass, *My Bondage and My Freedom* (1855; reprint, New York, 1968), 69.

[82] Ophelia S. Egypt, J. Masuoka, and Charles S. Johnson, eds., *Unwritten History of Slavery, Autobiographical Accounts of Negro Ex-Slaves* (Nashville, 1945), 68.

[83] Ibid., 8.

[84] Rawick, ed., *The American Slave*, Ark., 8: pt. 2, 319.

[85] Although historians Robert Fogel and Stanley Engerman cited the slave woman's age at first birth at 22.5, other historians, including Herbert Gutman and Richard S. Dunn, have found the age to be substantially lower. Dunn found the average at first birth at Mount Airy, a Virginia plantation, to be 19.22 years. Gutman found the range to be from 17 to 19. Economists James Trussell and Richard Steckel have found the age to be 20.6 years (Fogel and Engerman, *Time on the Cross*, 137–38; Richard S. Dunn, "The Tale of Two Plantations: Slave Life at Mesopotamia in Jamaica and Mount Airy in Virginia, 1799 to 1828," *William and Mary Quarterly*, 3d ser., 34 [1977]: 58; Herbert G. Gutman, *The Black Family in Slavery and Freedom, 1750–1925* [New York, 1976], 50, 75, 124, 171; James Trussell and Richard Steckel, "The Age of Slaves at Menarche and Their First Birth," *Journal of Interdisciplinary History* 8 [1978]: 504). The term *marriage* is used with the understanding that legal marriage among slaves was prohibited.

[86] See for example Botkin, ed., *Lay My Burden Down*, 64, 80; Woodward, ed., *Mary Chesnut's Civil War*, 213; Ronald O. Killion and Charles Waller, eds., *Slavery Time When I Was Chillun Down on Marster's Plantation: Interviews with Georgia Slaves* (Savannah, 1973), 37, 95.

[87] Botkin, ed., *Lay My Burden Down*, 145.

[88] Rawick, ed., *The American Slave*, S.C., 2: pt. 2, 51–52.

[89] Bibb, *Narratives of the Life and Adventures*, 72–73.

[90] Killion and Waller, eds., *Slavery Time*, 110–11.

[91] Northup, *Twelve Years a Slave*, 345.

[92] Bassett, *The Southern Plantation Overseer*, 129.

[93] Edward A. Pollard, *Black Diamonds Gathered in the Darky Homes of the South* (Washington, D.C., 1859), 24–25.

[94] Botkin, ed., *Lay My Burden Down*, 160.

[95] Bayside Plantation Records, 2: 8 January 1864, SHC.

[96] John W. Blassingame, ed., *Slave Testimony: Two Centuries of Letters, Speeches, Interviews, and Autobiographies* (Baton Rouge, 1977), 13.

[97] Olmsted, *Journey in the Seaboard Slave States*, 36.

[98] Woodward, ed., *Mary Chesnut's Civil War*, 526.

[99] Douglass himself knew very well that the cook had special advantages when it came to supplementing the family's food. One, Aunt Katy, always gave her own children extra food while denying the same rights to Douglass (Douglass, *My Bondage and My Freedom*, 27, 54–55, 75).

[100] Rawick, ed., *The American Slave*, Mo., 11:53.

[101] Ibid., Mo., 11:267.

[102] Ulrich B. Phillips and James David Glunt, eds., *Florida Plantation Records from the Papers of George Noble Jones* (Saint Louis, 1927), 63.

[103] J. Mason Brewer, *American Negro Folklore* (Chicago, 1968), 229.

[104] Olmsted, *Journey in the Seaboard Slave States*, 555.

[105] James Redpath, *The Roving Editor, or Talks With Slaves in Southern States* (New York, 1859), 27. The term *divorce* is used in this text with the understanding that legal marriage, and therefore divorce, among slaves was prohibited.

BLACK LIFE IN OLD SOUTH CITIES
David R. Goldfield

[1] Kathleen Bruce, *Virginia Iron Manufacture in the Slave Era* (1930; reprint, New York, 1968), 239–42.

[2] Fredrika Bremer, *The Homes of the New World; Impressions of America*, trans. Mary Howitt (1853; reprint, New York, 1868), 1:354.

[3] Quoted in Michael Tadman, *Speculators and Slaves: Masters, Traders, and Slaves in the Old South* (Madison, 1989), 102.

[4] J. Benwell, *An Englishman's Travels in America, His Observations of Life and Manners in the Free and Slave States* (London, 1853), 113.

[5] Adolph B. Benson, ed., *America of the Fifties: Letters of Fredrika Bremer* (New York, 1924), 96.

[6] Robert Russell, *North America, Its Agriculture and Climate; Containing Observations on the Agriculture and Climate of Canada, the United States, and the Island of Cuba* (Edinburgh, 1857), 151.

[7] *Richmond Daily Dispatch*, 18 Aug. 1853.

[8] Charles Weld, *A Vacation Tour in the United States and Canada* (London, 1853), 313–14.

[9] Quoted in Richard C. Wade, *Slavery in the Cities: The South, 1820–1860* (New York, 1964), 37.

[10] Quoted in Donnie D. Bellamy, "Macon, Georgia, 1823–1860: A Study in Urban Slavery," *Phylon* 45 (1984): 302.

[11] Quoted in Wade, *Slavery in the Cities*, 29.

[12] Ibid., 42.

[13] Quoted in Ulrich Bonnell Phillips, "The Slave Labor Problem in the Charleston District," *Political Science Quarterly* 22 (1907): 422.

[14] *Richmond Daily Dispatch*, 15 Apr. 1859; "Hiring Negroes," *Southern Planter* 12 (1852): 376; *Richmond Whig*, 27 Aug. 1852; *Norfolk Southern Argus*, 26 Sep. 1849, 23 Nov. 1858.

[15] Frederick Douglass, *My Bondage and My Freedom* (New York, 1855), 318, 328.

[16] William Johnson, *William Johnson's Natchez; Being the Ante-Bellum Diary of a Free Negro*, ed. William Ransom Hogan and Edwin Adams Davis (Baton

Rouge, 1951); Edwin Adams Davis and William Ransom Hogan, *The Barber of Natchez* (Baton Rouge, 1954).

[17]Whittington B. Johnson, "Andrew C. Marshall: A Black Religious Leader of Antebellum Savannah," *Georgia Historical Quarterly* 69 (1985): 173–92.

[18]For a sampling of the skilled trades available to nineteenth-century African-Americans see "Directory of Occupations Held by Black Artisans and Craftsmen Prior to 1865," in *The Other Slaves: Mechanics, Artisans, and Craftsmen*, ed. James E. Newton and Ronald L. Lewis (Boston, 1978), 243–45.

[19]Frederick Douglass. *Life and Times of Frederick Douglass* (1892; reprint, New York, 1962), 180.

[20]Quoted in Claudia Dale Goldin, *Urban Slavery in the American South, 1820–1860: A Quantitative History* (Chicago, 1976), 29.

[21]*Richmond Times and Compiler*, 28 May 1847, quoted in Charles B. Dew, *Ironmaker to the Confederacy: Joseph R. Anderson and the Tredegar Iron Works* (New Haven, 1966), 25.

[22]Leonard P. Curry, *The Free Black in Urban America, 1800–1850: The Shadow of the Dream* (Chicago, 1981), 34.

[23]*Richmond Enquirer*, 29 May 1847.

[24]Quoted in Marianne Buroff Sheldon, "Black-White Relations in Richmond, Virginia, 1782–1820," *Journal of Southern History* 45 (1979): 40.

[25]Quoted in Wade, *Slavery in the Cities*, 52–53.

[26]Randall M. Miller, "Aliens in the WASP Nest: Ethnocultural Diversity in the Antebellum Urban South" (Unpublished paper in the author's possession), 42 (first quotation), 45–46 (second quotation).

[27]Frances Anne Kemble, *Journal of a Residence on a Georgian Plantation in 1838–1839*, ed. John A. Scott (1961; reprint, Athens, 1984), 125.

[28]Charles G. Parsons, *An Inside View of Slavery: A Tour Among the Planters* (1855; reprint, Savannah, 1974), 9.

[29]James Stuart, *Three Years in North America* (New York, 1833), 2:68, 132.

[30]Henry Box Brown, *Narrative of Henry Box Brown, Who Escaped from Slavery Enclosed in a Box 3 Feet Long and 2 Wide* (1849; reprint, Philadelphia, 1969), 50.

[31]William Chambers, *Things as They Are in America* (Philadelphia, 1854), 271–72.

[32]Quoted in Wade, *Slavery in the Cities*, 70.

[33]Peter Randolph, *Sketches of Slave Life: or, Illustrations of the Peculiar Institution*, 2d ed. (1855; reprint, Philadelphia, 1969), 59.

[34]William Wells Brown, *Narrative of William W. Brown, An American Slave* (London, 1849), 34.

[35]Lionel H. Kennedy and Thomas Parker, *The Trial Record of Denmark Vesey* (1822; reprint, Boston, 1970); see also Robert S. Starobin, ed., *Denmark Vesey: The Slave Conspiracy of 1822* (Englewood Cliffs, N.J., 1970).

[36]Quoted in Wade, *Slavery in the Cities*, 158.

[37]Ibid., 152, 153.

[38]Marianne Finch, *An Englishwoman's Experience in America* (London, 1853), 295; see also John T. O'Brien, "Factory, Church, and Community: Blacks in Antebellum Richmond," *Journal of Southern History* 44 (1978): 520.

[39]Frederick Law Olmsted, *The Cotton Kingdom: A Traveller's Observations on Cotton and Slavery in the American Slave States*, ed. Arthur M. Schlesinger (New York, 1953), 37.

[40]Quoted in Wade, *Slavery in the Cities*, 126.

[41]Ibid., 130.

[42]Quoted in Ira Berlin, *Slaves Without Masters: The Free Negro in the Antebellum South* (New York, 1974), 25.

[43]Douglass, *Life and Times of Frederick Douglass*, 90; see also Clarence L. Mohr, "Slaves and White Churches in Confederate Georgia," in *Masters and Slaves in the House of the Lord: Race and Religion in the American South, 1740–1870*, ed. John B. Boles (Lexington, Ky., 1988), 154.

[44]Quoted in Wade, *Slavery in the Cities*, 83.

[45]Frederick Law Olmsted, *A Journey in the Back Country* (1860; reprint, Williamstown, Mass., 1972), 189.

[46]Philo Tower, *Slavery Unmasked: Being a Truthful Narrative of a Three Years' Residence and Journeying in Eleven Southern States* (Rochester, 1856), 252.

[47]Fredrika Bremer, *Homes of the New World*, 1:353.

[48]Johnson, "Andrew C. Marshall," 173–92.

[49]Benjamin Drew, *The Refugee: or the Narratives of Fugitive Slaves in Canada* (Boston, 1856), 180–81.

[50]James Stirling, *Letters from the Slave States* (London, 1857), 295.

[51]See for example James B. Browning, "The Beginnings of Insurance Enterprise Among Negroes," *Journal of Negro History* 22 (1937): 417–32; E. Horace Fitchett, "The Traditions of the Free Negro in Charleston, South Carolina," *Journal of Negro History* 25 (1940): 144–45, 150.

[52]Berlin, *Slaves Without Masters*, 307–8.

[53]Ibid., 307.

[54]Quoted in Harriet E. Amos, *Cotton City: Urban Development in Antebellum Mobile* (University, Ala., 1985), 99.

[55]Quoted in Berlin, *Slaves Without Masters*, 144.

[56]Quoted in Michael P. Johnson and James L. Roark, eds., *No Chariot Let Down: Charleston's Free People of Color on the Eve of the Civil War* (Chapel Hill, 1984), 88.

[57]Quoted in Wade, *Slavery in the Cities*, 107–8.

[58]Elizabeth Avery Meriwether, *Recollections of 92 Years, 1824–1916* (Nashville, 1958), 41; see also Randall M. Miller, "The Enemy Within: Some Effects of Foreign Immigrants on Antebellum Southern Cities," *Southern Studies* 24 (1985): 50.

[59]James M. Johnson to Henry Ellison, 28 Aug. 1860, quoted in Johnson and Roark, eds., *No Chariot Let Down*, 101.

[60]Quoted in Goldin, *Urban Slavery*, 29.

[61]*Richmond Daily Dispatch*, 15 Feb. 1853.

[62]Quoted in Johnson and Roark, eds., *No Chariot Let Down*, 136.

[63]Ibid., 145.

THE ARCHAEOLOGY OF SLAVE LIFE
Theresa A. Singleton

Much of the data presented is from either unpublished studies or research in progress and has been graciously provided by the following colleagues: David Babson, Kenneth Brown, Pamela Cressey, Matthew Emerson, Leland Ferguson, Joanne Bowen Gaynor, Christopher Hughes, Larry McKee, Kathleen Parker, Dennis Pogue, Stephen R. Potter, and Lesley Rankin-Hill. The author assumes full responsibility for any misrepresentations of their research.

Several colleagues graciously shared comments on earlier versions of this essay: Mark Bograd, Leland Ferguson, Joanne Bowen Gaynor, David R. Goldfield, Larry McKee, Dennis Pogue, and Stephen R. Potter. To Marcia Bakry, illustrator for the Department of Anthropology, National Museum of Natural History, Smithsonian Institution, the author extends special thanks for the line drawing of colonoware ceramics.

[1]James Agee and Walker Evans, *Let Us Now Praise Famous Men: Three Tenant Families* (1941; reprint, Boston, 1969), 13.

[2]The terms *African-American ethnicity* or *African-American ethnic patterns* refer here to behavior that is frequently found among African-American communities. This does not mean that these practices are found exclusively among African-Americans. Other ethnic groups may have developed similar behavior either independently or as a consequence of their interaction with African-Americans.

[3]A third and growing approach archaeologists use to study plantation life is the examination of the power relationships between slave owners and slaves. See for example Charles Orser, "The Archaeological Analysis of Plantation Society: Replacing Status and Caste with Economics and Power," *American Antiquity* 53 (1988): 735–51.

[4]For a detailed discussion of both value and reality culture, see Eric Wolf, "Culture: Panacea or Problem," *American Antiquity* 49 (1984): 393–400.

[5]Approximately thirty to thirty-five of the plantations investigated thus far have yielded information on slave life. While this essay does not mention each individual study, it does examine general patterns applicable to those sites as well as patterns peculiar to particular sites or groups of related sites. Most of the research in slave archaeology has been undertaken in Virginia, South Carolina, and Georgia.

[6]Numerous studies have examined the African-American communities in coastal Georgia and South Carolina. See for example Savannah Unit, Georgia Writers' Project, Work Projects Administration, *Drums and Shadows: Survival Studies Among the Georgia Coastal Negroes* (1940; reprint, Athens, 1986); Theresa A. Singleton, "The Archaeology of Afro-American Slavery in Coastal Georgia: A Regional Perception of Slave Household and Community Patterns" (Ph.D. diss., University of Florida, 1980).

[7]See for example Charles H. Fairbanks, "The Plantation Archaeology of the Southeastern Coast," *Historical Archaeology* 18, no. 1 (1984): 1–14.

[8]See for example John Solomon Otto, *Cannon's Point Plantation, 1794–1860: Living Conditions and Status Patterns in the Old South* (Orlando, Fla., 1984), 87.

[9]Archaeologists have unearthed cowrie shells at Monticello in Albemarle County, Virginia, the Stagville plantation near Durham, North Carolina, and the Ashland-Belle Helene plantation in Louisiana (William M. Kelso, "Mulberry Row: Slave Life at Thomas Jefferson's Monticello," *Archaeology* 39 [September–October 1986]: 30 [illustration]; Jennifer Garlid, "Stagville Field School in Historical Archaeology: A Nineteenth-Century Slave Cabin" [Site Report, Historic Sites Section, North Carolina Department of Archives and History, Raleigh, 1979], 22; David W. Babson, *Pillars on the Levee: Archaeological Investigations at Ashland-Belle Helene Plantation, Geismar, Ascension Parish, Louisiana* [Site Report, Midwestern Archaeological Research Center, Illinois State University, Normal, Ill., 1989], 86).

[10]Jerome S. Handler and Frederick W. Lange, "Plantation Slavery on Barbados, West Indies," *Archaeology* 32 (July–August 1979): 45–52.

[11]Kathleen A. Parker and Jacqueline L. Hernigle, "Portici, Portrait of a Middling Plantation in Piedmont Virginia," in *Occasional Reports #3, Regional Archaeology Program*, ed. National Capital Region, National Park Service (Washington, D.C., forthcoming), 213.

[12]Kelso, "Mulberry Row," 30 (illustration); Elizabeth Artemel, Elizabeth A. Crowell, and Jeff Parker, *The Alexandria Slave Pen: The Archaeology of Urban Captivity* (Washington, D.C., 1987), 121.

[13]See Matthew C. Emerson, *Decorated Clay Tobacco Pipes from the Chesapeake* (Ann Arbor, Mich., 1988), 130–38.

[14]Stephen R. Potter (National Capital Region, National Park Service, Washington, D.C.), communication with author, October 1990; Susan L. Henry, "Terra-Cotta Tobacco Pipes in 17th Century Maryland and Virginia: A Preliminary Study," *Historical Archaeology* 13 (1979): 15.

[15]Eric Klingelhofer, "Aspects of Early Afro-American Material Culture: Artifacts from the Slave Quarters at Garrison Plantation, Maryland," *Historical Archaeology* 21, no. 2 (1987): 112–19.

[16]*Colonoware* refers to a very broad category of ceramics of which numerous varieties have been identified. Not all archaeologists agree that African-Americans had a role in the manufacture of these ceramics.

[17]Archaeologists have uncovered evidence of colonoware manufacture at the Drayton Hall, Yaughan, and Curriboo plantations in South Carolina (Leland Ferguson, communication with author, May 1983; Patrick Garrow and Thomas Wheaton, "Colonoware Ceramics: The Evidence from Yaughan and Curriboo Plantations," in *Studies in South Carolina Archaeology: Essays in Honor of Robert L. Stephenson*, ed. Albert Goodyear III and Glen T. Hanson [Columbia, S.C., 1989], 176).

[18] Leland Ferguson, "The Cross is a Magic Sign: Marks on Pottery on Eighteenth-Century Bowls from South Carolina" (Paper delivered at the conference "Digging the Afro-American Past: Archaeology and the Black Experience," University of Mississippi, 17–21 May 1989).

[19] Matthew H. Hill, "The Ethnicity Lost? The Ethnicity Gained?: Information Functions of African Ceramics in West Africa and North America," in *Ethnicity and Culture: Proceedings of the Eighteenth Annual Chacmool Conference*, ed. Reginald Auger et al. (Calgary, 1987), 137–38.

[20] Parker and Hernigle, "Portici, Portrait of a Middling Plantation," 227.

[21] James Deetz, "American Historical Archaeology: Methods and Results," *Science*, 22 Jan. 1988, 365–67. Deetz's interpretation has, however, been highly criticized by archaeologists knowledgeable of Chesapeake ceramics.

[22] The one-pot meal is not unique to African-American cuisine, but certain southern dishes such as okra gumbo, hoppin John, red rice, or jambalaya appear to be African in origin. For a discussion of slave foodways and African origins see Stacy Gibbons Moore, "'Established and Well Cultivated': Afro-American Foodways in Early Virginia," *Virginia Cavalcade* 39 (1989): 70–83.

[23] Larry McKee, "Delineating Ethnicity from the Garbage of Early Virginians: Faunal Remains from the Kingsmill Plantation Slave Quarter," *American Archaeology* 6, no. 1 (1987): 36; Diana Crader, "Faunal Remains from the Slave Quarter at Monticello, Charlottesville, Virginia," *Archaeozoologia* 3 (1989): 3.

[24] Larry McKee, "Plantation Food Supply in Nineteenth-Century Tidewater Virginia" (Ph.D. diss., University of California, Berkeley, 1988), 131.

[25] Descriptions of African-styled architecture include W. E. Burghardt Du Bois, ed., *The Negro American Family*, Atlanta University Publications no. 13 (Atlanta, 1908), 49; George W. McDaniel, *Hearth and Home: Preserving a People's Culture* (Philadelphia, 1982), 34–44; Mechal Sobel, *The World They Made Together: Black and White Values in Eighteenth-Century Virginia* (Princeton, 1987), 119–23; John Michael Vlach, *The Afro-American Tradition in Decorative Arts* (1978; reprint, Athens, 1990), 122–38.

[26] Patrick Garrow and Thomas Wheaton, "Acculturation and the Archaeological Record in the Carolinas," in *The Archaeology of Slavery and Plantation Life*, ed. Theresa A. Singleton (Orlando, Fla., 1985), 243–48.

[27] Researchers recovered the charms during separate investigations (Samuel F. Smith, *An Archaeological and Historical Assessment of the First Hermitage* [Nashville, 1976], 210–11; Larry McKee [The Hermitage, Hermitage, Tenn.], communication with author, August 1990).

[28] Quoted in Julia F. Smith, *Slavery and Plantation Growth in Antebellum Florida, 1821–1861* (Gainesville, 1973), 199.

[29] Kenneth Brown, "From Slavery to Wage Labor Tenancy: Structural Continuity in an Afro-American Community" (Paper delivered at the conference "Digging the Afro-American Past: Archaeology and the Black Experience," University of Mississippi, 17–21 May 1989).

[30] William H. Adams, ed., "Historical Archaeology of Plantations at Kings Bay, Camden County, Georgia," in *Reports of Investigations 5*, ed. Department of Anthropology, University of Florida (Gainesville, 1987), 204.

[31] Kelso, "Mulberry Row," 30; Adams, "Historical Archaeology of Plantations at Kings Bay," 204; Dennis Pogue (Chief Archaeologist, Mount Vernon Ladies' Association of the Union, Mount Vernon, Va.), communication with author, August 1990; Klingelhofer, "Aspects of Early Afro-American Material Culture," 115–16; Parker and Hernigle, "Portici, Portrait of a Middling Plantation," 202.

[32] See for example McDaniel, *Hearth and Home*, 103.

[33] Adams, "Historical Archaeology of Plantations at Kings Bay," 204.

[34] Archaeologists differ in their interpretation of how slaves acquired certain possessions such as expensive ceramics and other housewares (See for example William Hampton Adams and Sarah Jane Boling, "Status and Ceramics for Planters and Slaves on Three Georgia Coastal Plantations," *Historical Archaeology* 23, no. 1 [1989]: 69–96).

[35] See for example McDaniel, *Hearth and Home*, 45–102; Edward A. Chappell, "Slave Housing," *Fresh Advices: A Research Supplement*, Nov. 1982, i–iv; Sobel, *The World They Made Together*, 100–26; Mark L. Walston, "'Uncle Tom's Cabin' Revisited: Origins and Interpretations of Slave Housing in the American South," *Southern Studies* 24 (1985): 357–73; Dell Upton, "White and Black Landscapes in Eighteenth-Century Virginia," in *Material Life in America, 1600–1860*, ed. Robert Blair St. George (Boston, 1988), 357–68.

[36] William M. Kelso, *Kingsmill Plantations, 1619–1800: An Archaeology of Country Life in Colonial Virginia* (Orlando, Fla., 1984), 104–10, 112–13, 121–23.

[37] Dennis Pogue, "Slave Lifeways at Mount Vernon," in *The Mount Vernon Ladies' Association of the Union: Annual Report 1989* (Mount Vernon, Va., 1990), 35–40.

[38] Garrow and Wheaton, "Acculturation and the Archaeological Record," 244.

[39] Kelso, *Kingsmill Plantations*, 120; William M. Kelso, "The Archaeology of Slave Life at Thomas Jefferson's Monticello: A Wolf by the Ears," *Journal of New World Archaeology* 6, no. 4 (1986): 13.

[40] Kelso, "The Archaeology of Slave Life," 14.

[41] Ibid.

[42] Charles L. Perdue, Thomas E. Barden, and Robert K. Phillips, eds., *Weevils in the Wheat: Interviews With Virginia Ex-Slaves* (1976; reprint, Bloomington, Ind., 1980), 116.

[43] Larry McKee, "The Ideals and Realities Behind the Design and Use of Nineteenth-Century Virginia Slave Cabins," in *Material Culture, World View, and Culture Change: Essays in Honor of James Deetz*, ed. Mary C. Beaudry and Anne Yentsch (Caldwell, N.J., forthcoming), typescript copy, 24.

[44] McKee, "Plantation Food Supply," 92; Genevieve Leavitt, "Slaves and Tenant Farmers at Shirley," in *The Archaeology of Shirley Plantation*, ed. Theodore R. Reinhart (Charlottesville, Va., 1984), 157–63.

45Christopher Hughes (Stagville Plantation Center, North Carolina Department of Archives and History, Durham, N.C.), communication with author, May 1990.

46Brown, "From Slavery to Wage Labor Tenancy," 6.

47Otto, *Cannon's Point Plantation*, 38.

48Frances Anne Kemble, *Journal of a Residence on a Georgian Plantation in 1838–1839*, ed. John A. Scott (1961; reprint, Athens, 1984), 257.

49By re-creating a mud-and-stick chimney, archaeologist William M. Kelso has demonstrated how slaves deliberately slanted chimneys away from the dwelling so that they could easily be pushed away in case of fire (Jonathan Dent, *Chronicle—Digging for Slaves*, BBC Production, 1989, presented as a segment on *Footsteps of Man*, Arts and Entertainment Network, 12 Jan. 1990). Tabby-brick chimneys, often used on plantations along the Georgia coast, were also highly susceptible to fire (Theresa A. Singleton, "Buried Treasure: Rice Coast Digs Reveal Details of Slave Life," *American Visions*, Apr. 1986, 38; Singleton, "The Archaeology of Afro-American Slavery in Coastal Georgia," 130–31).

50Archaeologists found evidence of a clock, for example, at Cannon's Point plantation on Saint Simons Island, Georgia (Otto, *Cannon's Point Plantation*, 76).

51See for example Fairbanks, "The Plantation Archaeology of the Southeastern Coast," 2–3.

52The recovery of plant-food, or botanical, remains is also possible but usually requires the implementation of special field techniques and the expertise of specialists. Since few archaeologists applied these techniques to slave sites, the subject is not included here.

53McKee, "Delineating Ethnicity from the Garbage of Early Virginians," 35; McKee, "Plantation Food Supply," 131.

54Crader, "Faunal Remains from the Slave Quarter at Monticello," 5.

55Parker and Hernigle, "Portici, Portrait of a Middling Plantation," 183.

56Elizabeth Reitz, "Vertebrate Fauna and Socioeconomic Status," in *Consumer Choice in Historical Archaeology*, ed. Suzanne Spencer-Wood (New York, 1987), 107–16.

57Joanne Bowen Gaynor, "Faunal Remains and Urban Household Subsistence," in *Material Culture, World View, and Culture Change: Essays in Honor of James Deetz*, ed. Mary C. Beaudry and Anne Yentsch (Caldwell, N.J., forthcoming), typescript copy, 14, 22.

58McKee, "Plantation Food Supply," 111.

59See especially Elizabeth Reitz, Tyson Gibbs, and Ted A. Rathbun, "Archaeological Subsistence on Coastal Plantations," in *The Archaeology of Slavery and Plantation Life*, ed. Theresa A. Singleton (Orlando, Fla., 1985), 163–91.

60Ibid., 184.

61Crader, "Faunal Remains from the Slave Quarter at Monticello," 4.

62Reitz, Gibbs, and Rathbun, "Archaeological Subsistence on Coastal Plantations," 185.

63Joanne Bowen Gaynor, "Preliminary Notes on House for Families Faunal Assemblage" (Typescript report, Mount Vernon Ladies' Association of the Union, Mount Vernon, Va., 1989).

64Reitz, Gibbs, and Rathbun, "Archaeological Subsistence on Coastal Plantations," 185.

65See for example Kelso, *Kingsmill Plantations*, 102. In the British West Indies, slaves may have been intentionally buried within slave villages (see Jerome Handler and Frederick Lange, *Plantation Slavery in Barbados: An Archaeological and Historical Investigation* [Cambridge, Mass., 1978], 174).

66Lesley M. Rankin-Hill, "Afro-American Biohistory: A Theoretical and Methodological Consideration" (Ph.D. diss., University of Massachusetts, 1990), 29.

67Ibid., 47.

68Other African-American populations studied by physical anthropologists include an antebellum Philadelphia community, a Union military encampment on Folly Island, South Carolina, and post-emancipation communities in Atlanta and Cedar Grove, Arkansas (See for example Rankin-Hill, "Afro-American Biohistory").

69For analyses of such research see Ted A. Rathbun, "Health and Disease at a South Carolina Plantation: 1840–1870," *American Journal of Physical Anthropology* 74 (1987): 239–53; Douglas W. Owsley et al., "Demography and Pathology of an Urban Slave Population from New Orleans," *American Journal of Physical Anthropology* 74 (1987): 185–97; Jennifer O. Kelly and J. Lawrence Angel, "Life Stresses of Slavery," *American Journal of Physical Anthropology* 74 (1987): 199–211.

70Rathbun, "Health and Disease at a South Carolina Plantation," 239, 246–47; Kelly and Angel, "Life Stresses of Slavery," 209; Owsley et al., "Demography and Pathology of an Urban Slave Population," 196.

71Kelly and Angel, "Life Stresses of Slavery," 207–8; Rathbun, "Health and Disease at a South Carolina Plantation," 248.

72Owsley et al., "Demography and Pathology of an Urban Slave Population," 195–96.

73Rathbun, "Health and Disease at a South Carolina Plantation," 247–48.

74Singleton, "Buried Treasure: Rice Coast Digs," 38.

75Roswell King, Jr., to Major Pierce Butler, 22 October 1803, Butler Family Papers, Box 2, Folder 12, No. 1447, Historical Society of Pennsylvania, Philadelphia.

76North of the slave South, James Deetz tentatively identified African-influenced architecture and foodways at the Parting Ways site in Plymouth, Massachusetts, which four free-black families occupied from 1783 to the 1840s (James Deetz, *In Small Things Forgotten: The Archaeology of Early American Life* [New York, 1977], 149–54).

77See for example Pamela Cressey, "The Archaeology of Free Blacks in Alexandria, Virginia" (Typescript report, Alexandria Archaeology, Office of Historic Alexandria, 1985); Robert J. Hurry, "An Archaeological and Historical Perspective on Benjamin Banneker," *Maryland Historical Magazine* 84 (1989): 361–69; Thomas Padgett, "The Final Report on Test Excavations at the William Johnson House, Natchez, Mississippi" (Mississippi Department of Archives and History, Jackson, 1978).

[78]Cressey, "The Archaeology of Free Blacks in Alexandria," 2.

[79]See for example Charles D. Cheek and Amy Friedlander, "Pottery and Pig's Feet: Space, Ethnicity, and Neighborhood in Washington, D.C., 1880–1940," *Historical Archaeology* 24, no. 1 (1990): 34–60.

[80]Cressey, "The Archaeology of Free Blacks in Alexandria," 2.

[81]Among the two studies of freedmen's communities is Michael Trinkley, ed., "Indians and Freedmen: Occupation at the Fish Haul Site, Beaufort County, South Carolina," in *Research Series 7* (Columbia, S.C., 1986). Another study, one of a James City, N.C., site, is in preparation (Thomas Wheaton [New South Associates, Stone Mountain, Ga.], communication with author, May 1990).

[82]Trinkley, ed., "Indians and Freedmen," 268–78, 310–11.

Checklist of
Illustrations

FIGURES

13. Cotton scale and stand
    Pine, iron, nineteenth century
    Louisiana State University Museum of
    Rural Life, Baton Rouge

14. Accounts with slaves, Bayside plantation,
    Bayou Teche, Louisiana
    Manuscript, 1849–1850
    Bayside Plantation Records, Southern
    Historical Collection, University of
    North Carolina, Chapel Hill

15. *Barbarity committed on a free African,
    who was found on the ensuing morning, by
    the side of the road, dead!*
    Alexander Rider, after Alexander Lawson
    (1773–1846)
    Engraving, in Jesse Torrey, *American
    Slave Trade* (London, 1822)
    Rare Book and Special Collections
    Division, Library of Congress

16. Portrait of Marie Lassus
    Louis Rousseau (fl. mid-nineteenth
    century)
    Albumen photoprint, 1860
    New Orleans Museum of Art, Museum
    Purchase through Laughlin
    Photographic Society Funds

17. Portrait of Frederick Douglass (1818–
    1895)
    Daguerreotype, ca. 1850
    The National Portrait Gallery,
    Smithsonian Institution

18. Portrait of Marlboro
    Ambrotype, ca. 1861–1864
    Raleigh S. Camp Collection, on loan to
    The Museum of the Confederacy,
    Richmond

19. "John Brown Pike"
    Attributed to Charles Blair
    Iron, wood, ca. 1859
    The Museum of the Confederacy,
    Richmond

20. Contraband camp, Baton Rouge Female
    Seminary, Louisiana
    G. H. Suydam
    Albumen photoprint, 1863
    Louisiana and Lower Mississippi Valley
    Collections, Louisiana State University
    Libraries, Baton Rouge

21. *The Negro in the War—Sketches of the
    Various Employments of the Colored Men
    in the United States Armies*
    C. E. F. Hillen
    Engraving, in *Frank Leslie's Illustrated
    Newspaper*, 16 Jan. 1864
    Private Collection

22. *Battery Marshall, Sullivan's Island*
    Conrad Wise Chapman (1842–1910)
    Oil on board, 1863
    The Museum of the Confederacy,
    Richmond

23. Fugitive slaves crossing the
    Rappahannock River, Virginia
    Timothy O'Sullivan (1840–1882)
    Stereograph, August 1862
    Prints and Photographs Division, Library
    of Congress

24. Horton Grove Quarter, Durham, North
    Carolina
    Katherine Wetzel
    Photograph, 1989

25. *A Plan of my Farm on Little Huntg.
    Creek & Potomk R[iver]*
    George Washington (1732–1799)
    Watercolor, ink, 1766
    Geography and Map Division, Library of
    Congress

26. View of Green Hill, Campbell County,
    Virginia
    Jack Boucher
    Photograph, March 1960
    Historic American Buildings Survey,
    Prints and Photographs Division, Library
    of Congress

27. South (front) and west elevations of
    Green Hill, Campbell County, Virginia
    Jack Boucher
    Photograph, March 1960
    Historic American Buildings Survey,
    Prints and Photographs Division, Library
    of Congress

28. *Rice Culture on Cape Fear River, N.C.*
    James E. Taylor (1839–1901)
    Engraving, in *Frank Leslie's Illustrated
    Newspaper*, 20 Oct. 1866
    Private Collection

29. *A Plan Exhibiting the shape & form of a
    Body of land called— Limerick*
    [Charleston District, South Carolina]
    Joseph Purcell
    Ink, March 1786
    Ball Family Papers, South Caroliniana
    Library, University of South Carolina,
    Columbia

30. *A Plan of a Plantation or Tract of Land*
    [Saint Helena Island, South Carolina],
    detail
    John Stapleton, after Joseph Purcell
    Ink, 1798
    John Stapleton Papers, South Caroliniana

Library, University of South Carolina, Columbia

31. Slave quarter, Fort George Island, Duval County, Florida
Stereograph, ca. 1870
Courtesy of George T. Bagoe Collection, The New-York Historical Society, New York City

32. Map of Fort George Island, Duval County, Florida
George G. Cellar
Ink, 1934
Historic American Buildings Survey, Prints and Photographs Division, Library of Congress

33. Mills plantation quarter, Port Royal Island, South Carolina
Timothy O'Sullivan (1840–1882)
Stereograph, 1862
Prints and Photographs Division, Library of Congress

34. Winnowing house (with rice mill in background), Mansfield plantation, Georgetown, South Carolina
Charles A. Bayless
Photograph, 1977
Historic American Buildings Survey, Prints and Photographs Division, Library of Congress

35. Rice threshing mill, Chicora Wood plantation, Georgetown, South Carolina
Charles A. Bayless
Photograph, 1977
Historic American Buildings Survey, Prints and Photographs Division, Library of Congress

36. Plot plan, Thornhill, Watsonia, Greene County, Alabama
W. A. Hotchkiss
Ink, ca. 1935
Historic American Buildings Survey, Prints and Photographs Division, Library of Congress

37. Servant's house, Thornhill, Watsonia, Greene County, Alabama
Kent W. McWilliams
Ink, n.d.
Historic American Buildings Survey, Prints and Photographs Division, Library of Congress

38. *Cotton press*
Alfred R. Waud (1828–1891)
Pencil, wash, ca. 1870
The Historic New Orleans Collection,

Museum / Research Center, Acc. No. 1977.137.4.11

39. Advertisement for the sale of Bellegrove, Donaldsonville, Iberville Parish, Louisiana
John Orr (1815–1887)
Engraving, ca. 1867–1868
The Historic New Orleans Collection, Museum / Research Center, Acc. No. 1970.13.1

40. Boat landing, unidentified plantation [perhaps Belair, Plaquemines Parish, Louisiana]
George Francois Mugnier (ca. 1857–1938)
Gold-chloride print, ca. 1884–1888
Louisiana State Museum, New Orleans

41. Airview of Uncle Sam Plantation, Convent, Saint James Parish, Louisiana
Joseph P. Marlow
Ink, 1940
Historic American Buildings Survey, Prints and Photographs Division, Library of Congress

42. Belair plantation quarter, Plaquemines Parish, Louisiana
George Francois Mugnier (ca. 1857–1938)
Gold-chloride print, ca. 1884–1888
Louisiana State Museum, New Orleans

43. Sugar mill, Belair plantation, Plaquemines Parish, Louisiana
George Francois Mugnier (ca. 1857–1938)
Gold-chloride print, ca. 1884–1888
Louisiana State Museum, New Orleans

44. Plot plan, Waring House, Mobile, Alabama
Kenneth Engwall
Ink, n.d.
Historic American Buildings Survey, Prints and Photographs Division, Library of Congress

45. Ward mansion, or Faber House, Charleston, South Carolina
Charles N. Bayless
Photograph, 1979
Historic American Buildings Survey, Prints and Photographs Division, Library of Congress

46. Plot plan, main floor, Robinson-Aiken House, 48 Elizabeth Street, Charleston, South Carolina
Mark W. Steele and Robert A. Busser
Ink, 1963

47. Service quarter, Robinson-Aiken House, 48 Elizabeth Street, Charleston, South Carolina
Charles N. Bayless
Photograph, 1979
Historic American Buildings Survey, Prints and Photographs Division, Library of Congress

48. Cow house, Robinson-Aiken House, 48 Elizabeth Street, Charleston, South Carolina
Charles N. Bayless
Photograph, 1979
Historic American Buildings Survey, Prints and Photographs Division, Library of Congress

49. *John E. Seabrooks Garden, Edisto* [Island, South Carolina]
Henry P. Moore (fl. 1853–1902, Concord, New Hampshire)
Stereograph, 1862
Moore Collection, New Hampshire Historical Society, Concord

50. Group of contrabands, "Mr. Foller's House," Cumberland Landing, Virginia
James F. Gibson
Stereograph, 14 May 1862
Prints and Photographs Division, Library of Congress

51. Horn, used on Andrew Jackson Donelson plantation, Bolivar County, Mississippi
Steer horn, ca. 1857
Mississippi State Historical Museum

52. *Stacking Wheat*
Edwin Forbes (1839–1895)
Pencil, 26 September 1863
Prints and Photographs Division, Library of Congress

53. Mortar and pestle
Orangeburg, South Carolina
Heart of pine, nineteenth century
South Carolina State Museum, Columbia

54. *Sugar Harvest in Louisiana and Texas*
Franz Holzlhuber (d. 1898)
Watercolor, 1859
Collection of the Glenbow Museum, Calgary, Alberta, Canada

55. *Two Slave Drivers and a Backwoodsman with his Rifle*, detail
W. H. Lizar, after Basil Hall (1788–1844)

Etching, in Basil Hall, *Forty etchings, from sketches made with the camera lucida, in North America, in 1827 and 1828 . . .* (Edinburgh, 1829)
Private Collection

56. Plantation clothing book, Washington, Georgia
W. A. L. Alexander
Manuscript, 1854–1860
Alexander-Hillhouse Papers, Southern Historical Collection, University of North Carolina, Chapel Hill

57. Portrait of "Mauma," a slave of the Patridge family, Florida
Daguerreotype, ca. 1850–1860
Florida Photographic Collection, Florida State Archives, Tallahassee

58. *Planting Sweet Potatoes, James Hopkinson plantation, Edisto* [Island, South Carolina]
Henry P. Moore (fl. 1853–1902, Concord, New Hampshire)
Stereograph, 1862
Courtesy of The New-York Historical Society, New York City

59. "Accounts of the Sick at Butlers Isld 1839" [McIntosh County, Georgia]
Manuscript, 4–7 February 1839
Butler Papers, Louisiana State Museum, New Orleans

60. "Directions &c in Treatment of the Sick," Araby plantation, Madison Parish, Louisiana
Haller Nutt
Manuscript, 1843–1850
Manuscript Department, William R. Perkins Library, Duke University, Durham, North Carolina

61. Slave pass, for Henry, assigned by Jefferson Davis (1808–1889)
Manuscript, 10 November 1863
Eleanor S. Brockenbrough Library, The Museum of the Confederacy, Richmond

62. Doll, Bennehan plantation, North Carolina
Attributed to slave(s)
Homespun cotton and cotton thread, ca. 1850
The Stagville Center, Durham, North Carolina

63. *An Affecting Scene in Kentucky*
Lithograph, 1836, probably published by Henry R. Robinson
The Library Company of Philadelphia

64. Pew bench, Salem Chapel, Fairntosh plantation, then Orange County, North Carolina
Pine, ca. 1826
The Stagville Center, Durham, North Carolina

65. Pulpit, Salem Chapel, Fairntosh plantation, then Orange County, North Carolina
Pine, ca. 1826
The Stagville Center, Durham, North Carolina

66. *Slave church in a cotton plantation*
Franz Holzlhuber (d. 1898)
Watercolor, ca. 1856–1860
Collection of the Glenbow Museum, Calgary, Alberta, Canada

67. Graveyard, Sapelo Island, Georgia
Photograph, ca. 1919–1920
Vanishing Georgia Collection, Georgia Department of Archives and History, Atlanta

68. Portrait of Omar ibin Said ("Uncle Moro") (1774–1864)
Photograph after ca. 1860 image
DeRossett Family Papers, Southern Historical Collection, University of North Carolina, Chapel Hill

69. Preparing cotton for the gin, J. J. Smith's plantation, Beaufort District, South Carolina
Timothy O'Sullivan (1840–1882)
Stereograph, 1862
Prints and Photographs Division, Library of Congress

70. Slave quarter, J. J. Smith's plantation, Beaufort District, South Carolina
Timothy O'Sullivan (1840–1882)
Stereograph, 1862
Prints and Photographs Division, Library of Congress

71. African-Americans, J. J. Smith's plantation, Beaufort District, South Carolina
Timothy O'Sullivan (1840–1882)
Stereograph, 1862
Prints and Photographs Division, Library of Congress

72. Five generations of an African-American family, J. J. Smith's plantation, Beaufort District, South Carolina
Timothy O'Sullivan (1840–1882)
Stereograph, 1862
Prints and Photographs Division, Library of Congress

73. "Negro Fields," Cornhill plantation, Sumter District, South Carolina, detail
John B. Miller
Manuscript, ca. 1840
McDonald Furman Papers, William R. Perkins Library, Duke University, Durham, North Carolina

74. Perryclear plantation quarter, Port Royal Island, South Carolina
Marked: "Hubbard and Mix"
Photographic print, probably from a stereograph, ca. 1870
Penn School Papers, Southern Historical Collection, University of North Carolina, Chapel Hill

75. Basket, with cover
Attributed to Florida slave(s)
Reed, ca. 1860
The Museum of the Confederacy, Richmond

76. Dining-room corner cupboard, Organ plantation, Bastrop, Texas
Attributed to slave(s)
Walnut veneer on pine and cedar, ca. 1840
Courtesy of the San Antonio Museum Association, San Antonio, Texas

77. Harness buckle, Mount Vernon, Virginia
Brass, ca. 1790
The Mount Vernon Ladies' Association of the Union, Mount Vernon, Virginia

78. Whipping tree, Frogmore plantation, Saint Helena Island, South Carolina
Photograph, ca. 1890
Penn School Papers, Southern Historical Collection, University of North Carolina, Chapel Hill

79. *The Plantation Police or Home-Guard Examining Negro Passes on the Levee Road Below New Orleans*, detail
Francis H. Schell (1834–1909)
[incorrectly credited to "F. B. Schell"]
Engraving, in *Frank Leslie's Illustrated Newspaper*, 11 July 1863
Private Collection

80. "$150 Reward. A Negro Man named Ben"
Broadside, 5 November 1827
Rare Book and Special Collections Division, Library of Congress

81. *Horrid Massacre in Virginia*, detail
Woodcut, in Samuel Warner, *Authentic and impartial narrative of the tragical scene which was witnessed in Southampton*

County (Virginia) . . . (New York, 1831)
Rare Book and Special Collections
Division, Library of Congress

82. *The Effects of the Proclamation* . . .
Engraving, in *Harper's Weekly*, 21
February 1863
Private Collection

83. Union Hospital No. 19, Nashville,
Tennessee
Albumen photoprint, 1863
National Archives

84. *Pickets of the First Louisiana "Native
Guard" Guarding the New Orleans,
Opelousas and Great Western Railroad*
Engraving, in *Frank Leslie's Illustrated
Newspaper*, 7 Mar. 1863
Private Collection

85. Portrait of a nursemaid and her charge
Daguerreotype, ca. 1850
Louisiana State Museum, New Orleans

86. *Drayton's* [plantation] *rear* [Edisto
Island, South Carolina], detail
Henry P. Moore (fl. 1853–1902,
Concord, New Hampshire)
Stereograph, 1862
Moore Collection, New Hampshire
Historical Society, Concord

87. Manumission document, signed Charles
A. Henry
Manuscript, 4 November 1841
Museum of the City of Mobile

88. *John E. Seabrooks Wharf / Edisto* [Island,
South Carolina] */ Century Plant*[ation] */
Drying Cotton*
Henry P. Moore (fl. 1853–1902,
Concord, New Hampshire)
Stereograph, 1862
Moore Collection, New Hampshire
Historical Society, Concord

89. Portrait of an African-American family
Alfred R. Waud (1828–1891)
Pencil, chinese white on paper, ca. 1861
The Historic New Orleans Collection,
Museum / Research Center, Acc. No.
1965.87

90. *"—but I did not want to go . . ."*
Alexander Rider, after Alexander Lawson
(1773–1846)
Engraving, in Jesse Torrey, *American
Slave Trade* (London, 1822)
Rare Book and Special Collections
Division, Library of Congress

91. *Slave Women Digging in Montgomery*
[Alabama]

George Fuller (1822–1884)
Pencil on paper, 21 February 1858
Private Collection

92. Nightshirt, slave-made, labeled "Andrew
Jackson," by Gracey Cotton, ca. 1830
The Hermitage: the home of Andrew
Jackson

93. Vest and trousers, slave-made
Cotton, ca. 1850
Shadows-on-the-Teche, New Iberia,
Louisiana, a museum property of the
National Trust for Historic Preservation

94. *Mothers with young Children at work in
the field*, detail
Woodcut, in *Illustrations of the American
Anti-Slavery Almanac for 1840* (New
York, 1839)
Rare Book and Special Collections
Division, Library of Congress

95. Account with slave Charlotte, Watson
family plantation, Louisa County, Virginia
Manuscript, 1858–1859
Watson Family Papers, Special Collections
Department, Manuscripts Division,
University of Virginia Library,
Charlottesville

96. *Laundry Yard With Two Laundresses*
George Fuller (1822–1884)
Pencil, ink wash on paper, 28 January 1858
Private Collection

97. *Noon on the plantation*
William Waud (d. 1878)
Watercolor, 1871
The Historic New Orleans Collection,
Museum / Research Center, Acc. No.
1977.137.4.10

98. *Interior of Negro Cabin, Spotsylvania
Court House, Virginia*
Edwin Forbes (1839–1895)
Pencil, 14 May 1864
Prints and Photographs Division, Library
of Congress

99. Names of male slaves, plantation book of
Charles Cotesworth Pinckney (1746–
1825), South Carolina
Manuscript, 1812–1861
Pinckney Family Papers, Manuscript
Division, Library of Congress

100. "By Hewlett & Bright. Sale of Valuable
Slaves, (On account of departure)"
Broadside, New Orleans, 13 May 1835
Courtesy of Bella C. Landauer
Collection, The New-York Historical
Society, New York City

[incorrectly credited to "Fred. B. Schell"]
Engraving, in *Frank Leslie's Illustrated Newspaper*, 30 Jan. 1864
Private Collection

121. Lucy Edwards
Carte de visite, ca. 1860
Eleanor S. Brockenbrough Library, The Museum of the Confederacy, Richmond

122. First African Baptist Church, Richmond, Virginia
Albumen photoprint, 1865
Prints and Photographs Division, Library of Congress

123. *The Presentation of a Gold Snuff Box to the Rev. R. T. Breckenridge*
Lithograph, 1845
Prints and Photographs Division, Library of Congress

124. Constitution and bylaws, Creole Fire Company No. 1, Mobile, Alabama
Manuscript, October 1858 [copy by John Trenier, Jr.]
Museum of the City of Mobile

125. Slave badge, "Charleston / No. 112 / Porter / 1815"
Copper, 1815
The American Numismatic Society, New York City

126. Free-black badge, "City of Charleston / Free"
Copper alloy, ca. 1848–1860
The American Numismatic Society, New York City

127. Petition, *Charleston Mercury*, 12 Dec. 1860
Serial and Government Publications Division, Library of Congress

128. *James Hopkinson's Plantation, Edisto Island*
Henry P. Moore (fl. 1853–1902, Concord, New Hampshire)
Stereograph, 1862
Moore Collection, New Hampshire Historical Society, Concord

129. Shoe buckle, cast brass *(above left)*
Buckle, cut brass *(above right)*
Watch fob, copper, clear glass intaglio *(below left)*
Button, brass *(below center)*
Button, bone *(below right)*
All: ca. 1790
All: The Mount Vernon Ladies' Association of the Union, Mount Vernon, Virginia

130. Sticks
Unidentified wood, ca. 1850
The Stagville Center, Durham, North Carolina

131. Cowrie shell
ca. 1800
The Stagville Center, Durham, North Carolina

132. Ring *(left)*
Horn, ca. 1840
Ring *(right)*
Ebony, ca. 1840
All: National Park Service

133. Portici plantation excavation, Manassas Battlefield Park, Virginia
Photograph, 1989
Courtesy, National Park Service, copy by Katherine Wetzel

134. Colonoware forms
Marcia Bakry
Computer-enhanced line drawing, 1990
Courtesy, Theresa A. Singleton

135. Bowl (partial) found at Pohoke site, Manassas, Virginia
Unglazed earthenware, ca. 1791–1840
National Park Service

136. Charm
Stamped brass, ca. 1820
The Hermitage: the home of Andrew Jackson

137. Beads
Glass, ca. 1800–1862
National Park Service

138. Chisel
Iron, ca. 1820–1862
National Park Service

139. Awl
Bone, ca. 1820
The Hermitage: the home of Andrew Jackson

140. *Group at Drayton's Plantation* [Hilton Head, South Carolina]
Henry P. Moore (fl. 1853–1902, Concord, New Hampshire)
Stereograph, 1862
Moore Collection, New Hampshire Historical Society, Concord

141. Knife-sharpening stones
Stone, ca. 1820
The Hermitage: the home of Andrew Jackson

COLOR PLATES

8. *A South View of Julianton Plantation, the Property of Francis Levett, Esqr.* [McIntosh County, Georgia]
John McKinnon
Watercolor, before 1803
Manuscript Department, William R. Perkins Library, Duke University, Durham, North Carolina

9. *Lynchburg—negro dance*
Lewis Miller (1795–1882)
Watercolor, 1853
Abby Aldrich Rockefeller Folk Art Collection. Photo courtesy of the Colonial Williamsburg Foundation, Williamsburg, Virginia

10. *Slave trader, Sold to Tennessee*
Lewis Miller (1795–1882)
Watercolor, 1853
Abby Aldrich Rockefeller Folk Art Collection. Photo courtesy of the Colonial Williamsburg Foundation, Williamsburg, Virginia

11. Cellarette
Attributed to Peter Lee
Pine, ca. 1850
Marengo County Historical Society, Demopolis, Alabama; photograph by Joseph C. P. Turner

12. Auction block
Wood, ca. 1850
Louisiana State Museum, New Orleans

13. Cane, or medicine(?) stick
Sweet gum, with honeysuckle vine, ca. 1799
The Stagville Center, Durham, North Carolina

14. Banjo and fiddle
Gourd, animal hide, wood, metal, Nineteenth century
Collection of Roddy and Sally Moore; © David Guerrero

15. Teapot, found on Hampton plantation, near McClellanville, South Carolina
Attributed to African-American(s)
Unglazed earthenware, late eighteenth century
Institute of Archaeology and Anthropology, University of South Carolina, Columbia

16. Tignon
Cotton, ca. 1840
Louisiana State Museum, New Orleans

17. Trousers and vest (jacket missing)
Attributed to African-American(s), John Burry plantation, Shreveport, Louisiana
Wool dyed with hickory nuts, ca. 1861–1865
Louisiana State Museum, New Orleans; gift of Mr. and Mrs. J. Parker Schneidau

18. *Preparations for the enjoyment of a fine Sunday among the Blacks, Norfolk*
Benjamin Henry Latrobe (1764–1820)
Pencil, ink, watercolor, 1797
Maryland Historical Society, Baltimore; photograph by Jeff D. Goldman

19. "No. 1. Git away from dat fence. . . . De Bottom rails on top now."
John J. Omenhausser (1831–1877)
Watercolor, 1863
Maryland Historical Society, Baltimore; photograph by Jeff D. Goldman

20. *A Plantation Burial*
John Antrobus (1831–1907)
Oil on canvas, 1860
The Historic New Orleans Collection, Museum / Research Center, Acc. No. 1960.46

Suggestions for Further Reading

Abrahams, Roger D., ed. *Afro-American Folktales: Stories From Black Traditions in the New World*. New York: Pantheon, 1985.

Andrews, William L. *To Tell a Free Story: The First Century of Afro-American Autobiography, 1760–1865*. Urbana: University of Illinois Press, 1986.

Anthony, Carl. "The Big House and the Slave Quarter." *Landscape* 20 (1976): 8–19; 21 (1976): 9–15.

Aptheker, Herbert. *American Negro Slave Revolts*. 5th ed. New York: International Publishers, 1983.

___. "Maroons Within the Present Limit of the United States." In *Maroon Societies: Rebel Slave Communities in the Americas*, edited by Richard Price. 2d ed. Baltimore: Johns Hopkins University Press, 1979.

Bancroft, Frederic. *Slave-Trading in the Old South*. Baltimore: J. H. Furst, 1931. Reprint. New York: Frederick Ungar, 1969.

Bassett, John Spencer. *The Southern Plantation Overseer as Revealed in His Letters*. Northampton, Mass.: Smith College, 1925.

Bayliss, John F., comp. *Black Slave Narratives*. New York: Macmillan, 1970.

Berlin, Ira, Barbara J. Fields, Thavolia Glymph, Joseph P. Reidy, and Leslie S. Rowland, eds. *Freedom: A Documentary History of Emancipation, 1861–1867*. Ser. 1, vol. 1, *The Destruction of Slavery*. Cambridge: Cambridge University Press, 1985.

Berlin, Ira. "The Slave Trade and the Development of Afro-American Society in English Mainland North America, 1619–1775." *Southern Studies* 20 (1981): 122–36.

___. *Slaves Without Masters: The Free Negro in the Antebellum South*. New York: Pantheon, 1974.

Beveridge, Charles E., and Charles Capen Mc-Laughlin, eds. *The Papers of Frederick Law Olmsted*. Vol 2, *Slavery and the South, 1852–1857*. Baltimore: Johns Hopkins University Press, 1981.

Bishir, Catherine W. "Black Builders in Antebellum North Carolina." *North Carolina Historical Review* 61 (1984): 423–61.

Blassingame, John W. *The Slave Community: Plantation Life in the Antebellum South*. 2d ed., rev. and enl. New York: Oxford University Press, 1979.

___, ed. *Slave Testimony: Two Centuries of Letters, Speeches, Interviews, and Autobiographies*. Baton Rouge: Louisiana State University Press, 1977.

___. "Using the Testimony of Ex-Slaves: Approaches and Problems." *Journal of Southern History* 41 (1975): 473–92.

Boles, John B. *Black Southerners, 1619–1869*. Lexington: University Press of Kentucky, 1983.

___, ed. *Masters and Slaves in the House of the Lord: Race and Religion in the American South, 1740–1870*. Lexington: University Press of Kentucky, 1988.

Bontemps, Arna Wendell, comp. *Great Slave Narratives*. Boston: Beacon Press, 1969.

Botkin, Benjamin A., ed. *Lay My Burden Down: A Folk History of Slavery*. Chicago: University of Chicago Press, 1945. Reprint. Athens: University of Georgia Press, 1989.

Breeden, James O., ed. *Advice Among Masters: The Ideal in Slave Management in the Old South*. Westport, Conn.: Greenwood Press, 1980.

Breen, T. H., and Stephen Innes. *"Myne Owne Ground": Race and Freedom on Virginia's Eastern Shore, 1640–1676*. New York: Oxford University Press, 1980.

Brewer, J. Mason. *American Negro Folklore*.

Chicago: Quadrangle, 1968.

Brewer, James H. *The Confederate Negro: Virginia's Craftsmen and Military Laborers, 1861–1865.* Durham: Duke University Press, 1969.

Chappell, Edward A. "Slave Housing." *Fresh Advices: A Research Supplement* (November 1982): 1–4.

Cohen, David W., and Jack P. Greene, eds. *Neither Slave Nor Free: The Freedmen of African Descent in the Slave Societies of the New World.* Baltimore: Johns Hopkins University Press, 1972.

Conrad, Alfred, and John R. Meyer. "The Economics of Slavery in the Ante-Bellum South." *Journal of Political Economy* 66 (1958): 95–130.

Coughtry, Jay. *The Notorious Triangle: Rhode Island and the African Slave Trade, 1700–1807.* Philadelphia: Temple University Press, 1981.

Courlander, Harold. *A Treasury of Afro-American Folklore: The Oral Literature, Traditions, Recollections, Legends, Tales, Songs, Religious Beliefs, Customs, Sayings, and Humor of Peoples of African Descent in the Americas.* New York: Crown Publishers, 1976.

Craven, Wesley Frank. *White, Red, and Black: The Seventeenth-Century Virginian.* Charlottesville: University Press of Virginia, 1971. Reprint. New York: W. W. Norton, 1977.

Creel, Margaret Washington. *A Peculiar People: Slave Religion and Community-Culture Among the Gullahs.* New York: New York University Press, 1988.

Curtin, Philip D. *The Atlantic Slave Trade: A Census.* Madison: University of Wisconsin Press, 1969.

Curry, Leonard P. *The Free Black in Urban America, 1800–1850: The Shadow of the Dream.* Chicago: University of Chicago Press, 1981.

Davis, Adwon Adams. *Plantation Life in the Florida Parishes of Louisiana, 1836–1846, as Reflected in the Diary of Bennet H. Barrow.* New York: Columbia University Press, 1943.

Davis, Charles T., and Henry Louis Gates, Jr., eds. *The Slave's Narrative.* New York: Oxford University Press, 1985.

Davis, David Brion. *The Problem of Slavery in the Age of Revolution, 1770–1823.* Ithaca: Cornell University Press, 1975.

Donnan, Elizabeth, ed. *Documents Illustrative of the History of the Slave Trade to America.* Washington, D.C.: Carnegie Institution of Washington, 1930–35.

Drew, Benjamin. *The Refugee: A North-Side View of Slavery.* In *Four Fugitive Slave Narratives,*

edited by R. W. Winks. Reading, Mass.: Addison Wesley, 1969.

Dunn, Richard S. "The Tale of Two Plantations: Slave Life at Mesopotamia in Jamaica and Mount Airy in Virginia, 1799 to 1828." *William and Mary Quarterly* 3d ser., 34 (1977): 32–65.

Egypt, Ophelia S., J. Masuoka, and Charles S. Johnson, eds. *Unwritten History of Slavery, Autobiographical Accounts of Negro Ex-Slaves.* Nashville: Fisk University Press, 1945.

Elkins, Stanley M. *Slavery: A Problem in American Institutional and Intellectual Life.* 3d ed. Chicago: University of Chicago Press, 1976.

Epstein, Dena J. *Sinful Tunes and Spirituals: Black Folk Music to the Civil War.* Urbanna: University of Illinois Press, 1977.

Escott, Paul D. *Slavery Remembered: A Record of Twentieth-Century Slave Narratives.* Chapel Hill: University of North Carolina Press, 1979.

Fairbanks, Charles H. "The Plantation Archaeology of the Southeastern Coast." *Historical Archaeology* 18, no. 1 (1984): 1–14.

Farley, Reynolds. "The Demographic Rates and Social Institutions of the Nineteenth-Century Negro Population: A Stable Population Analysis." *Demography* 2 (1965): 386–98.

Faust, Drew Gilpin. "Culture, Conflict, and Community: The Meaning of Power on an Antebellum Plantation." *Journal of Social History* 14 (1980): 83–97.

___, ed. *The Ideology of Slavery: Proslavery Thought in the Antebellum South, 1830–1860.* Baton Rouge: Louisiana State University Press, 1981.

___. *James Henry Hammond and the Old South: A Design for Mastery.* Baton Rouge: Louisiana State University Press, 1982.

Feldstein, Stanley. *Once a Slave: The Slaves' View of Slavery.* New York: W. Morrow, 1971.

Ferguson, Leland G. "Looking for the 'Afro' in Colono-Indian Pottery." In *Archaeological Perspectives on Ethnicity in America: Afro-American and Asian American Culture History,* edited by Robert L. Schuyler. Farmingdale, N.Y.: Baywood Publishing Company, 1980.

Fields, Barbara Jeanne. *Slavery and Freedom on the Middle Ground: Maryland during the Nineteenth Century.* New Haven: Yale University Press, 1985.

Fisher, Miles Mark. *Negro Slave Songs in the United States.* Ithaca: Cornell University Press, 1953. Reprint. New York: Citadel Press, 1969.

Fogel, Robert W. *Without Consent or Contract:*

The Rise and Fall of American Slavery. New York: W. W. Norton, 1989.

Foster, Frances Smith. *Witnessing Slavery: The Development of Ante-bellum Slave Narratives.* Westport, Conn.: Greenwood Press, 1979.

Fox-Genovese, Elizabeth. *Within the Plantation Household: Black and White Women of the Old South.* Chapel Hill: University of North Carolina Press, 1988.

Franklin, John Hope, and Alfred A. Moss, Jr. *From Slavery to Freedom: A History of Negro Americans.* 6th ed. New York: Alfred A. Knopf, 1988.

Fry, Gladys-Marie. *Stitched From the Soul: Slave Quilts From the Ante-Bellum South.* New York: Dutton Studio Books in association with the Museum of American Folk Art, 1990.

Genovese, Eugene D. *From Rebellion to Revolution: Afro-American Slave Revolts in the Making of the Modern World.* Baton Rouge: Louisiana State University Press, 1979.

___. *Roll, Jordan, Roll: The World the Slaves Made.* New York: Pantheon, 1974.

Gilbert, Olive, comp. *Narrative of Sojourner Truth, A Bondwoman of Olden Time.* 1878. Reprint. New York: Arno Press, 1968.

Gilmore, Al-Tony, ed. *Revisiting Blassingame's The Slave Community: The Scholars Respond.* Westport, Conn.: Greenwood Press, 1978.

Goldfield, David R. *Cottonfields and Skyscrapers: Southern City and Region, 1607–1980.* Baton Rouge: Louisiana State University Press, 1982.

___. *Urban Growth in the Age of Sectionalism: Virginia, 1847–1861.* Baton Rouge: Louisiana State University Press, 1977.

Goldin, Claudia Dale. *Urban Slavery in the American South, 1820–1860: A Quantitative History.* Chicago: University of Chicago Press, 1976.

Gutman, Herbert G. *The Black Family in Slavery and Freedom, 1750–1925.* New York: Pantheon, 1976.

Honour, Hugh. *The Image of the Black in Western Art.* Vol. 4, *From the American Revolution to World War I.* Pt. 1, *Slaves and Liberators.* Pt. 2, *Black Models and White Myths.* Cambridge: Harvard University Press in association with the Menil Foundation, 1989.

Huggins, Nathan Irvin. *Black Odyssey: The Afro-American Ordeal in Slavery.* New York: Pantheon, 1977.

Inscoe, John C. *Mountain Masters, Slavery, and the Sectional Crisis in Western North Carolina.* Knoxville: University of Tennessee Press, 1989.

Jacobs, Harriet A. *Incidents in the Life of a Slave Girl, Written by Herself.* Edited by Jean Fagan Yellin. Cambridge: Harvard University Press, 1987.

Johnson, Michael P., and James L. Roark. *Black Masters: A Free Family of Color in the Old South.* New York: W. W. Norton, 1984.

___, eds. *No Chariot Let Down: Charleston's Free People of Color on the Eve of the Civil War.* Chapel Hill: University of North Carolina Press, 1984.

Johnston, James Hugo. *Race Relations in Virginia and Miscegenation in the South, 1776–1860.* Amherst: University of Massachusetts Press, 1970.

Jones, Howard. *Mutiny on the Amistad: The Saga of a Slave Revolt and Its Impact on American Abolition, Law, and Diplomacy.* New York: Oxford University Press, 1987.

Jordan, Winthrop D. *White Over Black: American Attitudes Toward the Negro, 1550–1812.* Chapel Hill: University of North Carolina Press, 1968. Rev. and abr. *The White Man's Burden: Historical Origins of Racism in the United States.* New York: Oxford University Press, 1974.

Joyner, Charles W. *Down by the Riverside: A South Carolina Slave Community.* Urbana: University of Illinois Press, 1984.

___. *Remember Me: Slave Life in Coastal Georgia.* Atlanta: Georgia Humanities Council, 1989.

Katz, Bernard, ed. *The Social Implications of Early Negro Music in the United States.* New York: Arno Press, 1969.

Kelso, William M. *Kingsmill Plantations, 1619–1800: An Archaeology of Country Life in Colonial Virginia.* Orlando, Fla.: Academic Press, 1984.

___. "Mulberry Row: Slave Life at Thomas Jefferson's Monticello." *Archaeology* 39 (September–October 1986): 28–35.

Kemble, Frances Anne. *Journal of a Residence on a Georgian Plantation in 1838–1839.* Edited by John A. Scott. New York: Alfred A. Knopf, 1961. Reprint. Athens: University of Georgia Press, 1984.

Killion, Ronald G., and Charles Waller, eds. *Slavery Time When I Was Chillun Down on Marster's Plantation: Interviews with Georgia Slaves.* Savannah: Beehive Press, 1973.

Kipple, Kenneth F., and Virginia Himmelsteib King. *Another Dimension to the Black Diaspora: Diet, Disease, and Racism.* Cambridge: Cambridge University Press, 1981.

Klein, Herbert S. *The Middle Passage: Comparative Studies in the Atlantic Slave Trade.* Princeton: Princeton University Press, 1978.

Klingelhofer, Eric. "Aspects of Early Afro-American Material Culture: Artifacts from the Slave

Quarters at Garrison Plantation, Maryland." *Historical Archaeology* 21, no. 2 (1987): 112–19.

Kolchin, Peter. "Reevaluating the Antebellum Slave Community: A Comparative Perspective." *Journal of American History* 70 (1983): 579–601.

___. *Unfree Labor: American Slavery and Russian Serfdom.* Cambridge: Harvard University Press, Belknap Press, 1987.

Kulikoff, Allan. *Tobacco and Slaves: The Development of Southern Cultures in the Chesapeake, 1680–1800.* Chapel Hill: University of North Carolina Press, 1986.

Lane, Ann J., ed. *The Debate Over Slavery: Stanley Elkins and His Critics.* Urbana: University of Illinois Press, 1971.

Levine, Lawrence W. *Black Culture and Black Consciousness: Afro-American Folk Thought from Slavery to Freedom.* New York: Oxford University Press, 1977.

Lewis, Ronald L. *Coal, Iron, and Slaves: Industrial Slavery in Maryland and Virginia, 1715–1865.* Westport, Conn.: Greenwood Press, 1979.

Littlefield, Daniel C. *Rice and Slaves: Ethnicity and the Slave Trade in Colonial South Carolina.* Baton Rouge: Louisiana State University Press, 1981.

Litwack, Leon F. *Been in the Storm So Long: The Aftermath of Slavery.* New York: Alfred A. Knopf, 1979.

Lofton, John. *Insurrection in South Carolina: The Turbulent World of Denmark Vesey.* Yellow Springs, Ohio: Antioch Press, 1964. Reprint. *Denmark Vesey's Revolt: The Slave Plot That Lit a Fuse to Fort Sumter.* Kent: Kent State University Press, 1983.

McColley, Robert. *Slavery and Jeffersonian Virginia.* 2d ed. Urbana: University of Illinois Press, 1973.

McConnell, Roland C. *Negro Troops of Antebellum Louisiana: A History of the Battalion of Free Men of Color.* Baton Rouge: Louisiana State University Press, 1968.

McDaniel, George W. *Hearth and Home: Preserving a People's Culture.* Philadelphia: Temple University Press, 1982.

McElroy, Guy C. *Facing History: The Black Image in American Art, 1710–1940.* Washington, D.C.: Corcoran Gallery of Art, 1990.

Meier, August, and Elliott Rudwick. *Black History and the Historical Profession, 1915–1980.* Urbana: University of Illinois Press, 1986.

Mellon, James, ed. *Bullwhip Days: The Slaves Remember.* New York: Weidenfeld and Nicolson, 1988.

Menard, Russell P. "From Servants to Slaves: The Transformation of the Chesapeake Labor System." *Southern Studies* 16 (1977): 355–90.

Miller, Elinor, and Eugene D. Genovese, eds. *Plantation, Town, and County: Essays on the Local History of American Slave Society.* Urbana: University of Illinois Press, 1974.

Miller, Randall M., ed. *"Dear Master": Letters of a Slave Family.* Ithaca: Cornell University Press, 1978. Reprint. Athens: University of Georgia Press, 1990.

___, and John David Smith, eds. *Dictionary of Afro-American Slavery.* Westport, Conn.: Greenwood Press, 1988.

Mohr, Clarence L. *On the Threshold of Freedom: Masters and Slaves in Civil War Georgia.* Athens: University of Georgia Press, 1986.

Moore, Stacy Gibbons. "'Established and Well Cultivated': Afro-American Foodways in Early Virginia." *Virginia Cavalcade* 39 (1989): 70–83.

Morgan, Edmund S. *American Slavery, American Freedom: The Ordeal of Colonial Virginia.* New York: W. W. Norton, 1975.

___. "Slavery and Freedom: The American Paradox." *Journal of American History* 59 (1972): 5–29.

Morgan, Philip D. "Work and Culture: The Task System and the World of Lowcountry Blacks, 1700 to 1800." *William and Mary Quarterly* 3d ser., 39 (1982): 563–99.

___, ed. *"Don't Grieve After Me": The Black Experience in Virginia, 1619–1986.* Hampton, Va.: Hampton University, 1986.

Mullin, Gerald W. *Flight and Rebellion: Slave Resistance in Eighteenth-Century Virginia.* New York: Oxford University Press, 1972.

Newton, James E., and Ronald L. Lewis, eds. *The Other Slaves: Mechanics, Artisans, and Craftsmen.* Boston: G. K. Hall, 1978.

Noonan, John Thomas. *The Antelope: The Ordeal of the Recaptured Africans in the Administrations of James Monroe and John Quincy Adams.* Berkeley: University of California Press, 1977.

Northup, Solomon. *Twelve Years a Slave.* Edited by Sue Eakin and Joseph Logsdon. Baton Rouge: Louisiana State University Press, 1968.

Oakes, James. *The Ruling Race: A History of American Slaveholders.* New York: Alfred A. Knopf, 1982.

Oates, Stephen B. *The Fires of Jubilee: Nat Turner's Fierce Rebellion.* New York: Harper and Row, 1975.

Osofsky, Gilbert, ed. *Puttin' on Ole Massa: The Slave Narratives of Henry Bibb, William Wells Brown, and Solomon Northup.* New

York: Harper and Row, 1969.

Otto, John Solomon "A New Look at Slave Life." *Natural History* 88 (January 1979): 8–30.

———. *Cannon's Point Plantation, 1794–1860: Living Conditions and Status Patterns in the Old South.* Orlando, Fla.: Academic Press, 1984.

Owens, Leslie Howard. *This Species of Property: Slave Life and Culture in the Old South.* New York: Oxford University Press, 1976.

Parish, Peter J. *Slavery: History and Historians.* New York: Harper and Row, 1989.

Parry, Ellwood. *The Image of the Indian and the Black Man in American Art, 1590–1900.* New York: George Braziller, 1974.

Perdue, Charles L., Jr., Thomas E. Barden, and Robert K. Phillips, eds. *Weevils in the Wheat: Interviews With Virginia Ex-Slaves.* Charlottesville: University Press of Virginia, 1976. Reprint. Bloomington: Indiana University Press, 1980.

Phillips, Ulrich B. *American Negro Slavery: A Survey of the Supply, Employment and Control of Negro Labor As Determined by the Plantation Regime.* New York: D. Appleton, 1918. Reprint. Baton Rouge: Louisiana State University Press, 1966.

———, and James David Glunt, eds. *Florida Plantation Records from the Papers of George Noble Jones.* St. Louis: Missouri Historical Society, 1927.

———. *Life and Labor in the Old South.* Boston: Little, Brown, 1929.

———. *The Slave Economy of the Old South: Selected Essays in Economic and Social History.* Edited by Eugene D. Genovese. Baton Rouge: Louisiana State University Press, 1968.

Raboteau, Albert J. *Slave Religion: The "Invisible Institution" in the Ante-bellum South.* New York: Oxford University Press, 1978.

Rawick, George P., ed. *The American Slave: A Composite Autobiography.* 41 vols. Westport, Conn.: Greenwood Press, 1972–79.

Rawley, James A. *The Transatlantic Slave Trade: A History.* New York: W. W. Norton, 1981.

Rice, C. Duncan. *The Rise and Fall of Black Slavery.* New York: Harper and Row, 1975.

Ripley, C. Peter. *Slaves and Freedmen in Civil War Louisiana.* Baton Rouge: Lousiana State University Press, 1976.

Rose, Willie Lee, ed. *A Documentary History of Slavery in North America.* New York: Oxford University Press, 1976.

———. *Rehearsal for Reconstruction: The Port Royal Experiment.* Indianapolis: Bobbs-Merrill, 1964. Reprint. New York: Oxford University Press, 1976.

———. *Slavery and Freedom.* Edited by William W. Freehling. New York: Oxford University Press, 1982.

Rosengarten, Dale. *Row Upon Row: Sea Grass Baskets of the South Carolina Low Country.* Columbia, S.C.: McKissick Museum, 1986.

Savannah Unit, Georgia Writers' Project, Work Projects Administration. *Drums and Shadows: Survival Studies Among the Georgia Coastal Negroes.* Reprint. Introduction by Charles Joyner. Athens: University of Georgia Press, 1986.

Savitt, Todd L. *Medicine and Slavery: The Diseases and Health Care of Blacks in Antebellum Virginia.* Urbana: University of Illinois Press, 1978.

Scarborough, William K. *The Overseer: Plantation Management in the Old South.* Baton Rouge: Louisiana State University Press, 1966.

Schafer, Judith Kelleher. "New Orleans Slavery in 1850 as Seen in Advertisements." *Journal of Southern History* 46 (1981): 33–56.

Schopf, Johann David. *Travels in the Confederacy, 1783–1784.* Philadelphia: W. J. Campbell, 1911.

Schwarz, Philip J. *Twice Condemned: Slaves and the Criminal Laws of Virginia, 1705–1865.* Baton Rouge: Louisiana State University Press, 1988.

Sellers, James B. *Slavery in Alabama.* University: University of Alabama Press, 1950.

Singleton, Theresa, ed. *The Archaeology of Slavery and Plantation Life.* Orlando, Fla.: Academic Press, 1985.

———. "Breaking New Ground." *Southern Exposure* 16 (Summer 1988): 18–22.

———. "The Slave Tag: An Artifact of Urban Slavery." *South Carolina Antiquities* 16 (1984): 41–66.

Smedes, Susan Dabney. *Memorials of a Southern Planter.* Edited by Fletcher M. Green. New York: Alfred A. Knopf, 1965.

Smith, Edward D. *Climbing Jacob's Ladder: The Rise of Black Churches in Eastern American Cities, 1740–1877.* Washington, D.C.: Smithsonian Institution Press, 1988.

Smith, John David, comp. *Black Slavery in the Americas: An Interdisciplinary Bibliography, 1865–1980.* 2 vols. Westport, Conn.: Greenwood Press, 1982.

Smith, Julia Floyd. *Slavery and Plantation Growth in Antebellum Florida, 1821–1861.* Gainesville: University of Florida Press, 1973.

———. *Slavery and Rice Culture in Low Country Georgia, 1750–1860.* Knoxville: University of Tennessee Press, 1985.

Sobel, Mechal. *Trabelin' On: The Slave Journey to an Afro-Baptist Faith.* Westport, Conn.:

Greenwood Press, 1979.

___. *The World They Made Together: Black and White Values in Eighteenth-Century Virginia.* Princeton: Princeton University Press, 1987.

Stampp, Kenneth M. *The Peculiar Institution: Slavery in the Ante-Bellum South.* New York: Alfred A. Knopf, 1956. Reprint. New York: Vintage Books, 1964.

Starling, Marion Wilson. *The Slave Narrative: Its Place in American History.* 2d ed. Washington, D.C.: Howard University Press, 1988.

Starobin, Robert S., ed. *Blacks in Bondage: Letters of American Slaves.* 2d ed. New York: Markus Wiener Publishing, 1988.

___. *Industrial Slavery in the Old South.* New York: Oxford University Press, 1970.

___, ed. *Denmark Vesey: The Slave Conspiracy of 1822.* Englewood Cliffs, N.J.: Prentice-Hall, 1970.

Sterkx, H. E. *The Free Negro in Ante-Bellum Louisiana.* Rutherford: Fairleigh Dickinson University Press, 1972.

Stuckey, Sterling. *Slave Culture: Nationalist Theory and the Foundations of Black America.* New York: Oxford University Press, 1987.

Sutch, Richard. "The Breeding of Slaves for Sale and Westward Expansion of Slavery 1830–1860." In *Race and Slavery in the Western Hemisphere: Quantitative Studies,* edited by Stanley Engerman and Eugene D. Genovese. Princeton: Princeton University Press, 1975.

___. "The Care and Feeding of Slaves." In *Reckoning With Slavery: A Critical Study in the Quantitative History of American Negro Slavery,* edited by Paul A. David, Herbert G. Gutman, Richard Sutch, Peter Temin, and Gavin Wright. New York: Oxford University Press, 1976.

Tadman, Michael. *Speculators and Slaves: Masters, Traders, and Slaves in the Old South.* Madison: University of Wisconsin Press, 1989.

Tate, Thad W. *The Negro in Eighteenth-Century Williamsburg.* Williamsburg: Colonial Williamsburg Foundation, 1965. Reprint. Charlottesville: University Press of Virginia, 1985.

Taylor, Joe Gray. *Negro Slavery in Louisiana.* Baton Rouge: Louisiana Historical Association, 1963.

Taylor, Orville Walters. *Negro Slavery in Arkansas.* Durham: Duke University Press, 1958.

Thompson, Robert Farris. *Flash of the Spirit: African and Afro-American Art and Philosophy.* New York: Random House, 1983.

Tragle, Henry Irving. *The Southampton Slave Revolt of 1831: A Compilation of Source Material.* Amherst: University of Massachusetts Press, 1971.

Trussell, James, and Richard Steckel. "The Age of Slaves at Menarche and Their First Birth." *Journal of Interdisciplinary History* 8 (1978): 477–505.

Tyler, Ronnie C., and Lawrence R. Murphy, eds. *The Slave Narratives of Texas.* Austin: Encino Press, 1974.

Tyler-McGraw, Marie, and Gregg D. Kimball, *In Bondage and Freedom: Antebellum Black Life in Richmond, Virginia.* Richmond: Valentine Museum, 1988.

Van Deburg, William L. *The Slave Drivers: Black Agricultural Labor Supervisors in the Antebellum South.* Westport, Conn.: Greenwood Press, 1979.

Vlach, John Michael. "Afro-American Domestic Artifacts in Eighteenth-Century Virginia." *Material Culture* 19 (Spring 1987): 3–24

___. *The Afro-American Tradition in Decorative Arts.* Cleveland: Cleveland Museum of Art, 1978. Reprint. Athens: University of Georgia Press, 1990.

___. *By the Work of Their Hands: Studies in Afro-American Folklife.* Ann Arbor: UMI Research Press, 1990.

Wade, Richard C. *Slavery in the Cities: The South, 1820–1860.* New York: Oxford University Press, 1964.

Walston, Mark L. "'Uncle Tom's Cabin' Revisited: Origins and Interpretations of Slave Housing in the American South." *Southern Studies* 24 (1985): 357–73.

Webber, Thomas L. *Deep Like the Rivers: Education in the Slave Quarter Community.* New York: W. W. Norton, 1978.

Weekley, Carolyn J., and Stiles Tuttle Colwill. *Joshua Johnson.* Baltimore: Maryland Historical Society; Williamsburg: Abby Aldrich Rockefeller Folk Art Center, 1987.

White, Deborah Gray. *Ar'n't I a Woman?: Female Slaves in the Plantation South.* New York: W. W. Norton, 1985.

Wikramanayake, Marina. *A World in Shadow: The Free Black in Antebellum South Carolina.* Columbia: University of South Carolina Press, 1973.

Wiley, Bell I. *Southern Negroes, 1861–1865.* New Haven: Yale University Press, 1938. Reprint. Baton Rouge: Louisiana State University Press, 1974.

Williamson, Joel. *New People: Miscegenation and Mulattoes in the United States.* New York: Free Press, 1980. Reprint. New York: New York University Press, 1984.

Wish, Harvey, ed. *Slavery in the South: First-Hand Accounts of the Antebellum Southland from Northerners and Southern Whites, Negroes, and Foreign Observers.* New York: Farrar,

Straus, 1964.

Wood, Betty. *Slavery in Colonial Georgia, 1730–1775*. Athens: University of Georgia Press, 1984.

Wood, Peter H. *Black Majority: Negroes in Colonial South Carolina from 1670 through the Stono Rebellion*. New York: Alfred A. Knopf, 1974. Reprint. New York: W. W. Norton, 1975.

___, and Karen C. C. Dalton. *Winslow Homer's Image of Blacks: The Civil War and Reconstruction Years*. Austin: University of Texas Press in association with the Menil Foundation, 1988.

Wyatt-Brown, Bertram. "The Mask of Obedience: Male Slave Psychology in the Old South." *American Historical Review* 93 (1988): 1228–52.

Yetman, Norman R., comp. *Life Under the "Peculiar Institution": Selections from the Slave Narrative Collection*. New York: Holt, Rinehart and Winston, 1970.

Zelnick, Melvin. "Fertility of the American Negro in 1830–1850." *Population Studies* 20 (1966): 77–83.

Zierden, Martha, Jeanne Calhoun, and Lesley Drucker. *Home Upriver*. Charleston: Carolina Archaeological Services and Charleston Museum, 1987.

Index

Beaver Bend plantation (Ala.), 37

Beckie (slave), as nurse, *142*

Bectom, John (slave), on literacy, 88

Belair plantation (La.), *40*

Bell, Frank (slave), on wheat harvest, *53*

Bell, Louisa (runaway slave), 107

Bellegrove plantation (La.), *37*

Bennehan-Cameron plantation (N.C.), *21, 61, 69, 157*

Berkeley County (S.C.), 162

Berry, Fannie (slave), on Nat Turner rebellion, 97

Bertie County (N.C.), 1802 revolt in, 97

Bethel A.M.E. Church (Georgetown, S.C.), 88

Bethel Church (Baltimore), *145*

Betty (slave), as runaway's accomplice, 107

Bibb, Henry (slave): on courtship, 119; on care of deceased, 77; escape attempted by, 106; on physical punishment, 103; wife of assaulted, 103

Bibb, Malinda (slave): assaulted, 103; escape attempted by, 106

Bishop, Ank (slave), on child care, 59

Bishopville (S.C.), 5

Black Belt, 12, *68*

Black Culture and Consciousness (Lawrence Levine), 7

Black Family in Slavery and Freedom, The (Herbert Gutman), 7

Black Power movement, 6

Black, William (master), 119

Blassingame, John, 7

Boles, John B., on slave demography, 23

Bolivar County (Miss.), *52*

Bonner, James C., on plantation landscape, 21

Boré, Jean Etienne, on sugar, 37–38

Bosman, William (traveler), on African women, 102

Bost, W. L. (slave), on songs, 75

Boston (Mass.), 135, 140, 153

Bradfield, Nannie (slave), on clothing, 56

Bradley, Martha (slave runaway), on resistance, 95

Brady, Mathew, photographer of, *51*

Branch, Jacob (slave), on physical treatment, 90–91

Brazoria County (Tex.), 163

Breckenridge, Rev. Robert, and black church, *145*

Bremer, Fredrika (Swedish traveler): on Charleston African-American population, 127; Savannah church service described by, 146; on slave religion, 74; slave women described by, 104

Brent, Linda (slave), escape of, 107

Brewster, George (master), 73

Bristow, Josephine (slave), on child care, 114

Brooks, Sylvester (slave), on patrols, 81

Brown, Betty (slave), on diet, 120

Brown, Ebenezer (slave), work songs recollected by, 52, 82

Brown, Henry (slave), on literacy, 88

Brown, Henry Box (slave runaway): on Nat Turner rebellion, 97; on urban housing, 138

Brown, John, *16*, 18, 150

Brown, Katie, recollection of Moslem grandfather by, 81

Brown, Kenneth, 163–64

Brown, William Henry (artist), *vi*

Brown, William Wells (ex-slave): on sexual assault, 103; slave auctions described, 123–24, 139

Brown Fellowship Society (Charleston), 147, 148

Bruce, Henry Clay (escaped slave): on sexual assault, 61–62; on Nat Turner, 97

Bruh Rabbit, as folktale subject, 84–85, 92

Burleigh plantation (Ga.), 104

Burleigh plantation (Va.), 111

Burnett, Midge (slave): on holidays, 81; on Union soldiers, 98

Burnside, John (sugar planter), plantation described, 38–39

Burry, John (planter), *70*

Butler, Gabe (slave): on emancipation, 99; on physical treatment, 89; on superstition, 76

Butler, Pierce (rice planter), 31, 90

Butler's Island (Ga.), 31, *58*

Byrd, William II (Va. planter), 25

Camden (S.C.), 34

Camden County (Ga.), *168*

Camp, Maj. Raleigh S., *16*

Campbell County (Va.), *24*

Caroline (slave), on miscegenation, 73

Carter, Landon (Va. planter): plantation described, 25; on runaways, 94

Carter, Pharoah (Miss. planter): reaction to emancipation, 98–99; reaction to prayer meeting, 75; slave spy of, 56

Carter, Robert (Va. planter), 25

Cato (driver): report on crops by, 52; and religion, 74

Catoctin Furnace (Md.), 173

Celeste (slave), as truant, 107, 109

Charles (slave runaway), 119

Charleston (S.C.), and African-Americans: badges, *149;* benevolent societies, 147, 148; churches, 144; clothing, 142; community, 140, 141–42; free-black occupations, 133, 135; funerals, 147; Francis Pinckney Holloway, 146; Kitty, 150; liquor trade, 141; manumission, 150; Mary, 150; population, 14, *126,* 127, 132, 148; restrictions 136, 150, 151, 152, 153; Robinson-Aiken house, *44,* 45–47; schools, 146; slave artisans, 129; slave executed, 111; slave hiring, 130, 131; slave housing, 43, 44–47, 137, 138; slave resistance, 111; slave trade, *9,* 139; South Carolina Railway, 127; Denmark Vesey, 8, 14, 96, 140, 142, 144, 150; Ward house, *43,* 45; workers characterized, 134–35

Charleston City Gazette, plantation advertised, 31

Charlotte (slave), sexual assault on, 64

Charlotte (Va. slave cook), and clothing, *111*

Chattanooga (Tenn.), *128*

Cheatam, Henry (slave), on punishment, 90

Chesnut, Mary Boykin: child care observed, 120; on miscegenation, 62–63; on poisoning, 111

Chester District (S.C.), 95

Frances (slave), as master's spy, 56, 75

Franks, Dora (slave), on miscegenation, 73

Fredericksburg (Va.), 106

Free blacks: James Abbott, *130*; benevolent societies, 146–47; churches, 144–47, 148; class divisions, *14, 139*, 148; community, 140–42; Creoles, *147*, 148; Francis Pinckney Holloway, 146; housing and households, 140; Solomon Humphries, 132; infringements upon, *13*, 14, 125–26, 135–37, 141, 149–53; James M. Johnson, 152; William Johnson, 132, 133, 136, 148; Marie Laveau, *xi*; Henry Lee, *132*; Andrew Marshall, 123, 128, 132, 146; migration, 153; occupations and tasks, 132–34, 135; William Pencil, 140; political parties and, 149–50; population characterized, 132; Emmanuel Quivers, 123, 127, 132; schools, 146; urban demographics, 126, 127, 134; urban preference of, 132; and white immigrants, 136–37

Frogmore plantation (S.C.), *87*

Frowers, Frank (slave runaway), on physical treatment, 91

Fuller, George, sketch by, *108*

Fuqua, Moses (planter), 26

Fuqua, William (planter), 26

Gaillard, Henry (cotton planter), 34

Gantling, Clayborn (slave), on child rearing, 106

Gardner, Alexander (photographer), *79*

Garlic, Delia (slave), on physical treatment, 91

Garrison, William Lloyd, 97

Garrison plantation (Md.), 159, 164

Gaynor, Joanne Bowen, 172

General Commission of the Virginia Baptist Church, 143

Genovese, Eugene, 7

George (runaway slave), 95

Georgetown (S.C.), 26, 31, 88, 97

Georgia, and African-Americans (*see also* Savannah): Abraham, 119; Andrew, 74; Athens, 137; Nora August, *iv*; Augusta, 127, 143; Charles Ball, 90; birthrate, 104; building materials, 170; Burleigh plantation, 104; Butler's Is., 31, *58*; Cato, 52, 74; Christmas holiday, 81; impact of Civil War, 98; clothing, *55*, 56; Cockspur Is., *166*; as Confederate laborers, *17*; and cotton, 23, 33, 52, 81; dancing, 83; Darien, *iv, 66*, 81; David Dickson, 63; diet, 86; ethnicity, 157; funerals, *76, 77*, 81; Clayborn Gantling, 106; Hampton plantation, 170; Harmony Hall plantation, 164, *168, 169*; harvesttime, 81; health care, 58, 174; housing, 87, 88, *166*; hurricane houses, 33; Benjamin Johnson, 107; Julianton plantation, 31, *66*; Lucy, 113; Macon, 127, 132; Mollie Malone, 114; Marlboro, *16*; Sandy Maybank, 74; miscegenation, 62; Bilali Mohomet, 81; Moslem faith, 81; Robert Pinckney, 84–85; plantations characterized, 31, 33; punishment, 90; resistance, 92; rice, 26, 31, 33; Saint Simons Is., 74, 77, *169*, 170; Sapelo Is., 81; Sea Islands, *4*, 31, 77; Robert

Shepherd, 114; singing, 82; on slavery and the Constitution, 11; Terrell Co., 106; Viney, 114; Frances Willingham, 109; Wilmington Is., 84

Gery (runaway slave), 119

Ghana, material culture of, 158

Gibson, Ferdinand (planter), 114

Gone With the Wind (Margaret Mitchell), 21

Goree, Jordan (slave artisan), 37

Gracey (slave), clothing made by, *108*

Gracia Real Santa Teresa de Mose (Fla.), archaeology of, 175

Grandy, Charles (slave), on diet, 166–67

Green, Elijah (slave), on literacy, 88

Green Hill plantation (Va.), *24*, 26

Greene County (Ala.), 36

Grey, Josias (master), 63

Grove, William Hugh, Va. plantation described by, 25

Guendalos plantation (S.C.), 31

Guinea, native women characterized, 102

Gunston Hall (Va.), 25, 26

Gutman, Herbert, 7

Hall, Shadrach, recollection of Moslem grandfather, 81

Hammond, James Henry (cotton planter), 34, 63

Hampton plantation (Ga.), 170

Hansley, Samuel (master), 64

Harding, Captain (slaver), 110–11

Harmony Hall plantation (Ga.), 164, *168, 169*

Harper, William (educator), on slave women, 104

Harpers Ferry (Va.), *16*, 18, 150

Harriet (slave), childbirth encouraged, 104

Harris, Eliza (fictional slave), 107

Hemp, demographics of work force, 13

Henry (slave), and pass system, *61*

Henry (slave insurrectionist), 97

Henry, Charles, manumission by, *103*

Henry, Ida (slave), on physical treatment, 91

Henson, Josiah (runaway slave), 106, 111

Hermitage plantation (Tenn.), *161*, 162, *164*, 172, *174*

Higginson, Col. Thomas Wentworth, *79*

Hill, Matthew, 161

Hilton Head Island (S.C.), *163*, 175

Hodges, Smitty (slave), on health care, 59

Holloway, Frances Pinckney (free black), school of, 146

Hopkinson, James, plantation of, *57, 175*

Horry, Ben (slave): courtship of, 81; on food theft, 90; on literacy, 88

Horton Grove Quarter (N.C.), *21, 167*

Houston (Tex.), 163

Hubbell, L. C., as urban slave owner, *137*

Humphries, Solomon (free-black grocer), 132

Hunt, Gabe (slave), on harvesting tobacco, 53

Huntsville (Ala.), runaways, 106

Huntsville (Tex.), 37

Hurricane houses (Ga. and S.C.), 33

Incidents in the Life of a Slave Girl (Harriet Jacobs), 97

Robinson, John (urban slaveholder), Charleston house of, *44*, 45, *46*

Robinson, Manus (slave), on plantation landscape, 34

Robinson, Solon (journalist), plantation described by, 46–47

Rodney Plantation (Ala.), *68*

Roll, Jordan, Roll (Eugene Genovese), 7

Romeo (runaway slave), 119

Rose (slave), divorce of, 120

Rose, Willie Lee, 8

Royal African Company, 3

Rudd, John (slave), on resistance, 92–93

Ruffin, Edmund (planter), and arsonists, 92

Rufus (slave), arranged relationship of, 105

Russell, Benjamin (slave), on communication, 91–92

Russell, W. H. (English traveler), plantation described by, 39

Sabine Hall (Va.), 25

Said, Omar ibn (slave), as Moslem, *77*

Saint Augustine (Fla.), *iv*, 175

Saint Helena Island (S.C.), *1, 28*, 31, *87*

Saint James Parish (La.), 41

Saint Louis (Mo.), 103, 119, 126

Saint Luke's Parish (S.C.), 96

Saint Simons Island (Ga.), 74, 77, 170

Sam (La. slave), courtship of, 119

Sam (slave), marriage of, 119

Sam (S.C. slave), *115*

Samba's conspiracy (La.), 96

Sandy Island (S.C.), 26

Santee River (S.C.), 33

Sapelo Island (Ga.), 81

Savannah (Ga.), and African-Americans: churches, 123, 143, 146; community, 140; Charles Colcock Jones, 73; Andrew Marshall, 123, 128, 132, 146; population, 43, 132, 148, 149; restrictions, 136, 152; slave hiring, 131; slave housing, 137

Sea Islands (Ga. and S.C.), 4, 31, *66*, 77, *79*, 175

Seabrook, E. M. (planter), 31

Senegal-Mali, material culture of, 158

Senegambia, as source of slaves, 3

Shadrach (slave), funeral of, *77*

Sharper (slave runaway), 95

Shepherd, Robert (slave), on child care, 114

Sherman, William T., 98

Shirley plantation (Va.), archaeology of, 167

Shreveport (La.), *70*

Simms, Andrew (slave), on marriage, 60

Simms, William Gilmore, slavery characterized by, 62

Simon (slave runaway), 94

Slave Community, The (John Blassingame), 7

Slavery: in Africa, 1–2; Atlantic trade, *xiv*, 2, 3, 11, 110–11, 131; characterized, 11; impact of Civil War upon, 18–19; demographic division, 12–14, 18, 23, 126, 127, 148; demographic impact, 4, 6; established in English colonies, 2–3; in Europe, 1; historiography, 6–7, 14–15; impact of Mexican War, 16, 18

Slaves and slave communities: (*see also* specific names and states): abortion, 113–14; and alcoholic beverages, 86, 141, 142; in American Revolution, 8, 11; as artisans, *iv, 68, 70, 85, 86*, 88, 110, 128–29, *160, 161*; badges, *149*; birthrate, 102, 104–5, *114*, 117; childbirth, 59, 105–6, 113, 117; child rearing, 57, 60–61, 106, *109, 113*, 114–15, 117; children's games, 61; Christmas, 81–82; clothing and adornment, *x, 7*, 55–56, *70*, 109–10, *111*, 118–19, *141*, 142, *162*; colonoware, *69*, 159–61; communication between, 91–92, 113, 141–42; as Confederate laborers and servants, *16, 17*, 19, *96*, 98; corn shuckings, 82; cotton cultivation, *vi*, 33–34, 36–37, 52; courtship, 59, 118–19; cowrie shells, 157–58; dances, *7, 65, 66, 69*, 82–83, *141*; diet, *83*, 85, 86, 92, 120, 167, 171–73, 175; divorce, 120; drivers, *52, 55*; emancipation and manumission, *iv, 18*, 19, 98–99, *103*, 150; epithets, 56; families and female role, 7, 106, 109, 110, 114–15, 117, 120–21, 139–40; families and male role, 8, 106, 110, 120–21, 137, 139; folk remedies, 59, 174; folktales, 83–85; foodways, 85, 86, 161–62, 170–72, 175; funerals, *72, 76*, 77, 81, 147, *173*; furniture, 88; harvesttime, 81, 82; health care, 58–59, 112–13, 173–74; hiring, *129*, 130–32; holidays, 81–82; as house servants, 56–57, 120, 128, 138; household, 56–57, 109, 170; housing, 25, 26, *27, 28*, 31, 33, 34, *35*, 36, *37*, 39–40, 41, 43–44, 45–46, *84*, 87–88, 137–38, 162, 165–67, 169–70; hunting and fishing, 86, 120, *164*, 171; as iron workers, 123, 127, 135, 136; John Canoe festival, 82; language and speech, 83–85; literacy, 88, 92, 146; Maroons, 159; marriages, 59–60, *65*, 110, 119, *120*; masters characterized, 88–90; midwives, 105–6, 113; miscegenation, 61–64, 73; Moslem faith, *77*, 81, *164*; musical instruments, *xiv, 69*, 88; naming patterns, 7; as nursemaids, *101, 128, 142*; patrols, *89*, 92, 95; physical punishments, 51, *87*, 90–91, 103, 110, 111; population, 2, 11, 12, 148; proverbs, 83; as railway workers, 127; religion, *63*, 73–76, 81, 142–47, 148; resistance, 8, 91–97, 106–7, 110–12, 113–14, 140–41, 166; rice cultivation, 26, 31, 33, *53*, 54; sale and separation of, *ii, xiv*, 61, *66, 68*, 102, 104, 105, *107, 116, 118*, 119, 123–24, *138*, 139; sexual assault upon, 61–62, 64, 73, 102–4; songs of, 82; speech, 83; sugar cultivation, 40–43, 54–55; suicide, 92; superstitions and charms, *69*, 76–77, *157*, 162–64; tasks and labor, 55–56, 57, *71, 103*, 109, 110, 112–13; as textile workers, 127; tobacco cultivation, 13, 23, 25–26, 52–53; and Union soldiers, *16, 18, 96*, 98, 119; as Union soldiers, 19, *71*; urban landscape of, 43–47; urban restrictions on, 125, 131, 135–37, 150–53; voodoo, *xi*, 76–77

Smalls, Robert (slave): on master-slave relationship, *9*; as naval hero, 19

Acknowledgments

The idea for *Before Freedom Came* must be credited to members of the Board of Trustees of The Museum of the Confederacy and the Museum's former director, Elizabeth Scott Lux. Ms. Lux strongly supported this project from its beginnings in 1987 through the first National Endowment for the Humanities planning grant awarded the next year. Louis F. Gorr, the Museum's present director, embraced the idea upon his arrival in 1989 and immediately became one of the project's chief promoters. The Board also continued its strong backing of the endeavor over the years, especially under the leadership of Joan Massey and Jane Cecil. The encouragement and support of these important individuals is especially appreciated.

A team of seven consultants planned and shaped the interpretive component of the project, including this publication. Six of them are authors of the book's essays. The seventh, Edward A. Chappell, of the Colonial Williamsburg Foundation, made his presence felt in several important topic areas. Although each consultant made critical contributions regarding the exhibition, particular appreciation is due Theresa A. Singleton, of the Smithsonian Institution. Dr. Singleton (and her assistant, Mark Bograd) made archaeological reports and other information accessible and answered innumerable questions regarding specific objects.

The responsibility for a project of this size and detail rests on many shoulders. A special debt is owed the entire staff of The Museum of the Confederacy, in particular Malinda Collier, Howard Hendricks, Robin Reed, John Coski, and Clay Dye. Other contributions were made by staff members Guy Swanson, Cory Hudgins, Buddy Spencer, Tracie Williams, Beth Goldman, Rick Pougher, Lisa Middleton, Bobbie Jarrett, Margaret Jones, Elly Lewis, Becky Rose, Barbara Hyde, Sheryl Kingery, and Edie Whiteman. Janine Bell ably served as the community outreach coordinator for the project and planned the adult program component. Tucker H. Hill, the Museum's director of programs, guided the project on a daily basis with dedication, hours of hard work, and invariable good humor each step of the way.

Fortunately for the Museum, John McGuigan, acquisitions editor of the University Press of Virginia, showed a strong interest in this publication from its inception and made many helpful suggestions regarding the book's development. We also thank Mary Kathryn Hassett, Janet Anderson, and Nancy C. Essig, of the Press, for their contributions.

The project staff is very appreciative of the fine book design accomplished by Douglas W. Price and the many superb photographs taken by Katherine Wetzel. Donald Hirsch kindly acted as translator for the French material. We are grateful to Linda King, director of the Museum of Coastal History, for bringing "Nora" to our attention.

Without the generous and sustained financial support of the National Endowment for the Humanities, a federal agency, *Before Freedom Came* would not have been possible. We are grateful for the assistance of Tim Meagher and Marsha Semmel, of the Museums and Historical Organizations, Division of Public Programs, NEH. The project has also received generous support, as of this writing, from the Belle Bryan Day Nursery Foundation, Crestar Bank, the Massey Foundation, the Media General Foundation, the Memorial Foundation for Children, and the Metropolitan Life Foundation.

From Richmond the exhibition will travel in 1992 to the McKissick Museum at the University of South Carolina, in Columbia, and to the National Afro-American Museum and Cultural Center in Wilberforce, Ohio. Special thanks are extended to George Terry, Catherine Wilson Horne, and Janie Peeples, of the McKissick Museum, and to John Fleming and Barbara Andrews, of the National Afro-American Museum and Cultural Center, for their cooperation. The PRD Group, Ltd, of Fairfax, Virginia, served as the exhibition designers.

Hundreds of institutions, individuals, colleagues, and friends too numerous to list here participated in this project. Many, however, are named in the Checklist of Illustrations. Thank you very much for your cooperation and assistance.

Kym S. Rice, *Project Director*
Edward D. C. Campbell, Jr., *Editor*

Colophon:

Before Freedom Came: African-American Life in the Antebellum South was
designed by Douglas W. Price, of Goochland, Virginia. Katherine Wetzel,
of Richmond, Virginia, served as principal photographer and Tucker H.
Hill and John M. Coski, of The Museum of the Confederacy, as production managers. The editors prepared copy with the NBI OASys system and
converted text to WordPerfect 5.0 on the NBI Ethernet network. The text
was composed in Galliard roman and italic and Caslon 540 italic and
printed on acid-free Lithofect Plus Dull text & cover by the Carter
Printing Company, Richmond.